E. M. FORSTER: CENTENARY REVALUATIONS

E. M. FORSTER:
Centenary Revaluations

Edited by
Judith Scherer Herz and
Robert K. Martin

Department of English
Concordia University
Montreal, Quebec

University of Toronto Press
Toronto and Buffalo

Published in the United Kingdom 1982 by
The Macmillan Press Ltd

First published in Canada and the United States 1982 by
University of Toronto Press
Toronto and Buffalo

ISBN 0–8020–2454–8

Printed in Hong Kong

To the memory of

Oliver Stallybrass
1925–1978

'To those who knew and loved him,
he was more than a creator of books'.

'Forrest Reid', *Two Cheers for Democracy*

Contents

Preface

E. M. Forster, unlike Dickens, never visited Montreal. Indeed he never travelled further into Canada than Niagara Falls, a visit he excitingly recreated in *Marianne Thornton* by describing his cousin Inglis Synnot's much less tame expedition in 1859. But Concordia University, Montreal, was nonetheless the site in May 1979 of a centenary conference whose participants, the Dean of Dulborough conspicuously absent, came from Canada, the United States, England, Australia and India for a three-day critical scrutiny and reassessment.

The programme combined major addresses and seminar sessions, a writers' panel and a concert reading of excerpts from *Billy Budd*. Those who appeared on the programme were: Marcia Allentuck, Stephen Arkin, John Beer, Carl Behm III, Marie-Claire Blais, John Colmer, Peter Firchow, Philip Gardner, André Gerard, Kathleen Grant, Anthony Harding, Elizabeth Heine, Judith Herz, Linda Hutcheon, J. K. Johnstone, Robin Lewis, John Sayre Martin, Robert K. Martin, James McConkey, Frederick P. W. McDowell, Patricia Merivale, Bharati Mukherjee, Ira B. Nadel, Stacey Olster, Norman Page, John Plant, Paul Rivenberg, Barbara Rosecrance, S. P. Rosenbaum, Judith Ruderman, Vasant Shahane, Stella Slade, Elizabeth Spencer, Wilfred Stone, George Thomson, Molly Tinsley, Donald Watt and Eudora Welty.

The present volume contains a selection of the papers read at the conference chosen to represent the range of topics discussed. We have, in addition, included a few others that could not be delivered at the conference but nonetheless speak to the issues raised there.

We wish to thank all those who came to join us in Montreal. We extend our gratitude as well to the Provost and Scholars of King's College, Cambridge, and to the Society of Authors as the Literary Representatives of the Estate of E. M. Forster for permission to use unpublished materials; and for their generous assistance to the conference, Concordia University, the Humanities and Social Sciences Research Council of Canada, and the British Council, in particular its Montreal representative, Mrs Anna Lamarra. Sheila Lanthier, Ruth Portner, Michael Pacholka and Bill Reid all contributed enormously to the conference's success.

But the conference could not have taken place, nor the present book have been published, had there not been the demanding, exacting and inspiring work of Oliver Stallybrass. To his memory, renewed with each turning of the page, we dedicate this volume.

Montreal 1980   *JSH*
                                                      RKM

Notes on the Contributors

AHMED ALI is a Pakistani diplomat, novelist, poet and translator. His best known novel is *Twilight in Delhi* (1941). He is also the author of *Ocean of Night* (a novel, 1964) and *Purple Gold Mountain* (poetry, 1960) and many short stories. He has held several teaching posts, most recently as Fulbright-Hays Professor at Southern Illinois University.

ELIZABETH BARRETT is a graduate student at Concordia University, where she has written a thesis on the fiction of E. M. Forster.

JOHN BEER is Reader in English Literature at Cambridge and Fellow of Peterhouse and is the author of *The Achievement of E. M. Forster* and joint editor of the collection *E. M. Forster: A Human Exploration*. His other books include studies of Coleridge, Blake and Wordsworth.

MARIE-CLAIRE BLAIS is the author of fifteen novels, three plays and a book of poetry. Her best-known novel is *Une Saison dans la Vie d'Emmanuel* for which she received the Prix Médicis. Her other novels include *Le Belle Bête, Les Manuscrits de Pauline Archange, Le Loup*.

JOHN COLMER was educated at Oxford and has taught at Khartoum, Birmingham and Adelaide, where he is now Professor of English. He is the author of *E. M. Forster: The Personal Voice, E. M. Forster: A Passsage to India* and *Coleridge to 'Catch 22': Images of Society*.

G. K. DAS is Reader in English at the University of Delhi. He is the author of *E. M. Forster's India*, joint editor of *E. M. Forster: A Human Exploration* and has published several articles on E. M. Forster.

P. N. FURBANK is Reader in Literature at the Open University and author of *Samuel Butler 1835–1902, Italo Svevo: The Man and the Writer, Reflections on the Word 'Image'* and *E. M. Forster: a Life*.

PHILIP GARDNER is a Professor of English at the Memorial University of Newfoundland and the author of *E. M. Forster: The Critical Heritage*, *E. M. Forster* (British Council), and is at present editing *Forster's Commonplace Book*. His other books include studies of Norman Nicholson, William Empson and Kingsley Amis.

KATHLEEN GRANT has taught at the University of British Columbia and Acadia University. She is now a Killam Scholar at Dalhousie University, where she is writing a dissertation on Victorian religious novelists.

ELIZABETH HEINE has taught at the City University of New York, the University of Hawaii and the University of Texas at San Antonio. She has written studies of Forster, Virginia Woolf, Leonard Woolf, and is co-editor of Forster's *Arctic Summer and Other Fiction* and General Editor of the Abinger Edition.

JUDITH SCHERER HERZ is a member of the English Department of Concordia University. She has published essays on Chaucer, Shakespeare, seventeenth-century poetry, literary biography and E. M. Forster.

LINDA HUTCHEON is a member of the English Department of McMaster University. She has published essays on narrative technique, Camus, Pavese, Fowles and has translated several French-Canadian texts.

ROBERT K. MARTIN is a member of the English Department of Concordia University. He is the author of *The Homosexual Tradition in American Poetry* and has published essays on Crane, Whitman, Hawthorne and James.

JAMES McCONKEY is Professor of English at Cornell University. He is the author of *The Novels of E. M. Forster* as well as of numerous short stories and several novels, the most recent of which is *The Tree House Confessions*.

FREDERICK P. W. McDOWELL is Professor of English at the University of Iowa and the author of *E. M. Forster* and *E. M. Forster: An Annotated Bibliography of Secondary Writings About Him*. He has also written a book on Ellen Glasgow and essays on Shaw and Virginia Woolf.

BHARATI MUKHERJEE is the author of two novels, *The Tiger's Daughter* and *Wife*. With her husband, Clark Blaise, she wrote

Days and Nights in Calcutta.

IRA BRUCE NADEL is a member of the English Department of the University of British Columbia. He is co-editor of *Victorian Artists and the City* and the author of several essays on Victorian prose and prose fiction.

PAUL RIVENBERG is a graduate student at the University of Rochester, where he is working on modern British literature.

BARBARA ROSECRANCE is a member of the English Department of Cornell University and an assistant editor of *Partisan Review*. She has written essays on Forster, early modern British literature and poetry and music of the English Renaissance.

S. P. ROSENBAUM is a Professor of English at the University of Toronto. His books include *The Bloomsbury Group*, an edition of James's *The Ambassadors* and a concordance to the poetry of Emily Dickinson.

V. A. SHAHANE is Professor of English at Osmania University (Hyderabad). He is the author of *E. M. Forster: A Reassessment* and *E. M. Forster: A Study in Double Vision.*

ELIZABETH SPENCER is the author of *The Light in the Piazza* as well as of numerous other works, including most recently *The Snare*. Her *Collected Short Stories* was published in 1981.

WILFRED STONE is Professor of English at Stanford University and the author of *The Cave and the Mountain: A Study of E. M. Forster.* He is also author of a book on William Hale White and co-author of *Prose Style: A Handbook for Writers* and editor of several anthologies.

MOLLY TINSLEY teaches at the United States Naval Academy (Annapolis). She is the author of several articles and short stories.

EUDORA WELTY is the author of many works of fiction including *The Optimist's Daughter*, which won the Pulitzer Prize in 1972, *The Robber Bridegroom*, *The Golden Apples* and *The Ponder Heart*. She received the Howells Medal for fiction from the American Academy of Arts and Letters. Her book of essays and reviews, *The Eye of the Story*, was published in 1978.

1 Introduction: In Search of the Comic Muse

Judith Scherer Herz

'What special tribute shall we bring him?'[1] Forster wryly asked in 1927, speculating on the centenary of his untimely but immediate death. More than half a century later we can echo that question but without any of the irony that Forster implied in the question's supposed justification: 'He could scarcely have endured to put forth masterpiece after masterpiece had he not felt assured of the verdict of posterity'. Although verdict may have 'too much the atmosphere of the law courts' about it, he nonetheless could feel reasonably confident about the judgement of his contemporaries (he had just delivered the Clark lectures, *A Passage to India* had been translated into French, reviews, essays, appraisals of the contemporary novel increasingly spoke of his importance). Nonetheless he was far less certain of the epithet 'great' than were some of his more enthusiastic commentators. 'My novels will be either almost-successes or failures',[2] he wrote to Virginia Woolf in that same year and throughout his life he remained sceptical of the notion that his five published novels constituted a succession of 'masterpiece after masterpiece'. But despite Forster's own diffidence and his toying with the idea of greatness finally to put it aside, a cumulative verdict has been returned, in which at least one novel has been accorded that status and the entire œuvre an importance whose extent we are only beginning to recognize. Thus the question — 'what special tribute shall we bring him?' — remains still to be answered.

One tribute is, of course, a continued and excited reading. As with all writers one especially admires, there is the pleasure to be got from showing him to others, communicating one's own excitement and receiving the reflection of one's first enthusiasm often deepened as new eyes read newly. Perhaps that is special tribute enough. But the awareness of the necessity of an ever more discriminating reading, a realization that we have yet to sharpen our tools of analysis to a sufficient fineness for the continued study of Forster's writing are the necessary corollaries of our continued pleasure in the reading. This need for a renewed and renewing scrutiny may justify the offering of this collection in the way of special tribute as well.

It is offered with the sense of the ultimate stability of Forster's reputation, but reputation is nevertheless a flighty creature and there have been times over the past fifty years where she has seemed on the verge of flying away. Thus John Crowe Ransom could write in 1943 of a Forster 'revival' (in an essay that was in part a response to Trilling's study, itself the chief spark of that revival), implying that in the twenty years since *A Passage to India*, Forster had begun to slip into oblivion.[3] (This was, perhaps, more an American than an English phenomenon, considering his importance to Auden and Isherwood and his continued presence as an essayist and broadcaster.) Thirty-five years later there was again talk of a revival, especially in the reviews of P. N. Furbank's biography, many of which speculated on the vicissitudes of reputation, remarking, in particular, that Forster seems to have fallen behind Virginia Woolf as the two fly in and out of the clouds atop Olympus. They are, one suspects, moving more companionably above than the visible flight patterns of their reputations might presently suggest. This companionship, however, is based more on class, milieu, shared friends and experiences than on any crucial similarities as novelists. And I am not at all sure we can predict which reputation will alight on the higher bough twenty years, thirty years from now when reappraisals will again be in order. Their concerns with the nature of fiction aside, however, the strong likelihood is that they will neither be compared as novelists nor judged in relation to each other's accomplishments. What I am, of course, assuming is that they will be talked about and read, accorded the importance, dare one say the greatness, that many of the contributors to this collection assume (in posterity's name) for Forster's work.

There has always been, during these periods of revaluation, some tendency to separate the man and his writing, a tendency in part abetted by the seeming split in Forster's writing career. But we should be on guard against talking of Forster primarily in terms of how fine a human being he was as if his liberal humanism were somehow a quality distinct from and intrinsically more important than his performance as a novelist. (Paradoxically this tendency to admire Forster's political integrity often joins with almost the reverse attitude, a biographically based belittling of his accomplishments as one attends to his relationship with his mother, his sexual problems, his friends' gossip, as if these 'facts' were more worth the scrutiny than his writing. Either way his achievement as a novelist gets blurred.) But the whole of Forster's writing is unified to an extraordinary degree. One has always noted a touch of the essayist in the novels' narrators and the novelist's fiction-making is even more in evidence in essay, broadcast, biography. Moreover his contemporaries saw him in much the same way as we 'see' his narrators. There are countless descriptions that echo these essential characteristics: He had 'an appearance of retiring diffidence, of a desire only to be gentle, and charming, and amusing while in fact taking deadly aim'.[4] But however expert an essayist he was and complex, sharp, loving and fine a human being, it was the achievement of the novelist that prompted the centenary observances, not the other way around.

We are willing to believe what Forster says as an essayist because we have learned to trust him so implicitly in the fiction. This trust does not necessarily mean total agreement; in *Howards End* there is a margin for argument and, perhaps, in the outermost political and historical reaches of *A Passage to India* as well. But he never hides anything about a character nor is he evasive about his own beliefs. Words are utterly respected. As Meredithean as he is in some respects, he never Meredith-fashion piles up his words like a child playing with toys. It is in this sense he is most like a poet (not in the Meredith-like poetizing he sometimes indulges in). For Forster, as for his admired Jane Austen, words matter. Writing (like the inner life) pays.

And the reader pays too. There is not the luxury of detachment. We accept his judgements (or — and this is almost the same thing — we argue strenuously with them) whether or not we are of his philosophical-political persuasion. John Crowe Ransom may have shared a part of his beliefs (that part that Ransom labelled agrarian, what Forster ruefully referred to as feudal, knowing what the cost of real property was but wanting–not-wanting it at the same time), but Ransom by no means shared all of them. Yet there is no better description than Ransom's of the essential mechanism of a Forster novel: 'Five separate times he has taken a set of characters, indisputably alive, at least middling in virtue, and studied them, head and heart with uncanny and merciless intelligence'.[5] The crucial word there is *intelligence*, a quality which eschews sentimentality and allowed Forster to inhabit his created world with absolute assurance and authority. Intelligence of this order is not *parti pris*.

The voice that we most associate with this assurance of judgement is a comic one. It undermines and unmasks, its playfulness and charm turning on a sudden to more sombre tones. But it never loses balance and always produces a widening out of perception unlike many comic strategies which tend to work reductively. Its presence has been noticed from the start and not infrequently deprecated. It is a familiar position stretching from Leonard Woolf's reference to Forster's lapses into silliness in the early novels to Leavis's uneasiness with its re-emergence in *A Passage to India*.[6] Indeed, had he listened to his friend, Bob Trevelyan, this voice would have been silenced at the very beginning. For what Trevelyan objected to were just those qualities we most admire in Forster, his 'cool, hard, comic tone'[7] in Irving Howe's marvellously apt description of the unsentimental and continuous intelligence operating in all the fiction. Curiously, Trevelyan attacked the comic muse not for what she did, but for the way she said it. As unliterary a critic as he was, he did nonetheless address himself to what he begrudgingly supposed 'one must call style'.[8] Forster's he found 'too conversational and even slangy', not even appropriate for 'a slight and comic narrative' and he tried to convince Forster of the importance of the author's 'dignity'. His voice, Forster was instructed, should have a 'certain sameness of quality, and, if possible, beauty'. That end-of-the-sentence desideratum it had in abundance but in forms that Trevelyan could evidently not appreciate. Ransom's characterization of the 'beauty and purity' of Forster's style underlines this point exactly, and Ransom further links these qualities to 'the refreshing collocation of wit and poetry' (after the fashion of Meredith, but a Meredith transcended, for Forster has grace where Meredith has excess).[9] The point is, of course, that the 'beauty' is a function of the comedy, and in Forster's variation on a Keatsian theme, comedy is closely allied to truth. After all, Cecil Vyse, imagining himself a humorist, decided that 'in the interests of the Comic

Muse and of Truth'[10] he would bring the Emersons to Windy Corner. Both truth and comedy were indeed served but the humorist departed unsmiling.

That the Comic Muse covered more ground than Windy Corner we have long observed, but we have only now begun to map the extent of her territory. For as much as she is at home in *Where Angels Fear to Tread* and *A Room With a View,* she also flits across the landscape of all the others, taking up a surprisingly important residence in the last and greatest of all of Forster's major fictions. And she appears there not simply in the comic diminishings of the Turtons and Burtons, nor in the Oriental extravagances of the extras that hover about Aziz, but at the very heart of the novel. The expedition to the caves is the familiar Box Hill picnic but here small courtesies and familiar gestures have become syllables in an unknown — or a not yet invented — language: ou-boum. The event is unfolded as if it were tea on the vicarage lawn. The displacement is gradual. By the time the comic muse departs, only tragedy remains.

Although the near alliance of the comic and tragic modes has been recognized long before Polonius' recitative of generic distinctions, the special form it takes in Forster's writing has yet to be adequately explored. With increasing emphasis recently on a study of the Forsterian voice (several essays in this volume approach the problem through an examination of syntax, narrative voice, myth-making), we are beginning to assemble the tools for just such a study. There are nonetheless many obstacles in the way, not the least being the difficulties involved in talking about the sort of comedy Forster learned from Jane Austen. For both Austen and Forster nuance of language, verbal wit whose surprises are direct encounters with Truth, even the very rhythms of sentence and paragraph, all create a comic depth which makes the surface action of the characters often appear as pantomime. The characters can be very good by themselves, but the reader is primarily intent on catching the author's voice, for what he has to say about them is often more important than what they have to say for themselves. As he slides in and out of his characters he is able to appropriate even the language of their follies and pretensions, and he does this not in order to unmask them but to clarify them. It is essentially a comic process in which both reader and character are implicated along with the narrator.

Sometimes it is hard to tell them apart. Whose consciousness are we within, for example, when in *Where Angels Fear to Tread* we are made to feel Philip's almost physical pain as the vision of a dentist in fairyland explodes his false romanticizings? Our laughter there is directed not so much at Philip as at the comically incongruous patterns formed by his fragmenting consciousness (laughing gas and the Etruscan League). But partly because Philip himself had invested such faith in the comic muse our laughter is never reifying and it affords Philip as well a small space for recovery at the same time as it probes his absurdities and delusions. Forster even manages to absorb the central image of the passage into his own commentary when he speaks of Philip's spurious sentimentalizing as if it were a bad tooth to be extracted ('a touch will loosen it'). Narration becomes one with fiction. Dentistry has its uses (just as sons of dentists can be fallen in love with — a truth that Philip in appropriately subliminal fashion comes finally to acknowledge and Caroline not so subliminally). Thus the preposterous 'a dentist in fairyland' ceases to be a simply comic cry. The voice that comments 'the sooner it goes from us the better. It was going from Philip now and therefore he gave the cry of pain', (ii, 20) has directed our laughter in ways we were far from anticipating when we first encountered Philip's horrified reaction to Caroline's exhausted admission. It is an exquisite exercise in point of view, but we can imagine Lubbock's disapproval for the point of view is chameleon-like rather than constant. It is embedded in the language of the scene rather than within a single consciousness.

Our laughter co-ordinates the full range of our responses in such a passage, but occasionally, especially with characters like Harriet, it is simpler and more predictable. Then it is more nearly like the response of 'intellectual superiority' that Philip, invoking Meredith, found a congenial posture to adopt, a posture which Forster satirized so knowingly (and in some ways so fondly) in his portrait of 'Cecil as a Humorist' (*RWV*, x). However, we are usually not allowed Cecil's complacent, albeit aesthetic, detachment. More often our laughter is absorbed into the larger resonances of the fiction as we are forced to make ever finer discriminations in our attention to character, action, voice.

Even when our laughter is simple it can be enormously satisfying. When, during the conference, Elizabeth Spencer read the passage from *Where Angels Fear to Tread* in which Harriet gets the smut in her eye, the audience laughed heartily. We obviously heard something Trevelyan had not, for one of the passages he had singled out for special disapproval moved from the waltzing train to Harriet's notorious smut. The passage was completely familiar to most of us; yet the laughter was the response of a new delight.

But that was the only time during the conference when the Italian novels were more than passingly mentioned. The conference was by no means a sombre affair. Partly due to one's sense of the presence of Forster — would he not have thought the enterprise faintly comic we wondered — there was a pleasing friendliness, a lightness even in scholarly debate. Yet comedy itself was never a subject of that debate. It thus might seem somewhat perverse in an essay that purports to introduce papers mostly deriving from that conference to dwell at such length on the comic mode in Forster's writing. But if this is indeed to be a period in which Forster's somewhat unstable reputation will be fixed, then it is crucial that our revaluations do justice to his full accomplishment. That finely tuned laughter which is so probing a tool of moral analysis also provides us with our most accessible entrance into the fiction, and is one of our chief pleasures once we are within. As grateful readers and responsible critics we should acknowledge comedy's presence as we describe possible approaches to Forster's achievement.

The conference was, in part, celebration, in part, careful scrutiny, and, from a purely academic point of view, exceptionally productive as the essays included here suggest. The major emphasis remains, in this collection as it was at the conference, on the fiction, but the essayist and critic are present too. One crucial assumption is that the novelist and the humanist are a single person, so that, for example, the essay that sets out to assess the value of Forster's liberal humanism in the wake of the horrors of the Second World War accepts without question that his 'position as novelist is . . . forever secure'. And the essay that defines his distinctive philosophy finds a successful test of that philosophy in the considerable political influence he had both in regard to India and to civil liberties. The whole of Forster's life — its interior privacy as glimpsed in the letters, journals, the biography, its public expression as recorded in the fiction, the broadcasts, the essays and reviews — becomes the witness to, the validator of his beliefs. Thus the attempt to locate that which will endure as fashions change, both fashions of fiction and fashions of belief, provides an important focus for many of these discussions.

This linking of what we have learned about the 'facts' of Forster's life with a revaluation of his achievement occurs in several of the essays. In one the literary convention of marriage as well as its metaphoric significance is examined in nineteenth- and twentieth-century fiction and then set against Forster's reliance on 'friendship' as the primary relationship both in life and art. The theme of friendship is also given prominent place in that part of the discussion of Forster's philosophy that centres on *The Longest Journey*, but there it is directly tied to an evaluation of Forster's awareness of the issues raised in G. E. Moore's 'The Refutation of Idealism'. (This continues a discussion begun in *E. M. Forster: A Human Exploration*.) Philosophy is not the same as belief, however, and another essay emphasizes how little Forster's 'belief' had to do with institutions and churches. A man 'with a theological preoccupation [but] without a theology to satisfy it'[11] was Frederick Crews' description some years ago and that perception certainly accords with several of the points argued here.

But the analysis by means of biography, a reading of the life the more cannily to read the text, is only one of the approaches taken here. Two essays look for contexts of a very different sort. The dual consciousness of the romantic vision and the attempt of the *nouveau roman* to liberate 'readers from the tyranny of imported meanings' provide two frameworks for a single reading of *A Passage to India*. From this double perspective the novel becomes simultaneously a fulfilment of the romantic mode and an opening out from itself to a still uninvented form of fiction. A similar eclecticism, this time in terms of the relationship of *Aspects of the Novel* to formalist and anti-formalist ideas, is seen to characterize Forster's critical stance. But this placing of *Aspects of the Novel* within its contemporary critical and philosophic contexts also allows us to view it as an achieved literary text in its own right. Both as criticism and literature its success is seen to be a direct function of its eclectic form.

These arguments are picked up in several other essays. Intellectual contexts are emphasized in the essay that explores Forster's relationship with Roger Fry and Charles Mauron, and another nineteenth-century context is provided in a study of Forster's reading of Pater. Two readings of *Maurice* emphasize context as well. In one the emphasis is both biographical and generic in its examination of the novel's relationship to the genre of fantasy; in the other, *Maurice* is read in terms of its early twentieth-century social and intellectual milieu. *A Passage to India* is placed in a succession of frames — the mythological, the philosophical, the biographical. Forster's India is the home of friends, a source of mythological figures and a landscape congenial to the Plotinian speculations in which he had become interested in Alexandria.

In two of the essays on *A Passage to India*, text takes the place of context. In one the novel is examined as a complex linguistic system in which problems of syntax define problems of vision and ultimately challenge the ordering of art. In another the novel is read as a text which enacts by means of the manipulation of perspective its 'demonstration of discord . . . [in its] search for unity'. Text, this time the actual manuscript texts, is the subject of an essay that examines the editorial task itself, particularly the elucidating of doubtful readings involved in the preparation of *The Manuscripts of A Passage to India* (Abinger 6A). Editing is seen as a process of annotation which traces 'the paths followed by the author's imagination in creating the fiction'. Aspects of this process are also explored in the preparation of the general notes for *Arctic Summer* and *Nottingham Lace*. Another manuscript study discusses the evolution of *Maurice* from the original version through the successive alterations and revisions that extended over a fifty-five year period to the text finally published after Forster's death.

The essays on *A Passage to India*, however, are not so much revaluations as further minings of an incredibly rich vein, for there is no disputing the novel's place as one of the crucial modernist texts. The two essays on *Howards End*, by contrast, do pick up a much discussed question — how does one deal with the constant and some would claim intrusive presence of the author-narrator — but respond to it in new ways. Using different approaches, but both emphasizing the language of narration, these essays demonstrate the subtlety of this too easily denigrated narrative strategy.

One essay does stand apart from the others for it is personal witness rather than academic speculation. Its subject is memory, the author's recollection of his friendship with Forster and the experience of India they both shared and wrote about. This sense of personal connection and literary influence was also the essential subject of those writers who participated in the Writers' Panel held during the conference. Only two of the participants had had any direct contact with Forster but in varying degrees he was and is a presence in their writing. Although Forster in his many essays on writers he liked, admired, or merely felt called upon to comment on did not talk too often on the subject of influence, his remarks in the Butler essay ('A Book That Influenced Me') are directly to the point here. 'The only books that influence us are those for which we are ready and which have gone a little further down our particular path than we have yet got ourselves'.[12] The paths of the five writers who spoke in Montreal have by no means been the same but each writer testifies to encountering Forster somewhere along the way.

Nonetheless the decision to include their discussions in this book was made after an initial uncertainty. After all, how accurately can one catch the occasional speaking voice in print, how give form to the often casual and conversational tone? But finally it seemed that the personal reminiscence was indeed a most appropriate way to talk about one who invested such faith in people talking to one another, and who could, besides, speak of his own favourite writers in such casual and conversational tones as these: 'One's favourite book is certainly as elusive as one's favourite pudding, but there certainly are three writers whom I would like to have in every room, so that I can stretch out my hand for them at any moment'.[13] The stretching out of the hand to a book become a personal friend is surely a fitting emblem for the centenary activities themselves and for this volume that is their record.

NOTES

1. E. M. Forster, 'My Own Centenary', *Abinger Harvest* (London: Edward Arnold, 1961), p. 75.
2. P. N. Furbank, *E. M. Forster: A Life* (London: Secker and Warburg, 1978), II, 145.
3. John Crowe Ransom, 'E. M. Forster', *Kenyon Review*, V (1943), p. 618.
4. John Lehmann, *In My Own Time* (Boston: Little Brown, 1969), p. 327.
5. Ransom, p. 618.
6. Leonard Woolf, 'Arch Beyond Arch', *Nation and Athenaeum*, XXXV (1924), rpt. in Philip Gardner, *E. M. Forster: The Critical Heritage* (London and Boston: Routledge and Kegan Paul, 1973), p. 204. F. R. Leavis, *The*

Common Pursuit (London: Chatto and Windus, 1952), p. 274.

7. Howe uses that phrase to describe Hardy's manner in *Two on a Tower*. Hardy employed 'that cool, hard, comic tone which would later reach a kind of perfection in E. M. Forster's novels'. Irving Howe, *Thomas Hardy* (New York: Macmillan, 1967), p. 73.

8. 'Appendix A: "An Exchange Between Forster and R. C. Trevelyan"', in E. M. Forster, *Where Angels Fear to Tread*, ed. Oliver Stallybrass, Abinger edn. (London: Edward Arnold, 1975), p. 151.

9. Ransom, p. 621.

10. E. M. Forster, *A Room With a View*, ed. Oliver Stallybrass, Abinger edn. (London: Edward Arnold, 1977), p. 117.

11. Frederick Crews, *E. M. Forster: The Perils of Humanism* (Princeton, N.J.: Princeton University Press, 1962), p. 14.

12. E. M. Forster, 'A Book that Influenced Me', *Two Cheers for Democracy*, ed. Oliver Stallybrass, Abinger edn. (London: Edward Arnold, 1972), pp. 214–15.

13. E. M. Forster, 'In My Library', *TCD*, p. 298.

Part I

Politics and Philosophy

2 E. M. Forster's Subversive Individualism

Wilfred Stone

I

It is appropriate on this centenary of Forster's birth to take a look at some aspects of his social philosophy — his liberalism, his well-known creed of 'personal relations', his lifelong contention with the vexed problem of *power*. It is appropriate because Forster made his mark not just as a novelist, but also as a humanist; not just as an artist, but as a moral influence; not just as the author of *A Passage to India*, but also as the author of 'What I Believe'. It is appropriate as well because Forster's social attitudes are deeply personal, and now that P. N. Furbank's biography is out, and Forster is out of the closet in other ways, the materials are available for a reassessment. His position as a novelist is, I believe, forever secure, whereas his position as a humanist, as the liberal moral philosopher, is, I think, more problematical. But his influence in this role has been immense, and this centenary year will doubtless be the occasion for many people to re-evaluate the impact of Forster's influence upon them.

Let me begin with that striking statement Forster made in his post-war broadcast talk 'The Challenge of Our Time' (1946):

I belong to the fag-end of Victorian liberalism, and can look back to an age whose challenges were moderate in their tone, and the cloud on whose horizon was no bigger than a man's hand. In many ways it was an admirable age. It practised benevolence and philanthropy, was humane and intellectually curious, upheld free speech, and had little colour-prejudice, believed that individuals are and should be different, and entertained a sincere faith in the progress of society. The world

was to become better and better, chiefly through the spread
of parliamentary institutions. The education I received in
those far-off and fantastic days made me soft and I am very
glad it did, for I have seen plenty of hardness since, and I know
it does not even pay. Think of the end of Mussolini — the hard
man, hanging upside-down like a turkey, with his dead
mistress swinging beside him.[1]

I distinctly remember my shocked reaction when I first read that
statement — shortly after I had spent four years in an unwanted
military uniform. How, I wanted to cry out, did Forster suppose
that that hard man Mussolini got his comeuppance, except at
the hands of other hard men, or men who had been trained to be
hard? Did he suppose that some abstract force of history, operating automatically and inevitably, took care of these threats to
civilization without human intervention? What kind of bloodless
dream of history was this? And by what right did Forster the
non-combatant stand on the sidelines of conflict and assure us
that the hard ones always lost, just a few years after they had
come so desperately close to winning? To citizens of the twentieth
century who have known trenches and breadlines and concen-
tration camps for their inheritance, Forster's defence of 'softness'
can seem at best unrealistic and at worst infuriating. Yet the idea
of softness is at the heart of Forster's liberal philosophy; it is
literally soft at the centre.

So our question is: How valuable is a creed so centred? Is it a
responsible code or is it a cop-out — a denial of complexity and a
turning away from history? How seriously can we take Forster's
personal witness for softness in a world increasingly dominated
by the hard impersonality of gigantic armaments, gigantic
corporations, gigantic machines, gigantic populations, gigantic
cities? In engaging with that question, I shall consult Forster's
fiction and biography as different aspects of one record — as I
believe in essentials they are. And I shall approach the question
via Forster's personal experience, for it is that personal experience more than any theoretical belief that is written into 'What
I Believe' and those other credal pronouncements of Forster's
sixth decade. To ask what meaning that creed has for our day,
we must first ask what meaning it had for Forster himself.

II

As a child, Forster was brought up in virtual protective custody. Fatherless, surrounded by a doting mother and aunts, Forster ('the important one') was the centre of a charmed circle of love from which he never entirely escaped. That charmed circle was both a womb and a prison, a place of safety and of suffocation, and I believe that Forster's life can be largely described as a struggle between his desire to escape that confinement (to hold his own with hardness) and the temptation to return to that womb (to give in to softness). P. N. Furbank points out that Forster even as an adult had the sense of being one specially selected — 'one who, having been specially and royally favoured as a child, had magical feelings about his own life',[2] a sense of being set apart for something like divine favour. I think this magical sense was operating when Forster looked at the dead Mussolini and saw that hardness did not pay: he was looking out at a hard world and seeing, with relief, that his special Providence was at work, that the protectors were doing their job of making things safe for the favoured child. But living within this charmed circle was not all comfort, and Rickie in *The Longest Journey* is eloquent testimony that protective custody could be as much a prison as a paradise:

> The boy grew up in great loneliness. He worshipped his mother, and she was fond of him. But she was dignified and reticent, and pathos, like tattle, was disgusting to her. She was afraid of intimacy, in case it led to confidence and tears, and so all her life she held her son at a little distance. Her kindness and unselfishness knew no limits, but if he tried to be dramatic and thank her, she told him not to be a little goose. And so the only person he came to know at all was himself.[3]

To break out of that feminine confine, Forster could expect help from no-one but himself, and there is real anger at the father who, psychologically, abandoned him. When I was gathering photographs for *The Cave and the Mountain*, Forster gladly gave me pictures of the mother but would not give me one of the father; I felt he simply did not want the father represented in his life story. It is clear, I think, that Forster as a young man fought a kind of losing battle for his own manhood and that his homosexuality is a direct result of his early smothering — a kind of victory in that it was a defiance of the guardians, a kind of defeat in that it was a denial of fatherhood. But Forster did fantasize breaking out: I think those scenes of physical violence in his fiction (like Gino and Philip in *Angels*) and those outbursts of hardboiled petulance in his essays ('the strong are so stupid') are ways he asserted his masculinity. And that story 'The Machine Stops' is nothing but a fantasy of violent escape from the mother's realm. D. H. Lawrence identified Forster's central crisis, I believe, when in 1915 he wrote to Bertrand Russell (when Forster was 36): 'Will all the poetry in the world satisfy the manhood of Forster, when Forster knows that his implicit manhood is to be satisfied by nothing but immediate physical action?'[4] To become a man, Forster had to fight clear, to use his muscles, to test his courage, to endure pain, to act as a sexual being. Forster knew this, but he also knew the temptation of a powerful tug in the reverse direction, towards softness, pacifism, non-involvement, and what he called 'decadence' — all values that, throughout his life, he accorded deep respect.

The Longest Journey dramatizes this struggle. The essential plot of the book shows Forster killing off a soft, weak, half-wanted self, Rickie, in favour of a hard, strong, longed-for self, Stephen. Stephen the half-brother is the continuator, the stud who breeds the child that continues the family line through the beloved mother. But Rickie, Forster's direct representative in the novel, suffers deterioration and death, and through him the hated father's line is allowed to die out. Thus Forster gets revenge — on the father, and on certain qualities he loathed in himself. That Rickie and Stephen represent two sides of Forster seems to me evident: on the one side is weakness, ugliness, dependency; on the other a craving for strength (even brutality), beauty and heroism. Even relatively late in life Forster looks in his own mirror and sees these two personae contending. Here is part of his New Year's 'summing-up' for 1925:

> Jan. 2 Famous, wealthy, miserable, physically ugly — red nose enormous, round patch in middle of scalp which I forget less than I did and which is brown when I don't wash my head and pink when I do. Face in the distance . . . is toad-like and pallid . . . My stoop must be appalling yet I don't think much of it . . . and am surprised I don't repel more generally: I can still get

to know any one I want and have that illusion that I am charming and beautiful.[5]

Stephen is less Rickie's anti-self than he is a wished-for alter ego, another self that could defend and protect the central self. It is significant that in all of Forster's fiction where weak Prufrock-like men appear they save themselves (when they don't simply run away) through the acquisition of protectors. There are two great exceptions — the short stories 'Dr. Woolacott' (1927) and 'The Other Boat' (1957) — but in most of the fiction protection comes from outside, in the form of guardians, class privileges, wealth, 'civilization', or tough guys like Stephen who happen to be on the right side. Meanwhile, outside of fiction, in real life, Forster was deeply drawn to strong men who could be enticed into friendship or love. Perhaps the ideal in this direction was T. E. Lawrence, that close friend who combined heroism and sensitivity,[6] and whom Forster sought in vain as a lover. But there were other hard ones, notably the police officer Bob Buckingham, with whom Forster had more success, to say nothing of the 'reformed and unreformed burglars' and others with whom Forster had affairs.[7] Whatever these affairs mean, they do represent the kind of physical engagement D. H. Lawrence called for — an effort to move out of his *cordon sanitaire* and engage with a hard world.

But the hard ones, as Forster experiences them, usually come as enemies, not as friends, and to confront them in the flesh was a terror of his young life. Stephen's opposite in *The Longest Journey* is Gerald the bully, who persecutes rather than protects the weak. This is how Rickie remembers him, years after his school days:

> The horror disappeared, for, thank God, he was now a man, whom civilization protects. But he and Gerald had met, as it were, behind the scenes, before our decorous drama opens, and there the elder boy had done things to him — absurd things, not worth chronicling separately. An apple-pie bed is nothing; pinches, kicks, boxed ears, twisted arms, pulled hair, ghosts at night, inky books, befouled photographs, amount to very little by themselves. But let them be united and continuous, and you have a hell that no grown-up devil can devise. Between Rickie and Gerald there lay a shadow that darkens life more often than we suppose. The bully and his victim never quite forget their first relations. (iii, 43)

The one who has been bullied desires revenge, and Forster openly used the pen as a weapon to avenge himself on those who had hurt him. 'In no book', he said, 'have I got down more than the people I like, the person I think I am, and the people who irritate me'.[8] And in his 1920 essay 'The Consolations of History', Forster expresses frank delight in paying off old scores against the military — a form of organized hardness that, along with bureaucracy generally, he wholeheartedly loathed:

> It is pleasant to be transferred from an office where one is afraid of a sergeant-major into an office where one can intimidate generals, and perhaps this is why History is so attractive to the more timid amongst us. We can recover self-confidence by snubbing the dead.[9]

Yet we should not conclude that Forster disapproved of hardness or even brutality. He just wanted it to be on his side, operating as his vicar. Howard Sholton in 'The Purple Envelope' (1905), for example, 'loved to take life, as all those do who are really in touch with nature'.[10] And in another passage from *The Longest Journey* we are told that Rickie believes 'something can be said' for cruelty and brutality:

> Athletes, he believed, were simple, straightforward people, cruel and brutal, if you like, but never petty. They knocked you down and hurt you, and then went on their way rejoicing. For this, Rickie thought, there is something to be said: he had escaped the sin of despising the physically strong — a sin against which the physically weak must guard.   (iii, 42)

The school scenes in *The Longest Journey* reflect the spirit if not the letter of Forster's actual experiences at school. Furbank tells us of Forster's profound unhappiness at the various schools he attended from the age of 11. At 'The Grange', for example, where he spent the summer of 1892, Forster learned what it was to be bullied, and his letters home from this place are desperate pleas to be rescued: 'O what is going to happen? . . . I feel utterly wretched, I would like to come away. Every one is against me . . .' Furbank comments:

> There was nothing for it but to withdraw him from the school,

and he returned to 'Rooksnest' in floods of tears. His beloved Maimie was there, and between them the two women soon comforted him; but he could tell from his mother's manner that she was ashamed of him as a cry-baby. It had been impressed on him when he went to 'The Grange' that it was a school for the sons of gentlemen, and all through his troubles there the refrain ran through his mind: 'If they were not the sons of gentlemen they would not be so unkind'.[11]

At Tonbridge, where he spent the next eight years and where the 'sons of gentlemen' came a notch lower on the social ladder, he was not so cruelly bullied but was miserable, bored and, as Furbank says, keenly wounded by 'the general atmosphere of unkindness'.[12] 'School was the unhappiest time of my life',[13] he wrote later. He came away from the experience with a life-long 'horror of gangs', and his device for recovering his balance after being bullied was, as Furbank reports, 'mentally resolving the gang back into individuals'.[14] He was a day student at Tonbridge, so the mother's protection was still extended, one result of which was that he was permitted to ride a bicycle instead of engaging in games — an unprecedented relaxation of the rules. Tonbridge failed utterly to harden Forster; he simply would not rise to the bait. To the degree that the Kiplingesque school anthem expressed the spirit of the place, to that degree Forster despised it, and one of the finer touches in *The Longest Journey* is the the small boy who refused to sing the anthem on the grounds that 'it hurt his throat'. Two couplets that Forster exposed to special ridicule were these:

> Here shall Tonbridge flourish, here shall manhood be,
> Serving God and country, ruling land and sea . . .
> Choose we for life's battle harp or sword or pen;
> Perish every laggard, let us all be men.[15]

The religiosity, the patriotism, the muscularity of those verses all rubbed Forster the wrong way. They were tainted by the bullying that went with them, and Forster's notion of 'manhood' differed fundamentally from the school ideal. To the school's hardness he opposed — with considerable pluckiness — his own softness, and over the years made a creed of it. But his rejection of those school ideals confirmed him forever as an outsider, a pariah, to the main ranks of his own class.

After Tonbridge came Cambridge which, of course, was every-thing Tonbridge was not. Here too was a muscular 'best set', but it did not dominate, and here Forster the pariah felt welcomed and warmed — particularly after he became accepted as a member of the Apostles. This was the Cambridge of Lord Acton who was saying that 'All power corrupts and absolute power corrupts absolutely', and here were friends who cultivated a pose of *ir*reverence towards the very values extolled in the Tonbridge anthem. The following lines published in *Basileona*, an undergraduate magazine, caught the new mood perfectly:

> I fail to see the reason why
> Brittania should rule the waves,
> Nor can I safely prophesy
> That Britons never shall be slaves;
> It always gives me quite a pain
> Ever to *think* about the main.
>
> Elusive prospects of renown
> Do not excite me in the least,
> A Lion fighting for a Crown
> Is hardly an attractive beast.
> If you are anxious to be shot
> For Queen and Country, I am not.[16]

Cambridge was once again a kind of charmed circle for Forster, an *alma mater* offering a new kind of protective custody; but it was within those protected bounds that Forster's liberalism, an existential experience, found its first deep reinforcement.

Time permitting, we could trace Forster's contention with the issue of crude power through all his novels, particularly in *Howards End* and *A Passage to India*. Suffice it to say that the issue of softness vs. hardness, sensitivity vs. brutality, is central and that Forster — to his credit — does his best as author to guard against the sin of the physically weak — that of 'despising the physically strong'. He has Margaret marry the redblood Henry and insists on honouring the Wilcox energy and grit: 'If Wilcoxes hadn't worked and died in England for thousands of years, you and I couldn't sit here without having our throats cut'.[17] And Aziz tries to be friends with the English, his imperial oppressors, until the pressures of politics force them apart. In both novels the forces of alienation prove stronger than those of connection, for the reason that the hard ones — those grown-up public school boys — behave too badly. One speech by Ronny Heaslop tells it all:

> I am out here to work, mind, to hold this wretched country by force. I'm not a missionary or a Labour Member or a vague sentimental sympathetic literary man. I'm just a servant of the Government . . . We're not pleasant in India and we don't intend to be pleasant. We've something more important to do. [18]

Forster is, of course, characterizing himself in that 'vague sentimental sympathetic literary man', and at least one distinguished Indian critic has testified that if Forster's ideal of a 'democratic Empire' had been tried in India — a society based on equal rights and privileges for Indians and Englishmen alike — the British Empire could have been an enduring institution. [19] But the imperialist, as Forster tells us in *Howards End*, is a 'destroyer' — and in retrospect, when Forster's ideas for governing India are compared with those that were actually tried, Forster begins to look like a practical politician! But we must return to biography.

The event that perhaps tested Forster's liberal humanism most acutely and painfully was the First World War. All Bloomsbury felt, says Furbank, that 'it was not *their* war', [20] and Forster aligned himself with this attitude. The war filled him with nothing less than 'panic and emptiness', and his first response was to find refuge in friends, exercising the old pattern of dissolving the 'gang' into individuals. 'He was doubly disturbed', Furbank tells us, '— by the war itself, and by the inadequacy of his own response to it'. [21] That response *was* inadequate. Essentially he just ran away — to the safety of a cushy job with the Red Cross in Alexandria — and when in 1916 he was threatened with conscription (technically, the duty to 'attest'), he simply went to pieces. Here is Furbank's account:

> He was now in a serious dilemma. He was determined not to attest, yet could not easily explain his reasons — for he knew that, in a strict sense, he was not a conscientious objector. For a few days he was badly thrown by the contretemps, and — as once or twice later in life in times of stress — he developed a

kind of falling sickness and had bouts of hurling himself against the furniture. [22]

He finally managed to stay out of the army through some wire-pulling with high-ranking friends—a conspicuous instance of using his social rank as a 'protector'. 'I am quite shameless over this wirepulling', Forster wrote to his mother in 1916; 'If I can't keep out of the army by fair means then hey for foul! Let alone that there conscience. I know I should be no good, and haven't the least desire to pacify the parrots who cry "All must go"'. [23] One cannot, of course, fail to share Forster's horror of the war and his desire to escape it, but neither can one refrain from asking the obvious, embarrassing question: What about those hundreds of thousands who had no high-ranking friends and no wires to pull? This is but one of the many times in his life that Forster invoked special privilege in order to save himself— and is but an extended pattern of that tearful escape home from school.

During these war years in Alexandria Forster experienced an intense retreat inward. There was, of course, a movement out-ward as well — to an interest in the history and politics of Egypt that led to *Alexandria: A History and A Guide* (1922), *Pharos and Pharillon* (1923), and his long essay 'The Government of Egypt' for the Labour Research Department (1920). It was this period, as Lionel Trilling has said, that gave Forster 'a firm position on the Imperial question'. [24] But I think these outgoing efforts were, in part at least, a kind of moral compensation for having so narcissistically sought sanctuary during the war years. [25] Part of that inward retreat expressed itself as an embrace of 'deca-dence'. After having read Huysmans' *A Rebours* and Eliot's *Prufrock* in 1917, he wrote: 'Oh, the relief of a world which lived for its sensations and ignored the will . . . Was it decadent? Yes, and thank God'. [26] And speaking specifically of Prufrock he wrote: 'Here was a protest, and a feeble one, and the more congenial for being feeble. For what, in that world of gigantic horror, was tolerable except the slighter gestures of dissent?' (*AH*, 107). Eliot would have been surprised, I think, to know that anyone read *Prufrock* as a 'protest'. Forster's reasons are interesting:

> He who measured himself against the war, who drew himself to his full height, as it were, and said to Armadillo-Armageddon 'Avaunt!' collapsed at once into a pinch of dust. But he who

could turn aside to complain of ladies and drawing-rooms preserved a tiny drop of our self-respect, he carried on the human heritage. (*AH*, 107)

This is salvation via nostalgia. What Forster is saying is that he felt safe in such rooms with such ladies — perhaps even saved — and there is little question that his embrace of 'decadence' as a value in this period is a kind of fantasy return to the womb. He loved Eliot's poems because they 'were innocent of public-spiritedness: they sang of private disgust and diffidence, and of people who seemed genuine because they were unattractive or weak' (*AH*, 106). Can there be any doubt that this is Forster looking into his own mirror? He is building a defence for the 'unattractive or weak', for softness, and I think that it is during these years that Forster crystallized that defence into something like a principle — and into a political position that touched more than the Imperial question. He was confronted with the clear choice of either being ashamed of himself or being proud of himself, and he elected to be proud of himself. Unless the world is made safe for the soft individual it cannot, for Forster, be a tolerable world: he wanted a literal translation of the hope that the meek should inherit the earth. Decadence? Forster refuses to hear it as a bad word. Years later, in 1939, when these conflicts had been reduced to a creed, Forster declared that decadence is what some people call those intervals in history when 'force and violence' do not 'get to the front'. Forster calls those absences 'civilization' and finds in such interludes 'the chief justification for the human experiment'.[27]

But Forster did not arrive at such views easily. His letters to friends out of Alexandria are full of trouble and sadness, and he by no means managed to 'let alone that there conscience'. Alexandria was a time of sexual awakening for Forster and he was excited by the streams of soldiers pouring into the Montazah Convalescent Hospital where he worked; but he was conscious as well that they came from a hell he had no part of. 'It makes me very happy yet very sad', he writes to Lowes Dickinson in July 1916; 'they come from the unspeakable all these young gods, and in a fortnight at the latest they will return to it . . .' But what comes next? Does Forster consider joining them? Partaking of their suffering like a brother? On the contrary, he clings to his privileged position, and his conscience erodes into a daydream of what might be: 'Why not a world like this?' (referring to the comforts the soldiers knew at the hospital). Why not a world 'that should not torture itself by organized and artificial horrors?'[28] This is no way to 'face facts', and friends who were not pacifists (as Dickinson was) criticized Forster for his evasions; but during this period that dream of a world without violence became, in some strange way, confused in Forster's mind with moral action. He looked out on the 'real' world as if from a kind of hibernation, a drugged quarantine; and though he sensed that there was something 'unreal' about his position, he clung to it. Thus he writes to Bertrand Russell in 1917:

> Here I have been for nearly two years. Harmless and un-harmed. Here in Egyptian hospitals. I live in their wards, questioning survivors. It has been a comfortable life. How unreal I shan't know till I compare it with the lives others have been leading in the period. I don't write, but feel I think and think I feel. Sometimes I make notes on human nature under war conditions . . . I love people and want to understand them and help them more than I did, but this is oddly accompanied by a growth of contempt. Be like them? God, no.[29]

There is class snobbery here and maybe something worse, but this passage gives us a glimpse at the workings of Forster's 'conscience'. Love warring with contempt measures the degree of Forster's self-contempt — and the guilt (evaded rather than suppressed) arising from his position of special privilege. But such exclusiveness is inseparable from Forster's liberal human-ism, for the softness it defends is his own softness, and in that defence Forster again and again implicitly declares himself to be a special case and deserving of special treatment. In spite of having 'magical feelings about his own life' and feeling in some way exempted from the common human fate, he at the same time felt that his situation was somehow 'unreal'. But Forster is never openly apologetic over a position that some people saw as plain cowardice; and Alexandria, I believe, was the testing place where he gained the confidence to accept himself as he was, and to be his own kind of liberal.

During the war, Forster felt that history was sweeping him away, that he could not get anywhere by the exercise of will, that in all the big things he was helpless. Like Cavafy (and perhaps with Cavafy's help), he reduced history to personal relations, to relations — in his case — based on homosexual love. And he elevated 'decadence' to something like an ideal.

But the germ of an opposing attitude was alive in him. And after the war, as if to make up for his wartime retreat, he came out of his cocoon and engaged in a wide variety of political actions. Throughout the 'twenties he was an active critic of England's imperialistic crimes in India and Egypt; as first president of the National Council for Civil Liberties, he did what he could to defend free speech on the BBC and elsewhere; he led a wide-ranging assault with his pen on bureaucracy, in the military and in government offices (hitting a high point with that fine satire, 'Our Deputation'); he was active in fighting literary censorship and the prudery behind it, defending Radclyffe Hall's *Well of Loneliness* (1928) and, much later, Lawrence's *Lady Chatterley's Lover* (1960); he was active in the PEN Club and in 1928 became the first president of the 'Young PEN', a club for young and unknown writers; he continually spoke out against homosexual and racial prejudice. As another war loomed, Forster became somewhat disillusioned with activism, and on the eve of the Munich crisis he was asked by Goronwy Rees, assistant editor of the *Spectator*, 'Why have you given up politics?' He replied, 'Because I want just a *little* result'.[30]

To be sure, Forster was an activist only in liberal causes, which is to say only causes for which words are weapons. But he had emerged from hiding and become a fighter with words, and he no longer acquiesced in the belief that history operated by its own forces and could not be affected by the will. If Forster became less organizationally engaged in the late 'thirties and early 'forties, he assuredly did not become less articulate. In these years Forster uttered a flood of speeches, broadcasts and essays defining his liberal humanist position — the greatest of which is 'What I Believe' in 1939. In them all, Forster stood his ground in defence of softness, but it was a position toughly held and not weakly acted out. Julian Bell, before he was killed in the Spanish Civil War in 1937, had challenged Forster's pacifism as an archaic posture in a world threatened by Hitlers and Mussolinis. But in reply Forster refused to 'chuck gentleness' and went on to say, 'If one has been gentle, semi-idealistic, and semi-cynical, kind, tolerant, demure, and generally speaking a liberal for nearly sixty years, it is wiser to stick to one's outfit'.[31] And it was about this time that Christopher Isherwood in *Lions and Shadows* (1938) had talked about the need for the 'Truly Weak Man' to submit himself to what he called the 'Test'. Forster would have none of this, and wrote to Isherwood in February 1938:

> *Bother the Test* — am so certain I shall fail mine that I can't think about it. Now and then I get toward facing facts, but get too tired to keep on at it. I only hope I shan't let any one down badly: *that* thought does present itself rather alarmingly.[32]

If this is still somewhat self-indulgent, it is at least honest; Forster is sure of who he is and unabashed about acting the part.

During the second war, Forster's stance became one of 'keeping calm and cheerful'. He did not succumb to despair — though he had a tragic sense that the old order had forever 'vanished from the earth'[33] and he turned out, during the war years, a steady stream of propaganda broadcasts, one of them beginning memorably with the words, 'This pamphlet is propaganda'![34] But throughout the war he concerned himself less with winning battles than with reminding his countrymen and women that it was 'civilisation' they were fighting for, not victory. What would be gained if in defeating the Nazis we allowed our culture to become 'governmental' like theirs? All would be lost. And his PEN speech in the autumn of 1941 — to a hall full of anti-Hitler writers and refugees, all highly committed — began, 'I believe in art for art's sake'.[35]

III

But all these utterances can be glossed by reference to the one classic statement of 1939, 'What I Believe'. It is all there. Forster in his level speaking voice and colloquial vocabulary, without pomposity or prophetic intonation, made a statement that has become a classic in the modern liberal/humanist tradition. Since most readers probably know this essay almost by heart, I shall dip into it only briefly. He comes out as the defender of weakness ('the strong are so stupid'); of a saving élite ('an aristocracy of the sensitive, the considerate and the plucky'); of free speech ('I believe in [Parliament] *because* it is a Talking Shop'); of something like deconstruction ('The more highly public life is organized, the lower does its morality sink'); and, of course, of personal relations, the key to the whole creed:

> . . . there is even a terror and a hardness in this creed of personal relationships, urbane and mild though it sounds. Love and loyalty to an individual can run counter to the claims of the State. When they do — down with the State, say I, which means that the State would down me.
>
> (*TCD*, 68, 70, 67, 71, 66)

These are tough statements. If this author is not much good with his fists or the sword, he has learned to be very good with words. And if this is a creed born of weakness and dependency, it no longer sounds like a cry from the beleaguered schoolboy. Forster lived in a free country and would not be jailed — not yet — for sounding treasonous. Nevertheless, these are radical things to say on the eve of a war and it took courage to say them. No one could accuse Forster of playing it safe or of currying favour with the powerful.

But — to return to the question with which we began — how viable is such a creed as a programme of action, as creed to be *followed*? In attempting to answer that, I should like to invoke the name of a writer behind the Iron Curtain, the Hungarian novelist George Konrád. In Konrád's career and words, superficially so different from Forster's, I find Forster's creed validated in some critical ways. Konrád as a writer assumes an oppositional stance against the state that, in interesting ways, parallels Forster's — and dramatizes how Forster's creed could be put to work in a 'real' confrontation. Konrád is an Eastern European and a Jew who has known repression first hand. Only four of the one hundred students who attended his small-town Jewish elementary school are alive today. 'I have known ever since', he writes, 'that you cannot trust the state, only a few friends at best.'[36] Those who ran the death camps were loyal citizens of the state and that, writes Konrád, is the greater part of their evil. On the dangers of bureaucracy and the power of the non-violent individual in opposing it, Konrád agrees with Forster down the line. Forster we remember, in 'What I Believe', addresses not an age of anarchy but an age of 'faith', not a world unorganized, but a world too highly organized and growing more so — in which the top dog is the bureaucrat, civil or military. Both Forster and Konrád would agree with Max Weber in seeing the threat to the future as coming not from the left or the right but from the bureaucracy; and Konrád extols friendship as a value in the face of a cruelly oppressive state in words that virtually paraphrase Forster's. Forster says, 'If I had to choose between betraying my country and betraying my friend, I hope I should have the guts to betray my country' (*TCD*, 66). Konrád says, 'The true symbol of the totalitarian state is not the executioner, but the exemplary bureacrat who proves to be more loyal to the state than to his friend'.[37]

Konrád utters many more words that could have come from Forster's own mouth. This dissenting spokesman from Soviet-occupied Hungary believes in the efficacy of ideas as weapons with something of the fervour of a Victorian liberal. Let us gloss a few of his statements:

Let us not want to win; let's just try to curtail each other's power. It's better to talk than fight.[38]

[Compare Forster: I realize that all society rests upon force. But all the great creative actions, all the decent human relations, occur during the intervals when force has not managed to come to the front.] (*TCD*, 68)

You can use violence with everyone, but the inner chambers of consciousness cannot be touched by violence; it's much too crude for that.[39]

[Compare Forster: So that is what I feel about force and violence. It is, alas! the ultimate reality on this earth, but it does not always get to the front. Some people call its absences 'decadence'; I call them 'civilisation' and find in such interludes the chief justification for the human experiment.] (*TCD*, 68)

We represent the truth, our enemies the opposite, believed the old-time revolutionaries. We awakened from this adolescent dream.[40]

[Compare Forster: They have Faith, with a large F. My faith has a very small one, and I can only intrude it because these are strenuous and serious days, and one likes to say what one thinks while speech is comparatively free . . .] (*TCD*, 72)

Here are a few more of Konrád's statements that cannot be glossed so precisely but that nevertheless echo the spirit of Forster's creed:

> Whether I survive or not, this war is as absurd as all the others. I would like to drink, not fire a gun; there isn't an army I wouldn't desert.[41]

> I never hated my class. Having been brought up in it I was merely ashamed of it.[42]

> For me the lesson learned from the war was this: we must make the individual citizen less dependent on the state, and make the state more dependent on the individual.[43]

Here is a freedom fighter who believes in personal relations, who loathes violence, and who is convinced that the 'guerrillas of the typewriter'[44] can, if persistent, win every time in the face of superior armed might. 'This quiet revolution begins', writes Konrád, 'with people who do not subordinate their conscience to the needs of the state.'[45] Konrád's prediction is that 'during the fourth quarter of this century citizens in their slow and cunning ways, will "humanize" the state'.[46] They will do this not through violence, but through being a yeast, a kind of Arnoldian 'saving remnant', that will spread its virtue like an ink blot or a beneficent disease. It is the same faith that Forster places in his 'aristocracy of the sensitive, the considerate and the plucky' — an aristocracy not of power but of those elect souls found in all ages, classes, and nations who represent 'the true human condition, the one permanent victory of our queer race over cruelty and chaos' (*TCD*, 70).

Is this faith naïve? Well, obviously, it would only work under certain conditions. In opposing an Idi Amin or a Shah of Iran — two overthrown despots who depended on torture rather than words as the instruments of their power — such a faith would have no more effect than, as Forster might say, love or a flower. It is a creed potent only in societies that have some respect for law and tradition, some sensitivity for human rights, some reluctance simply to wipe out or jail their dissidents. Apparently modern-day Hungary, however precariously, qualifies as this kind of society, for Konrád — though he was briefly arrested in 1973 for collaborating on a book about the rise of intellectuals to class power — has managed to stay out of prison while continuing to turn out novels and essays severely critical of the state. To be sure, Konrád walks a tightrope that Forster, in his much freer society, never had to. Nevertheless, the fact that Konrád puts his beliefs to risk in an active political arena — and against a formidable state power — for me authenticates Forster's position in important ways. They both hold creeds admirably designed to wear away the establishment, to keep it off balance, to remind it that governments exist to serve human beings and not for their own sakes. It may not always be true that 'the strong are . . . stupid' or that 'the more a society is organized, the lower does its morality sink' (Forster, *TCD*, 71), or that 'An ideal is deformed as soon as it is adopted by a system'[47] (Konrád), but it is true much of the time, and these are useful precepts in the unending war for decency in human society. So, though Forster's creed of liberal humanism in large part grew out of his own sense of dependency and weakness, it need not be soft at the centre. Though Forster was never tested as Konrád was tested — and both are essentially men of words and not of action — it is clear to me that in the Second World War Forster was quite ready to stand and die for what he believed if called upon to do so. That hope that he should 'have the guts' to betray his country before he betrayed his friend would have been, I believe, a fulfilled hope. Forster's dream of 'civilisation' repudiates the fighting attitude, but Forster could fight — with words — when he had to; his dream was of a womb, a quiet place, but over the years Forster had learned that huddling there was not the way to solve problems or find self-respect. He became a fierce non-combatant — most impressively in 'What I Believe'. The great social need of the modern world is to keep bureaucracy human, to bring bigness down to size, to keep power from becoming abstract. Both Forster and Konrád are evidence that the weak can be strong in this task — especially if they hold on to their faith as artists — the faith, in Konrád's words, that 'The act of creation is always a radical act'[48] and in Forster's that 'Creation lies at the heart of civilisation like fire in the heart of the earth'.[49]

After making that claim for 'creation', Forster went on to say, 'In this difficult day [1939] . . . it is a comfort to remember that violence has so far never worked' (*TCD*, 41–42). It is virtually

the same statement he made in 1946 when he said that 'hardness
. . . does not even pay'. What Forster means is that violence and
hardness do not, in his mind, work in *the long run*, and those words,
appropriately enough, make up the title of an essay Forster wrote
in 1938 that I would like to close with. He is talking back to the
Communists:

> Talking with Communists makes me realise the weakness of
> my own position and the badness of the twentieth-century
> society in which I live. I contribute to the badness without
> wanting to. My investments increase the general misery, and
> so may my charities. And I realise, too, that many Communists
> are finer people than myself— they are braver and less selfish,
> and some of them have gone into danger although they were
> cowards, which seems to me finest of all . . . [But] their
> argument for revolution — the argument that we must do evil
> now so that good may come in the long run — it seems to me to
> have nothing in it. Not because I am too nice to do evil, but
> because I don't believe the Communists know what leads to
> what. They say they know because they are becoming con-
> scious of 'the causality of society'. I say they don't know, and
> my counsel for 1938–39 conduct is rather: Do good, and
> possibly good may come from it. Be soft, even if you stand to
> get squashed.[50]

If one is really ready to be squashed rather than fight — as both
Forster and Konrád in different ways claim they are — one has,
in a sufficiently liberal society, some heroic potentialities. It is the
role of the hero as nuisance, as gadfly — and perhaps as martyr.
If, more formally speaking, ours is the age of the anti-hero, then
the hero might well be the victim who carefully picks the cause he
suffers or dies for. Both Forster and Konrád fall in that role — or
potentially fall in it. The advice to 'Be soft, even if you stand to
get squashed' is Forster's way of defending his personal inheritance and experience, but it is also his way of saying to a violent
world that he will not 'do evil now so that good may come in the
long run'. He has no faith in such futures; he has faith only in
the individual and in personal relationships — and in the love
and loyalty that make them vital.

Once again we ask; Is this a viable faith? The answer, I think,
is yes, but it is not a creed for everyone — especially not for those

sentimentalists who can embrace the 'aesthetic' Forster, the believer in art for art's sake, but who deny or forget Forster the serious humanist and moralist. To stand up and say that goodness equals softness, as Forster does, carries conviction only when we are persuaded that the speaker has the 'guts' to live his creed to the uttermost, to pay the ultimate price for being soft in a hard world. I believe that Forster, by 1939, stood ready to pay that price if need be — to betray his country before his friend, to be squashed rather than resort to violence. The creed stands or falls on whether Forster's personal witness to this belief is convincing. To me it is. Forster did not always pay the price that hardness demands of softness, but I believe that by 1939 he had matured to a point where he was ready to pay it. One cannot prove this, for Forster was never tested *in extremis*, but the whole bent of his experience points in this direction. Forster *is* a special case. More than most men he lived his life in terms of ends rather than means, in terms of final values rather than of movements or causes — and this aspect of his fortune makes him seem, at times, not one of us. But Forster did not exempt himself. He went into spiritual danger although he was a coward, and 'What I Believe' is the distilled testimony of how he made himself brave for others. It is one of the best reminders I know that human beings may, after all, possess the power of redeeming themselves.

NOTES

1. 'The Challenge of Our Time', *Two Cheers for Democracy*, ed. Oliver Stallybrass, Abinger edn. (London: Edward Arnold, 1972), p. 54.
2. P. N. Furbank, *E. M. Forster: A Life* (New York: Harcourt Brace Jovanovich, 1977), II, p. 131.
3. E. M. Forster, *The Longest Journey*, World's Classics, No. 578 (London: Oxford University Press, 1960), pp. 27–8.
4. Letter dated 12 February, 1915. See Harry T. Moore, ed., *Collected Letters of D. H. Lawrence* (New York: Viking, 1962), p. 318.
5. Furbank, II, p. 134.
6. P. N. Furbank points out that T. E. Lawrence's *Seven Pillars of Wisdom* 'supported him in a cherished belief that sensitiveness and introspection could exist side by side with vigour, active heroism and largeness of vision'. Furbank, II, pp. 119–20.
7. Furbank, II, p. 185.
8. E. M. Forster, 'The Art of Fiction', *The Paris Review*, I (1953), 37.
9. E. M. Forster, 'The Consolations of History', *Abinger Harvest* (London: Edward Arnold, 1961), p. 191.

10. E. M. Forster, *The Life to Come and Other Stories*, ed. Oliver Stallybrass, Abinger edn. (London: Edward Arnold, 1972), p. 36.
11. Furbank, I, p. 40.
12. Furbank, I, p. 42.
13. E. M. Forster, 'Breaking Up', *The Spectator*, LXI (July 1923), 110.
14. Furbank, I, p. 43.
15. Quoted in Furbank, I, pp. 41, 42.
16. *Basileona*, 1900. The verses were found in a *Scrapbook* of Forster's which he let me examine in the autumn of 1957.
17. E. M. Forster, *Howards End*, ed. Oliver Stallybrass, Abinger edn. (London: Edward Arnold, 1973), p. 171.
18. E. M. Forster, *A Passage to India*, ed. Oliver Stallybrass, Abinger edn. (London: Edward Arnold, 1978), p. 44.
19. G. D. Das, *E. M. Forster's India* (London: Macmillan, 1977), p. 25.
20. Furbank, II, p. 1.
21. Furbank, II, p. 1.
22. Furbank, II, p. 26.
23. Furbank, II, p. 27.
24. Lionel Trilling, *E. M. Forster* (Norfolk, Conn.: New Directions, 1943), p. 138.
25. In 1917 Forster wrote to G. Lowes Dickinson: 'I have never had the energy or intelligence to understand contemporary civilisation, have never done more than loaf through it and jump out of its way when it seemed likely to hurt me' (Furbank, II, p. 26). In 1939, in 'What I Believe', Forster wrote, 'I look the other way until fate strikes me. Whether this is due to courage or to cowardice in my own case I cannot be sure' (*TCD*, p. 68). These are not simple avoiding reactions, but part of a struggle in Forster, a life-long struggle, between courage and cowardice.
26. E. M. Forster, 'T. S. Eliot', *Abinger Harvest*, p. 106.
27. Forster, 'What I Believe', *TCD*, p. 68.
28. Furbank, II, p. 34.
29. Quoted in Jane Lagoudis Pinchin, *Alexandria Still: Forster, Durrell and Cavafy* (Princeton: Princeton University Press, 1977), p. 99.
30. Furbank, II, p. 222.
31. Furbank, II, p. 224.
32. Furbank, II, p. 223.
33. E. M. Forster, 'They Hold Their Tongues', *TCD*, p. 29.
34. E. M. Forster, *Nordic Twilight* (London: Macmillan, 1940), p. 3.
35. E. M. Forster, 'The New Disorder', *Horizon*, IV (1941), 379.
36. George Konrád, 'The Long Work of Liberty', *The New York Review of Books*, XXIV (26 January 1978), 38.
37. Konrád, p. 38.
38. Konrád, p. 40.
39. Konrád, p. 40.
40. Konrád, p. 39.
41. Konrád, *The City Builder*, trans. Ivan Sanders (New York: Harcourt Brace Jovanovich, 1977), p. 61.
42. Konrád, p. 75.
43. Konrád, p. 77.

44. Konrád, 'The Long Work of Liberty', p. 39.
45. Konrád, p. 39.
46. Konrád, p. 38.
47. Konrád, p. 39.
48. Konrád, p. 38.
49. E. M. Forster, 'What Would Germany do to Us?', *TCD*, p. 41.
50. E. M. Forster, 'The Long Run', *New Statesman and Nation* (n.s.), XVI (1938), 971–2.

3 The Philosophy of E. M. Forster

P. N. Furbank

The word 'philosophy' in my title is the right one, I think. E. M. Forster had a philosophy in the sense in which D. H. Lawrence and Blake possessed one (and in which H. G. Wells on the one hand, and Virginia Woolf on the other, did not). I mean that he had a set of theories (not just beliefs) about existence which had multiple application and formed a worked-out system. You could become a 'Forsterian' as you could a Lawrentian or a Blakeian. And though he was a natural or 'born' novelist, I cannot think of another equally considerable one who wrote so exclusively in the interests of a philosophy.

Because it is his philosophy I am concerned with, rather than just his beliefs, I shall refer rather less than might have been expected to his 'What I Believe' (anyway, I am assuming that the reader will know it pretty well). And, in general, my essay will have rather a skeletal quality, since I am only writing about the basic principles of his system (the principles of 'multiple application') whereas of course much of his best and most original thinking was done in the application of this system to particular topics. For instance, he made a persistent and lifelong study of the problem of money and the right ethical attitude to be taken towards it. And again, through all the latter part of his life he kept returning (in letters and diary-entries) to the question of whether a case could be made out for Asceticism — and if so, what kind of case. He had original views, certainly related to his philosophy, on Self-Pity, Proportion, Chastity, Nature-worship and a hundred other topics, and I do not mean to touch on them here. In fact my essay is a fairly humdrum piece of exposition, but still it may have a sort of use.

The centre or foundation of his philosophy, it seems to me, is a proposition about death — the one which figures so prominently in *Howards End*: 'Death destroys a man; the idea of Death saves him'.[1] I call it the foundation of his philosophy because, it seems clear, his self-discovery as a man and a writer came at the moment of his embracing this as a truth. Deaths, of course, proliferate in his early novels and almost the best-known line in his whole work is 'Gerald died that afternoon'.[2] It puzzled me that critics and readers should jib at it, as they sometimes do, for the novel *The Longest Journey* is inconceivable without it. (Though I see there might be reason to jib at the succeeding sentence, 'He was broken up in the football match'.) Forster, when taxed on the subject of Gerald's death, said 'It had to be passed by',[3] which puts the point exactly. He needed to convey, and succeeded marvellously in doing so, that the transition from life to death may be as simple and unexpected as that four-word sentence. And if we add to this his very early, but fine and 'central', story 'The Road from Colonus', of which the message is that an offered death may be a saviour in disguise, we have identified one essential portion of his vision. The vision seems to have come to him in very early manhood, as a revelation, enabling him to integrate the different fragments of his personality, releasing his powers, and giving him a sense of potential 'greatness' in life. And the message he drew from it was that, given the enormous fact of death, the things that are taken for granted in ordinary life have to be reappraised. As Helen Schlegel says to Leonard Bast, 'Injustice and greed would be the real thing if we lived for ever. As it is, we must hold to other things, because Death is coming. I love Death — not morbidly, but because He explains. He shows me the emptiness of Money. Death and Money are the eternal foes. Not Death and Life' (*HE*, xxvii, 235). The acceptance of the idea of death spiritualizes life. And it is by the route of this notion that Forster finds his own way to the theory, shared by D. H. Lawrence, that the warring principles in existence are not spirit and body but the human and mechanical, the living spirit and the dead letter.

It is to be seen that this philosophy of death is an optimistic one. It has of course no connection with theistic philosophies, or at least those with doctrines about what happens after death; nor has it any connection with 'fatalism'; and it is only connected with hedonism by its stress on living in the moment. And why it is optimistic is that, according to it, the idea of death redirects human thoughts and energies on to the right objects — the large concerns like Love and Beauty — instead of the petty ones, and those objects shine more vividly in its light.

A continual reminding onself of the 'great change', death — so the theory continues — brings home to one the ubiquity of change, the truth that everything in existence is in a ceaseless state of flux, even dizzyingly so, and moving or hurled in unknowable directions. For this reason one cannot be too foreseeing in life, and it is no use *preparing* too hard, for life is full of false clues and signposts that lead nowhere. What counts is not preparedness but responsiveness and a sense for fact. For life does, after all, all unexpectedly, offer fateful challenges and 'eternal moments', to respond to which is salvation and to ignore which may mean damnation. I am here, of course, rehearsing wellknown themes of Forster's novels, but I mean also to evoke a characteristic of his style — I mean the extraordinary precipitateness and swiftness of transformation of his narrative. There is, for instance, something peculiar and original in his handling of conversations. Hardly any characters exchange two sentences before they have changed in relation to each other, and also changed in themselves, often for ever. He comments on this himself on occasion, as when Henry Wilcox confides his troubles in his son Charles and, says Forster, 'somehow liked him less as he told him more' (*HE*, xiii, 323). He is also explicit about the place of conversations in his world-view, the distracting vistas opened up by them of a restless and prodigy-crammed cosmos. 'He [Henry Wilcox] simply did not notice things, and there was no more to be said . . . he never noticed the lights and shades that exist in the grayest conversation, the finger-posts, the milestones, the collisions, the illimitable views' (xxii, 184). And it is only a brief step, hardly a step at all, from the unpredictability of conversations to the futility of overpreparing for events. Here we may take as our example the comedy of Mrs Munt at the beginning of *Howards End*. She arrives in Hertfordshire determined to rescue Helen Schlegel from a rash engagement, and within minutes, disconcerted by the car's bouncing and by the Wilcox son's rudeness, has quite forgotten what she came for and has become an ardent champion of the supposed lovers.

I have spoken of the importance, in Forster's scheme, of living in the moment. To live in the Now belongs to those who, in Helen Schlegel's words, are capable of saying 'I'. — 'No superman ever said "I want", because "I want" must lead to the question, "Who am I?" and so to Pity and to Justice. He only says "want"' (*HE*, xxvii, 232). The 'business' mind, likewise, is incapable of saying 'I', the place which should be occupied by 'I' being filled instead with 'panic and emptiness'. And of Mr Wilcox, Forster writes, 'No Pagan he, who lives for the Now, and may be wiser than all the philosophers. He lived for the five minutes that have passed, and the five to come; he had the business mind' (*HE*, xxix, 245). To live in the Now, it is necessary to possess the whole of oneself. And here comes in the doctrine of 'connection', or one part of it. For in order to possess the whole of oneself, one needs to recognise the connection of all the pieces of oneself, of the 'beast' with the 'monk' and the 'prose' with the 'passion' (xxii, 183). And here the theme of death returns; for it is the idea of death, of one's personal death, that gives one a vantage point from which to survey oneself as a whole.

I have also spoken of the need for a 'sense of fact'. A quotation from the essay 'The Game of Life' puts us on the right track.

> Once started on the subject of Life they ['the men of good will'] lose all diffidence, because to them it is ethical. They love discussing what we ought to be instead of what we have to face — reams about conduct and nothing about those agitating apparitions that rise from the ground or fall from the sky.[4]

With this we may connect a memorable passage of his about Ibsen's 'so-called symbolism'.

> To his impassioned vision dead and damaged things, however contemptible socially, dwell for ever in the land of romance, and this is the secret of his so-called symbolism: a connection is found between objects that lead different types of existence; they reinforce one another and each lives more intensely than before. Consequently his stage throbs with a mysteriousness for which no obvious preparation has been made, with beckonings, tremblings, sudden compressions of the air, and his characters as they wrangle among the oval tables and stoves are watched by an unseen power which slips between their words.[5]

His immediate point arises from a certain dislike of the literary-critical term 'symbolism', in that it carries a suggestion of some opposition between symbols and realities and encourages a concern, which must be fruitless, with *un*realities. He once similarly objected to the term 'levels' as applied to a work of literature, saying that he preferred the term 'aspects' — with the same implication that realities are all that count, and realities are whole and indivisible: they do not have separable 'levels', they merely appear different according to where you look at them from. But these two eloquent passages tell us much more; they depict the universe as it presented itself to Forster: an unfathomably strange collection of the most varied objects, which objects one is wise to take as much notice of as one can, and which seem in some cases to take notice of oneself, and of which at all events one is oneself a member, not just a spectator. And to get into right relation to this universe it is essential to respond and to discriminate. The power of discrimination is evoked by Forster in his tribute to the Emperor Babur, who, so unexpectedly in a conqueror, actually noticed things for their own sakes and used his senses to discriminate among them, recording in his memoirs many years later that 'the first time a raft struck, a china cup, a spoon, and cymbal fell into the water, whereas the second time the raft struck, a nobleman fell in, just as he was cutting up a melon'. The emperor's admirers, says Forster, call him merely 'charming' and 'quaint' . . . 'not realising that Babur knew what he was about, and that his vitality was so great that all he had experienced rang and glowed, irrespective of its value to historians'.[6] For, as an object in the universe, one can give vitality to other objects as well as receiving it from them.

Such catalogues of heterogeneous details as Babur recorded were dear to the Bloomsbury imagination; they are common in Virginia Woolf and have a 'modernist' quality, vaguely recalling, though with great and essential differences, the 'details set in order' of Ezra Pound's *Cantos*. What we may note here, however, is an unexpected and important connection with Forster's view of death. Babur, having renounced the desire to live, perhaps discovered, says Forster, 'that the so-called Supreme Moment is, after all, not supreme, but an additional detail, like a cup that falls into the water, or a game of chess played with both hands, or the plumage of a bird, or the face of a friend' (*AH*, 337). This was no mere *belle-lettrist* conceit but was what Forster sincerely felt about death and succeeded in realizing in his own life; and it is logically connected, in ways I am not sure that I can spell out, with his general proposition that 'Death destroys a man; the idea of death saves him'. One is moving in the right direction if one says that he realized Matthew Arnold's dictum about 'seeing life steadily and seeing it whole' more literally than Arnold ever did. By adding death to the picture, the relationship of all the other details is transformed, and death itself is revealed as only a detail, with no special status.

Discriminations loom large in *The Longest Journey*. The novel, as Forster has said, is about the contrast between reality and unreality (tragedy being associated with the failure to face reality). And by a trick familiar in Forster, we are offered false examples of 'facing reality' which we must discriminate from the true — in particular Mrs Failing, who goes in for 'unconventionality' and 'truth-telling' and who 'imagined herself to be a cold-eyed Scandinavian heroine', whereas 'Really she was an English old lady, who did not mind giving other people a chill provided it was not infectious' (*LJ*, xiii, 145). Thus according to the novel, two things are essential in this connection: the willingness to face realities, and the ability to recognize them. The novel, further, distinguishes between two approaches to reality and truth-finding. There is the abstract way, as represented by Ansell, who is no good at the 'concrete'. ('Ansell could discuss love and death admirably,' reflects Rickie, 'but somehow he would not understand lovers or a dying man, and in the letter there had been scant allusion to these concrete facts' [*LJ*, vi, 65].) And then there is the concrete way, as represented by Rickie, who, when a cow is introduced into a philosophical argument, can make no sense of it until he has imagined a real flesh-and-blood cow, and if one cow, other cows too. Soon 'The darkness of Europe was dotted with them, and in the far East their flanks were shining in the rising sun' (*LJ*, i, 3). Both approaches are presented as valid and, in this most systematic book, neat parallels are drawn between them — as when, in the British Museum scene, 'Ansell shook his head, and looked up at the dome as other men look at the sky' (*LJ*, xx, 209–10).

Forster's conception of reality should be growing clearer. He had no tendency to see the universe as resolving, Platonically, into a One, or as revealing itself, Buddhistically, as an illusion and mere 'veil of Maya'. He believed, indeed, that things were not as they seemed, especially as they seemed to the inactive eye;

and also, a thought connected with the preceding, only certain of them mattered. And for him what supremely mattered was human relationships, which he could imagine to be the sole true material of history. For him people mattered, but only relatively, for people are inevitably in a ceaseless state of flux and dissolution; the thing which may contain more reality and permanence is found in *relationships* between people. By common consent the climax of *A Passage to India*, philosophically speaking, is Mrs Moore's breakdown and degeneration after the incident in the Marabar caves. And it is important to notice that the vision which has begun to dominate her before the time of her breakdown is the exact opposite of Forster's own. The feeling comes over her ('vision or nightmare?') that 'though people are important, the relations between them are not'.[7] We are to regard this as an expression of illness, and the illness can be called 'psychological' or 'metaphysical' according to choice; it is, at all events, one to which a humanist like Forster was peculiarly liable. Which explains why it is part of his scheme to show that it was not after all a true vision and *was* a nightmare. The real Mrs Moore was not the peevish and egotistical old lady who dies aboard ship on her journey home; she existed more truly in her legacy or posthumous influence, which was her gift for human relationships. The legacy in another sense is Ralph Moore, who represents supremely a life lived according to feeling. We are here, of course, moving from philosophy to fiction, and the question whether Forster believed in such an 'inheritance' is not one we are called upon to answer.

To hold that personal relationships are the thing of supreme importance must have much influence on one's political beliefs. And there is something odd in Forster's career in this respect. For he had considerable political influence, notably in regard to the Indian empire and in regard to civil liberties, and this despite the fact that he felt unable to understand politics and had no answer to political problems. I see a successful test of his philosophy here; for he had a theory of politics, and this, though extremely negative, was clear-cut, original and logically perfectly consistent with his other theories. The best statement of it is a remark in a letter to Bertrand Russell of 28 July 1918, à propos of Russell's *Principles of Social Reconstruction*:

For a time I thought you would shake me out of my formula —

that though of course there is a connection between civilisation and our private desires and impulses and actions, it is a connection as meaningless as that between a word and the letters that make it up. But the formula holds.[8]

There is a rigour about this, despite its almost absurd negativity, which served him well in the 1930s, when his honesty became a support to politically-minded friends like Isherwood and Auden and saved him from the disillusionment with politics which overtook them.

For Forster, personal relationships and love were an example, the highest one, of things that are intrinsically good — good in themselves and not to be valued just as a means to something else. And what he valued in Cambridge, a place he was in many respects critical of, was that it was somewhere where, above all, things could be valued for themselves. He refers to this Cambridge in his preface to the World's Classics edition of *The Longest Journey* as 'the Cambridge of G. E. Moore . . . the fearless uninfluential Cambridge that sought for reality and cared for truth' (p. xi). S. P. Rosenbaum has recently published, in *E. M. Forster: A Human Exploration*, an article, '*The Longest Journey*: E. M. Forster's Refutation of Idealism' in which he makes extensive claims for Moore's influence on Forster. His argument is in part a criticism of my own remark, in *E. M. Forster: A Life*, that 'too much had been made' of the influence of Moore on Forster, in view of the fact that Forster never read Moore and moreover was bored by technical philosophical discussions.[9] Rosenbaum argues, with some support from Forster himself, that Forster received Moore's influence through friends.[10] He holds that the discussion with which *The Longest Journey* opens, about whether the cow is there when there is no one perceiving it, is 'a fairly direct allusion' to a famous early paper of Moore's, 'The Refutation of Idealism',[11] and the novel shows considerable understanding of the issue raised in Moore's paper — indeed that 'Forster's general philosophical outlook is derived mainly from Moore's ethics and epistemology'. In *The Longest Journey*, according to Rosenbaum, Forster 'imaginatively converts an epistemological point from the essay into a moral one'.[12]

Rosenbaum has written an excellent paper, yet it does not convince me. No amount of reading *The Longest Journey* or the account of the Apostles' society in *Goldworthy Lowes Dickinson* gives me any feeling that Forster followed, or was even aware of, Moore's mode of argument about Idealism. And moreover I suspect that Moore's rather 'scholastic' and arithmetical way of talking of 'organic unities' — e.g. 'Thus if we compare the value of a certain amount of pleasure, *existing absolutely by itself*, with the value of certain "enjoyments", containing an equal amount of pleasure, it may become apparent that the "enjoyment" is much better than the pleasure, and also, in some cases, much worse' — would have repelled him had he encountered it. All one can find about Berkeleyan idealism in Forster, surely, is what any educated person of this century or the previous one knew: that is to say the idea summed up in the famous limerick about the tree in the Quad. [13] Forster in this sense was philosophically naïve, though only in this sense.

This said, Rosenbaum has cleared up at least one point most satisfactorily. I said in my biography that it was puzzling that the problems which Ansell and his friends were discussing in that opening scene seemed to belong more to the age of Berkeley than that of Moore and Russell; and Rosenbaum's explanation is quite convincing:

> It was not Forster, then, who was looking back to the age of Berkeley but Moore and Russell, who found Berkeley's idea being used to support Idealism at the turn of the century in Cambridge.

This provides an excellent reason why Forster should, at this period, have heard discussions which centred on Berkeley. And it lends plausibility to the conclusion Rosenbaum draws from it.

> Their refutation of this Idealism is part of the revolution they worked in philosophy, and Forster's novel is an imaginative interpretation and extension of that refutation. Indeed, Russell's account of how liberating Moore's refutation was could have come from *The Longest Journey*: 'With a sense of escaping from prison, we allowed ourselves to think that grass is green, that the sun and stars would exist if no one was aware of them, and also that there is a pluralistic timeless world of Platonic ideas'. (pp. 33–4)

In the novel, according to Rosenbaum, 'Ansell is, with some

inconsistencies, a philosophical Realist [like Moore] . . . and Rickie's waverings between Idealism and Realism mark crucial stages in his education' (p. 37). And Rosenbaum identifies that 'idealism' which Forster, following Shelley, associates with monogamous love — an evil tendency which denies the independent reality of all but the loved one — with the Berkeleyan idealism (the view that 'to be' is equivalent to 'to be perceived') from which Moore offered liberation. This seems helpful in a way. But difficulties arise in the attempt to fit Moore's 'Refutation' and Forster's novel together more systematically. For instance, Rosenbaum admits that Ansell really ought not, if he is to be a heroic Moore-ite Realist, to deny the existence of Agnes Pembroke; and to explain this, he has to posit a complicated scheme by which Ansell is also 'flawed with Idealism' (through having, as we learn in the novel, read too much Hegel) and has to have his sense of reality 'corrected and completed by Stephen Wonham'. And the trouble with this is that, whenever Ansell's philosophical inconsistencies are noted in the novel, Forster's tone suggests that they do not matter in the least — Ansell's position, humanly speaking, is absolutely sound. But what is much more damaging to Rosenbaum's theory is that it forces him to admit that 'little of Moore's actual argument finds its way into the novel' (p. 37), and that 'Forster's use of Moore will undoubtedly strike some philosophers and even some critics as hopelessly naïve' (p. 53). Now, I do not in the least consider Forster's novel as naïve, and neither does Rosenbaum; so if his approach invites such a notion, it suggests to me that it is a wrong one.

That *The Longest Journey* is an intricately and systematically worked out philosophical novel, as Rosenbaum argues, is certainly true. Indeed Forster himself feared his novel might be *too* systematic, too full of ingenious symbolism, at the expense of flesh and blood. However, the philosophy, to my mind, is (so much as this can ever be the case) original to Forster. Unlike Rosenbaum, who sees the novel as a 'refutation' of Idealism, I would see the emphasis, philosophically speaking, as resting not so much on Idealism versus Realism (though of course this theme features in the book) as on the damage to our perceptions of the world fostered by monogamous love. To ignore the variety of the loves and friendships offered to one, as do the members of that 'great sect' condemned by Shelley, cuts one off from the qualities that one may need to complete one's own makeup (a psychological point); but it also (a philosophical point this) encourages 'slovenly perceptions'[14] and a general failure in discrimination and response to the world.

Rosenbaum persuades me that I have underestimated Moore's influence on E. M. Forster.[15] However, the influence that I now think I see is of a slightly different kind from what he suggests, and certainly much less direct. It was, as we know, characteristic of Moore that he should approach Ethics by way of a survey of 'intrinsic' goods or things that are good in themselves. This, as he says in *Principia Ethica*, Chapter 6, is 'the fundamental question of Ethics — the question "What things are goods and ends in themselves?"' And this was so much Forster's own attitude to life and ethics — he so explicitly repudiated the 'Wilcox' approach, which concerned itself with things merely as means and with the use they could be put to; and he attached so much importance to the discrimination of the various intrinsic goods offered by the universe — that I would suspect we can detect in him the general climate of thought of Moore's Cambridge. In a way which may well be related to Moore, Forster insisted always on thinking in terms of 'positives' — it is indeed this insistence that is one of the things which gives his thought originality. We may take as an example that little quotation from an entry on 'Resentment' which I gave in my Introduction to the facsimile edition of his Commonplace Book: 'Resentment . . . can only be killed by crowding it out with healthier growths. Middleton Murry . . . makes the mistake of trying to pull out of himself what he considers bad'.[16] Or to put it in other language, the way to deal with evil tendencies in the mind is not to try to negate them but to oppose other 'positives' to them. Then again, there is his doctrine, stated in 'What I Believe', that the hope for the world, if there is any hope, lies not in a change of heart but (on the analogy of economics) on regulating and redistributing the resources of good will already existing. 'Not by becoming better, but by ordering and distributing his native goodness, will Man shut up Force into its box . . .'[17]

Discussion of *The Longest Journey* prompts me to say even a little more about Forster's attitude to 'fact' and 'realities'. For it is perhaps in this novel that one is most made aware of his habit of seeing the 'position' or 'situation' of his characters in, as it were, topographical terms. In that remarkable scene among

Cadbury Rings, in which Mrs Failing makes her revelation to Rickie, it is extraordinary by how many touches the landscape (its shapes, its view or lack of view, and the siting of the characters in it) is given symbolical force; or again how, in the succeeding scene, when Rickie has a second chance to acknowledge Stephen, Forster with perfect consistency makes Agnes stand quite literally in his way ('She was stopping his advance quite frankly, with widespread arms' [*LJ*, xiv, 161]), masking his view of Stephen. We can make no useful distinction, in terms of what is metaphorical as opposed to literal, between this and the comment about Stephen Wonham and Mrs Failing: 'He could not see into her: she would have puzzled an older and cleverer man. He may have seen round her' (*LJ*, x, 102). And there fits in here the remark or protest of Forster's that I quoted in my biography. Challenged to 'face facts', he replied with passion: 'Don't say "face facts" to me. Everyone keeps saying it now; but the fact is, it's impossible to face facts. They're like the walls of a room, all round you'.[18] In *The Longest Journey* the snobbish Tilliard is neatly satirized for his belief (an analogue, for Forster, of the 'aesthetic' heresy) that you could 'see life' without forming part of it. ('Tilliard's *couche sociale* permitted experiences. Provided his heart did not go out to the poor and the unorthodox, he might stare at them as much as he liked. It was seeing life' [*LJ*, xv, 167].) And the great internal consistency of Forster's outlook can be seen in the parallel with his judgement on Mrs Failing's truth-telling. She believed, again quite falsely, that you could go in for truth-telling in an 'experimental' spirit, being yourself quite uninvolved.

I would further draw a connection with Forster's habit or principle of always 'realising' his metaphors and allowing them to take him where they would — another version of respect for what is real. I have written of this elsewhere;[19] but, to make a related point, how intensely characteristic of Forster, in its referring back to reality of an unexamined and trite phrase, is this slight touch in *A Room With a View*:

> 'I love weather like this', said Freddy.
> Mr. Beebe passed into it.[20]

What of course is noticeable, too, in the Cadbury Rings chapter, and in many other places in Forster, is a way of talking as if landscape and inanimate things had purposes of their own. He habitually makes the features of the landscape the subject governing an active verb: 'one village had clustered round the source and clothed itself with trees . . . into it the road to London slipped, covering the bushes with white dust' (*LJ*, xiii, 147–8). This brings us close to those 'objects leading different types of existence' of his essay on Ibsen.

The 'as if', whatever its status as a belief, expressed for him the most truthful and also morally salutary way of regarding the relation of the world to ourselves. And I am not forgetting that it is just this 'as if' which Leavis, in commenting admiringly on some sentences in *A Passage to India*, identifies as their characteristic weakness. Of Forster's sentence 'How indeed is it possible for one human being to be sorry for all the sadness that meets him on the face of the earth, for the pain that is endured not only by men, but by animals and plants, and perhaps the stones' (*PI*, xxvi, 235), Leavis, referring to the last six words, asks 'can one do anything but reflect how extraordinary it is that so fine a writer should be able, in such a place, to be so little certain just how serious he is?'[21] Leavis's question is a just and pertinent one, and I'm not sure if I have an altogether good answer to it. But anyway I am not required to here, and what I hope is, rather, that the present essay will have shown that Forster *meant* such sentiments — that they were not just a novelist's whim but part of a coherent philosophical outlook.

NOTES

1. E. M. Forster, *Howards End*, ed. Oliver Stallybrass, Abinger edn. (London: Edward Arnold, 1973), p. 236.
2. E. M. Forster, *The Longest Journey*, World's Classics, 578 (London: Oxford University Press, 1960), p. 58.
3. P. N. Furbank and F. J. H. Haskell, 'The Art of Fiction: E. M. Forster', *Paris Review*, No. 1 (Spring 1973), 27–41.
   Interviewer: 'I have always been worried by the suddenness of Gerald's death in *The Longest Journey*. Why did you treat it in that way?'
   Forster: 'It had to be passed by. But perhaps it was passed by in the wrong way.'
   I think the question must have been one of Francis Haskell's and Forster's 'perhaps it was passed by in the wrong way' was most probably said out of politeness to his interviewers.
4. E. M. Forster, 'The Game of Life', *Abinger Harvest* (London: Edward Arnold, 1965), p. 72.

5. E. M. Forster, 'Ibsen the Romantic', *Abinger Harvest*, p. 102.
6. E. M. Forster, 'The Emperor Babur' *Abinger Harvest*, p. 334.
7. E. M. Forster, *A Passage to India,* ed. Oliver Stallybrass, Abinger edn. (London: Edward Arnold, 1978), p. 127.
8. P. N. Furbank, *E. M. Forster: A Life* (London: Secker and Warburg, 1977, 1978), II, p. 46.
9. Furbank, I, p. 77.
10. Rosenbaum also rightly corrects me for the foolish remark that 'it was a cardinal tenet of Moore's theory of ethics that the only things in the world possessing intrinsic value were good states of mind', which, as he points out, is to make exactly the error which Moore attacked (there being, in fact, many different things in the world to which we apply the epithet 'good', this being the only attribute they have in common). What I ought to have said, of course, was that, according to Moore, *'By far the most valuable things*, which we can know or imagine', are good states of mind.
11. G. E. Moore, 'The Refutation of Idealism', *Mind*, October 1903.
12. S. P. Rosenbaum, *'The Longest Journey*: E. M. Forster's Refutation of Idealism', *E. M. Forster: A Human Exploration*, ed. G. K. Das and John Beer (London: Macmillan, 1979), p. 38.
13. There once was a man who said God
    Must find it exceedingly odd,
       If he finds that this tree
        Continues to be
    When there's no-one about in the Quad.
14. 'Out of these he constructed a repulsive figure, forgetting how slovenly his own perceptions had been during the past week, how dogmatic and intolerant his attitude to all that was not Love'. (*The Longest Journey*, xv, 163).
15. I have recently come across an unpublished Apostles' paper of Moore's, dated 9 November 1900 (two months before Forster's formal admission to the Society) entitled, 'Is it a Duty to Hate?' (It was in the sale of Moore papers at Sotheby's on 17 December 1979.) Moore argues that it is, or can be, a duty to hate and attempts to refute two of the main opposing doctrines: first, the view, which he attributes to Tolstoy, that hatred never has good effects; and secondly, the view, which he associates with Walt Whitman and George Meredith, that hatred is never a good state of mind in itself, and everything is good if you only look at it in the right way, i.e. a loving way. One cannot help being strongly reminded by this of that exchange in Chapter 2 of *The Longest Journey*:

    '. . . what right have they to think us asses in a pleasant way? Why don't they hate us? What right has Hornblower to smack me on the back when I've been rude to him?'
    'Well, what right have you to be rude to him?'
    'Because I hate him. You think it so splendid to hate no one. I tell you it is a crime.'

16. E. M. Forster, *Commonplace Book*, ed. P. N. Furbank, facsimile edition (London: Scolar Press, 1978), p. ix.

17. E. M. Forster, 'What I Believe', *Two Cheers for Democracy*, ed. Oliver Stallybrass, Abinger edn. (London: Edward Arnold, 1972), p. 72.
18. Furbank, II, 2.
19. P. N. Furbank, 'Forster and "Bloomsbury" Prose', *E. M. Forster: A Human Exploration*, ed. G. K. Das and John Beer (London: Macmillan, 1979).
20. E. M. Forster, *A Room With A View*, ed. Oliver Stallybrass, Abinger edn. (London: Edward Arnold, 1977), p. 189.
21. F. R. Leavis, *The Common Pursuit* (London: Chatto and Windus, 1952), p. 274.

Part II

Literary History

4 *Aspects of the Novel* and Literary History

S. P. Rosenbaum

I

'Let there be those "formidable erosions of contour" of which Nietzsche speaks'.[1]

Among the notes that E. M. Forster made in his *Commonplace Book* while working on *Aspects of the Novel* is a quotation from *Tristram Shandy* that asks a hard question:

> Shall we be destined to the days of eternity, on holy-days as well as working-days, to be shewing the *relicks of learning*, as monks do the relicks of their saints — without working one — one single miracle with them? (p. 122)

This is just the kind of awkward question Forster enjoyed asking, and it may help us to avoid some of the customary centenary pieties that would have irritated him. Do Forster's writings still work miracles for us, or are they really now relics of learning that we parade on academic holidays? What about *Aspects of the Novel* itself? For a quarter of a century after its publication in 1927 it was the most widely read English critical work on the most popular literary form of the time. Since the Second World War the criticism of fiction has grown enormously in complexity, seriousness, sensitivity — and bulk. After *Scrutiny*, the New Criticism, Chicago Aristotelianism, structuralism, hermeneutics, what is *Aspects of the Novel* if not a relic of learning?

In the following pages I would like to try to indicate how *Aspects of the Novel* might be looked upon as something more than just a relic, though I do not promise any miracles. I will try to show how *Aspects of the Novel* ought to be read in conjunction with a number of other texts, and not just as a theory of the novel but as a piece of writing in its own right. It is now time, in short, to look at *Aspects of the Novel* under the aspect of literary history.

It is not an aspect Forster felt very friendly towards. Time is the avowed enemy throughout *Aspects of the Novel*, and nowhere is it more disliked than in the chronicles of the pseudo-scholar:

> Everything he says may be accurate but all is useless, because he is moving round books instead of through them, he either has not read them or cannot read them properly. Books have to be read (worse luck, for it takes a long time); it is the only way of discovering what they contain. A few savage tribes eat them, but reading is the only method of assimilation revealed to the West. The reader must sit down alone and struggle with the writer, and this the pseudo-scholar will not do. He would rather relate a book to the history of its time, to events in the life of its author, to the events it describes, above all to some tendency. As soon as he can use the word 'tendency' his spirits rise, and though those of his audience may sink they often pull out their pencils at this point and make a note, under the belief that a tendency is portable. (p. 8)

Forster's mockery of pseudo-literary history is a warning to us all because we cannot escape literary history if we want to understand not just what Forster's writing means to us but what it meant to his contemporaries and to himself. Like the discussion of fiction, literary history has also developed considerably since *Aspects of the Novel*, though more recently. Old literary history with its source-hunting, tendency-labelling evasions of analysis and evaluation has been giving way to a newer literary history that attempts to move through books as well as around them. Recent literary history has been asking questions about forms as well as origins, as it tries to interrelate texts rather than just talk about influences. It has been examining manifestations of the new along with continuities of the old; it has been looking at the assumptions about the literariness of a piece of writing that are held by authors and readers, and it sees texts as combining quite different kinds of literary statements.[2]

There is another reason for looking at *Aspects of the Novel* under the aspect of literary history besides recent developments in the

theory of literary history. Over the past fifteen years or so the
materials of modern English literary history have become widely
and extensively available in the manuscript collections of libra-
ries and in the publication of bibliographies, biographies, auto-
biographies, letters, diaries, and scholarly editions of Forster
and his literary friends. These materials offer opportunities to
pursue the answers to the new kinds of questions that literary
history has been asking. The Abinger Edition of Forster's work
is an excellent example of this new material, and I am considerably indebted to its late editor, Oliver Stallybrass, whose
fine edition of *Aspects of the Novel* has made my discussion possible.

II

The literary history of *Aspects of the Novel* begins in Bloomsbury. In
the 1920s Forster's closest Bloomsbury friends were Leonard and
Virginia Woolf. They were the first people he wrote to, thanking
them for their encouragement, when he finished *A Passage to India*
in 1924.[3] In December 1925, Forster's most important statement
on the nature of literature before *Aspects of the Novel* appeared in
the Hogarth Essay series of the Woolfs' press. *Anonymity: An
Enquiry* is alluded to in *Aspects of the Novel* for its theory of
inspiration but it also anticipates some of the basic assumptions
of Forster's theory of the novel, such as the autotelic nature of
imaginative literature ('a poem points to nothing but itself'),
the mixed form of the novel (part atmosphere, part information),
the limits of literary study (it is only a serious form of gossip) and
the unimportance of personality or biography in that anonymous
state of imagination in which the reader approaches the inspiration of the writer.[4] It was also in December of 1925 that Forster
declined Leonard Woolf's proposal that he write a book on
psychology and fiction for a new Hogarth series — perhaps the
Hogarth Lectures on Literature — that was under consideration.
Leonard Woolf's suggestion may have influenced the topic that
Forster chose when, several months later, he was offered the
Clark Lectureship at Cambridge. If so the influence was to be
reciprocal, for the lectures that Forster gave and then published
as *Aspects of the Novel* clearly left their mark on more than one of
the works in the Hogarth Lectures on Literature series that began
appearing shortly after Forster's book. We shall come back to

the significance of the lecture form in the literary history of *Aspects of the Novel* later.

In May 1926, Forster wrote to Virginia Woolf that he was going to give some lectures at Cambridge, he thought on the novel, and he would like her advice on two points: how could one lecture on novels — what, for example, should such a course of lectures be called? And what were the best novels? (Forster did not mention in his letter that he had been offered the Clark Lectureship, whose first incumbent had been Virginia Woolf's father.) They had tea together next day and argued about novel-writing, Virginia Woolf wrote to her sister, adding that she found Forster 'limp and damp and milder than the breath of a cow'.[5] There was some further correspondence between the novelists about Virginia Woolf's essay on *Robinson Crusoe*, which she had published in February. Forster wrote that he found the piece very interesting, but in his *Commonplace Book* he noted its 'dreary Bloomsbury conclusion' (p. 128). Virginia Woolf had argued in words Forster would echo in his criticism of pseudo-scholars, that biography or the history of the novel does not help increase the pleasure or the intelligence with which we read fiction because,

> however we may wind and wiggle in our approach to books, a lonely battle awaits us at the end. There is a piece of business to be transacted between writer and reader before any further dealings are possible . . .

That business involved seeing 'those cardinal points of perspective — God, man, nature' on which novelists gaze; but Defoe's ruthless commonsense snubs these and leaves us instead with an earthenware pot which, nevertheless, pulls the universe into harmony as completely as if it had been man himself. If a writer believes in a pot with enough intensity, Forster paraphrased Virginia Woolf, it can be as satisfying as the universe.[6]

What Forster meant in calling this a 'dreary Bloomsbury conclusion' immerses us in aesthetics. It was just before the turn of the century, Forster later recalled, that he first heard Roger Fry lecture and detected the essential Bloomsbury undertone that it was the treatment that counted and not the subject.[7] In his 1920 retrospect to *Vision and Design* Fry put his formalism this way:

I conceived the form of the work of art to be its most essential quality, but I believed this form to be the direct outcome of an apprehension of some emotion of actual life by the artist . . .[8]

Earlier Clive Bell had polemicized the formalism that he had developed with Fry out of their responses to French post-impressionist painting. Bell argued that 'Significant Form' — which he defined as lines and colours combined into forms that cause aesthetic emotion in us — was the essential quality of a work of art; 'if a representative form has value', he insisted, 'it is as form, not as representation'.[9] In her essay on *Robinson Crusoe* Virginia Woolf is using this formalism as a metaphor: Defoe's commonsense belief in the pot is intense enough to produce a form that harmonizes his vision of the universe. Perhaps it was this metaphorical application of visual to literary art that Forster found dreary. At issue here is a central problem in Bloomsbury's literary aesthetics, and that is how the doctrine of significant form in the visual arts is applicable to words. The apprehension and evaluation of form in literature is very different from that in pottery, and in the novel Forster would argue form was even less important than in drama or poetry. Clive Bell originally thought the cognitive content of literature prevented that art from having significant form; Fry, who believed in the unity of the arts, tried at various times to demonstrate how literary form could be the essential quality of words.

In 1924 I. A. Richards attacked Bloomsbury's formalism in *Principles of Literary Criticism*, denying that form is the source of value in art, dismissing aesthetic emotion as part of 'the phantom aesthetic state', disagreeing with what he took to be Bell's and Fry's separation of art from life.[10] Richards surprisingly has nothing to say in his book about the principles of criticism that apply to the novel. Perhaps his silence also helped Forster to his subject. In *Anonymity: An Enquiry*, however, which came out the year after Richards' book, Forster was closer in several respects to Bloomsbury's dreary conclusions than to Richards' — particularly in the conclusion that poetry was autotelic. Richards had gone back to A. C. Bradley's well known lecture 'Poetry for Poetry's Sake', which he delivered in 1901, as an illustration of the inadequacies of literary formalism. Fry and Bell used it as support in their respective replies to Richards.[11] It is worth noting that Bradley's lecture contains the phrase 'significant form', and that when Forster came to write the address entitled 'Art for Art's sake' that he gave in 1941, he adopted Bradley's careful distinction between art as an end in itself and art as the supreme end of life. From *Anonymity: An·Enquiry* to 'Art for Art's Sake' Forster was an ambivalent formalist, and nowhere is this more manifest than in his most influential critical work.

III

It may also have been in Bradley's 'Poetry for Poetry's Sake' that Forster found the answer to the question he had asked Virginia Woolf about what lectures on the novel could be called. At the end of his introductory lecture Forster explains that he has adopted the word 'aspects' because it is a free, scientifically vague term that allowed him to consider the different ways both reader and writer look at a novel. It is an enlightening explanation, for it tells us something about the form of Forster's lectures and also reveals something of their value for us now. Forster as reader is but one way he approaches the novel; Forster as writer is another — and not just as a writer of novels. It was, of course, Forster's reputation as a novelist that made him an authority on novels for his audience, and his subsequent critics have been helped by *Aspects of the Novel* to understand his own novels. But Forster is also a writer in *Aspects of the Novel* itself. We will turn to this aspect of his lectures after considering them as an illustrated theory of fiction conceived of mainly from the reader's or critic's point of view.

In 'Poetry for Poetry's sake' Bradley argued that the unity of a literary work has various 'aspects' rather than separable parts; the true critic does not separate form and content: 'the whole, the poetic experience, of which they are but aspects is always in mind . . .'.[12] When aspects are distinguished for purposes of evaluation, however, Bradley points out they become components and the heresies of separable substance and form arise, as indeed they do in *Aspects of the Novel*. Forster enumerates seven aspects in his lectures: story, people, plot, fantasy, prophecy, pattern and rhythm. He is not always clear about the nature of these aspects, for in one place he defines them as demands made upon the reader (pp. 74–5) but elsewhere he says that five of the aspects are critical tools, while fantasy and prophecy are something else (p. 101). There is a shift here, in other words, between aspects of fiction and kinds of novels, as Forster is aware. He speaks of the discussions of the novels he has classified as fantastic or prophetic as 'interludes' in his lecture, interludes that even call for a new invocation (pp. 102, 76).

But if Forster is inconsistent about what he means by the term 'aspects' he is unwaveringly clear that one of his aspects is more important than all of the others. It is a curious reflection of the form of *Aspects of the Novel* that few of its readers remember that it has a single unifying idea. We forget the whole in the familiarity of some of its parts — the familiarity of the Forsterian tone of voice in which we must say 'Yes — oh dear Yes — the novel tells a story' in the discrimination of flat and round characters, in the battle between plot and characters, in the possibilities of rhythm in fiction. Specific insights into particular novels and novelists also remain in the memory longer than what amounts to Forster's thesis. We recall his comments that time is the hero of *The Old Wives' Tale* and muddle the hidden god in *Tristram Shandy*; we do not quickly forget the description of the fluffy, lush home counties posing as the universe in the work of that suburban roarer Meredith, nor how the clothes of those Egyptian deformities, the characters of Henry James, 'will not take off'. But who remembers half so clearly the dualism that Forster insists characterizes the novel? 'The idea running through these lectures is plain enough', he says quite accurately after the lectures on story, people, and plot, and it is

> that there are in the novel two forces: human beings and a bundle of various things not human beings, and it is the novelist's business to adjust these two forces and conciliate their claims. (p. 73)

There could hardly be a clearer instance of Bradley's heresy of separable substance and form. Again and again in his lectures Forster returns to the primacy of the aspect he calls people — the only aspect to be given two lectures. Moll Flanders, for example, is a fictive rather than a human being not because she is embodied in a self-contained work of art but because she is psychologically unreal: we can know all about her inner life in a way we can never know that of people, and this is how novels give us 'the illusion of perspicacity and of power' (p. 44). But Forster does not want to distinguish too sharply between the fictive and the human in fiction. His aim in theorizing about novels is the same as it was when he was creating them: to conciliate the human and the non-human. Thus, though he calls his lectures on the aspect of character in fiction simply 'People', his famous distinction between flat and round characters brings us back to the realm of art. It will not do to call them flat and round people.

The inconsistencies of Forster's dualism arise from his diminishing the value of art in fiction relative to the value of the characters whom Forster isolates from their aesthetic embodiments. In her reviews and subsequent correspondence, Virginia Woolf objected to Forster's theory not because of its emphasis on the centrality of character — she agreed with him and with Arnold Bennett about that — but because of his devaluing of art. 'In most literary works there are two elements', Forster stated early in his lecture on plot, 'human individuals . . . and the element vaguely called art' (p. 59). This almost sounds like a doctrine of insignificant form in fiction, particularly when, as Virgina Woolf complained, the talk of art was so vague.[13]

There is another basic distinction in *Aspects of the Novel*, however, that is surprisingly formalistic in its consequences — consequences that Virginia Woolf, as we shall see, could not accept. Readers of *Aspects of the Novel* most likely remember Forster's radical separation of art from history better than they do his distinction between people and art because of his delightful image of all the novelists in the history of the novel sitting timelessly around the reading room of Bloomsbury's British Museum writing their novels synchronically. If separating people from art in novels reduces the significance of form in fiction, distinguishing history from fiction clearly enhances the work itself and therefore by implication its aesthetic form. 'History develops, Art stands still . . .' (p. 14). It is a crude even vulgar motto, Forster admits, only a partial truth but one he quite cheerfully embraces and in this he is in agreement with Bell's and Fry's aesthetic theories. '. . . Assuredly, to understand art we need to know nothing whatever about history', Clive Bell had claimed in *Art*,[14] and Forster assumes in talking about novels that no mists from the river of time will obscure our apprehension of their significance. Thus the title of his lectures is very apt. Novels rather than novelists or traditions are what he mainly speaks about, and aspects are not developments; each stands still to be contemplated like a painting or a sculpture. Time is the enemy of value throughout *Aspects of the Novel*, not just in the literary history of pseudo-scholars.

IV

Forster's lectures on the novel are thus a mixture of formalistic and non- or even anti-formalistic ideas. He would not find much sympathy in Bloomsbury for this mixture, and yet it displayed a quintessential Bloomsbury characteristic — eclecticism. It was Clive Bell, the most uncompromising formalist of the Group, who maintained in *Civilisation* (which he finished the year Forster gave his lectures) that the civilized man would be an eclectic.[15] The clearest statement of eclecticism in Bloomsbury can be found in *Aspects of the Novel*. Forster's attitude towards it is more pessimistic than Bell's would have been. He reluctantly concluded, after expressing reservations about the double vision in his lecture on prophecy that most of us will keep the single vision and therefore,

> be eclectics to this side or that according to our temperament. The human mind is not a dignified organ, and I do not see how we can exercise it sincerely except through eclecticism. And the only advice I would offer my fellow eclectics is: 'Do not be proud of your inconsistency. It is a pity, it is a pity that we should be equipped like this. It is a pity Man cannot be at the same time impressive and truthful'. (p. 101)

The engrained eclecticism of *Aspects of the Novel* has indeed struck some critics as pitiful, and yet it is basic for his comparative critical method. The subject of *Aspects of the Novel*, Forster stated in the middle of his lectures, was 'the books we have read', (p. 73) and he worried that they had escaped him as he theorized about the novel. He need not have worried, for the books we have read in *Aspects of the Novel* include works of criticism as well as novels. Forster's juxtaposition of novels or novelists may appear sadly eclectic to those with monolithic notions of traditions in fiction; for others, however, Forster's bringing together of novels is the most stimulating aspect of his criticism. The comparison of anonymous quotations from the fiction of Richardson and James,

Wells and Dickens, Sterne and Virginia Woolf in the introductory lecture establishes the critical procedure which Forster continues in his other lectures. *The Antiquary, The Old Wives' Tale* and *War and Peace* are brought together in the lecture on story; *Moll Flanders* and *Mansfield Park* are the chief examples in the lectures on people. Plot sets the novels of Meredith alongside those of Gide, among others, and fantasy compares rather fantastically Sterne, the completely forgotten Matson, Beerbohm and Joyce. Prophecy pairs George Eliot and Dostoyevsky, to begin with, and then brings in Melville, Lawrence and Emily Brontë. Finally Anatole France, Percy Lubbock, James and Proust all come together in the last lecture.

Forster's eclectic use of critical works in *Aspects of the Novel* has naturally attracted less attention than the novels he compares, yet these texts provide the critical ideas, the aspects, that bring the compared novels into focus. It is a matter not merely of the extrinsic sources for *Aspects of the Novel* but of the intrinsic critical structure of the work. 'The books we have read' — the subject, that is, of *Aspects of the Novel* — include, in addition to novels, critical texts of T. S. Eliot, Aristotle, Alain, Lubbock, Wells and Henry James. They are specifically referred to but there are others present that do not get mentioned: Virginia Woolf's essay on *Robinson Crusoe*, Bradley's 'Poetry for Poetry's Sake', and the work of the critic to whom Forster dedicated *Aspects of the Novel*. Forster's lectures depend significantly on the interpretation of these texts as on the works of fiction that he discusses, and a literary history of *Aspects of the Novel* needs to examine Forster's eclectic use of them. And while it is not possible to discuss all of them in detail, I want at least to note Forster's use of them and to analyse briefly his interpretations of several of them. This should still leave us time to consider *Aspects of the Novel* as a literary text in its own right and to glance at its interesting relation with what may be in the English-speaking world today the most widely read book about fiction.

V

In his introductory lecture Forster mentions three books on the novel, none of which he makes much use of. From Abel Chevalley's 'brilliant little manual', *Le roman anglais de notre temps*, he adopts the unhelpful definition of the novel as 'a fiction in prose of a certain extent', (p. 3) and then never refers to the book again. (It is hard to see what Forster found so brilliant in Chevalley's survey unless it was all the novelists he was prepared to generalize about, including Forster himself who is described as full of ideas and talent; Chevalley's attack on Henry James may have appealed to Forster too.) Walter Raleigh's *The English Novel* is referred to as a work of genuine scholarship; he is able to contemplate the river of time, though Forster does not remark that Raleigh's river stops with Scott. After a satirical digression in which Clayton Hamilton's *Materials and Methods of Fiction* is anonymously cited as a particularly egregious example of the substitution of classification for understanding — it is a work Virginia Woolf also reviewed with ridicule[16] — Forster comes back to his argument for the timelessness of fiction, and here he invokes T. S. Eliot.

Eliot was Forster's immediate predecessor in the Clark Lectureship (Raleigh was another Clark Lecturer), and he is cited to support Forster's ignoring of literary history. Though Eliot's lectures on metaphysical poetry were never published, Forster quotes, from *The Sacred Wood*, Eliot's remarks on the business of a critic, part of which is to preserve tradition (which Forster feels he cannot do) and part of which is 'to see literature steadily and to see it whole; and this is eminently to see it as *not* consecrated by time but to see it beyond time . . .' (p. 15). This part Forster gladly accepts as support for his own efforts to view the novel synchronically. Eliot had also observed in *The Sacred Wood* that the critic's tools are analysis and comparison.[17] Much of modern criticism since Eliot has favoured analysis at the expense of comparison, though this cannot be said of *Aspects of the Novel* which does the opposite. Eliot's comments on tradition, quoted by Forster, disclose of course another text, one that Forster had already used in *Howards End*. Eliot's discussion of the business of the critic at the beginning of *The Sacred Wood* is in the context of making amends to Matthew Arnold, whose famous lines on Sophocles are echoed and whose essay 'The Function of Criticism at the Present Time' is approvingly quoted by Eliot. 'How astonishing it would be,' Eliot went on, 'if a man like Arnold had concerned himself with the art of the novel . . .'.[18] Forster does not pursue any of the topics in the criticism of the novel that Eliot wishes Arnold had, but Eliot's remarks may also have influenced

Forster's choice of subject for the Clark Lectures. Arnold was Forster's favourite Victorian, after all, and he may have accepted a little advice from him, such as the now rather quaint suggestion that English critics should pay some attention to foreign thought.

Forster's references, direct and indirect, to Eliot and Arnold almost invoke their critical protection at the outset of his enterprise. These critical allusions can remind us of Forster's share in Bloomsbury's early response to so different a mind and sensibility as Eliot's, and also of the continuities between Bloomsbury and the Victorians — continuities sometimes ignored in accounts of Bloomsbury's ironic attitudes towards the world of their fathers.

VI

Aristotle's *Poetics* might not count as an example of foreign thought in English criticism, so domesticated has his influence been, but the same cannot be said of the work of the French philosopher and essayist Alain, who is still an unfamiliar name to many students of English literature. Forster combines critical ideas from Aristotle and Alain in a theory of the novel that describes how timeless works of art represent time-bound human beings. Aristotle's influence is the more important, for several of the central features of Forster's theory of the novel appear to have been developed in response to Aristotelian theory of poetry and psychology.

Forster begins his lecture on plot by quoting Aristotle on character and happiness and then disagreeing with him. Forster argues that we know better than Aristotle, who said character gives us qualities but happiness or misery takes the form of action. We believe it is in our inner secret lives that we are happy or unhappy, and therefore Forster looks for a more psychological aesthetics, such as Alain's. Bloomsbury's concern with states of mind, which they derived from the philosophy of G. E. Moore, coincides with Forster's dissatisfaction with Aristotle. The *Poetics* with its analysis of tragedy into six parts may nevertheless have suggested for Forster a model for organizing his lectures into seven aspects of fiction. A comparison of the two sets of analysis quickly brings out the distinctive features of Forster's theory of the novel. Aristotle's dominant idea of plot is broken into plot and story by Forster. Aristotle's character and Forster's people are where the two theories converge most closely. Aristotle's thought and diction have no corresponding aspects in Forster — and the absence of any consideration of ideas or of language in *Aspects of the Novel* is among the serious defects of Forster's analysis, a defect all the more surprising when one thinks of his own novels. Forster's aspects of fantasy and prophecy are non-Aristotelian, except perhaps as functions of the chorus, but pattern and rhythm are parts that could be included in Aristotle's conception of plot. (They also resemble faintly Aristotle's melody and spectacle, which were not parts of the epic, the genre that Aristotle discusses which is closest to the novel.) It should be clear from this brief comparison that by exalting the role of character in fiction and rejecting Aristotle's primary emphasis on action in life and art, Forster divides Aristotle's idea of plot into various aspects. As a consequence, the conception of structure in the novel — the closest analogue to significant form in painting — is also fragmented in Forster's theory.

This fragmentation can be illustrated by Forster's familiar but puzzling distinction between story and plot. By defining story as a narrative of events in their time sequence, and plot as a narrative of events in their causal sequence, Forster obscures their relationship — though at one point, when discussing pattern and rhythm, he does say, almost in an aside, that plot is actually derived from, 'springs out of the story' (p. 102). But he never makes it clear why the arrangement of a story's incidents that is to be designated as the plot has to be limited to those incidents in a causal sequence. (And Forster does not confine his discussions of plot in Meredith, Hardy, or Gide to causally arranged sequence of events.) Plot for Aristotle is σύνθεσιν τῶν πραγμάτων or τῶν πραγμάτων σύστασις. Butcher translates these phrases as 'the arrangement of incidents' and 'the structure of incidents'.[19] The incidents or happenings have to occur in a temporal sequence, of course, which can also be a causal one. But 'there is a great difference', Aristotle notes, 'between a thing happening *propter hoc* and *post hoc*' — thus possibly giving Forster the idea for his distinction between plot and story.[20] Forster, who knew Greek, indicates by his quotations from Aristotle that he was using Bywater's translation of the *Poetics*, and Bywater translates Aristotle's definition of plot as 'the combination of incidents or things done in the story', and again as 'the combination of incidents in the story'.[21] Thus he appears to make two things out of one, translating τῶν πραγμάτῶν not just as incidents or happenings, but as incidents or happenings *of the story*, and Forster seems to follow Bywater here.

Time outside the novel can be ignored by putting all the novelists together in the British Museum, but inside the novel Forster knows 'there is always a clock' (p. 20). In distinguishing between plot and story, Forster appears to be trying to confine the clock to one aspect of the novel, the story, which he nevertheless concedes is 'the fundamental aspect of the novel' (p. 17). In another image Forster describes the story as 'the naked worm of time' (p. 19). When *Aspects of the Novel* is juxtaposed with the *Poetics* it becomes apparent that Forster's plot is ultimately only another species of worm.

Forster's disagreements with Aristotle are not, as we have seen, merely about the meanings of plot. They extend all the way from literary criticism to happiness. The *Poetics* brings out the degree to which *Aspects of the Novel* is an anti-critical work of criticism. Forster hardly conceals the suspicion and distaste with which he regards critical methodology. They are summed up in his remark that questions about literary method of the kind Aristotle liked to ask 'have too much the atmosphere of the law courts about them' (p. 59).

VII

Alain's *Système des beaux-arts*, in spite of its title, was far less methodological in intent than Aristotle. At one point in his *Commonplace Book* Forster drew up two columns in order to compare Aristotle and Alain on character (p. 137). In one column he wrote down the passsage from Aristotle he had quoted at the beginning of the lecture on plot; but the other column remained blank. Forster might have put there the beginning of his quotation from Alain that he gives in the first lecture on people: 'What is fictitious in a novel is not so much the story as the method by which thought develops into action, a method which never occurs in daily life' (p. 32). For both Forster and Alain character not plot is the soul of fiction. But Forster is uneasy about Alain's sharp division between history and fiction. In history, according to

Système des beaux-arts, we are spectators but in fiction we are actors because there is always one character with whom we identify, who thinks for the reader, whose interior life presents in perspective other characters and objects in life. Forster agrees with Alain's discussion of character, however, because it gives him an aesthetic explanation of what makes characters real in fiction. It is a matter of knowing all about their inner, mental existences.[22] There is something of Kant's formalistic argument for the autonomy of the aesthetic in Alain's distinction between historcal and fictive prose that also comes into Forster's theory.

There is, I believe, another theory of fiction that comes into *Aspects of the Novel*, one that helped Forster more than Alain did to a non-Aristotelian conception of character. It comes from Charles Mauron, another modern French aesthetician. Mauron's name appears not in Forster's text but before it. It is to him that *Aspects of the Novel* is dedicated. A month after Forster delivered his lectures, Virginia and Leonard Woolf published, a part of their second Hogarth Essay series, a pamphlet of two essays by Mauron entitled *The Nature of Beauty in Art and Literature*. They were translated with an introduction by Roger Fry. Mauron himself had been introduced into Bloomsbury by Fry who shared with him the conviction that aesthetics ought to be thought about scientifically. Forster came to know Mauron better than anyone else in Bloomsbury did, except Fry; he once wrote that after Fry Mauron was the friend who helped him most to look at pictures. There would have been ample opportunity for Forster to read Mauron's two essays in French or English while he was preparing his lectures, which he delivered early in 1927. Fry had used Mauron's essays in *Transformations*, published in the autumn of 1926, to help answer Richards' *Principles of Literary Criticism*.[23]

The second of Mauron's essays, entitled 'Beauty in Literature', consists of an attempt to show how post-impressionist aesthetic theory can be used to discuss literary beauty. Mauron's hypothesis is that an exact analogy can be drawn between spatial volumes in painting and psychological or spiritual volumes in literature. In the spatial world,

> there remains the vast crowd of complex volumes: in the spiritual there remain the everyday realities of our soul, all the forms of our inner life.

> 'As the painter creates a spatial being, the writer creates a

psychological being'. Such, I think, is the hypothesis that we might admit as the basis for all literary criticism.[24]

The purpose of what used to be called plastic arts is the creation of spatial being, for Mauron, whereas the end of literature is the creation of psychological beings. These psychological beings are of three general types: the simplest psychological volumes are states of mind or moments of the spirit (they predominate in lyric poetry); the second are characters in drama and fiction; the third type consists of relations between psychological types, or what we call situations. 'Moments of the spirit, characters, situations and their complexes — these, . . .' it seems to Mauron, 'all literature envisages'.[25] Then carrying further the analogy to sculpture, Mauron finds that the written text is the equivalent of surface in plastic art, and thought the equivalent of volume.

Mauron did not follow up his theory, but it indicates the direction of his future criticism that was to make him a leading psychological critic of French literature. He never clarified the precise nature of his notion of psychological volumes (the relationship of words to psychological volumes does not seem at all analogous to that of lines and colours in spatial volumes) nor did he show how they could be arranged to display significant form in literature. Yet his theory suggests how post-impressionism provided aesthetic analogies for Forster in *Aspects of the Novel*. It is surely not just a coincidence that the most famous distinction in *Aspects of the Novel* — whose very title is a visual metaphor, albeit a faint one — consists of describing characters in terms of volume. The volumes of flat and round characters illustrate their psychological and moral dimensions. And earlier in his lectures Forster had remarked that the novelist, unlike other kinds of artists, uses what he calls 'word-masses' to describe himself, and these become in turn his characters (pp. 30–1).

Neither Mauron nor Forster reveals exactly how the formal relations between psychological volumes can be beautiful though Forster implies that through round characters the novelist harmonizes human beings with other aspects of his form. Mauron's 'Beauty in Literature' nevertheless offered Forster a post-impressionist literary aesthetic that suggested form in literature was a matter not just of structure or even style, but of character — the aspect of fiction Forster claimed was most significant. Thus the formalism of 'Beauty in Literature' was less dreary to Forster than other Bloomsbury theories of literary beauty. The dedication of *Aspects of the Novel* was more than a gesture of friendship.[26]

VIII

The right arrangement of flat and round characters in a novel was more important, Forster concluded, than the point of view, and this brings us to the last group of critical texts in relation to which Forster eclectically developed *Aspects of the Novel*. Inevitably they have to do with Henry James. Forster's ambivalence about the value of form in fiction is nowhere more clearly apparent than in his discussions of James's theory and practice. The theory is considered mainly in relation to Percy Lubbock's exposition of the master's method in *The Craft of Fiction*, which was published in 1921. Forster quotes Lubbock's statement that method in fiction is governed by 'the question of the relation in which the narrator stands to the story', (p. 54) and then disagrees. For Forster 'the whole intricate question of method' — he is echoing Lubbock's words here — 'resolves itself not into formulae but into the power of the writer to bounce the reader into accepting what he says . . .' (p. 54). Lubbock's exposition of point of view in fiction is rather more than a matter of formulae, but the disagreement between *The Craft of Fiction* and *Aspects of the Novel* is not really about this so much as the broader issue that disturbs Forster throughout his lectures. Lubbock is concerned that readers and novelists will ignore the art of the novel and treat it as a piece of life, whereas Forster worries that in treating it as art we shall forget life. Apart from their disagreements over the achievement of Tolstoy or Dickens, it is not a very illuminating critical dispute, especially as neither critic-novelist has anything to say about language or style. Forster once called words in *Aspects of the Novel* 'the minutiae of style' (p. 86). The two most influential English books on fiction in the early modern period move without hesitation between originals and translations, as if there were no differences between them.

It is for Lubbock's master that Forster reserves his most sustained criticism. In the first lecture of *Aspects of the Novel* James is parodied by Forster himself, and in the last lecture it is Wells's parody that is quoted. *The Ambassadors* is held up as an example of a novel that sacrifices life to pattern. The grounds for Forster's dislike are rather involved, I think. They have to do with both James's content and form. Forster's unease with James's content is illustrated by the sexual imagery that he uses to criticize James in both the text of *Aspects of the Novel* and his *Commonplace* notes. James's characters' clothes 'will not take off . . . this castrating is not in the interests of the Kingdom of Heaven', he keeps among the vegetables 'because their reproductive organs are not prominent' (pp. 110–11, 125). The comparison of James first with Wells and then with Proust also suggests that James's fictive sexuality bothers Forster, and in more than just one way.[27]

Forster's formal objections to the art of James's fiction are more interesting for the history of criticism than his unhappiness with its sexual implications. As with the other critical works Forster uses in *Aspects of the Novel*, those connected with James help Forster to bring out his own theory. This emerges in the way Forster favours Wells in the famous controversy that began when James criticized Well's novels for being without form and then was continued by Wells in *Boon* where he attacked James's novels for being without content. Forster quotes Wells's lethal comparison of a James novel to an empty church with a dead kitten, an egg shell and a bit of string on the altar, but not the ensuing correspondence which ended with Wells saying that James thought of literature as painting whereas he likened it to architecture. Wells's spokesman in *Boon* claimed that 'James never discovered that a novel isn't a picture . . . That life isn't a studio . . .'[28]

The aspect of the novel that is the context for Forster's criticism of James is pattern. Pattern expresses completion, Forster claims, whereas rhythm — the aspect under which Proust is discussed — conveys expansion and allows the novelist to give his characters a good run and achieve 'something else at the same time' (p. 116), that something else being artistic form. The distinction being made here between pattern and rhythm is somewhat invidious, and it suggests that one of the principal objections that Forster, like Wells, had to James's theory and practice, and also more generally to Bloomsbury's aesthetics, was that their artistic analogies came from painting and sculpture. Music was a deeper art than these for Forster. One of his conclusions in *Aspects of the Novel* is that 'in music fiction is likely to find its nearest parallel'

(p. 116). The distinction between aesthetic analogies carries over into the differences between fantasy, which just glances about, and prophecy, which gives the sensation of sound or song. Virginia Woolf's likening of *Robinson Crusoe* to a pot was 'a dreary Bloomsbury conclusion' at least partly because of the visual nature of the comparison. (It may also help to explain why, when her latest novel was *Mrs. Dalloway*, Forster classified Virginia Woolf as a fantastist.) But Forster's reaction to post-impressionist aesthetics should not be exaggerated. In terms of Roger Fry's binary formulation, Forster concentrated more on vision and tended to deprecate design. Yet the title of his lectures stresses the viewing of fiction. Here again Forster was eclectic.

IX

A literary history of *Aspects of the Novel* needs to do more, however, than examine the eclectic uses to which Forster put the texts of fiction and criticism with which his lectures are concerned. It should examine the form of the lectures themselves if only because Forster's eclecticism like Bloomsbury's extends beyond the ideas in his writing to the writing itself. The Nietzschean erosions of contour that Forster admired in Gide's *Les Faux-monnayeurs* can also describe what is happening in *Aspects of the Novel*, and not just with the texts that Forster has used to construct his lectures. The Bloomsbury writers combined in various ways forms of fiction and non-fiction, eroding the boundaries between them. This has not always been understood or appreciated by their critics, especially when the erosions are ironic. The mixing of forms is clear enough, perhaps, in a work like *Orlando* but not always in Virginia Woolf's *Common Reader* essays. Lytton Strachey's biographies still await adequate analysis as writing that combines fictive and non-fictive genres. And with Forster critics have discussed a work like *Aspects of the Novel* in the same dichotomous spirit in which he looked at the novel. His lectures have been read as if they themselves were composed of two forces: a theory of fiction and a bunch of other things. Those other things are essential to our experience of reading *Aspects of the Novel*. The art of Forster's lectures distinguishes them from the critical texts they use and discloses to us why *Aspects of the Novel* has not become in literary history merely a relic of learning. To appreciate this we need to look more closely at *Aspects of the Novel* as a form of writing.

How can novels be lectured on? Forster had asked Virginia Woolf. The genre of the public literary lecture presented Forster with opportunities and difficulties. The public lecture form renders ineffective any prolonged or involved argument. The possibilities of exemplification are so limited that there can be little or no close textual analysis. And of course there is no place for a scholarly apparatus of notes and bibliographies. These limitations were all advantages to Forster, who contentedly classified himself and most other lecturers as pseudo-scholars. The problem of exemplification Forster handled very effectively by emphasizing the comparison of passages or novels. There was another aspect of lectures that Forster exploited with great skill, and that is their colloquial opportunities. In his 'Author's Note' Forster justifies his colloquial informality by appealing to the subject of his lectures, the novel, which 'may possibly withold some of its secrets from the graver and grander streams of criticism, and . . . reveal them to backwaters and shallows' (p. xvii). Here once again in *Aspects of the Novel* Forster connects the informality of lectures, the colloquialness of the novel, and the inadequacies of criticism.

Forster's defence of the talkative tone of his lectures stresses from the very outset the voice in *Aspects of the Novel*. A lecture is, of course, a script for performance. In their printed form Forster's lectures still call upon us to respond to that voice as readers, since we cannot be hearers. And in this respect Forster's lectures resemble his essays, which are unapologetically talkative. The tone of the lectures is quite close to that of the familiar essay as Forster practised it, but there is also a difference to be found in the centrality of voice in the lectures. Voice becomes more prominent in a sustained work like *Aspects of the Novel* than in the essay, which in Forster's writings is a quite short form. The recurring voice in Forster's lectures sounds in the end more familiar to us than the brief voices of the essays, however familiar their essay form is. Identifying the voice of *Aspects of the Novel* by listening to its various tones is as important to the appreciation of Forster's book as comprehending his theory of the novel is. In fact they cannot be completely separated. We first hear Forster's voice distinctly in the invocation of the first lecture. Invocations are not exactly customary in lectures, certainly not one that calls upon the donor of the lectures as a kind of god whose integrity and *in*attention are solicited! And I think, by the way, that we must describe it as Forster's voice here and not his persona's because in a lecture the voice is the author's. In the absence of a poetics of the lecture we have to be tentative, but there does seem to be no persona in a lecture, only personality.

The prominence of voice in the form of *Aspects of the Novel* appears in the second lecture, where Forster gives us three vocal reactions to the place of story in the novel. The third of these, described as 'a sort of drooping regretful voice' that says 'Yes — oh dear yes — the novel tells a story' (p. 17) is identified as the author's. And it is his voice again that we are asked to join in a kind of chorus at the end of the lecture. We hear that voice at various times in the lectures, most notably in the passage on eclecticism when we are advised in quotation marks not to be proud eclectics. But there are other voices or tones of voice in *Aspects of the Novel* besides the deprecating one — voices that are affectionate, deflating, giggly, mocking, admiring, dismissive. Attending to them is one of the chief pleasures of reading Forster's text.

The images of *Aspects of the Novel* are another of its pleasures: the novelists in the British Museum, the flatness and roundness of characters, the fantastic and prophetic bars of light, and of course the water imagery. The novel for Forster is 'one of the moister areas of literature', and water runs through these lectures from the opening streams and shallows of criticism through the 'spongy tract' that is the novel (a rather neat pun), to the humanity with which the novel is sogged, and finally down to the open seas of prophecy. Characters also appear in *Aspects of the Novel*, and not only those from novels. The bus conductor and the golfer offer us opinions about the place of story in the novel. Curiosity is personified in the man who, when you meet him again in a year's time, will probably 'ask you how many brothers and sisters you have, his mouth sagging open, his eyes still bulging from his head' (p. 60). Finally, there are Forster's parodies of criticism as well as fiction, often done devastatingly in paraphrase.

Forster, we should remember, entitled his lectures 'aspects' because the term included the ways that both the reader and the novelist can regard the novel. The features of Forster's text that I have been reminding you of — and they are to be found in his essays as well — are not those we usually expect to find in modern criticism. They are more novelistic than critical. They tend in fact quite deliberately to undermine the seriousness of *Aspects of the Novel* as a work of critical theory. How earnest is Forster in visualizing all the novelists synchronically at work on their novels round the reading room of the British Museum? He is certainly serious about time as an enemy of value in life and art but the image is surely at least partly ironical. Forster's critical vision here is double, as Virginia Woolf had said of his fictive vision.[29] His misgivings about criticisms are manifest throughout *Aspects of the Novel*. We even have the standard romantic allusions to peeping and botanizing on our mothers' graves and enumerating the rainbow's warp and woof. Some of Forster's doubts about the value of criticism derive from his disillusionment with the novel itself. This emerges clearly in his argument with Virginia Woolf about the importance of art in fiction. Forster was not disillusioned about criticism because he was never illusioned about it. But he wrote no more novels after he lectured on them in 1927. He continued to write criticism, however. The next set of lectures he gave after *Aspects of the Novel* was also given in Cambridge; they were lectures for the tripos in 1930, and there are autobiographical resonances in Forster's entitling them 'The Creator as Critic'.

Despite his scepticism about formalistic and historical criticism and his doubts about the novel, Forster succeeds through its eclectic form in making *Aspects of the Novel* a worthwhile work on the criticism of fiction. But here again Forster is characteristically ambivalent. A course of lectures, he tells his audience at the beginning of the sixth one, 'tends in its parasitic way to lead a life of its own and it and the ideas running through it are apt to move in one direction while the subject steals off in another' (p. 73). This does not happen in *Aspects of the Novel* because of the way Forster erodes the contours between subject and treatment, between criticism and creation. The erosion may limit the value of the lectures as criticism, but it augments them as writing. A novel, Forster said in *Anonymity: An Enquiry*, is part atmosphere, part information. Criticism of the novel is similarly divided in *Aspects of the Novel*, and the atmosphere in which the theory and criticism of fiction are presented there is largely one of comic irony. The comic irony of Forster's lectures is his principal means of mixing creative and critical writing. How many of the novels he mentions are comedies.

Forster of course was not the only early modern writer to make literary criticism funny. If he had not read Ezra Pound, he certainly knew D. H. Lawrence's *Studies in Classic American Literature*, which appeared in 1923.[30] A similar relationship exists between the criticism and poetry or fiction of all these writers; Forster's own critics have shown how illuminating his ideas are when applied to his own novels. *Aspects of the Novel* is a particularly useful commentary on *A Passage to India*, for example. But unlike Pound's and Lawrence's critical humour, Forster's is not polemical in his lectures. The irony is far gentler. Yet irony it remains, and a number of reviewers complained that *Aspects of the Novel* diminished the art of its subject. Perhaps it does. But if we attend to Forster's lectures as a work in its own right, a work that will be read and enjoyed longer than the critical writings of probably all but one of his reviewers, we should be able to see how Forster's comic irony eclectically combines not only the texts of novelists and critics but also the forms of fictive and critical writing to create the art of *Aspects of the Novel*.

X

The literary history of *Aspects of the Novel* remains radically incomplete without an account of how it became, in turn, a text in subsequent discussions of the novel. And again this involves the form of Forster's book as well as its content — its significance, that is, as a work *of* literature as well as one *on* literature. There are, for example, the reviews of *Aspects of the Novel* by Arnold Bennett, E. F. Benson, L. P. Hartley, Ford Madox Ford, Edmund Wilson, I. A. Richards, and of course Virginia Woolf. But also very relevant to the literary history of Forster's lectures is the Hogarth Press series entitled 'Lectures on Literature' that began appearing shortly after *Aspects of the Novel* was published. One of the early works in this series, Edwin Muir's *The Structure of the Novel*, is designed in part as a direct reply to Forster. Another work announced as forthcoming in the series but never published in it, is even more interesting. It is Virginia Woolf's long essay 'Phases of Fiction', which was serialized in the spring of 1929 but never published as a book. It can then be read, I think, as another response to *Aspects of the Novel* and therefore belongs to the debate

about fiction that really began when Forster wrote to Virginia
Woolf for advice about lecturing on novels.

The literary history of that debate is at least a chapter in itself
but two dimensions of it need to be briefly mentioned here
because they extend the significance of this Bloomsbury debate
as well as confirm the usefulness of a literary history that concerns
itself with intertextual relations and the development of forms.

Virginia Woolf's disagreements with Forster in her two reviews
of his lectures, in their ensuing correspondence (only a part of
which has been described in their respective biographies[31]), and
in the works on fiction Virginia Woolf subsequently wrote recapitulate and extend two very well known earlier twentieth-
century disagreements over the novel. Woolf's complaint that
Forster was too concerned with human emotion and not enough
with aesthetic emotion in his lectures is a continuation of the
dispute between James and Wells a half generation earlier.
James's closing words to Wells, 'it is art that *makes* life, makes
interest, makes importance . . .'[32] could have come from Woolf's
review, and Wells's reply that he did not know what James meant
by art is exactly how Forster responds. Henry James and Virginia
Woolf are fond of drawing analogies between fiction and the
visual arts; Wells and Forster find them misleading (though
Forster uses them) and turn instead to parallels in architecture
and music. In 1914 James criticized his Edwardian successors
Wells, Bennett and others for their saturation approach to fiction.
Just a few years later we find Virginia Woolf attacking her
Edwardian predecessors for their materialistic conceptions of
character. Even Forster, Woolf observes in *Mr Bennett and Mrs
Brown*, which she wrote in the early twenties, had somewhat
spoiled his early novels by compromising with Edwardian
materialism in his characterization.

Virginia Woolf's quarrel with Bennett resembles James's
argument with Wells even more closely than her quarrel with
Forster. As with the James/Wells debate, it was basically about
how novels should be written rather than how they should be
criticized. Bloomsbury's epistemology, ethics and aesthetics had
shown Woolf that Bennett's fiction was inadequate in content
as well as in form.[33] We now know that she also attacked Bennett's
notion of Mrs Brown because Bennett had revealed, in an earlier
book on women, that he did not understand them or their
situation.[34] We shall see this theme recurring in her debate with

Forster. The point to be emphasized here is that the disagreement between Mr Bennett and Mrs Woolf cannot properly be reduced to a conflict between ordinary life in fiction and high-brow art.[35] Similarly, the disagreement between Forster and Woolf is not just a life-versus-art opposition.

These three debates disclose modern critic-novelists of different generations in recurrent disagreement about the value of their form and its nature. Half a century later the vocabulary of our debates about fiction is different but not, perhaps, the underlying concerns.

XI

The second dimension of the subsequent literary history of *Aspects of the Novel* that needs to be mentioned here is involved in the first. When Forster complained to Virginia Woolf that if his notion of life in his lectures was vague, so was her notion of art — she replied that she was not writing a book on fiction, only reviewing one. We have noted that Woolf was, in fact, at work on a book about fiction at this time that was announced for years but never appeared as a book.[36] One of the reasons why 'Phases of Fiction' was not finally published in the Hogarth Lectures on Literature may have been because of another book on fiction that Woolf began to write at the same time she was supposed to be finishing 'Phases of Fiction'.

It was a year and a half after Forster gave his now widely acclaimed lectures on the novel, in Cambridge, that Virginia Woolf was herself in Cambridge and lecturing on the novel. These lectures were reworked into the book she called *A Room of One's Own*. It was her last and most interesting response to *Aspects of the Novel* and very different from her earlier ones. Woolf's subject in *A Room of One's Own* is women and fiction but the cultic fame of the book has tended to obscure the second of her two subjects. It is in her discussion of fiction, however, that Virginia Woolf implicitly, though never directly, challenges an aspect of Forster's theory of fiction that she had not mentioned before. In *A Room of One's Own* she questions not Forster's devaluing of form in fiction but his formalistic rejection of the history of the novel. Forster, after comparing passages from six novels in his opening lecture, had defended his timeless discussions of the novel in the following words:

> Does not chronology seem less important now that we have
> visualized six novelists at their jobs? If the novel develops, is
> it not likely to develop on different lines from the British
> Constitution, or even the Women's Movement? I say 'even the
> Women's Movement' because there happened to be a close
> association between fiction in England and that movement
> during the nineteenth century — a connection so close that it
> has misled some critics into thinking it is an organic con-
> nection. As women bettered their position the novel, they
> asserted, became better too. Quite wrong. A mirror does not
> develop because an historical pageant passes in front of it. It
> only develops when it gets a fresh coat of quicksilver — in other
> words, when it acquires new sensitiveness; and the novel's
> success lies in its own sensitiveness, not in the success of the
> subject-matter. Empires fall, votes are accorded, but to those
> people writing in the circular room it is the feel of the pen
> between their fingers that matters most. (p. 13)

Forster's obliviousness here to how the conditions of life affect the
novel and determine the opportunities of its authors to become
novelists in the first place displays a more extreme version of
formalism than anything to be found in Virginia Woolf's various
defences of the art of fiction. In *A Room of One's Own* the women
novelists are not with the men under the dome of the British
Museum. They are in drawing rooms and kitchens and — in the
future, it is to be hoped — in their own rooms. The British
Museum in *A Room of One's Own* is the place not where writers write
timelessly but where the narrator goes from Cambridge to find
out why women are poor.

Woolf's rejection of Forster's assumption that history develops
but art stands still is all the more interesting in *A Room of One's Own*
because of its form and its conclusion. The conclusion is that a
woman needs five hundred pounds a year and a room of her own
so that she can live in the presence of reality, think of things in
themselves. To do this she must attain that unself-consciousness,
that unsex-consciousness, that resembles what Forster described
as the anonymous state of creation in his pamphlet *Anonymity: An
Enquiry*. 'All literature tends toward a condition of anonymity'
for both Forster and Virginia Woolf.[37]

The resemblance in form between *A Room of One's Own* and *Aspects of the Novel* connect these two works as illuminatingly as do their critical assumptions and conclusions. The erosions of contour that *A Room of One's Own* achieves are more formidable than those in *Aspects of the Novel*. Both works combine genres in such a way that they cannot be fully understood or appreciated simply as works of criticism or non-fiction. Virginia Woolf rewrote her two lectures in a fictive form of one giant lecture that has six chapters, various personae, a narrative structure, symbolic motifs, a peroration, etc. And the lecture form is insisted upon throughout. Again we have an emphasis on voice, on the role of the audience, and on the identity of the lecturer not just as critic but as novelist. Both *A Room of One's Own* and *Aspects of the Novel* use comic irony throughout, mocking for example the academic setting and the very genre in which they are taking place. Virginia Woolf's lecture is more radical in its implications than Forster's; as well, its mixture of fiction and non-fiction is more original than Forster's. There is also an important difference in their interest in the novel, for Forster is looking at present and past novels while Virginia Woolf is chiefly concerned with unwritten future ones. Nevertheless these two works complement each other when brought together through literary history.

Today *A Room of One's Own* works miracles for many readers. Forster's lectures are unlikely to do so very often, yet they are, in an important literary historical sense, a part of Virginia Woolf's lectures, just as the texts of Bradley, of Eliot and Arnold, of Aristotle and Alain, of Mauron, Lubbock, James and Wells are parts of Forster's — not to mention all the novels that Virginia Woolf and Forster allude to, including their own.

But time must have a stop even in literary history. My moral is simply that we need to re-examine where we stop it in modern literary history.

NOTES

1. E. M. Forster, *Aspects of the Novel*, ed. Oliver Stallybrass, Abinger edn. (London: Edward Arnold, 1974), p. 71. All page references in the text are to this edition of Forster's work.
2. For an account and demonstrations of new literary history see Ralph Cohen's forthcoming book on the theory of literary history.

3. Forster's letters to the Woolfs are in the Sussex University Library and the Berg Collection of the New York Public Library.

4. *Anonymity: An Enquiry* (London: Hogarth Press, 1925; rpt. *Two Cheers for Democracy*, ed. Oliver Stallybrass, Abinger edn. (London: Arnold, 1972), pp. 77–93.

5. *The Letters of Virgina Woolf, 1923–1928*, ed. Nigel Nicolson and Joanne Trautmann, III (London: Hogarth, 1977), p. 266.

6. Extracts from Forster's *Commonplace Book* have been published as an appendix to Stallybrass's edition of *Aspects of the Novel*. The *Commonplace Book* itself was published in a facsimile edition by the Scolar Press in 1978.

7. See *The Bloomsbury Group: A Collection of Memoirs, Commentary and Criticism*, ed. S. P. Rosenbaum (Toronto: Univ. of Toronto Press, 1975), p. 25.

8. Roger Fry, *Vision and Design* (London: Chatto, 1920), p. 194.

9. Clive Bell, *Art* (London: Chatto, 1914), p. 8, p. 25.

10. I. A. Richards, *Principles of Literary Criticism* (1924; rpt. London: Routledge, 1961), Chapters I, II, and III.

11. See Roger Fry, *Transformations* (London: Chatto, 1926), Chapter I, and Clive Bell, *Landmarks in Nineteenth-Century Painting* (London: Chatto, 1927), pp. vii–x.

12. A. C. Bradley, 'Poetry for Poetry's Sake', *Oxford Lectures on Poetry* (London, 1909; rpt. Bloomington, Indiana: Indiana Univ. Press, n. d.), pp. 16, 16–17.

13. For Virginia Woolf's reviews of *Aspects of the Novel* see B. J. Kirkpatrick, *A Bibliography of Virginia Woolf*, Revised Edition (London: Hart-Davis, 1967). For the correspondence between Forster and Virginia Woolf see *The Letters of Virginia Woolf, op. cit.*, III, pp. 437–9; Quentin Bell, *Virginia Woolf: A Biography* (London: Hogarth, 1972), II, pp. 134–5; and P. N. Furbank, *E. M. Forster: A Life* (London: Secker and Warburg, 1978), II, pp. 146–7.

14. Bell, *Art*, p. 98.

15. Clive Bell, *Civilisation* (London: Chatto, 1928), p. 170.

16. Forster's review is included as an appendix to Stallybrass's edition of *Aspects of the Novel*; for Virginia Woolf's see Kirkpatrick, *op. cit.*

17. T. S. Eliot, *The Sacred Wood* (London, 1920; rpt. London: Methuen, 1960), p. 37.

18. Eliot, p. xiii.

19. Aristotle, *The Poetics*, trans. S. H. Butcher, ed. John Gassner, 4th ed. (n. p.: Dover, 1951), VI, 6 and VI, 9. 1450a.

20. Aristotle, X. 3. 1452a.

21. Aristotle, *De Poetica*, trans. Ingram Bywater in *The Basic Works of Aristotle*, ed. Richard McKeon (New York: Random, 1941), pp. 1460–1.

22. Alain's discussions of history and fiction are in Chapters 5 to 8 in Part 10 of *Système des beaux-arts* (Paris, 1920; rpt. Paris: Gallimard, 1926), pp. 316–28.

23. In April 1925, Forster met Mauron in France to work on a translation of *A Passage to India* (Furbank, *Forster*, II, 138). Fry heard Mauron read 'Beauty in Literature' in Pontigny in September 1925, and wrote to Virginia Woolf that he had arranged to translate it. (Fry's unpublished letters to Virginia Woolf are at the University of Sussex.)

24. *The Nature of Beauty in Art and Literature*, trans. Roger Fry (London: Hogarth, 1927), pp. 66–7.

25. Mauron, p. 78.

26. Mauron in turn translated *Aspects of the Novel* in *Mesures* in 1928, though the translation is not listed in B. J. Kirkpatrick's bibliography of Forster.

27. Forster thought that in *The Turn of the Screw* James was 'merely declining to think about homosex, and the knowledge that he is declining throws him into the necessary fluster' (p. 134).

28. *Henry James and H. G. Wells: A Record of Their Friendship, their Debate on the Art of Fiction, and their Quarrel*, ed. Leon Edel and Gordon N. Ray (Urbana: Univ. of Illinois Press, 1958), p. 244. (The ellipses are Wells's.) According to Edel and Ray, James review of contemporary fiction, 'The Younger Generation' started the debate. Forster was, surprisingly, not mentioned at all by James in this 1914 survey written for the *Times Literary Supplement*, though he had published four novels by then. James's ignoring of Forster may have contributed to Forster's dislike of him.

29. See 'The Novels of E. M. Forster', *Collected Essays* (London: Hogarth, 1966), I, pp. 342–51.

30. Forster refers to Lawrence's articles on Melville in *Aspects*, p. 99.

31. Bell and Furbank mention only a single exchange of letters. There are two more letters from Forster and one from Virginia Woolf about *Aspects of the Novel*.

32. *James and Wells*, p. 267.

33. See my 'The Philosophical Realism of Virginia Woolf', *English Literature and British Philosophy*, ed. S. P. Rosenbaum (Chicago: Univ. of Chicago Press, 1971), pp. 320–3.

34. See *The Diary of Virginia Woolf*, ed. Anne Oliver Bell (London: Hogarth, 1978), II, pp. 339–42.

35. See for example Samuel Hynes, 'The Whole Contention between Mr Bennett and Mrs Woolf', *Edwardian Occasions* (New York: Oxford Univ. Press, 1972), pp. 24–38. Hynes is right to stress that the debate between Virginia Woolf and Arnold Bennett has a broad context but it is even broader than he suggests, as Virginia Woolf's reactions to Bennett's *Our Women* (see previous note) and Forster's *Aspects of the Novel* indicate. Bennett was clearly a more self-conscious artist in writing novels than Wells was and perhaps even Forster; he also realized the potential importance of post-impressionism for literature, and that is more than can be said of Henry James.

36. See J. Howard Woolmer, *A Checklist of the Hogarth Press, 1917–1938* (London: Hogarth, 1976), p. 165.

37. *Anonymity: An Enquiry*, p. 81.

5 'Sublime Noise' for Three Friends: Music in the Critical Writings of E. M. Forster, Roger Fry and Charles Mauron

Linda Hutcheon

'It will be generally admitted that Beethoven's Fifth Symphony is the most sublime noise that has ever penetrated into the ear of man.' That, of course, is the well-known opening of, appropriately, the *fifth* chapter of *Howards End*. Forster's biographer, P. N. Furbank, has suggested that this passage and what follows recall a dialogue written in 1904, six years earlier, by Forster's friend and mentor, Goldsworthy Lowes Dickinson.[1] In that piece, a poet returns in an exalted mood from hearing this same music, and finds himself attacked by two friends, a musician and a painter who resembles Roger Fry, for using music as a substitute for living. In his defence, the poet offers an allegorical interpretation of the Beethoven that is not unlike that offered by Helen Schlegel in the novel: goblins and elephants, 'panic and emptiness'. Forster's use of Beethoven in this novel is worth stressing in conjunction with Dickinson, Fry, and the possible functions of music if only because when we think of Bloomsbury and its Cambridge roots, it seems more natural to think of literature, and perhaps even painting, than it is to think of music. Yet the images and structures of that third art significantly inform the writings, both critical and creative, not just of Forster, but also of other members of the Bloomsbury Group.

Two figures are of particular interest, however. The well-known art critic, Roger Fry, and the less well-known French aesthetic theorist, Charles Mauron, are two men whose use of musical associations and analogies in their writings casts an interesting light on Forster's own. It is M. H. Abrams' view, in *The Mirror and the Lamp*, that the analogy used for art in a given period plays an important role in shaping the structure of critical theory. If this is so, to go one step back and study both the use of analogue and the perspective taken on the art form from which it is drawn might prove revealing in discovering the underlying theoretical structures of a group of writers. The present choice of music as both the art to be discussed and as the source of images and structures, was one motivated by the three men's personal tastes and talents. However, it is also significant that music, which was a mimetic art for Aristotle, one to be discussed in formal terms, also came to be a major aesthetic analogue for the Romantics because of its non-mimetic qualities and therefore expressive possibilities.

Forster, in the company of other Bloomsbury figures, appears to manifest an attraction for both of these seemingly contrary perspectives. For him, music was certainly 'the deepest of the arts and deep beneath the arts',[2] yet in his critical writings, he appears to waver between two reasons for this exalted status of music. Sometimes he held the view that it was the form or the order of the art, as indeed believed Roger Fry. At other times he also seemed to want to attribute music's power to something that reminded him of something else, or even to something ineffable, almost mystical in it. The formal and the impressionistic impulses seem to be at war in Forster, and Charles Mauron, despite a strong formal concern instilled in him by his own training and by his friend Fry, continued the battle, a battle in a war that may indeed still be in progress.

It is obvious that these three men differed in age, temperament, background and profession. Forster, the quiet novelist and man of letters, shared little on the surface with the more flamboyant and older Fry who was a painter, art expert and aesthetician, although both had been at King's College, Cambridge and both had been Apostles. They also shared Cambridge and Bloomsbury friends, among them Dickinson and the Woolfs. Mauron was a younger French chemist who, because of failing eyesight, was forced to return to his first loves, poetry and aesthetics. He was discovered in Provence after the First World War by Fry and set to work translating Forster's *A Passage to India*. Unlike

Forster, Fry and Mauron both began as scientists, turned to critical and also creative work, while retaining a strong commitment to the value of the experimental method in aesthetic theorizing. What is most important here in the close friendship of both Fry and Forster with Mauron is the fact that it was things musical and literary that forged the links between them. Mauron translated into French most of Forster's work, originally at Fry's instigation. Together Fry and Mauron translated Mallarmé, and Fry translated Mauron's essays and poems into English and arranged for their publication. From the published letters, it is clear that the two Englishmen frequently discussed literary and aesthetic matters with their mutual friend in France. These interchanges of ideas and mutual debts are implied perhaps in such details as Forster's dedication of *Aspects of the Novel* to Mauron.

Music was another potent link among the three friends. Forster and Fry shared the friendship of Lowes Dickinson, a serious lover of music. All three men, and Dickinson too for that matter, were not only appreciators of music in concert, but attempted to play keyboard music for themselves as well. And it was Forster, on his first visit to his French translator in 1925, who arranged for Fry to buy a gramophone for Mauron. These points of literary and musical connection through work and friendship are not only of some biographical interest, but they also serve to make us aware of the similar roots of what turn out to be quite different attitudes to and interpretations of this particular art form.

Aside from the writing of the libretto to *Billy Budd*, Forster's appreciation of music, like Fry's, was largely that of a serious amateur. In his critical writings on other authors, the language and images of music appear frequently, often in the context of praise for some formal accomplishment. For instance, he compliments Proust for his use of Vinteuil's phrase as a literary as well as musical structuring device.[3] Virginia Woolf's biography of Roger Fry is ordered like a 'musical composition', and *To the Lighthouse* is 'a novel in sonata form'.[4] In 'Ibsen the Romantic', Forster wrote: 'with Ibsen as with Beethoven, the beauty comes not from the tunes, but from the way they are used and worked into the joints of the action'.[5] Forster himself wanted to play the Romantic Beethoven piano sonatas in order to capture their 'architecture', even at the expense of the sensuousness heard in the concert hall. (This same concern for form can be seen in terms of painting, not music, in Forster's idea of characters as flat or round 'word-masses',[6] a notion perhaps inspired by his friend Charles Mauron's contemporaneous theory of psychological volumes in literature.)[7]

In *Aspects of the Novel* Forster again wrote, in formal terms, that music,

> though it does not employ human beings, though it is governed by intricate laws, nevertheless does offer in its final expression a type of beauty which fiction might achieve in its own way. Expansion. That is the idea the novelist must cling to. Not completion. Not rounding off but opening out. When the symphony is over we feel that the notes and tunes composing it have been liberated, that they have found in the rhythm of the whole their individual freedom (p. 116).

Forster's concept of the 'intricate laws' of music, of the 'rhythm of the whole' that gives the parts both their freedom and their meaning, is one that he shared with Roger Fry. But the post-impressionist art theorist had a different notion of what was involved in that 'expansion,' to use Forster's term. Art did indeed have effects on its perceiver, but the most important of these was the response to form itself. And for Fry music provided the best proof. The emotions induced by music were abstract and universal and were created by the contemplation of formal, harmonious relations of notes, one to the other. The value of this 'aesthetic emotion' for Fry was unquestionable; it was more important and more profound than those 'accessory' feelings aroused by less 'pure' art forms. By 'purity', Fry intended no value judgement but simply a formal notion of almost 'chemically' pure relations of parts with as little reliance on representation or subject matter as possible. For Fry, as for those nineteenth-century poets he so admired, music was the purest, the most formal of the arts; as such, it became, in his general art theory, the ideal model and goal for all the others. As he wrote to Marie Mauron in 1920, 'Always think of music where the problem is less complicated, for all arts, being one, are parallel ways of reaching the goal of satisfying the needs of the spirit'.[8] A few years later, her husband, Charles, was to repeat these same ideas in his first English publication.

If music was the purest art form, the one least reliant on

representation, literature, and the novel in particular, was obviously another matter, for Fry and Forster both. Nevertheless Fry always argued that 'first-rate novels' owe their delight for the reader to something akin to the pleasure of music, to 'the recognition of *inevitable sequences*; a pleasure which . . . corresponds to the pleasure . . . found in marking the inevitable sequence of the notes in a tune'.[9] Forster too uses a musical image in his discussion of fiction in *Aspects of the Novel*. His idea of 'rhythm' concentrates less on sequence for its musical parallel than on those very formal relations which Fry so prized. Proust's novel 'hangs together because it is stitched internally, because it contains rhythms' (p. 113). 'Rhythm' is not, however, a fixed 'pattern' (which potentially 'shuts the doors on life' [p. 112]); it is rather repetition plus variation and operates structurally to create beauty in the text. It is this formal idea of rhythm, the use of the musical structure of relations between parts, that leads Forster to suggest that 'in music fiction is likely to find its nearest parallel' (p. 116).

Fry certainly found in music the nearest parallel to what he valued in the art of painting: Picasso is praised for trying to create 'a purely abstract language of form — a visual music'.[10] But while Fry remained a 'formalist', in this sense of the word, modifying his views only slightly over the years, Forster's concept of 'rhythm' seems subtly to alter in the thirteen years that separate the Clark lectures that became *Aspects of the Novel* and the 1939 piece called 'Not Listening to Music' where the term 'rhythm' takes on a somewhat less rigorously formal meaning, in music, at least: 'There's an insistence in music — expressed largely through rhythm; there's a sense that it is trying to push across at us something which is neither an aesthetic pattern nor a sermon' (*TCD*, p. 124). He never specifies what that 'something' is, and this lack of explanation, this opting for the suggestively unexplained, is also a feature of Forster's use of musical analogies in his more literary writings.

The 'mysticism' that Roger Fry lamented in Forster's fiction might be seen to play a role in Forster's general critical frame of reference as well. He wrote in his Commonplace Book around the time of *Aspects of the Novel* that music and poetry ('words under their musical aspect') could be timeless in a way that the novel, written in linear prose, could never be. Because of this, perhaps, music (and some forms of literature) could provide an escape from the present; listening to Beethoven's Seventh Symphony later during the Second World War, he wrote that music like that could never be stopped. It moved through tanks and guns to its own close.[11] These ideas were written for Charles Mauron who was himself in the process of developing a theory connecting what he perceived as a contemporary desire for mysticism and mystery, with the immense power of music.

Music also offered to Forster, however, the possibility of another kind of transcendental moment, a moment actually endangered by 'rhythm', by the recognition of formal relations. Upon finding a parallel between Beethoven's Sonata Op.31, No.3, Scherzo movement and his Appassionata, Forster noted the danger of making such a discovery, in that it removed him from Beethoven's state when he was composing. But most often it was less some spiritual identification with the composer that Forster achieved than a more simple sort of 'wool-gathering' by the listening but 'wandering' mind, as it made associations, as did Helen Schlegel in *Howards End*. The listener, if not the composer, then, could transform even music into a representational art form. In this transformation Forster departs from strictly structural concerns.

This departure does not deny the strong interest in formal principles that is revealed in Forster's criticism. Indeed the echo of Gautier in the title of the essay, 'Art for Art's Sake', prepares us for his statement that the work of art is a 'self-contained entity, with a life of its own imposed on it by its creator' (*TCD*, p. 88). But the example of music clearly reveals that there is an underlying divergence in Forster's criticism from what we have called the 'formalism' of Fry. Roger Fry felt that the aesthetic emotion aroused by music was caused solely by the 'recognition of formal design', and that we could be moved most deeply 'by certain sequences of notes which arouse no suggestion of any experience in actual life',[12] Music became the paradigm for 'pure', that is, non-representational, art. Today Fry would be classed more an 'absolutist' than as a 'referentialist' by musical theorists, since to him music did have meaning, emotional and intellectual meaning, though it used no linguistic signs; it operated as a closed system, to use modern terminology, with no signs related to a non-musical world. While Forster at his piano, trying to learn a little about musical construction, might have agreed in part, it was the 'wool-gatherer' who usually won out, and Forster would have to be labelled as a 'referentialist' or at least as an impressionist.

This difference between formal and impressionistic interpretations is perhaps best illustrated by looking briefly at a theory that Forster, Fry and Mauron all toyed with, that of a parallel between the arts of music and painting, between sounds and colours. Although Forster was careful in 'Not Listening to Music' (in 1939) to separate what he called 'music itself' from 'music that reminds me of something', a separation Fry himself always made in order to denigrate the latter, he found that Debussy kept reminding him of Monet, for he translated sounds into colours (*TCD*, pp. 122–3). A few years later, in 'The C Minor of that Life', he was still writing, 'I continue to wonder whether keys have colours, . . . whether they tint the tunes which are played in them . . .' (*TCD*, p. 119). This same impressionistic vagueness can be seen in the later writings of his friend Mauron on painters: Van Gogh's mind reveals '[l']ivresse d'une musicalité colorée' and René Seyssaud is a 'musicien de la couleur'.[13] But as early as 1925, Mauron, then more under Fry's influence, perhaps, had been playing with this notion. While finding the idea 'profoundly useful for aesthetics', Fry the painter, as well as Fry, the formalist and former scientist, took a rather less vague stand on Mauron's notion, as his language reveals: 'There is an acoustic phenomenon which corresponds closely to colour. The timbre of the instruments', he wrote to Mauron. And he went on to write of the 'qualitative diversity' of sounds and colours and the problems of 'apprehension of gradation', contrasting the keyboard to colours arranged in spectral order.[14]

This attempt at almost scientific precision characterizes the search for accuracy that obsessed Fry. In a similar way, the opposite quality, the vagueness of Forster's 'wondering' is representative of a certain quality of his thinking. That this difference between the two men should be revealed clearly in the discussions on music is perhaps inevitable, given that the process of verbalization of responses to music is traditionally accepted as being a difficult one, one prone to garbling and to perverting experiences that are thought too subtle or at least too varied for language. Forster seemed to sense this linguistic limitation, but the artist in him found a partial solution in the translating of wordless feelings into images, thereby making music a form of representational art in yet another sense.

The manuscript of Forster's so-called 'analyis' of Beethoven's piano sonatas at King's College Library is full of such literary or metaphorical translations. The last bars of one piece are called a little smile which irradiates backwards over the rest. In another, the arpeggios, we are told, rush up and down like brooms until any sense of continuity is swept away. Then the brooms are put away and their swing is lost. In yet another piece, a fish swims against the D Minor stream. The next key loses the fish. In other words, where one expects formal analysis of the sonatas, since this is what Forster, inspired by Mauron, set out to do, one finds instead impressionistic description, suggestive images. Here even the narrative impulse of Forster the novelist is called into play by the music. The frequently repeated adjective, 'ravishing', takes its full meaning as he notes a series of bars in a piece in which lusciousness is unexpectedly 'raped'. We are told to contrast this to a very different rape at the end of the first movement of the Appassionata which Forster feels had been planned from the opening bar. This one is a thorough and thoroughly 'serious' act of sex. This referentialism is far from a formalist response to the contemplation of structural relations in art.

Fry, too, frequently used images from one art to describe another, but it was out of a conviction that all the arts were as one, from a formal point of view, at any rate. The relation of art to 'reality' was an issue Fry never ignored, but it was one that interested him, as a theorist and as a painter both, less than did the contemplation of formal, aesthetic relations in art and the emotions evoked by this contemplation. He was alternately amused and annoyed by Forster's insistence that paintings 'reminded' him of something before he even noticed some structural significance. That they should argue about music (in fact, the music to be sent to Mauron) was perhaps inevitable. Forster forbade Fry to choose records for their mutual friend, and Fry responded by criticizing Forster's subsequent choice (Holst) as a 'picturesque kind of music' that bored him 'considerably'.[15] The theoretical objection to such art had earlier been formulated by Fry regarding painting: art that relies on association of ideas (or representation) is not 'pure', in that it encourages an imagined practical activity rather than a 'disembodied functioning of the spirit' in the contemplation of forms. As Fry put it, 'The disadvantage of such an art of associated ideas is that its effect really depends on what we bring with us: it adds no entirely new factor to our experience'.[16]

Fry's theory proved useful for music, for architecture, for post-impressionist painting, and to some extent for Mallarmé's verse. But mixed forms, such as opera and song, turned out to be more complex, and more representational. Fiction was even more of a problem. 'Even in the novel', wrote Fry,

> which as a rule has pretensions to being a work of art, the structure may be so loose, the esthetic effects may be produced by so vast an accumulation of items that the temptation for the artist to turn aside from his purpose and interpolate criticisms of life, of manners or morals, is very strong. Comparatively few novelists have ever conceived of the novel as a single perfectly organic whole.[17]

While Forster, in *Aspects of the Novel*, also valued the beauty of the 'whole' of a work of fiction, he also admitted the 'intensely, stiflingly human quality of the novel', a quality not to be ignored, or exorcized, or else 'the novel wilts, little is left but a bunch of words' (pp. 15–16). And as he later wrote, he actually did not mind if 'the pot of art gets cracked here and there, and sheds a few drops into life'.[18] These two views of fiction, related closely to those two opposing views of the referential nature of music, are seen clearly even in the early work of Mauron, who wrote in 1927,

> Music has been for long the purest art, the art of which the effects are apprehended by the purest feeling; painting and sculpture are today almost approaching this. But literature remains encumbered with accessories, philosophical, psychological, social demonstrations, with sentimentalities and opinions. A great step would be made if we could savour, appreciate, and discuss pure literary qualities.[19]

This last wish reveals Fry's strong influence at this time, but there was a side to Mauron that responded strongly to Forster's impressionist vagueness, to what Fry loosely called his 'mysticism' as well.

This vagueness is perhaps best seen in the use of another musical analogy in *Aspects of the Novel*. This time it is not the formal concept of 'rhythm' that is in question, but the more indeterminate if suggestive notions of 'voice' and especially 'song'. Story is called 'the repository of a voice' (p. 27), of 'something' that appeals to the ear, 'something we should lose if the novel were not read aloud', yet is not melody or cadence. This 'something' evidently lies in the story, but what it is is unclear. This same vagueness characterizes the discussion of 'prophecy', which is also called a 'tone of voice'. The difference between George Eliot and Dostoyevsky is clear, writes Forster, to 'anyone who has an ear for song' (p. 88). But what does this mean? And how helpful is it, in literary terms, to say that prophetic literature such as Dostoyevsky's 'gives us the sensation of a song or of a sound' (p. 94), or that the 'essential' of *Moby-Dick* is its 'prophetic song', even though 'we cannot catch the words of the song' (p. 95)? The almost mystic quality of Forster's vague defining characteristic of song comes to light as he goes on to write, 'Nothing can be stated about *Moby-Dick* except that it is a contest. The rest is song'.

It is this same impressionistic use of music that is seen at times in Mauron's critical writing. In *Mallarmé l'obscur*, he writes that 'Petit Air II' of Mallarmé is marked by a 'passage rapide de la réalité à rien, du son au silence, d'un seul trait en *rubato*, fusée et retombée en éparpillement qui font penser à Chopin'.[20] Perhaps it was because the poet in question was Stéphane Mallarmé that Mauron felt the need to turn to musical associations, for Mallarmé himself wrote many poems and essays on music and gave a lecture on 'La musique et les lettres' at Oxford and Cambridge. It was Mallarmé's poetry, of course, that Mauron and Fry translated together. But for Fry, this French poet's work represented the formally purest shape poetry could take, and therefore it was in terms of music that this literary purity was expressed; that is, in terms of the 'harmony' of the 'aural complex', the 'melodic effect' of sounds, the 'mental tune'. And when co-translator and commentator Mauron picked up Fry's notion of the conditions of pure art with regard to Mallarmé, the first condition he named was the 'establishment of a keyboard' which was nothing but a system of transitions'.[21] Mauron vacillated, then, between a vague impressionistic use of musical associations and a precise structural one. It was probably more the formal line of Fry's influence as well as a reinforcement of his own scientific penchant that led to the definition of 'psychocritique', Mauron's later version of literary psychoanalysis, as a musical analysis of obsessive themes and their variations in literature.

It seems that when Mauron, like Forster, wrote about aesthetic structure, he shared Fry's interest and concern for form. However, it was when questions of aesthetic response and aesthetic creation arose that the paths diverged. This explains what might appear to be a formalist/impressionist contradiction in some of Mauron's writing. For instance, he wrote of the role of the poet's 'moi orphique' in uniting the conscious and the unconscious: 'l'oeuvre littéraire apparaît comme un contrepoint à deux voix; les deux voix s'ignorent par définition; or, elles sont harmonisées',[22] This statement, dating from 1952, might appear to be using a structural image, but in 1950, Mauron had already made it clear that the Orpheus image of the poet attracted him because it combined 'les deux figures du chanteur et de l'initié mystique'.[23] In a note a page later, he went on to say that it took him years to realize than 'en général les vérités de l'art s'expriment sans effort dans la langue mystique'. By this Mauron meant something more than a Forsterian impressionism or subjectivism; he actually meant the language of the Oriental mystics, and of the Tao in particular. This early mystic theory of aesthetic creation for Mauron was set upon a notion, like Fry's, of the first step to a formal aesthetic response as a disinterested 'intensity' of contemplation that is the result of the cutting off of action in the 'real world'. For Fry this was true of creator and audience both; at this state, Mauron's interest was more in aesthetic creation: 'la poésie qui, comme la musique et en général toute expression artistique, a pour principe la contemplation, tend à revenir au silence', a direction he saw as parallel to 'l'ascension mystique'.[24] The contemplative poet, composer, painter, like the saint or mystic, renounced the 'real world'. Fry's view of contemplation, however, extended to aesthetic response as well as creation. It was also less mystic than Mauron's, perhaps because its roots lay not in the Tao but probably in Fry's own Quaker background, or in Bloomsbury ideals generally, as formed by G. E. Moore's *Principia Ethica.* In the famous chapter on 'The Ideal', Moore wrote that the most valuable things we know or can imagine are certain 'states of consciousness', one of which is 'the enjoyment of beautiful objects'.[25] For Moore, as for Fry, the value of aesthetic response lay in both a cognitive element (formal relations, for

Fry) and 'some kind of feeling or emotion' which had no practical value at all. Though there is certainly no direct influence here, and though Fry thought Moore and his followers were 'mystics', the similarity in perspective is an interesting one, and one shared by other members of Bloomsbury.

Yet Forster and Mauron both differ here from Fry in that the practical aspects (both social and personal) of aesthetic response, if not creation, are implicit in their critical impressionism. Formal principles appear in both men's works when they write of the structure of a work of art, although when Mauron addresses himself to the process of creation, his mysticism (and later his psychologism) is evident. And there is decidedly an unwillingness on both Forster's and Mauron's parts to surrender to formalism the actual mechanisms of aesthetic response. Unlike Fry, both seemed to want to claim for art a pragmatic value outside itself. And once again their use of music is revealing. The concluding pages of Mauron's *L'Homme triple* offer an image of music as a paradigm of all art, exercising a social function outside itself. At a concert, writes Mauron, 'chacun y écoute seul, et pourtant la société ne nous offre rien d'aussi unanime. Et n'oublions pas que pour réaliser le miracle, pour trouver en lui la musique, le compositeur a dû fuir le bruit pour lui infernal, de la société'.[26] Seen here are the two functions of contemplation, pragmatic for the listener and yet almost mystical for the creator. Music as a model for social order through some sort of mystic communion was an idea that Forster too entertained at this time. In 1946 he wrote that the value of art lay in its order, its internal 'harmony', a musical image, that at least offered some symbol of hope 'in the bosom of this disordered planet'.[27] This of course sounds like a formal principle though it is used to a practical end that Fry would have scorned.

Music, being perhaps the least mimetic or representational of art forms, may be the one most immediately expressive of feeling, and therefore almost most open to subjective responses, social or personal. Witness, for instance, Forster's account of listening to some previously unknown music late in the dusk: 'When the music stopped I felt something had arrived in the room; the sense of a world that asks to be noticed rather than explained was again upon me'.[28] This same almost mystic, suggestive vagueness is characteristic too of the musical analogies used in *Aspects of the Novel* in the discussion of 'prophecy', as it is defined in terms of aesthetic response — the reader will recognize it by its 'song'. But in that same book there is also that formalistic use of another image from music, the rhythm or order of the novel's structure as a whole, that gives meaning to the parts and beauty to the whole. The mixture of the impressionistic and the structural is even more striking in some of Mauron's writing, especially when music is in any way involved. For example, in the course of a few paragraphs, he once defined melody with a Forster-like image of a 'journey in the land of music' (and extended the image at length) and then redefined it, as might Fry, as 'the sequence of . . , modifications, *perceived in relation to the constants*'.[29]

It was suggested at the start that the way in which a writer uses an analogy might serve to reveal an underlying pattern in his critical theory. If so, Mauron's mixture of the structurally precise and the suggestively vague (or even mystical) in his musical associations and analogues would point to a critical duality, one that he shares with Forster. But if placed in the context of literary history, such a two-way pull between an interest in objective form and a concern for subjective responses is reminiscent of the struggle between classicism and romanticism, or perhaps between Aristotelian and Longinian impulses in critical thinking. Longinus, as Abrams has remarked, was the spiritual antecedent of critical impressionism, and Aristotle, with his structural view of the inner order of parts in a work of art, might be said to have been among the first to focus interest on form. The fact that this duality should appear in Forster's and Mauron's writings in their references to music therefore is not at all surprising in the light of this particular literary framework. Music for Aristotle was a mode of imitation of emotion whose formal medium included rhythm and harmony (*Poetics* I:2), a view Roger Fry might have agreed with. But music was also one of the most important analogies used by the Romantics, not for its structural properties, but on the contrary for its suggestivity, imprecision and availability to subjective impressionism.

In the almost paradoxical use of music in their critical writings, then, Mauron and Forster are showing a critical ambivalence that cannot be explained only by mutual influence or accidents of talent or interest. Instead, one might want to speculate that their dualism partakes of what Stephen Spender has called the 'struggle of the modern', and as such both might be seen as representative of their age. Spender points to a critical paradox in terms of literary history as seen in the works of Eliot, Joyce, Pound and others. He sees a reaction against Romanticism and a return to a more classical critical consciousness about writing, yet a recouping on another level of the subjectivity and impressionism we associate with Romanticism.[30] Though in many ways different from these writers, Forster and Mauron also reveal, as an underlying structure beneath their use of musical analogies, this same ambivalence, this same attraction to objective formal critical criteria and yet also to personal subjective values in art. Music may indeed be the 'purist' of the arts, but it is also 'sublime noise', at least for Forster.

NOTES

This paper was originally published in *Modernist Studies* 3(1979) pp. 141–50.
1. P. N. Furbank, *E. M. Forster: A Life* (New York: Harcourt Brace Jovanovich, 1977), I, 173.
2. E. M. Forster, 'The Raison d'Etre of Criticism', *Two Cheers for Democracy*, ed. Oliver Stallybrass, Abinger edn. (London: Edward Arnold, 1972), p. 105.
3. E. M. Forster, 'Our Second Greatest Novel?', *TCD*, p. 218.
4. E. M. Forster, 'Virginia Woolf', *TCD*, pp. 240, 243.
5. E. M. Forster, *Abinger Harvest* (London: Edward Arnold, 1936), p. 84.
6. E. M. Forster, *Aspects of the Novel*, ed. Oliver Stallybrass, Abinger edn. (London: Edward Arnold, 1974), p. 30.
7. S. P. Rosenbaum suggested this link in his essay '*Aspects of the Novel* and Literary History', printed elsewhere in this book. See Mauron's 'Beauty in Literature' (first read at the Décades de Pontigny, September 1925 and later translated by Fry) in *The Nature of Beauty in Art and Literature*, trans. Roger Fry (London: Hogarth Press, 1927), pp. 66–9; 76–9. This book was published a month after Forster's Clark lectures which were later published as *Aspects of the Novel*. Fry, too, mentions Mauron's 'ingenious analogy of literature with the plastic arts' in 'Some Questions in Esthetics', *Transformations* (London: Chatto and Windus, 1926). pp. 8–9, 11.
8. Denys Sutton, ed., *Letters of Roger Fry*, II (London: Chatto and Windus, 1972), pp. 497–8.
9. Roger Fry, *The Artist and Psycho-analysis*, Hogarth Essays (London: Hogarth Press, 1928), p. 292, italics his.
10. Roger Fry, 'The French Post-Impressionists', *Vision and Design* (London: Chatto and Windus, 1920), p. 157. Benedict Nicolson, as Denys Sutton reminds us ('Introduction' to *Letters of Roger Fry*, I, p. 40) claimed that this item of Fry's was a 'streak of "Expressionism"' influenced by Julius Meier-Graefe. (See 'Post-Impressionism and Roger Fry', *Burlington Magazine*, 93 [January 1951], 11 ff.) It would appear rather to be the perfect example of Fry's formalism, given his many remarks on the formal purity of music as an art form.

11.   In a note concerning Charles Mauron's fate in war-torn France in the manuscript (King's College Library) of analyses of Beethoven's piano sonatas, p. 23 verso.
12.   *The Artist and Psycho-analysis*, p. 301.
13.   Charles Mauron, 'Vincent et Monticelli' in the catalogue of the Vincent Van Gogh exhibit at the Musée Cantini, Marseilles (12 mars–28 avril 1957), not paginated; and in *René Seyssaud, mon ami*, lecture of 13 February 1954 at the Musée Cantini, Marseilles and published later (St. Rémy-de-Provence: l'Escolo des Aupiho, 1959), p. 18.
14.   Roger Fry, letter to Mauron, 9 July 1925, in *Letters of Roger Fry*, II, pp. 574–5.
15.   Forster's letter (dated 5–5–25) is at King's College Library; Fry's to Mauron, 9 July 1925, is in *Letters of Roger Fry*, II, p. 575.
16.   'The French Post-Impressionists', p. 159.
17.   'Some Questions in Esthetics', p. 7.
18.   E. M. Forster, 'Word-Making and Sound-Taking', *Abinger Harvest*, p. 101.
19.   'Beauty in Literature', p. 87.
20.   Charles Mauron, *Mallarmé l'obscur* (1941; rpt. Paris: José Corti, 1967). p. 111.
21.   See Fry's 'Early Introduction', published in his translation of Mallarmé's *Poems* (London: Chatto and Windus, 1938), pp. 296, 300n, and Mauron's 'Introduction', p. 37.
22.   Charles Mauron, 'L'Art et la psychanalyse', *Psyché*, 7 (1952), p. 32.
23.   Charles Mauron, *Introduction à la psychanalyse de Mallarmé* (Paris: La Baconnière, 1950), p. 204.
24.   Charles Mauron, *Sagesse de l'eau* (Paris: Laffont, 1945), p. 42.
25.   G. E. Moore, *Principia Ethica* (1903; rpt. Cambridge: Cambridge University Press, 1922), p. 188.
26.   Charles Mauron, *L'Homme triple* (Paris: R. Laffont, 1947).
27.   E. M. Forster, 'The Challenge of our Time', *TCD*, p. 57.
28.   E. M. Forster, 'The Last of Abinger', *TCD*, p. 357.
29.   Charles Mauron, *Aesthetics and Psychology* (London: Hogarth Press, 1935), pp. 82, 84, italics his.
30.   Stephen Spender, 'Imagination is Personal', *The Struggle of the Modern* (London: Methuen, 1963), p. 48.

6 The Paterian Mode in Forster's Fiction: *The Longest Journey* to *Pharos and Pharillon*

Robert K. Martin

He sat down in an olive-garden, and, all around him and within still turning to reverie, the course of his own life hitherto seemed to withdraw itself into some other world, disparted from the spectacular point where he was now placed to survey it, like that distant road below, along which he had travelled this morning across the Campagna. Through a dreamy land he could see himself moving, as if in another life, and like another person, through all his fortunes and misfortunes, passing from point to point, weeping, delighted, escaping from various dangers. That prospect brought him, first of all, an impulse of lively gratitude: it was as if he must look around for some one else to share his joy with: for some one to whom he might tell the thing, for his own relief. Companionship, indeed, familiarity with others, gifted in this way or that, or at least pleasant to him, had been through one or another long span of it the chief delight of the journey.
. . .

The purely material world, that close, impassable, prison-wall, seemed just then the unreal thing, to be actually dissolving away all around him: and he felt a quiet hope, a quiet joy, dawning faintly, in the dawning of this doctrine upon him as a really credible opinion. It was like the break of day over some vast prospect with the 'new city', as it were some celestial New Rome, in the midst of it. That divine companion figured no longer as but an occasional wayfarer beside him; but rather as the unfailing 'assistant', without whose inspiration and concurrence he could not breathe or see, instrumenting his bodily senses, rounding, supporting his imperfect thoughts. How often had the thought of their brevity spoiled for him the most natural pleasures of life, confusing even his present sense of them by the suggestion of disease, of death, of a coming end, in everything! How he had longed sometimes that there were indeed one to whose boundless power of memory he could commit his own most fortunate moments, his admiration, his love . . . one strong enough to retain them even though he forgot, in whose more vigorous consciousness they might subsist for ever, beyond that mere quickening of capacity which was all that remained of them in himself! . . . To-day at least, in the peculiar clearness of one privileged hour, he seemed to have apprehended that in which the experiences he valued most might find, one by one, an abiding-place.[1]

It has often been remarked that Pater's concept of the 'privileged hour' is one which has reverberated throughout the literature of the Modern Movement. Joyce's epiphanies, James's moments of realization, Mann's ecstatic recognitions, Woolf's instants of visionary penetration, Proust's penetrations of time (his *moments bienheureux*), Eliot's 'awful daring of a moment's surrender' — all owe something to Pater's appropriation for fiction of Wordsworth's 'spots of time' and to his transformation of the visionary experience from a moment of transcendental encounter with the world beyond to a moment of ecstatic encounter with the world within. But while the relationship of Pater to the other great modernists is usually recognized (although rarely pursued), his relationship to Forster goes virtually unrecognized. The reasons for this are fairly easy to identify, and relate primarily to the history of Forster criticism, rather than to any qualities inherent in Forster's work. Put most baldly, it comes down to this: Forster has been read as a liberal humanist, and such a reading must inevitably place most of the weight upon his last two novels (*Howards End* and *A Passage to India*) rather than upon the earlier novels or the short stories. In these novels, Pater's influence on Forster is least clear and further away in time. A preference for the 'late Forster' has clouded the essential sources of Forster's vision, including the sources of his humanism. For Pater criticism has been unable to remove from Pater the simplifying label 'Decadent' or 'Aesthete', indeed has (thanks to Yeats) seen Pater as a kind of prose poet, singing a Rossetti-like Dark Lady. In fact, however, as the passage cited above illustrates, Pater's strong sense of human community, his passionate avowal of friendship as the highest goal, is directly related to the view of one's own life-journey afforded by the 'privileged hour'; in that moment Marius passes beyond the fear of death, not through a commitment to art, but through a religious commitment to 'companionship', one which brings him to Pater's very special form of Christianity and enables him finally to die, not for the world, but for Cornelius.

Forster himself had little to say about Pater, aside from recognizing in the introduction to *Aspects of the Novel* that any definition of the novel must be able to encompass *Marius the Epicurean* as well as *Ulysses* and *Pilgrim's Progress*, among others.[2] Since it has been so often said that Forster would have classed Marius among the 'flat' characters (without, however, pointing out that Forster, who had an admirable opportunity to do so, did not make use of it), let me likewise speculate that Forster could have classed Pater among the prophetic novelists, those who convey to us 'the sensation of sinking into a translucent globe and seeing our experience floating far above us on its surface, tiny, remote, yet ours' (*Aspects*, p. 93). Forster did not, of course, place Pater in that rare category of prophetic novelist because, I suspect, by 1927 Pater's influence had been left relatively far behind. Not, however, forgotten entirely, for in 1923 Forster published one of his most Paterian books, *Pharos and Pharillon*.[3] In any case, the relationship between Pater and Forster cannot be considered in the usual terms of influence. One will not find a passage in Forster that echoes a specific one in Pater. What one finds is a shared set of ideas, some of which may be assumed to have travelled indirectly from Pater to Forster, others of which seem to indicate a pattern sufficiently similar that one may safely conclude that Pater resonated somewhere in Forster's mind as he wrote. What Forster inherited from Pater were these ideas: that knowledge is conveyed suddenly, through an apperception of the divine, which places the individual outside himself (*ex-stasis*) and enables him to view himself from a radically new perspective; that history is an antithetical struggle between two forces, or two tendencies, which we can call classic and romantic, or Hebrew and Hellene, or even England and Italy; that in the nineteenth (or twentieth) century the gods are in exile, still existing, but hidden away beneath the surface of things, waiting to be called forth again; that the central myths of Greece which can be re-enacted in modern England are those of Dionysus and Demeter, the priest-consort and the earth-mother; and that what the myths convey, in only barely concealed form, is a homosexual romance.

Forster's 'The Point of It' shows his use of a Paterian visionary moment. The story is reminiscent of the concluding episodes of the first book of *Marius*, in which Marius and his friend Flavian sail 'further than they had ever done before to a wild spot on the bay, the traditional site of a little Greek colony' and Flavian actually becomes a Greek in Marius' mind: 'The life of those vanished townsmen, so brilliant and revolutionary . . . associated itself from the actual figure of his companion' (*Marius*, vol. 1, pp. 108–9). In this very moment of transcendence, Flavian is stricken with the onset of his fatal disease. One easily recognizes a pattern common in Forster's early fiction: a symbolic journey to Italy or Greece, the realization of an identity with the Greek spirit, and a sudden transformation, into madness or death. Forster's Harold is the ideal Greek athlete, who indeed seems hardly to exist beyond his physical self: 'Harold melted the more one thought of him. Robbed of his body, he was so shadowy'.[4] He has close links to Housman's 'athlete dying young' and perhaps even to Melville's Billy Budd, and he plays a major role in Forster's imagination as the Gerald of *The Longest Journey*. Harold's death is not a defeat but a victory (the point is repeated in Joyce's 'The Dead'), as he reaches the ecstatic consciousness of the athlete: 'he was approaching the mystic state that is the athlete's true though unacknowledged goal: he was beginning to be' (p. 91).

Micky betrays that vision by accepting a life of convention, by becoming successively Michael and Sir Michael. A tasteful essayist, he denies the passion that drove Harold to row beyond human limitations. He realizes after his death that he has been willing to sacrifice critical rigour for polite mendacities: 'he was suffering for all the praise that he had given to the bad and mediocre upon the earth; when he had praised out of idleness, or to please people, or to encourage people; for all the praise that had not been winged with passion' (p. 113). Sir Michael has betrayed the call resoundingly issued by Pater in the 'Conclusion' to *The*

Renaissance:

> We have an interval, and then our place knows us no more.
> Some spend this interval in listlessness, some in high passions,
> the wisest, at least among 'the children of this world', in art
> and song. For our one chance lies in expanding that interval,
> in getting as many pulsations as possible into the given time.
> Great passions may give us this quickened sense of life, ecstasy
> and sorrow of love, the various forms of enthusiastic activity,
> disinterested or otherwise, which come naturally to many of
> us. Only be sure it is passion — that it does not yield you this
> fruit of a quickened, multiplied consciousness.[5]

Micky's passionlessness, his muffling of 'the keen, heroic edge'
will condemn him to an eternity in the waste land, where 'he lay
sunk in the sand of an illimitable plain' (p. 111).

Two myths are evoked by Forster to give contrast to Michael's
lack of passion: Castor and Pollux, and Orion. The first evokes
the sacrificial love of one brother for another, a willingness to
die which is rewarded by eternal life. It links heroism with the
sacred male couple and warns of the dangers of the death-in-life
of heterosexual marriage. Orion is the spirit of youth, the
embodiment of the passionate ideal: 'not a star but a nebula, the
golden seed of worlds to be' (p. 115). While neither of these myths
is abandoned by Forster (Orion recurs prominently in *The Longest
Journey*), their central role is taken by the myth evoked by Pater
in the death of Flavian, the myth of Dionysus, whose death
accomplished the refertilization of the world. For Flavian's death
is a sacred marriage with the earth goddess, his final words 'a
kind of nuptial hymn, which, taking its start from the thought of
nature as the universal mother, celebrated the preliminary
pairing and mating together of all fresh things, in the hot and
genial spring-time' (*Marius*, vol. 1, p. 113). Harold is a 'merry
guide'[6] 'to a not too terrible hereafter', who awaits Micky and
then accompanies him across the bar, toward the final vision of
'a farm, full to the brim with fire' (p. 125). That final image
underscores Forster's sense that the death of Harold and Micky
accomplishes a rejuvenation and refertilization of the world ('a
farm, full to the brim') through the assertion of the creative and
phallic fire (Pater's 'plumage of tender, crimson fire' comes to
mind). Once Micky accepts the heroic mission of Orion and

returns to his beloved Castor, harmony is restored, the earth replenished, and death no longer fearful. By the end of his journey, Marius too has learned the lesson of Flavian: he

> seemed to understand how one might look back upon life here, and its excellent visions, as but the portion of a race-course left behind him by a runner still swift of foot: for a moment, he experienced a singular curiosity, almost an ardent desire to enter upon a future, the possibilities of which seemed so large (*Marius*, vol. 2, pp. 220–1).

Forster's title for another of the stories from his first volume as well as for the volume itself (and, wonderful irony, for the first volume written by the heroine of the story), 'The Eternal Moment', has obvious associations with Pater. Forster's view of that moment, embodied as it is in the figure of Miss Raby, is mildly ironic. From her first words, 'Do you see that mountain just behind Elizabeth's toque? A young man fell in love with me there so nicely twenty years ago. Bob your head a minute, would you, Elizabeth, kindly' (p. 179), we are warned that a comic misproportion is at work. For there is little of Pater's 'privileged hour' in Miss Raby's 'eternal moment'. Rather there is the confusion of a frightened and virginal woman who imagines a rape when there is none (and anticipates of course the monumental misunderstandings of *A Passage to India*) and then imagines an eternal devotion (also absent), and finally retreats to the illusion of memory. Her triumph is 'cold, hardly human' (p. 244), a victory over life which is far from the passionate commitment of Pater's 'Conclusion'. But there are other elements in Forster's story which indicates his indebtedness to Pater and show that his mock-Paterian heroine nonetheless inhabits a Paterian universe.

Forster's story is largely one of place, and his use of place is similar to that of Pater: place, no matter how accurately described, remains symbolic place, the physical rendering of the *genius loci*. Vorta, the place of Miss Raby's 'eternal moment' is located almost precisely at the point at which the Latin world and 'Teutonia' meet. Although apparently inside Austria, it is still spiritually part of Italy and politically part of 'Italia Irredenta'. Most of the comedy of the story derives from the misunderstandings caused by the confrontation of two cultures which do not, metaphorically as well as actually, speak the same language. The Northern spirit, represented at its worst in Colonel Leyland, and its merely foolish self in Miss Raby, imposes an order and a literal spirit upon the expansive and disorderly South. The encounter, which of course has its resonances from *Where Angels Fear to Tread* to *A Passage to India*, is not only comic, its tragedy lies in the imposition of a new, coarser spirit upon the once naïve South, a fatal corruption.

The terms of this fall from innocence are part of a particular tradition of seeing the Anglo-Saxon/Latin encounter, one which would seem to trace its path from Hawthorne to James to Forster. But another strain of that tradition can be seen clearly in Pater's 'Denys l'Auxerrois', even though Italy is never explicitly its subject or setting. The three towns of 'Denys' — Troyes, 'rich, almost coarse', Sens, 'far graver . . . almost English austerity' and Auxerre, 'Perfect type of that happy mean between northern earnestness and the luxury of the south' — represent the opposite pulls of the Northern and Southern sensibilities. And Denys, who embodies the spirit of Auxerre, passes from gentleness to coarseness. But the change makes possible a third stage, to Pater the highest or 'Renaissance' stage, a 'seriousness' 'as if the gay old pagan world had been *blessed* in some way'.[7] In the light of Pater's 'Denys', we can make better sense of Forster's story. Miss Raby begins as a foolish and naïve observer, linked to the militarist Colonel; she encounters a comic-opera hero, a foolish and naïve version of the Southern lover; but out of it all she gains her vision. Feo and the Colonel are finally accomplices, while only she can 'triumph' over the mutable. Her 'eternal moment' is not the moment of passion she has previously imagined, but a moment of realization and self-knowledge. She transcends the two opposed worlds and creates her own, based upon her 'vision of herself'. For Miss Raby, unlike, say, the narrator of 'Ansell' or Harold in 'Albergo Empedocle', there can be no complete return to the world of ancient simplicity. As Pater put the problem in the opening lines of 'Denys',

since we are no longer children, we might well question the advantage of the return to us of a condition of life in which, by the nature of the case, the values of things would, so to speak, lie wholly on their surfaces, unless we could regain also the childish consciousness, or rather unconsciousness, in our-

selves, to take all that adroitly and with the appropriate
lightness of heart.[8]

Although both Forster and Pater were tempted by the dreams of
a return to the primitive, in all of Pater's work and in most of
Forster's major work, the Northern and Southern, the primitive
and the civilized, came together to form a new consciousness, a
new self neither too primitive nor too civilized (this is the explicit
meaning of the ending of *Howards End* and of *Maurice*, as well as
of *The Longest Journey*).

The tripartite structure of 'Denys l'Auxerrois' is used by
Forster in *The Longest Journey* as well (and, much later, in *A Passage
to India*). Just as the three cathedral towns of 'Denys' represent
three stages of development and three modes of art, so the three
settings of *The Longest Journey* represent spiritual places and sets
of values. Cambridge is the place of ideas, the flourishing of
friendship, Sawston the place of cant, the home of marriage and
school, and Wiltshire the place of things, the 'real' England of
the past. It will be helpful to note that Forster's use of the
tripartite structure corresponds to the same seasons of the Greek
year, in which Cambridge represents the Spring/Summer,
Sawston represents the Fall/Winter, and Wiltshire represents the
Winter/Spring. The novel thus encompasses the cycle of the year,
stressing Rickie's role as the year-daimon whose death is required
in order to ensure the continuation of the earth. Rickie, the
winter-Dionysus, gives way to Stephen, the summer-Dionysus,
Persephone is returned to Demeter, and the earth can flourish
again. The world of Cambridge, the homosexual summer of the
symposium and Theocritus, is short-lived. From the beginning
we see the signs of oncoming fall: 'The great elms were motion-
less, and seemed still in the glory of midsummer, for the darkness
hid the yellow blotches on their leaves . . .'[9] The passage out of
Cambridge is a loss of innocence, a symbolic recreation of the
fall of man, seen as part of a large cyclical pattern in which man
must be reconciled with the earth (hence the novel's associations
with *Oedipus at Colonus*) before he can be redeemed from experience. The dell, too, site of Rickie's 'symbolic moment', is in a
brief season of flourishing, its summer also tainted by the
knowledge of an oncoming fall: it was 'the brief season of its
romance . . . its divine interval between the bareness of boyhood
and the stuffiness of age' (ii, 20). That brief interval of life

('interval' is Pater's word as well, and for him it is a symbol 'of the splendour of our experience and of its brevity') is identical with the Greek ideal of adolescence, the perfect male beauty found only between boyhood and manhood. But it also represents the perfect mean, for it brings together the boy and the old man, the spirit of play and the spirit of earnestness, into a new form of joyful wisdom. The dell's perfect blooming is the world about to be abruptly shattered for Rickie and so arduously regained.

The principal myth on which Forster calls is that of Dionysus. Forster's mythmaking is syncretic, so it is always dangerous to attempt precise identifications of his characters with a single mythic equivalent. Like Pater in his famous passage on the Mona Lisa, in which he identifies her with figures as different as Leda and St Anne (and which Yeats borrowed for his poem on Leda), Forster conceives of 'a perpetual life, sweeping together ten thousand experiences' (*The Renaissance*, p. 130). Thus Rickie is sometimes Siegfried, sometimes the Fisher King, while Stephen is sometimes Pan, sometimes Hermes, sometimes Triptolemus, and Agnes is Medea, Cleopatra, or Medusa. But the Dionysus pattern is pervasive, it makes sense of the conclusion to the novel which has otherwise seemed so troublesome to commentators, and it was one of Forster's greatest debts to Pater. Those critics who take seriously Forster's mythmaking (and they are still a minority) have generally been slightly vague about his sources, citing the general interest in anthropology at Cambridge at the turn of the century. The fullest treatment of the subject, for instance, comments on Forster, 'The archaeological discoveries that were synthesized by Cambridge scholars were embodied, hot off the press, into the young student's short stories'.[10] The same article remarks of Forster, 'As an archaeology student at Cambridge during this period' and 'he, like Rickie, was a classics student at Cambridge when immense syncretic treaties issued yearly from the university halls'. Forster may well have known the work of Frazer, Rouse, Harrison, Cornford, and others, but he took most of the mythological structure of *The Longest Journey* from Pater's essays in *Greek Studies* and his recreation of the Dionysus myth in 'Denys l'Auxerrois'.

It was Pater, in 'A study of Dionysus',[11] who pointed out the relationship between Demeter and Dionysus (both wine and grain being harvest symbols — as in Christian myth) and who emphasized the dual symbols of Dionysus, fire and water (wine, as fire-water, unites the two). These symbols dominate *The Longest Journey* ('In full unison was Love born, flame of the flame, flushing the dark river beneath him' [iii, 46], and, at the end of the novel, 'The paper caught fire from the match, and spread into a rose of flame . . . they laid it flower-like on the stream . . . Stephen, who knelt in the water, declared that it was still afloat, . . . burning as if it would burn forever' [xxxiii, 313]). It was also Pater who indicated that Dionysus took the place of Persephone as the lost child of Demeter.[12] Thus the mourning mother goddess of *The Longest Journey* (principally Mrs Elliot but also upon occasion Mrs Failing) can be comforted by the return to her of Rickie/Dionysus, whose death in turn frees Stephen to assume his role as the new child, the summer Dionysus. Although Stephen is to be understood, particularly at the conclusion, as the restored Dionysus, he is also, as we have observed, Triptolemus. Pater's comments on that figure are to the point: he 'was a quite Boeotian divinity, of the ploughshare' linked to Hermes by his 'broad country hat' and the 'airy, mercurial wheels of his farm instrument, harrow or plough'. Although he begins as a 'delicate, fresh, farm-lad' he becomes 'a king's son' and finally a priest of Demeter (*Greek Studies*, pp. 106–7). One can observe the same transformation in Stephen, from Mrs Failing's 'plough-boy' to the orphaned divine child of the 'King', Robert, and finally to the priest of the novel's conclusion: 'he believed that he guided the future of our race, and that, century after century, his thoughts and his passions would triumph in England. The dead who had evoked him, the unborn whom he would evoke — he governed the paths between them' (xxxv, 332).

If one bears in mind, then, that Rickie is drawn on the model of the recurring Dionysus of Pater, 'the consort or priest of humanity', as Pater's leading critic has put it,[13] one can recognize the symbolic patterns operative in the conclusion of *The Longest Journey*. It is by no means true that, as some readers have suggested, Forster or even Rickie accepts 'the coarse animality of Stephen'.[14] Rather the Stephen of the conclusion is a new, integrated being who brings together the best of Rickie and Stephen, a figure of the union of body and mind. Under the sign of the mystic rose, figure of marriage, the two are wed, much like Ishmael and Queequeg, and a new self is born of the sacred union. When Rickie looks at Stephen, he sees a 'transfigured face. He believed that a new spirit dwelt there, expelling the crudities of youth. He saw steadier eyes, and the sign of manhood set like a bar of gold upon steadier lips' (xxxiii, 313). Like Pater, Forster used the death of the winter-Dionysus not as a means to a return to the primitive but as a means to the creation of an integrated self, represented by the sacred male couple.

That theme remained important throughout Forster's work (it is expressed in the conclusion of *A Passage to India*, wistfully, and in the conclusion to *Maurice*, triumphantly). It is the major theme of *Pharos and Pharillon*, Forster's ignored and Paterian series of sketches drawn from the history of Alexandria. The mood of Pater is clear in Forster's evocation of the *genius loci*, his 'Baedeker' opening (reminiscent, say, of the opening of 'Denys'), and his antithetical structure. Alexandria, more perhaps than the Wiltshire of *The Longest Journey*, is the place where two worlds come together and form a new world. Forster's oppositions have been the new England and the old, or between England and Italy (as they will be between England and India), but here he draws upon the nineteenth century's central pair of historic tendencies — the opposition between Hebrew and Hellene. The central definition of that opposition is given, of course, by Matthew Arnold, but it is one which marks the work of Pater, James, Forster, Wilde and Lawrence as well. In almost all of these writers, except Pater and Forster, that opposition is rendered in largely symbolic terms, as the opposition of aesthetic or moral attitudes, but it was Pater who began to situate the conflict in an historic and geographical place (France in the late middle ages), and it was Forster who built upon this tradition until he came upon the place of their actual meeting in Alexandria.

The first chapter of *Pharos and Pharillon* evokes the two spirits under the watchful eye of the lighthouse. For Alexandria is the city of Alexander, the triumph of Hellenism, but it is also a city of Jews. It is the city of the Septuagint translation, but it is also a city sacred to the love of Alexander for Hephaestion, whose shrine was located at the *pharos*. It thus brings together the ideals of moral earnestness and physical beauty, finding a place for homosexual love among the moral codes of the West. It is to Alexandria that he turns in hope of restoring sexuality to its proper place, neither moralized nor philosophized away, just as Forster had come to a full acknowledgement of himself as a homosexual in Alexandria. 'And in that curious city, which had never been young and hoped never to grow old, conciliation must have seemed more possible than elsewhere, and the graciousness of Greece not quite incompatible with the Grace of God'.[15] The second half of the book suggests the same sort of reconciliation, here turning to much more primitive mythic sources as he evokes the Rue Rosette, running between the gate of the sun and the gate of the moon: 'In the evening the western vista can blaze with orange and scarlet, and the eastern, having darkened, can shimmer with a mysterious radiance, out of which, incredibly large, rises the globe of the moon' (*PP*, p. 74).

Unity is given to Forster's sketches by the use of place itself, but also by the book's dedication and by the figure of Cavafy, who closes both halves. The dedication is to Hermes Psychopompos, the Hermes also evoked in the introduction to *The Eternal Moment* and, later, to *The Collected Short Stories*. The mischievous god is appropriate to the wry tone which Forster adopts, but his role as psychopomp is also taken seriously. Like *The Longest Journey* or 'The Point of It', *Pharos and Parillon* points toward the hereafter. The poem of Cavafy's chosen to conclude the first section, 'The God Abandons Antony', evokes Bacchus, a Roman deity, who seems to assume something of Hermes' function as a conductor of souls, leading man finally to an acceptance of the mutability of things. Cavafy's lines,

> listen to the notes, to the exquisite instruments of the mystic choir, and bid farewell to her, to Alexandria whom you are losing

gloss Forster's concluding statement of this section, 'The Pharos, the Temple of Seraphis — these have perished, being only stones, and sharing the impermanence of material things. It is ideas that live' (*PP*, p. 45). If Alexandria is the city of the death of love (because of the death of Hephaestion), it is also the city of the birth of love. Cavafy is its spirit, for while he sings of Greek love and hymns the young men of his 'Nights', he also has the unworldliness of the Hebraic spirit, 'of the recluse, who, though not afraid of the world, always stands at a slight angle to it' (p. 79). In Cavafy Hebrew and Hellene come together. To live with passion, to face death with joy, to renounce this world for the next, these were ideas which came first to Forster from Pater and to which he responded enthusiastically as he found them again in the poet of Alexandria who sang, with Pater, the 'divine companion'.

NOTES

1. Walter Pater, *Marius the Epicurean* (London: Macmillan, 1910 [1885]), vol. 2, pp. 66–7, 70–1.

2. E. M. Forster, *Aspects of the Novel*, ed. Oliver Stallybrass, Abinger edn. (London: Edward Arnold, 1974), p.3.

    Forster apparently first read *Marius* in 1905 and was put off by it. (See P. N. Furbank, *E. M. Forster: A Life* [New York: Harcourt, Brace Jovanovich, 1978], I, p. 132.) He found Pater both squeamish and morbid. However, by the end of 1907 he may have reconsidered, since he included Pater in what appears to be a reading list of homosexual authors. (Furbank, I, p. 159 n.l.; Furbank does not give any explanation for the list.) I would speculate that Forster's awareness of Pater as a homosexual artist altered his own relationship to him and enabled him to see Pater in a new light.

    After this paper was first read in Montreal, Elizabeth Heine was kind enough to point out to me Forster's reference to Pater in his unfinished and unpublished novel, *Nottingham Lace*. The hero reads Pater as a sign of his alienation from his stuffy aunt. But Forster is also ironic about 'the Oxford don who found undergraduates too boorish to speak to'.

    Clearly Forster's attitude had changed by the time he was in Alexandria. In 1918 he wrote to Florence Barger of 'The Will as Vision', cited at the beginning of this essay, as 'that touching chapter', in a digression in a letter concerned with Edward Carpenter. (This reference has kindly been communicated to me by Elizabeth Heine and by Michael Halls, Archivist, King's College Library.)

    I am delighted that manuscript evidence supports my contention, based solely on Forster's published writing, that Forster used Pater as an important point of reference in his early fiction and again when writing *Pharos and Pharillon* in Alexandria.

3. Although this study concludes with *Pharos and Pharillon*, Forster's use of Pater continues for at least a few years beyond that. In *Anonymity: An Enquiry* (London: Hogarth Press, 1925) Forster's 'crucial point', that 'all literature tends toward a condition of anonymity' (p. 14), is a striking echo of Pater's famous judgement that 'all art constantly aspires to the condition of music' (*The Renaissance*, p. 140). Forster's echo of Pater here involves both an indebtedness to Pater's formalism (reinforced by Fry's) and an ironic distancing from Pater's strong sense of personal communication between the artist and the perceiver.

4. E. M. Forster, 'The Point of It', *The Eternal Moment* (New York: Harcourt Brace, 1928), p. 95.

5. Walter Pater, *The Renaissance: Studies in Art and Poetry* (New York: Macmillan, 1906), pp. 251–2.

6. See Housman's poem of this name.

7. Walter Pater, 'Denys l'Auxerrois', *Imaginary Portraits* (London: Macmillan, 1922 [1887]), pp. 48–9, 51, 70–1.

8. *Ibid.* p. 47. Pater's style here clearly foreshadows James's late style in its use of almost parenthetical qualifiers.

9. E. M. Forster, *The Longest Journey*, World's Classics, N. 578 (London:

Oxford University Press, 1960), p. 3.
10. John Magnus, 'Ritual Aspects of E. M. Forster's *The Longest Journey*', Modern Fiction Studies XIII (Summer, 1967), pp. 195–210.
11. Walter Pater, 'A Study of Dionysus: The Spiritual Form of Fire and Dew', *Greek Studies: A Series of Essays* (London: Macmillan, 1904 [1895]), pp. 9–52.
12. Cf. Pater's comment about Persephone: 'Her story is, indeed, but the story, in an intenser form, of . . . the king's blooming son, fated, . . . to be wounded to death'. ('Demeter and Persephone', *Greek Studies*, p. 109.)
13. Gerald Cornelius Monsman, *Pater's Portraits: Mythic Pattern in the Fiction of Walter Pater* (Baltimore: Johns Hopkins, 1967), p. 20.
14. John Colmer faults Forster for his squeamishness in refusing Stephen. *E. M. Forster: The Personal Voice* (London: Routledge & Kegan Paul, 1975), p. 82.
15. E. M. Forster, *Pharos and Pharillon* (London: The Hogarth Press, 1923), p. 34.

7 Marriage and Personal Relations in Forster's Fiction

John Colmer

By common consent E. M. Forster is a master of domestic comedy. His self-confessed model was Jane Austen. 'I was more ambitious than she was', he declared in an oft-quoted passage, 'and tried to hitch it on to other things',[1] to social criticism, symbolism and prophecy, in fact. Intimate as the rapport with Jane Austen proved, the adoption of domestic comedy as a main fictional mode involved commitment to an institution in which he had little faith: marriage. His own belief was in personal relations. Although logically there was no reason why ideals of personal relations should be embodied in matrimony, biographically there were. Male friendship, not marriage, lay at the centre of his world-view. Thus we have in Forster an interesting case of the creative tension between a personal ideology only belatedly raised to full consciousness and an alien social ideology enshrined in a literary form to which he was strongly attracted on stylistic grounds. Fortunately the traditional form proved sufficiently malleable for him to discover a personal voice and vision within it. This paper seeks to place the process of discovery in broad historical perspective and to examine the positive and negative effects of the tension between literary tradition and personal vision, between individual and social ideology.

Marriage serves different functions in the structure of three fairly distinct types of nineteenth- and twentieth-century fiction: in Jane Austen's domestic comedies, in the Victorian Condition of England novel, and in the modern prophetic, symbolist novel, as practised by D. H. Lawrence and others. In Jane Austen's novels the characters have to learn that happiness comes from conforming to society and making prudential marriages. For her charming and witty heroines, the reward is not sexual fulfilment but self-knowledge and social integration. Their education consists in learning to avoid pride and prejudice, to balance the rival claims of sense and sensibility, and to distinguish between sober fact and Gothic fiction. In *Mansfield Park* the characters come to learn the difference between theatrical emotions and social decorum. In *Emma* the heroine's marriage to Mr Knightley signals the abandonment of her well-intentioned egotism and the development of a wider experience of life and society, while in *Persuasion* Anne Elliot discovers that an apparently lost happiness can be recaptured in marriage to her former suitor, Captain Wentworth. Marriage for the heroines in Jane Austen's domestic comedies is a reward for good conduct. It marks the full entry of the individual into society, the final emancipation from illusion, egotism and proud self-sufficiency. It celebrates the mature acceptance of social norms, the harmony achieved between temperament and tradition. Many of the married couples are certainly foolish, but the institution of marriage remains the highest social good. Through it the characters attain personal happiness and social harmony. In Jane Austen there is no conflict between the function of marriage as a happy ending to the comic form and as the embodiment of the highest social good. In Forster, by contrast, the tension between the two functions is great and he frequently girds against marriage both in his novels and in his critical writings, especially in the paper on 'Pessimism in Literature', delivered at the Working Men's College in 1906. There he argues that, for the modern writer, marriage as a happy ending is the enemy of truth. [2] His discussion is more narrowly focused than Virginia Woolf's rebellion against the tyranny of plot and character, and prompted by personal as well as literary antipathy towards marriage.

The second type of fiction in which marriage serves a major structural and thematic function is the Victorian Condition of England novel. In many of these novels the marriages people make and the houses and cities they inhabit come to assume a representative social significance. For Dickens in *Hard Times* and Mrs Gaskell in *North and South*, marriages become a vital part of the author's critique of society. Louisa's arid marriage to Bounderby is the natural outcome of her education in hard facts by her father Mr Gradgrind; and the failure of her marriage expresses the emptiness of Mr Gradgrind's whole system. Louisa, having been tempted to look for love outside her loveless marriage, confronts her father in the melodramatic scene that brings the second book of *Hard Times* to its arresting climax. 'Now father', Louisa cries, 'you have brought me to this. Save me by some other means!'

> He tightened his hold in time to prevent her sinking on the floor, but she cried out in a terrible voice, 'I shall die if you hold me! Let me fall upon the ground!' And he laid her down there, and saw the pride of his heart and triumph of his system, lying an insensible heap, at his feet.[3]

This well-known scene is a reminder that in a certain type of novel the emptiness of a marriage can express the sterility of a whole social system.

Marriage in Mrs Gaskell's novel *North and South* symbolizes the need to combine the virtues of South of England culture and North of England practical energy. The heroine, Margaret Hale, leaves her sheltered upbringing in the South of England to encounter the harsh realities of the industrial scene at Milton Northern, where she meets and falls in love with the stubborn factory owner Mr Thornton. But she can only accept him in marriage after he has come to sympathize with the workers' demands and to see the need for a more humane relationship between masters and men. Again, as in Dickens' *Hard Times*, marriage serves an emblematic function in the structure of the novel, signifying the limits of various social philosophies and the possibility of reconciling opposite views. These brief references to two well-known Victorian Condition of England novels conveniently establish the fact that in the structure of a certain type of fiction marriage may become a metaphor for a whole way of life and that the quality and durability of a marriage may express a profound truth about a social philosophy.

In some respects this type of fiction represents a deepening and expansion of Jane Austen's domestic comedy, just as the modern symbolist, prophetic novel represents a deepening and expansion of the Victorian Condition of England novel. If we take Lawrence's *Women in Love* as an example of this third form we are immediately aware of significant changes that have taken place in the structural function of marriage. The first difference is that the value of marriage is no longer unquestioningly accepted and that values are, in general, no longer socially derived as they are in Jane Austen and the Victorian novelists; instead they are individually discovered through personal conflict and apocalyptic vision. Now, the gifted individual, not society, is the judge of what is good. His vision of a new type of marriage expressed the need for a total regeneration of man and society. Homes are no longer seen as centres of traditional value, as in *Mansfield Park*, *North and South* and *Howards End*, but as prisons from which to escape. When Gudrun and Ursula return to their family home, they become aware that 'the whole place seemed to resound about them with a noise of hollow, empty futility'.[4] For both of them life presents itself as a restless journey into the unknown.

Another main difference between this type of fiction and those glanced at earlier is that life's journey does not end in a socially approved marriage. The journey is open-ended and so is the literary form. The theme of the contrary pulls between man-to-man relationships and man-to-woman in *Women in Love* remains unresolved. And one might add there is a third radical difference, which Forster's definition of prophecy in Dostoyevsky describes very well: 'the characters and situations always stand for more than themselves; infinity attends them, though they remain individuals they expand to embrace it and summon it to embrace them'.[5] Thus, in the visionary prophetic novel, as in Blake's poetry, marriage becomes an emblem of cosmic spiritual principles, not social ideologies, as in the Victorian Condition of England novel.

This brief survey, oversimplified as it necessarily is, serves a double purpose. By sketching in the place of marriage in the structure of three different kinds of domestic novel, it demonstrates the resilient strength, the capacity for further development, of a particular literary genre. It also creates the appropriate perspective for understanding Forster's own creative struggle. To some extent, Forster's movement from the Jane Austen-like comedy of *A Room With a View* through the condition of England seriousness of *Howards End* to the visionary and prophetic resonances of *A Passage to India* parallels the historical development already traced.

Forster showed great inventiveness and ingenuity in adapting the conventions of domestic comedy to express his personal vision in his early fiction, and the characters and stories develop a subterranean level of meaning, which is both psychologically complex and socially subversive, as the result of the tension between literary convention and the author's world-view. The rescue party and the escape from an unsuitable marriage or liaison occupies a limited place in the domestic comedies of Jane Austen, appearing in Darcy's offstage rescue of his sister Georgiana and the story of Lydia Bennet, but not much elsewhere. Forster's development of this minor motif of domestic comedy is one of his main methods of adapting the genre to his own needs. As Miss Beaumont's escape from her possessive and materialistic suitor in the short story 'Other Kingdom' shows, the desirability of escape from one kind of marriage may easily seem to imply the desirability of escape from marriage itself, indeed from any restrictions on individual freedom and spontaneity, from any barriers to complete identification with nature itself. Miss Beaumont, the narrator informs the reader,

> danced away from our society and our life, back, back through the centuries till houses and fences fell and the earth lay wild to the sun. Her garment was as foliage upon her, the strength of her limbs as boughs, her throat the smooth upper branch that salutes the morning or glistens to the rain.[6]

However acceptable such a poetic metamorphosis may be within the conventions of the *fin de siècle* short story, it has little place in the novel of ironic domestic comedy. The plots of *A Room With a View* and *Where Angels Fear to Tread* turn on engagements and marriages, and the rescue party motif is vital in both novels; but the only metamorphosis comes when Forster finds it easier to transform George and Lucy into spirits of youth or earth spirits than to realize their actual happiness and requited love in marriage.

Where in Jane Austen the wise forces of society protect the innocent from unwise marriages and bless their prudential unions, in Forster the conventional forces of society send out rescue parties to bring young lovers to their senses and to enforce false values. But they usually fail. Mrs Herrington's unwilling agent Philip arrives too late to rescue Lilia from marriage to Gino, and Harriet's melodramatic sense of familial duty is partly responsible for the death of Lilia's and Gino's baby. Indeed, *Where Angels Fear to Tread* gains much of its strength and delicacy from the ironic juxtapositon of the false values associated with conventional marriage and the true values associated with personal relations, seen in the tangled love and hatred between Philip and Gino, and most clearly exemplified in the discovery by Caroline and Philip of values that lie outside society's notions of duty, that transcend conventional notions of good and evil. The promise of salvation comes from being true to the inner self, from trusting the dictates of instinct, love and imagination; it does not come from a socially prompted and blest marriage. Yet, paradoxically and illogically, Forster retains marriage as the happy climax of his Italian novel *A Room With a View*. This accounts for a certain falsity of tone that impairs its ending. But apart from this blemish, he transmutes the conventions of domestic comedy in the Italian novels to express his deeply rooted faith in personal relations and the sober honesty of the concluding conversation between Charlotte and Philip in *Where Angels Fear to Tread* foreshadows the ending of *A Passage to India*.

The conflict between personal relations and marriage finds clearest expression in Forster's most autobiographical novel, *The Longest Journey*. Rickie's marriage to the devious Agnes produces a fatal desertion from the high ideals of personal relations that he had experienced at Cambridge. It is not just that Agnes is a scheming and untruthful person who forces Rickie into mean compromises with worldly standards. The structure of the novel develops an implicit contrast between the marriage of true minds represented by the friendship of Rickie and Stewart Ansell and the unholy alliance for selfish and corrupt ends represented by the Silts' marriage and by Agnes's marriage to Rickie. After the breakfast departure of Agnes and her chaperone from Ansell's rooms, another undergraduate remonstrates with him for his exaggerated misogyny. '"They pay a civil visit to your rooms and you see nothing but dark plots and challenges to war." "War!" cried Ansell, crashing his fists together. "It's war, then!" '[7] His pedantic letter advising Rickie not to marry because unfitted in both body and soul conflates Byronic and Shavian sentiments. 'Man wants to love mankind; woman wants to love one man. When she has him her work is over' (ix, 94). Although this Apostle of Cambridge truth and homosexual love is often shown in an ironic light, he nevertheless articulates the world-view that gives form and meaning to the novel as a whole. This rests on Forster's faith in a spiritual aristocracy of male comrades. But the literary form demands marriage as a happy ending. And so Forster devises an ingenious pastoral coda that formally celebrates a happy marriage but which in fact releases Stephen Wonham from its limiting bonds and allows him to follow his natural instincts to sleep in the woods at night and not in his wife's bed. Significantly Stephen's wife has no name, no character; she is only a disembodied voice, chiding her wilful, errant husband.

The posthumously published *Maurice* makes it clear, as the other novels do not, that it was Forster's homosexuality that prevented him from embodying his ideals of personal relations in marriage. Because it was originally written for a small circle of friends and not for general publication, it should have been possible to ignore the restraints imposed by social morality and by the conventions of domestic comedy. But this is not entirely the case. In the 'Terminal Note' to the novel Forster said that 'a happy ending was imperative'.[8] In obedience to the demands of domestic comedy he shapes his simple polemical plot to end with a happy marriage, the somewhat implausible happy homosexual marriage of Maurice Hall and Alec Scudder. To establish the superiority of this union of male comrades he feels obliged to disparage Clive's marriage to Anne. Unfortunately insufficient grounds are supplied to justify Maurice's scorn for their union, although some attempt is made to suggest the superficiality and worldliness of the heterosexual couple. Forster later recognized the weakness. In the 'Terminal Note', he confesses that Clive's conversion 'annoyed' him.

> He has annoyed me. I may nag at him over much, stress his aridity and political pretensions and the thinning of his hair, nothing he or his wife or his mother does is ever right. This works well enough for Maurice, for it accelerates his descent into Hell and toughens him for the final reckless climb. But it may be unfair on Clive who intends no evil and who feels the last flick of my whip in the final chapter, when he discovers that his old Cambridge friend has relapsed inside Penge itself, and with a gamekeeper. (p. 237)

In Forster's novels characters go out of focus as soon as they marry. What in *Howards End* he revealingly describes as the 'glass shade' that falls and 'cuts off married couples from the world',[9] comes down and blurs the reader's vision of Clive and Anne. The irrational antipathy Maurice feels towards the married couple has an interesting parallel in Forster's initial reaction to Bob Buckingham's marriage to May which, P. N. Furbank remarks, produced 'flares of misogyny', and 'hysterical rages, when he would throw himself against the furniture'.[10] In *Maurice*, Forster makes an awkward compromise between his personal ideology and the combined demands of a social ideology and a literary form.

In *Howards End*, when, following the example of the Victorian Condition of England novelists, he wrote a novel in which marriage becomes an emblem of social harmony, it is not surprising that there is a sense of strain. In *Howards End*, as in the slightly later novel *Maurice*, the glass shade comes down as soon as the marriage occurs. Margaret is allowed her magnificent outburst against the hypocrisy of her morally obtuse husband, she also retains something of her original individuality, but we lose sight of precisely those characteristics in her husband that constituted his fictional life and symbolic significance. At the purely human level the marriage seems a poor thing, since it first rests on Henry's jaunty masculine condescension and later on Margaret's maternal solicitude in nursing the broken Henry. As Frieda Lawrence remarked, 'broken Henrys remain Henrys as I know to my cost'.[11] At the symbolic level the marriage between Margaret the representative of culture and Henry the broken capitalist is not a very impressive image of potential social harmony. The main flaw in the novel is that the symbolic marriage between the opposed forces in English society rests upon two shaky and implausible unions, that between the eternal spinster Margaret and the blustering businessman Henry Wilcox, and that between the heroic Helen and the timid clerk, Leonard Bast, which largely consists of an improbable one-night stand.

Neither union very satisfactorily illustrates the virtues of personal relations and therefore the significance of the novel's epigraph as it is expounded by Margaret.

Only connect! That was the whole of her sermon. Only connect the prose and the passion, and both will be exalted, and human love will be seen at its highest. Live in fragments no longer. Only connect, and the beast and the monk, robbed of the isolation that is life to either, will die.   (xxii, 183)

In fact, personal relations triumph only between persons of the same sex, not within matrimony. They triumph between Margaret Schlegel and Mrs Wilcox and they triumph between the two Schlegel sisters when, among the familiar furniture at Howards End, the past comes to sanctify the present and the sense of the continuity of life gives promise for the future.

If we seek an explanation for the persistence of the marriage motif in Forster's fiction it is not to be found exclusively in the strength and resilience of a literary form, domestic comedy. It is to be found in his abiding adherence to the idea of continuity. The equation between marriage and continuity is made explicitly in his autobiographical confession that if he had not been suddenly cast out of the much loved family house, Rooksnest, at the age of fourteen he would have been 'a different person, married',[12] and become part of the continuity of English life. For the development of the theme of continuity there had to be marriages, and children, and ancestral homes, as well as descriptions of the unchanging English countryside. Where *A Passage to India* differs from all the earlier novels is not only in its treatment of nature but in its radical questioning of the value of both marriage and personal relations. On the rail journey to the Marabar Caves, we are told, Mrs Moore 'felt increasingly (vision or nightmare?) that though people are important the relations between them are not, and that in particular too much fuss has been made over marriage; centuries of carnal embracement, yet man is no nearer to understanding man'.[13] Although these sentiments are dramatically placed, they express the radical questioning that India forced on the novelist himself. The novel ends on a note of separation, not of union or the triumph of personal relations. It had taken Forster eighteen years to break from the happy endings of domestic comedy and become a modern. In the 1906 paper on 'Pessimism in Literature', he had written: 'Separation, then, is the end that best pleases the novelist or dramatist of today — the erection of a barrier, spiritual or physical, between the people in his book'.[14] The famous ending of *A Passage to India* exemplifies the ideal.

'Why can't we be friends now?' said the the other, holding him affectionately. 'It's what I want. It's what you want.'

But the horses didn't want it — they swerved apart; the earth didn't want it, sending up rocks through which riders must pass single file; the temples, the tank, the jail, the palace, the birds, the carrion, the Guest House, that came into view as they issued from the gap and saw Mau beneath: they didn't want it, they said in their hundred voices, 'No, not yet,' and the sky said, 'No, not there.'   (xxxvii, 312)

This passage holds in prophetic balance the tension implicit in Forster's personal ideology, the belief that male friendship is the highest ideal but that it is challenged and threatened by the cumulative forces of both nature and society.

In view of all I have said about the alien nature of marriage in Forster's life and writings it comes as something of a surprise to find him reminding Angus Wilson in an interview that he once 'put forward the golden wedding as one of the great achievements of civilization'.[15]

NOTES

1. P. N. Furbank and F. J. H. Haskell, 'E. M. Forster', *Writers at Work: The Paris Review Interviews*, ed. Malcolm Cowley (New York: The Viking Press, 1958), p. 34.
2. 'Pessimism in Literature', *Albergo Empedocle and other Writings*, ed. George H. Thomson (New York: Liveright, 1971), pp. 135–8.
3. Charles Dickens, *Hard Times* (New York: Rinehart and Co., 1958), Book II, Ch. 12, p. 201.
4. D. H. Lawrence, *Women in Love* (New York: The Modern Library, 1922), Ch. 27, p. 427.
5. E. M. Forster, *Aspects of the Novel*, ed. Oliver Stallybrass, Abinger edn. (London: Edward Arnold, 1974), p. 91.
6. E. M. Forster, 'Other Kingdom', *Collected Short Stories of E. M. Forster* (1947; rpt. London: Sidgwick & Jackson, 1965), p. 86.
7. E. M. Forster, *The Longest Journey*, The World's Classics, No. 578 (London: Oxford University Press. 1960), p. 93.
8. E. M. Forster, *Maurice* (London: Edward Arnold, 1971), p. 236.
9. E. M. Forster, *Howards End*, ed. Oliver Stallybrass, Abinger edn. (London: Edward Arnold, 1973), p. 255.
10. P. N. Furbank, *E. M. Forster: A Life* (New York: Harcourt Brace Jovanovich, 1977), II, p. 182.
11. Furbank, II, p. 8.
12. 'Memory', a paper delivered to the Bloomsbury Memoir Club in the early 1930s. Quoted in John Colmer, *E. M. Forster: The Personal Voice* (London: Routledge and Kegan Paul, 1975), p. 3.

13. E. M. Forster, *A Passage to India*, ed. Oliver Stallybrass, Abinger edn. (London: Edward Arnold, 1978), p. 127.
14. 'Pessimism in Literature' in *Albergo Empedocle*, p. 137.
15. Angus Wilson, 'A Conversation With E. M. Forster', *Encounter*, 9 (November 1957), p. 55.

8 *A Passage to India*, the French New Novel and English Romanticism

John Beer

When I first wrote about *A Passage to India* some years back, I was mainly concerned to trace the continuities within Forster's fiction as a whole and their relationship to some central themes in English romanticism. His interest in the human imagination, with its power to betray those who indulged it too easily and to act as an important guide to the nature of reality in those who knew how to and on what terms to trust it, had emerged for me as an important clue in understanding his achievement as a whole, and I argued that it was still at work within the largely negative vision of his Indian novel, contributing to its unusual shape and organization.[1] In a more recent essay I have taken a closer look at some romantic images, notably those involving echoes and reflections, which are used in that novel and help suggest the ambiguous status of the individual in the universe.[2] I want now to approach it from a different point of view again, looking primarily at those elements in it which have led critics to acclaim it as one of the first great 'modern' novels. In spite of all that has been written about it in recent years, there has been comparatively little attempt to determine its nature as a body of fiction.

A definitive reading obviously is neither desirable nor possible. In an age when, as Frank Kermode has pointed out, we value works for their hermeneutic versatility,[3] there is a good deal to be said for allowing diversity of interpretations to flourish. Yet it remains a part of the critic's task to indicate important contours in the novel's landscape, to draw attention to points of complexity that might otherwise be missed, and to ask what *kind* of novel we are reading.

If we approach *A Passage to India* in formal terms, with this question in mind, the first and most obvious point that is likely to strike us is that it is a failed detective story. To those familiar with detective fiction, the set-up seems familiar enough: the description of scene and characters, the mysterious and sinister event, and the investigation towards a solution. Yet in these terms we are thwarted: there is no 'solution', and we never know what, if anything, happened in the cave.

To readers of a later time, however, this is not quite the frustrating experience it might have been when the novel was first issued since we have become familiar with such a situation by our readings in contemporary fiction and particularly in the French new novel, as practised for example by Robbe-Grillet. In such novels, and their equivalent films, a similar situation is often met with: it is only gradually that the reader comes to see that the expectation of a solution was after all the mark of a false attitude on his part. And even some things which Robbe-Grillet has said about the new novel strike one, at least at first sight, as things that might be said also about *A Passage to India*. He talks, for instance, of a common effect to be found in a thriller:

> . . . the plot starts to thicken alarmingly: witnesses contradict one another, the suspect multiplies his alibis, new factors crop up which had previously been overlooked . . . . And you have to keep coming back to the recorded evidence: the exact position of a piece of furniture, the shape and frequency of a fingerprint, a word written in a message. The impression grows on you that nothing else is *true*. Whether they conceal or reveal a mystery, these elements that defy all systems have only one serious, obvious quality — that of being *there*.[4]

Whether or not that is true of the average thriller, it is true in an important sense of *A Passage*: the existence of the mystery drives us back to a sense less of what might have happened in the Marabar caves than of the evidence: the smashed binoculars, Adela Quested's shock and above all the caves themselves, described as exactly as possible by the author and presented as preceding by thousands of years not only the petty fates of individual human beings but the human race itself.

Robbe-Grillet goes on to describe the traditional forms of

narrative — 'the systematic use of the past definite tense and of the third person, the unconditional adoption of chronological development, linear plots, a regular graph of the emotions, the way each episode tended towards an end, etc.' — and sees them as all having been devoted to the imposition of 'the image of a stable universe, coherent, continuous, univocal and wholly decipherable', commenting that 'as the intelligibility of the world was never even questioned, the act of narration raised no problems'.

When we recall a later comment of Forster's on his novel: 'I tried to indicate the human predicament in a universe which is not, so far, comprehensible to our minds', it is not perhaps surprising to discover that the use of the past definite tense, and of strict chronological definition is sometimes violated, that the plot though more or less linear leads not to a conclusion but to an uncertainty, and that the picture of the universe is, to adapt Robbe-Grillet's phraseology, incoherent, discontinuous, multivocal ('India in her thousand voices') and largely undecipherable.

Again, we might turn to Robbe-Grillet's comments on solitude:

Let us as an example, recapitulate the functioning of 'solitude'. I call. No one answers me. Instead of concluding that there is no one there — which could be an observation, pure and simple, dated and placed, in space and time — I decide to act as if someone were in fact there, and as if, for one reason or another, he were refusing to answer. From then on the silence that follows my appeal is no longer a real silence, it has become pregnant with content, with depth, with a soul — which immediately plunges me back into my own soul. The distance between my cry, as I hear it, and the mute (perhaps deaf) interlocutor to whom it is addressed, becomes a sort of anguish, my hope and my despair, a sense to my life. Henceforth nothing will count for me save this false vacuum and the problems it causes me. Should I go on calling? Should I call more loudly? Should I use other words? I try again . . . . I very soon realise that no one is going to answer, but the invisible presence that I continue to create by my cry forces me to go on, for all eternity, sending out my unhappy cry into the silence. Its echo soon starts to deafen me.[5]

It is hard to read these words without recalling the well-known passage in which Forster describes the effect upon Mrs Moore's consciousness of the echo she had heard in the Marabar cave:

> The crush and the smells she could forget, but the echo began in some indescribable way to undermine her hold on life. Coming at a moment when she chanced to be fatigued, it had managed to murmur: 'Pathos, piety, courage — they exist, but are identical, and so is filth. Everything exists, nothing has value.' If one had spoken vileness in that place, or quoted lofty poetry, the comment would have been the same — 'ou-boum'. If one had spoken with the tongues of angels and pleaded for all the unhappiness and misunderstanding in the world, past, present, and to come, for all the misery men must undergo whatever their opinion and position, and however much they dodge or bluff — it would amount to the same, the serpent would descend and return to the ceiling.[6]

This effect is reinforced when we turn back to the original manuscript and discover that in that version, in which a physical attack on Adela is described, she found her cries for help met simply by the Marabar echo; we also learn that the passage about the power of the echo to negate values was at first associated with Fielding — and that Fielding actually went into a cave and started declaiming noble and resonant poetry (the opening of *Paradise Lost*, a poem by Meredith, a Persian poem taught him by Aziz), only to find each greeted and replied to by the same dull noise.[7] In the final version Forster simply made this scene a *possibility*, to be contemplated by Mrs Moore's (or perhaps merely the reader's) consciousness, but it remains one of the key-statements in the novel. Although we cannot ignore the difference in what Robbe-Grillet is saying (in his novel it is the silence that echoes, not a cave) we recognize a common predicament.

Perhaps the most striking point of correspondence between Robbe-Grillet's novels and *A Passage to India*, however, lies in a common feature of their construction as a whole. Some commentators (including Robbe-Grillet himself) have noted that there is in most of his novels an important gap at the heart of what is going on. In terms of the plot it is often no more than a gap in the chronology of events, but it may also be given a visual correlative. Roger Sturrock has discussed some of these: in *Les Gommes*, there is a gap between the drawbridge and the road as the drawbridge finally settles, quaveringly, into position, and the impossibility of being certain just when there is a gap and when there is not emphasizes the precarious condition of all perceptual interpretations of events. In *La Maison de Rendez-vous*, more strikingly, the events take place in a restaurant anchored in the harbour (and so surrounded by water) in the middle of which there is a hole, a square pool in whose green water may be seen 'a multitude of huge fish, blue, violet, red or yellow'. Sturrock argues that this pool corresponds to the gap at the centre of the narrative which gives the fantasies of his characters space to breed.[8]

Encounter with such a gap, a gap which cannot be controlled, induces a situation in which the very thing that is not there can assume a size out of all proportion to its own significance — what Robbe-Grillet himself calls 'the void which overruns, which fills everything'.[9] We may compare Adela Quested's reaction to the echo:

> The noise in the cave, so unimportant intellectually, was prolonged over the surface of her life . . . . The sound had spouted after her when she escaped, and was going on still like a river that gradually fills the plain. Only Mrs. Moore could drive it back to its source and seal the broken reservoir.
>
> (xxii, 185)

Adela Quested also manifests something which one recognizes from Robbe-Grillet's novels: the tendency of those who have become aware of such a void or gap to indulge in obsessive activity. While the cactus spines are being plucked from her body she is haunted by the phrase, 'In space things touch, in time things part' (xxii, 184), which she repeats over and over again, uncertain whether it is a philosophy or a pun. It is neither, perhaps, but it does remind us of something that Blake also wrote about: the tendency of the mind that has become aware of an uninterpretable void to concentrate on finding a firm point of organization, if possible in terms of space and time.[10]

Adela Quested's obsessive activity transcends the kind described by Robbe-Grillet or Blake, however, since she retains awareness of the problem that she is facing. Rather, the activity of her mind is a circular process, first wrestling honestly with the problem and then being overtaken for a time by the irrational powers of her personality:

> Adela was always trying to 'think the incident out', always
> reminding herself that no harm had been done. There was 'the
> shock', but what is that? For a time her own logic would
> convince her, then she would hear the echo again, weep,
> declare she was unworthy of Ronny, and hope her assailant
> would get the maximum penalty. After one of these bouts, she
> longed to go out into the bazaars and ask pardon from everyone
> she met, for she felt in some vague way that she was leaving
> the world worse than she found it. She felt that it was her crime,
> until the intellect, reawakening, pointed out to her that she
> was inaccurate here, and set her again upon her sterile round.
>
> (xxii, 185)

We recall Blake again:

> If it were not for the Poetic or Prophetic character the Philo-
> sophic & Experimental would soon be at the ratio of all things,
> & stand still, unable to do other than repeat the same dull
> round over again.[11]

Adela Quested attains the 'Poetic or Prophetic character' only
once in the novel, however, in the courtroom; and then the
pressure of the context is such that her poetic and prophetic
utterance can articulate itself only in the statement 'I am not
quite sure' (xxiv, 217).

This kind of obsessive activity in Adela's mind is richer and
more complex than that of Robbe-Grillet's characters, where the
obsessive activity is more strictly cerebral, falling back upon
some simple inviolable order. I am thinking for instance of the
husband in *La Jalousie* who occupies himself in counting and
organizing in his mind the banana trees on his plantation, only
to find that the pattern will never quite come together; or still
more closely the bicyclist salesman in *Le Voyeur* who occupies
himself in calculating how long he can devote to selling each of
his watches if he is to sell eighty-nine during the time he has to
spend on the island, only to be seized by panic when talking to
a boy who he thinks may have seen him assaulting a young girl:

> He began to talk at such a rate that objections — or regret at his

own words — became quite impossible. In order to fill in the gaps he often repeated the same sentence several times. He even surprised himself reciting the multiplication table.[12]

This kind of activity seems to be paralleled in Forster's novel rather by the behaviour of Mrs Moore after the visit to the caves. Her speech, it will be remembered, becomes highly repetitive:

> . . . all this rubbish about love, love in a church, love in a cave, as if there is the least difference, and I held up from my business over such trifles!
> 'What do you want?' he said, exasperated. 'Can you state it in simple language? If so, do.'
> 'I want my pack of patience cards.'   (xxii, 192)

And so Mrs Moore sidesteps any possibility of facing the un-faceable by retreating to the strictly organized code of a solitary card game, played over and over again, obsessively. And yet in her presence, Adela becomes convinced that Mrs Moore has in some way proclaimed Aziz's innocence — so much so that Ronny in the end asks her.

> She replied: 'I never said his name', and began to play patience.
> 'I thought you said, "Aziz is an innocent man," but it was in Mr. Fielding's letter.'
> 'Of course he is innocent,' she answered indifferently; it was the first time she had expressed an opinion on the point.
> 'You see, Ronny, I was right,' said the girl.
> 'You were not right, she never said it.'
> 'But she thinks it.'
> 'Who cares what she thinks?'
> 'Red nine on black ten — ' from the card-table. (xxii, 195)

When the others force her back into conversation her talk be-comes apparently irrelevant, rambling and repetitive; but when Adela asks if the case cannot now be withdrawn, and is told by Ronny 'the case has to come before a magistrate now; it really must, the machinery has started', Mrs Moore chips in with

'She has started the machinery; it will work to its end.'

It is at this moment that Ronny decides that she ought to leave India: 'she was doing no good to herself or to anyone else there' (xxii, 196).

So far it might seem that the drift of the argument is pushing *A Passsage to India* more and more into the role of precursor to the new novel, as it has emerged in France since the Second World War. It is time to point out some differences. It shares with them a defeat of the normal expectation that a plot will end in some clear resolution; it also shares a tendency (associated with the first, perhaps) to bring into question the whole process of fiction itself. We might, for instance, consider the opening to Chapter 14 of Forster's novel:

> Most of life is so dull that there is nothing to be said about it, and the books and talk that would describe it as interesting are obliged to exaggerate, in the hope of justifying their own existence. (xiv, 125)

In such a statement Forster might seem to be aligning himself with those novelists who have argued for the total deconstruction of plot on the grounds that plot does violence to the unorganized, plotless nature of most human experience.

Yet of course Forster deconstructs his plot a good deal less than he would if he were pursuing the implications of that remark in any determined manner. Whereas in the *nouveau roman* we are left in serious doubt as to what has been happening — and in some cases whether anything at all has happened throughout the plot — Forster localizes such uncertainties to one place and one time. One might indeed wonder whether there is any uncertainty at all, particularly when it is discovered that in the manuscript version Adela Quested *was* assaulted physically. Yet if we stick to the final text and that alone, the uncertainty is clearly there, and we know that Forster meant it to be there, from an important letter which he wrote to Lowes Dickinson shortly after the novel appeared. Even here, however, it will be noticed that he is concerned to limit the range of possibilities quite strictly to three, instead of allowing them to proliferate as a later novelist might. Dickinson had asked what had happened in the cave. Forster replied:

> In the cave it is *either* a man, *or* the supernatural, *or* an illusion.

If I say, it becomes whatever the answer a different book. And even if I know! My writing mind therefore is a blur here — i.e. I will it to remain a blur, and to be uncertain, as I am of many facts in daily life. This isn't a philosophy of aesthetics. *It's a particular trick I felt justified in trying because my theme was India.* It sprang straight from my subject matter. I wouldn't have attempted it in other countries, which though they contain mysteries or muddles, manage to draw rings round them. Without the trick I doubt whether I could have got the spiritual reverberation going. I call it 'trick': but 'voluntary surrender to infection' better expresses my state.[13]

This letter is important not only because it seems to settle, once and for all, what Forster's own view of the event, or non-event, in the cave was; it also openly disavows any deliberate generalizing intent. His creative posture, he implies, was passive: he adopted this course because his subject was India, and this uncertainty suited it, was to some extent forced upon him by it.

This very limited disorganization of plot is matched by an equally limited disruption of chronology. So far as chronology within the plot-structure is concerned, there are no problems: everything seems to fit neatly and exactly. But if we begin to ask just when the events of the novel as a whole took place, it is not altogether easy to be sure. Some details of the novel, like the Lieutenant-Governor and the dog-carts, belong to an earlier period, while references to the Amritsar massacre place the timing of the novel as contemporary with its first publication. Yet again we suddenly find Forster saying in Chapter 29 that after Aziz had generously renounced his claim for compensation,

> . . . it won him no credit with the English. They still believed he was guilty, they believed it to the end of their careers, and retired Anglo-Indians in Tunbridge Wells or Cheltenham still murmur to each other: 'That Marabar case which broke down because the poor girl couldn't face giving her evidence — that was another bad case.'   (xxix, 250)

If we adopt the time-scale presupposed by that remark we find ourselves suddenly transported to a vantage point in, say, the 1960s. But such literal-mindedness would be out of place; it would be truer to say that we are being invited to view the events from an Olympian standpoint which takes us out of time altogether, while at the same time suggesting that we are dealing with permanent human obtusenesses.

Another place in the novel where the sense of time is noticeably affected has something of the same quality. It is the beginning of the 'Temple' section, where Forster originally wrote as his opening sentence,

> Some hundreds of miles westward of the Marabar Hills, and two years later in time, Professor Narayan Godbole stood in the presence of God.[14]

He then changed 'stood' to 'stands', and goes on to take us out of time in the next sentence as well: 'God is not born yet . . . but He has also been born centuries ago, nor can He ever be born, because He is Lord of the Universe . . . He is, was not, is not, was' (xxxiii, 274).

It is in this extension of the Olympian attitude to time that we begin to discover another important difference between Forster's novel and the new novel of Robbe-Grillet and others which can be traced also in their relative attitudes to mythology.

Some critics have found a 'mythological' element in Robbe-Grillet's novels; in such cases they are read as presentations of Freudian mythology, with its strangely self-destructive quality. By this I mean that the most dominant myths of Freud's writing, such as the myth of Oedipus, have a powerful and even looming presence there; yet in the end the logic of the argument would seem to turn back on the myths themselves, to see them, too, as projections of human needs and desires. They do not have the authority of myths that are presented as having a more general or objective status. And Robbe-Grillet's novels present Oedipal imagery with a certain priority, but without allowing the reader to accord them more than a provisional status. Their status, in other words, refers them back to the individual human being, and Oedipus remains a riddle. Even in the work of a novelist such as Michel Butor, who gives mythology more play, there are limitations: a myth is defined as 'a form of social hygiene' and the need for it is seen as a bulwark against the dissolution of society that must otherwise come about; it is seen as essentially something that we make up ourselves and for particular purposes.

Forster's approach, by contrast, gives mythology a greater life of its own. He allows for a possible metaphysical validity of myth in a way that psycho-analytic accounts, at least of the Freudian kind, normally do not. And at this point it is profitable to turn to another of Forster's accounts of his novel, given some thirty or so years later in an unpublished talk entitled 'Three Countries'. Here, as in the programme note quoted from earlier, he acknowledges the political significance of his novel, but also draws attention to further elements in it which transcend local questions:

> . . . the book is not really about politics, though it is the political aspect of it that caught the general public and made it sell. It's about something wider than politics, about the search of the human race for a more lasting home, about the universe as embodied in the Indian earth and the Indian sky, about the horror lurking in the Marabar Caves and the release symbolized by the birth of Krishna. It is — or rather desires to be — philosophic and poetic. [15]

When Forster says that the novel is about the search of the human race for a more lasting home, about the universe as embodied in the Indian earth and the Indian sky, and the horror lurking in the Marabar Caves, we can recognize elements which might well make up a *nouveau roman*. But when he speaks of a release, 'symbolized by the birth of Krishna', it is harder to see any correlative in that kind of novel. Release is precisely what seems often to be lacking. And it is Forster's willingness to allow the Hindu element in his novel to flourish so fully that gives a quite different kind of shape to his conclusion. The reader feels that the Hindu values are hovering on the point of being accepted and affirmed by the novelist himself. 'No man could say where was the emotional centre of the Hindu festival, any more than he could locate the heart of a cloud' — but it is hard to resist the sense that it had one, all the same.

The novel can be read in orthodox Hindu terms with some fidelity. On this reading of the novel, the English characters find the caves horrifying simply because they have not been initiated into the larger sense of the universe that a fuller acquaintance with Hinduism would have given them.

For a Hindu the cave would not be horrifying: it would rather be the retiring place of the individual which he enters in order to commune with God. The Barabar caves which Forster visited were not, like the Marabar caves of his novel, untouched by human hand; they had served as monastic cells for those who wished to meditate alone and were, as he later acknowledged in his notes, ornamented. Several writers have pointed out similarly, that the pronouncing and meditating upon the syllable 'Om' is part of the meditative discipline in certain forms of Indian religion, so that even the sinister 'ou-boum or bou-oum' could for such a meditator become simply a natural echo of his own deepest meditations, a reverberation of 'Om'.[16]

At the same time this seems to be a set of significances that exist outside the novel rather than within the text that is presented to us. Forster later described his own delight on discovering that the symbolism of the Hindu temple was that of a world-mountain enclosing a central cavern where the individual could be alone with his god, but that was evidently a subsequent recognition.[17] The English in this novel are caught rather (as perhaps he himself was at the time) between the decline of their own religion and a failure to apprehend any other. The religious associations of the caves are deliberately eliminated by Forster; equally deliberately he sets his characters in a place which is, in its essence, older than any human religion.

Some critics, pursuing a different line of thought, have noted the physiological reference of the 'fists and fingers' and seized upon the possible interpretation of the caves as wombs. The point finds natural support in Freudian analysis and has been developed by Wilfred Stone in a memorable discussion which quotes among other things Norman Douglas on cave-worship as the cult of the feminine principle.[18] At the same time I have come across no source in Hindu thought which would ascribe such meaning to the cave, and it is noticeable that this is a significance that Forster himself never suggests in his imagery. What he does say many years later in looking back at the planning of the incident is that the caves 'were something to focus everything up; they were to engender an event like an egg'.[19] And in a later incident of the novel, it will be remembered, Aziz, looking to see the cave into which Adela has disappeared, finds that 'Caves appeared in every direction — it seemed their original spawning-place . . .' (xvi, 145). Forster once again delicately balances disgust and delight in fecundity by that word 'spawning'; but as soon as one focuses more sharply on the image one sees that while caves which spawn may be eggs, they are also, by definition, hollow eggs.

My point here is not to discount either Hindu or Freudian interpretations of the novel, but to suggest that they hardly have Forster's own authority behind them: they are significances which one may discover in the novel, just as one may discover them in Forster's own personality, but which he himself would seem to be excluding — perhaps deliberately. His various descriptions of the caves combine to resist any identification of them with the womb — at least if that is thought of as a source of warmth and life. Rather, they focus his questionings of the significance of the universe, once there is removed from it the normal pattern of birth, generation and death by which most human beings live, and it is an essential feature of that questioning that it should resist the imposition of any significance derived from a traditional religion.

Nothing I have said, obviously, is intended to derogate from the centrality of the cave imagery in the novel: on the contrary it needs to be examined with extreme care. The need for vigilance is intensified, moreover, by Forster's refusal (a refusal which, it will be recalled, Dr Leavis found disturbing)[20] to write to a consistent degree of seriousness or to signal clearly his transitions from whimsy to something more ambiguous. In this context it is useful to recall one of Furbank's observations on Forster: that he had a habit of realizing images with an unexpected literalness. On one occasion, for instance, he described how he had, like a rat, deserted the sinking ship of fiction, 'and *swam* towards bio-graphy'. Or again, when a friend said to him 'One must face facts', he replied 'How can I, when they're all about me?'[21] When he opens his chapter on the Marabar caves with the words, 'The Ganges, though flowing from the foot of Vishnu and through Siva's hair, is not an ancient stream' we are tempted to read the statement in much the same way that we read his joke in the first chapter, 'There are no bathing-steps on the river-front as the Ganges happens not to be holy here'. If so, we may still not take him very seriously when a few lines later we find him saying of the caves themselves

They are older than anything in the world. No water has ever covered them, and the sun who has watched them for countless aeons may still discern in their outlines forms that were his before our globe was torn from his bosom . . . .   (xii, 116)

Further attention to the image, allowing the sentence to resonate in its own right, causes a quite different vision to emerge — particularly when Forster continues, 'If flesh of the sun's flesh is to be touched anywhere, it is here, among the incredible antiquity of these hills'. For in what sense can either the caves, or at the opposite extreme the sun be thought of as having *flesh*? Realize the image and you are left with a stark dialectic: an eye of everlasting life gazing at the dead flesh of its own body. The idea can temporarily take over and interpret the whole universe: we recognize that all human beings are in moments of starker awareness eyes of everlasting life which are forced to contemplate the necessary death of their own flesh.

Close attention of this kind, involving expansive interpretation, is further justified by evidences of calculation in Forster's handling of his material. We have already noted that the Barabar caves of actuality had different kinds of entrance, some simple squares, others elaborately ornamented, each showing strong human influence; the Marabar caves, by contrast, are described as all alike and apparently untouched by human art. Forster suggests also that there are a great number of them — and still more perhaps which have no entrance from the outside world; at the Barabar caves there were only seven, and none at all at the Kawa Dol, the place where they are actually visited in the novel. (*PI*, Notes, 356–7). In an author who tries where possible to be precise and factual, this emphasis on the non-human is likely to be a calculated effect.

Close reading at this point in the novel also reveals an 'echoing' effect in the use of certain keywords. That is, the word or phrase will impress itself upon the mind in one way, but then, attended to again will reveal another meaning, and then perhaps another. The word 'extraordinary', read first in its normal sense of 'out of the ordinary', can return to the eye in the sense of '*extra* ordinary' — that is even more ordinary than usual; and then again simply as extra, ordinary — that is, no more than a simple addition to the sum of ordinary events. The visitor returns from the Marabar caves says Forster, uncertain whether he has had an interesting experience, or a dull one or no experience at all. He does not know, in other words, whether what he found there was extraordinary, *extra* ordinary or just extra, and ordinary.

This is not, perhaps, a kind of reading commonly called for in Forster's writings. It is invited in this novel, however, and at this point of the novel, by the very way in which the author himself refers to his key-word:

> It is as if the surrounding plain or the passing birds have taken upon themselves to exclaim 'Extraordinary!' and the word has taken root in the air, and been inhaled by mankind.
>
> (xii, 117)

A word that can behave like that is clearly to be looked at with some care. Another, more complicated example of a phrase echoing in the mind to reveal different layers of significance comes in the description of that archetypal Marabar cave, the one supposed to subsist within the hollow boulder of the Kawa Dol that sways in the wind:

> . . . a bubble-shaped cave that has neither ceilings nor floor, and mirrors its own darkness in every direction infinitely. If the boulder falls and smashes, the cave will smash too — empty as an Easter egg.
>
> (xii, 118)

On its first impact that smashing has a rather appalling effect, since a void which had at least possessed form is suddenly transformed into utter non-existence. Yet the image of the Easter egg, on the echo, limits the feeling of appalledness by domesticating it. We are reminded rather of the disappointment of a child at discovering that the marvellous looking egg turns out to have nothing but hollowness inside it — a sharp disappointment for the moment, perhaps, but one that is quickly mitigated by the pieces of chocolate that remain. No sooner has that softening of the blow been registered, on the other hand, than a third echo of the phrase brings us up against the word Easter and reminds us that *this* Easter egg is an empty cave. We are reminded of the empty cave that might transform human experience by realizing an unthinkable possibility of resurrection but is more likely to confirm humanity in its own scepticism. The swaying of the boulder itself emphasized, meanwhile, the instability and fragility of human conceptions of the universe and man's place in it.

A striking feature of Forster's description of the caves is his use of images that bring out different possible significances but also fall away from one another, so thwarting any one overall pattern of interpretation. Take, for instance, the first approach to the caves, which comes after the small contretemps between Adela and Dr Aziz. The slight coldness that has overtaken their relationship is registered in a single, formal Jane Austen-like sentence: 'The first cave was tolerably convenient'. Then,

> The small black hole gaped where their varied forms and colours had momentarily functioned. They were sucked in like water down a drain.

Following this the scene without humanity is described — the scene as it must always have looked — after which we read

> And then the hole belched, and humanity returned.
>
> (xiv, 138)

The hole which a moment ago was like a drain, so connecting with an imagery of excretory functions, has turned into a rejecting mouth — but humanity is not spewed forth, it is belched forth. The suggestion that emerges here is of silent water disappearing down a drain — which comes back now as noise in the belching.

Other ambiguities, which are actually dramatized in the text, respect this duality of invited response. As elephants take the party up to the Marabar hills, for example, mounds are seen by the track which might be either graves or breasts of the goddess Parvati (the villagers give both explanations); these alternative explanations of death or superfecundity then modulate into something doubly sinister when Adela Quested sees a thin dark object which she identifies as a snake, only to see through her field-glasses that it is the withered and twisted stump of a toddy-palm. The alternative here is between the deadly and the deathly — and the fact that the villagers continue to insist that it is a snake now that the idea is in their heads merely assists the underlying sense of hollowness and nullity which is already there in the spiritual silence of the journey, where 'sounds did not echo or thoughts develop' (xiv, 132). It is as if the villagers are wantonly superimposing interpretation upon a void.

This underlying, further sense is reinforced by the increasing use of an imagery which is on the point of becoming uninterpretable, such as the drain imagery cited above, or that of caves which are 'spawned' yet have 'orifices'. It reaches its apogee, perhaps, in the moment when Aziz realizes that it is of no use to shout, 'because a Marabar cave can hear no sound but its own' (xvi, 145). Robbe-Grillet's account of 'solitude' is marvellously caught, and extended, here.

I have spoken up to now as if the ambiguities of the experience in the cave normally showed a bias either towards the sinister or at least the life-denying, and that is no doubt true of the novel's main effect. There is however one indication of positive value in the caves which is not checked or negated anywhere else, though by the end of the paragraph its effect has been carefully restricted. I am thinking of the moment when a visitor strikes a match in the cave:

> Immediately another flame rises in the depths of the rock and moves towards the surface like an imprisoned spirit; the walls of the circular chamber have been most marvellously polished. The two flames approach and strive to unite, but cannot, because one of them breathes air, the other stone. A mirror inlaid with lovely colours divides the lovers, delicate stars of pink and gray interpose, exquisite nebulae, shadings fainter than the tail of a comet or the midday moon, all the evanescent life of the granite, only here visible. Fists and fingers thrust above the advancing soil — here at last is their skin, finer than any covering acquired by the animals, smoother than windless water, more voluptuous than love. The radiance increases, the flames touch one another, kiss, expire. The cave is dark again, like all the caves. (xxii, 117–18)

The final emphasis, as so often in this novel, is upon limitation. The flames can never unite; the power of physical surface intervenes, light is surrounded by, and yields to darkness. Yet that need not close the reader's eyes to what has opened out in the course of the paragraph. It is only under the rules of time which govern sequential fiction that the darkness triumphs; in another sense the beauty, inherent in the very rock itself, has opened another dimension. It has intimated the possible existence of a timeless order which might have an eternal value, and so gestured towards an absolute romanticism.

This theme in the novel is reflected in the aftermath of Mrs Moore's collapse. Even as she falls under the rules of time and yields to the limitations of her body her spirit remains alive in a strange, disembodied manner. Even while she is talking on repetitively in her weary, irritable voice, Adela hears her as declaring Aziz's innocence; and even when she is dead, there continues in the chant of the crowd outside the courtroom, and in the remembering consciousness of her friends a sense of connection — that 'connection' which is of chief importance to Forster and which is for him one of the mysteries in a nature whose mechanical processes might otherwise seem to confirm the existence of impenetrable surfaces between individuals.

What is no more than a hint with Mrs Moore, moreover, becomes actual momentarily, in Adela, in her experience in the courtroom, where the whole baffling experience of the caves is seen by her transformed into unity, and even as splendid.

> Why had she thought the expedition 'dull'? Now the sun rose again, the elephant waited, the pale masses of the rock flowed round her and presented the first cave . . .   (xxiv, 216)

The effect of this passage, like that of some words discussed earlier, depends on the reader's willingness or otherwise to change his mode of reading. Cast into sequence it is quickly lost in the flow of the events of the courtroom; lingered on and contemplated, it offers the hint of a different psychic order, an alternative vision of humanity which might stand in judgement on time's processes just as the naked punkah-wallah who rouses Adela from her state of unreality stands in separation from all that is going on in the courtroom.

The existence of such passages and images throughout the novel are the mark of a persistent trait in Forster, a willingness to be sceptical about his own scepticism and to acknowledge the existence of a possible metaphysical dimension in human experience which is accepted and acknowledged by the human imagination itself under certain conditions.

It is here that his debt to the early Romantics is most evident. In his essay 'My Own Centenary',[22] Forster drew upon the coincidence that the centenaries of Beethoven and Blake both fell in the year (1927) in which he was writing, to project a sermon in 2027 by the Dean of Dulborough which would compare him with those two predecessors. The self-effacing irony of that comparison, emphasized by the Dean's platitudes, swings upon its axis to reveal a further depth when one recalls their importance as presences in his own art. His devotion to Beethoven, which he never lost, was evidenced memorably in *Howards End*; it was to him that he owed some of the continuing energy and explorative impulses in his work as a whole. But it is Blake, perhaps, who is a better guide to the mazes of *A Passage to India*. We have argued that Forster's novel is characterized by moments of transforming imagination, such as Adela's experience in the courtroom, which the reader is invited to set outside the narrative of the novel, in interpretative transcendence. The novel works to its fullest effect for readers who are willing to allow themselves this degree of flexibility and for such a reading one can think of no better preparation than an acquaintance with Blake. Forster's own attitude to him was best indicated, perhaps, in a review of his poems which began 'Blake is a man whom one is ashamed to review. One's feelings lie deep and are vague . . .'.[23] He was forced to be 'vague' since he could not altogether endorse Blake's commitment to the imagination, however much he might admire it; the 'depth' of feeling referred to was based both on a respect for Blake the individual and on an unusually good grasp of Blake's philosophy — which may well have been reflected in detail in the novel. When he describes Aziz cycling through the 'arid tidiness' of the British houses in Chandrapore, he also comments,

> The roads, named after victorious generals and intersecting at right angles, were symbolic of the net Great Britain had thrown over India.   (ii, ll)

Blake had used his image of the net of Urizen in precisely the same way: Urizen imposed a mathematical grid over the universe which then turned into a net in which humanity struggled. There is even an illustration in the *Songs of Innocence and Experience* which shows the process in action.[24] The British Raj, on this reading, takes on the attributes of an obsessive work of self-confirmation, undertaken by an occupying power whose philosophy is blinkered by a narrow nationalism.

The suspicion that Forster is drawing on Blake's philosophy

here to suggest the precarious foundations of the British attitude (strong, like Urizen's, in the short term but constructed ultimately upon a conception of human nature which must end in despair), finds support in the review just referred to, where he goes on to say of Blake:

> To handle him from the outside is to fall into the error of his demiurge Urizen, who withdrew from the primal unity, and, applying laws to the universe, brought everything, himself included, to destruction. Urizen saw that his rule was wrong, he 'wept and called it pity', but, entangled in chains meant for others, he supposed that the alternative to law is lawlessness, he could not imagine the service of perfect freedom.

Forster's conception of what that service might be like was nourished by a sharp sense, derived from the Romantic poets generally, of the energies and illuminations which enabled human beings to signal to one another across the barriers that divided them. The overall tone of his later works would be one of kindly scepticism, but it would be accompanied by many touches which transcend that scepticism and which derived from what he had learnt in his earlier creative achievement. The duality of vision which had not only survived but had even been strengthened by his encounter with India gave him, in fact, both an unusual insight into the nature of individual freedom and a tenacious energy in serving it.

It is at such points that Forster's purposes diverge most radically from those of the new novelists. To believe that the human heart can find any valid response in nature, or that the imagination can enjoy privileged knowledge would be beyond the terms of their presuppositions. Yet the divergence is not quite so deep as one might think, since by very reason of being creative writers they all share the kind of knowledge that can come from practice of the novelist's art. In *The Hill of Devi*, Forster tells how he took his unfinished Indian chapters to India with him in 1921, hoping that renewal of the experience would help set the novel in motion again. On the contrary,

> as soon as they were confronted with the country they purported to describe, they seemed to wilt and go dead and I could do nothing with them. I used to look at them of an evening in

my room in Dewas, and felt only distaste and despair. The gap between India remembered and India experienced was too wide.[25]

There is something very like this in Robbe-Grillet's description of how, when he was writing *Le Voyeur*, as he was trying to describe in detail the flight of seagulls and the movement of waves, he made a brief trip to the Brittany coast:

On my way there I said to myself: this is a good opportunity to observe things 'from life' and to 'refresh my memory' . . . . But the moment I saw my first sea bird I realised how wrong I had been: on the one hand the seagulls I was now seeing had only the vaguest connection with the ones I was describing in my book, and on the other hand I was quite indifferent to this fact. The only seagulls that mattered to me at that moment were the ones in my mind. They too had probably come, in one way or another, from the external world, and perhaps even from Brittany, but they had been transformed, and at the same time had seemed to become more real, *because* they were now imaginary.[26]

Robbe-Grillet's statement suggests that he is acknowledging the right of imagination to its own autonomous play. It is an acknowledgement which bears not only on the novelist's art, but on that of the reader, who thus turns out to be making contact, not primarily with an objective reality, but with the novelist's imagination.

It can indeed be argued that such a novelist's very negations and denials set up conditions of imaginative freedom for the reader. One is reminded of Keats's comment on the lack of precise detail in Milton's description of Pandaemonium:

What creates the intense pleasure of not knowing? A sense of independence, of power, from the fancy's creating a world of its own by the sense of probabilities.[27]

The statement looks forward to much in modern fiction, where novelists have learned to exploit the 'intense pleasure of not knowing'. It also suggests ways in which the new novel, despite an apparent bias towards determinism, serves the cause of individual freedom.

Forster's own passage to freedom took him by a different route. In so far as he could find a firm historical tradition for his belief in the value of the imagination it would have been the platonism of his friend Lowes Dickinson. Lowes Dickinson however, who accompanied him on his first visit to India, found his sense of values stifled and oppressed by what he found there: 'I remember how he used to cower away from those huge architectural masses, those pullulating forms, as if a wind blew off them which might wither the soul',[28] At that level, Forster evidently shared his reaction to some degree. It is not only enacted dramatically in Mrs Moore's collapse but also acknowledged even in his Indian characters. By comparison with the real-life Rabindranath Tagore, who had written (in a poem published the year Forster visited India for the first time) 'Many a song have I sung in many a mood of mind, but all their notes have always proclaimed, "He comes, comes, ever comes"',[29] Forster's Godbole is less positive:

> 'I say to Shri Krishna, "Come! Come to me only". The God refuses to come . . . .'
> 'But He comes in some other song, I hope?' said Mrs. Moore gently.
> 'Oh no, he refuses to come . . . I say to Him, "Come, come, come, come, come, come", He neglects to come.'   (vii, 72)

Godbole's rueful yet accepting avowal presents yet another response to the conflict between imaginative affirmation and sceptical recognition which is central to this novel. Forster's own solution, as we have traced it, takes two forms. Against the despair induced by the recognition that 'in India nothing is identifiable' or that 'nothing comprehends the whole of India, nothing, nothing' he would set the recognition, carried over from *Howards End*, that 'it is private life that holds out the mirror to infinity; personal intercourse, and that alone, that ever hints at a personality beyond our daily vision'.[30] Mrs Moore's survival in the consciousness of others reaffirms his belief in the magic of personal relationships; but it needs for its full effect to be reinforced by the other hints of a link between 'infinity' and 'the personality beyond our daily vision' that are inherent in the descriptions of beauty and culminate perhaps in Adela's court-room vision.

We have also seen, however, how the structure of the novel works to enclose that vision, imposing the language and imagery of limitation so strongly that a conventional reading of the narrative might end with a conviction that they had been finally negated. The very instabilities in the novel help focus the reader's attention upon that which does not change, upon the resistancies of things. The sense of inevitable separateness which is induced by the caves is given further point by the failure of the flames to cross the polished barrier that reflects them and (most memorably) by the rocks that the earth sends up in the last sentence of the novel to force riders into single file.

In these respects, Forster's novel foreshadows effects which are later to be made central to the new novel. Robbe-Grillet, indeed, sees their development as the only possible way forward for fiction, as several of his own statements testify:

> In the construction of future novels, gestures and objects will be *there*, before they are *something*; and they will still be there afterwards, hard, unalterable, ever-present, and apparently quite indifferent to their own meaning . . .
> But from now on . . . objects will gradually lose their instability and their secrets, they will forego their false mystery . . .
> . . . the future hero will in the contrary remain *there* . . .[31]

The rhetoric of such expressions is such as to suggest a finality in these new perceptions, a final arrival at the truth of things, uncluttered by the affections or the search for ultimate meanings. This is natural enough, since most artists need the security that derives from the sense of driving towards an ultimate truth, a point of achieved precision. Yet there is no logical reason why the assertions that Robbe-Grillet is making must be finally valid for all time; elsewhere, indeed, he acknowledges the danger of predicting the course of fiction too far ahead, emphasizing the overall importance of development. 'Form in the novel has to evolve to stay alive', he writes, and

> There is no question . . . of establishing a theory, a pre-cast mould in which to pour the books of the future. All novelists, and all novels, must invent their own form. No recipe can replace this continual thought.[32]

For his own part, however, he can visualize only one direction for this intensive thought, a direction dictated by his belief that the romantic exploration of the relationship between the human mind and nature represents a form of tyranny. Writing of the effect of the film on the novel, he indicates the ideological significance of what he is doing as he contends that the actual presentation of objects, a chair, the movement of a hand, the bars to a window, reduces the amount of symbolism that can be associated with them: 'Instead of monopolizing our attention it seems just like one more attribute'. 'It seems in fact as if the conventions of photography . . . liberate us from our own conventions' — he goes on:

> . . . from now on . . . objects will gradually lose their instability and their secrets, they will forego their false mystery, and that suspect inner life that an essayist has called 'the romantic heart of things'. They will no longer be the vague reflection of the vague soul of the hero, the image of his torments, the shadow of his desires. Or rather, if it does still happen that things are used for a moment as a support for human passions, it will only be temporarily, and they will only be making a more or less derisive show of accepting the tyranny of meanings, the better to indicate how far they remain alien to man.[33]

In reading *A Passage to India* one is bound to be reminded of things that are said in that passage. Indeed, there are moments when Forster himself might seem almost to be ushering his readers towards a similar position. I am thinking in particular of Mrs Moore's journey to Bombay, and the scenes she sees from the train:

> She watched the indestructible life of man and his changing faces, and the houses he has built for himself and God, and they appeared to her not in terms of her own trouble but as things to see. There was, for instance, a place called Asirgarh which she passed at sunset and identified on a map — an enormous fortress among wooded hills. No one had ever mentioned Asirgarh to her, but it had huge and noble bastions and to the right of them was a mosque. She forgot it. Ten minutes later, Asirgarh reappeared. The mosque was to the left of the bastions now. The train in its descent through the

Vindhyas had described a semicircle round Asirgarh. What could she connect it with except its own name? Nothing; she knew no one who lived there. But it had looked at her twice and seemed to say: 'I do not vanish'. (xxiii, 199)

Once again, however, the position is not quite the same as in Robbe-Grillet's work. There the object is to be repeatedly observed and registered, unchanging, by the reader; at Asirgarh, by contrast, the object insists on its own stability, yet offers no point from which it can be viewed as a stable unit — it is either bastions and mosque or mosque and bastions: we understand the optical illusion that has disturbed Mrs Moore but are not permitted to focus on the object in its own identity. If we go on in spite of that to create our own stable image of Asirgarh, we are immediately brought up short by the next incidents. Mrs Moore too 'has started the machinery; it will work to its end' (xxii, 196). Just as the mechanical train, regarded as the point of her stability, made the identity of Asirgarh unnecessarily problematic to her, so her arrival at Bombay impresses her suddenly with a sense of what the machine is taking her away from:

'I have not seen the right places', she thought, as she saw embayed in the platforms of the Victoria terminus the end of the rails that had carried her over a continent and could never carry her back. (xxiii, 199)

As she drives through Bombay she has a sudden longing to 'disentangle the hundred Indias that passed each other in its streets'. And then finally, as she boards the mechanical steamer that will take her back to England, she sees thousands of coconut palms waving her farewell.

'So you thought an echo was India; you took the Marabar Caves as final?' they laughed. 'What have we in common with them, or they with Asirgarh? Goodbye!' (xxiii, 200)

Forster has directed our attention to a particular object in space only to remind us immediately afterwards not only that there are myriads of objects to focus upon, but that the quality of our perception itself may change: that to hear an echo in a Marabar cave is not the same kind of experience as to respond to Asirgarh, and that even if we were to identify Asirgarh it would not be the same as to identify a myriad of coconut trees.

Forster's attitude to the stability of objects is, in that respect, diametrically opposed to Robbe-Grillet's. While recognizing their ineluctable presence it would regard any attempt to give them finality as a form of enslavement. And he was sustained in this conviction by what he had learnt in pursuing the ways of the imagination. Like the early Romantics, he had come to know that the effort to hold together in the mind apparently irreconcilable modes of thought, called for by loyalty to different areas of one's psychic experience, could be, however oppressive in the short run, ultimately bracing and sustaining. The formula 'Each thing has a life of its own and we are all of one life'[34] had almost destroyed Coleridge by driving him to explore simultaneously the ultimate implications of objective and subjective states of mind, along with their moral implications, but it had also kept him faithful to the full range of human experience. Wordsworth's recognition in the Simplon Pass that the impossible contradictions of the landscape were yet held in unity by the imagination, that 'awful power' which could turn them into 'workings of one mind, the features/Of the same face, blossoms upon one tree' was equally liberating; the image of the journeying traveller could henceforth continue to alternate with that of the halted one. Blake's insistences on the supremacy of the imagination might lead him into grave impasses, but sustained him, equally, in his role as 'mental traveller'.[35]

This kind of dual consciousness is most fully sustained in *A Passage to India* by Professor Godbole, who continues to sing, even though the god neglects to come. His resilience and pursuant energy are demonstrated not only in the climactic dance scene (xxxiii, 276–7), where the contradictions of the world are almost (but not quite) brought into one, but also in his love of paradox — another trait shared with the Romantics. When asked his opinion about the alleged assault in the cave, for instance, he replies,

> 'My answer to that is this: that action was performed by Dr. Aziz.' He stopped and sucked in his thin cheeks. 'It was performed by the guide.' He stopped again. 'It was performed by you.' Now he had an air of daring and coyness. 'It was performed by me.' He looked shyly down the sleeve of his own coat. 'And by my students. It was even performed by the lady

herself. When evil occurs, it expresses the whole of the universe. Similarly when good occurs.'   (xix, 169)

In the same way Forster comments on the birth of Krishna,

God is not born yet — that will occur at midnight — but He has also been born centuries ago, nor can He ever be born, because He is the Lord of the Universe, who transcends human processes. He is, was not, is not, was.   (xxxiii, 274)

I catch something of the same note in a recorded remark of Blake's. Talking to Crabb Robinson, he said firmly, 'Jesus is the only God' — and then he added, 'and so am I, and so are you'.[36]

Where Robbe-Grillet seeks to liberate his readers from the tyranny of imported meanings by directing them to see objects as ineluctably there, Forster seeks to liberate them by encouraging them to consider alternative meanings. His is ultimately a fiction of possibilities, of imaginative explorations which encourage his readers to be sceptical, yet also to be sceptical concerning their own scepticism. Perhaps there is something ultimately self-destructive about such a fictional enterprise, since consciousness of the multiplicity of meaning may lead rather to the fields of biography, criticism and social comment, which Forster himself came to prefer. But it may also be that Forster, with his acute awareness of the possible play between imagination and object, ultimately was indicating a way forward for the novel to which the new novel, also, will prove to have been pointing. If so, the 'alertness to what has not yet been experienced' which provides the chief positive note in *A Passage to India* will come to have vindicated itself still more fully.

NOTES

1. John Beer, *The Achievement of E. M. Forster* (London: Chatto and Windus, 1962), Ch. 6.
2. John Beer, 'Echoes, Recollections, Correspondences: Some Central Romantic Themes and *A Passage to India*', in Forster centenary papers edited by V. A. Shahane. These papers were presented at the Forster centenary conference held in Hyderabad, India, January 1979.
3. See especially, Frank Kermode, *The Classic* (London: Faber and Faber, 1975).
4. Alain Robbe-Grillet, *Snapshots, and Towards a New Novel*, trans. B. Wright

(London: Calder and Boyars, 1965), p. 56.

5. Robbe-Grillet, pp. 83–4.

6. E. M. Forster, *A Passage to India*, ed. Oliver Stallybrass, Abinger edn. Abinger edn. (London: Edward Arnold, 1978), pp. 267–8.

7. E. M. Forster, *The Manuscripts of A Passage to India*, ed. Oliver Stallybrass, Abinger ed. (London: Edward Arnold, 1978), pp. 267–8.

8. John Sturrock, *The French New Novel: Claude Simon, Michel Butor, Alain Robbe-Grillet* (London: Oxford University Press, 1969), pp. 178–9; 187–8.

9. Robbe-Grillet in Sturrock, p. 194.

10. See, for example, Burgundy in 'The French Revolution', ll. 83–105 and Urizen in *The Four Zoas*, ii, ll. 135–200 in Geoffrey Keynes, ed., *Complete Writings of William Blake* (London: Nonesuch Press, 1957), pp. 138–9; 282–5. Cf: my *Blake's Humanism* (Manchester: Manchester University Press, 1968), pp. 98–102; and *Blake's Visionary Universe* (Manchester: Manchester University Press, 1969), pp. 139–47, etc.

11. 'There is no Natural Religion' in Keynes, p. 97.

12. Sturrock, quoting *Le Voyeur* (Paris: Editions de Minuit, 1955), p. 216.

13. Letter to G. Lowes Dickinson (26 June 1924), quoted in the introduction to E. M. Forster, *A Passage to India*, ed. Oliver Stallybrass, Abinger edn. (London: Edward Arnold, 1978), p. xxvi.

14. Forster, *The Manuscripts of A Passage to India*, p. 499.

15. 'Three Countries', cited in the introduction to *A Passage to India*, pp. xi and xxv.

16. See G. O. Allen, 'Structure, Symbol and Theme in E. M. Forster's *A Passage to India*', *PMLA*, LXX (1955), 942–3; and Wilfred Stone, *The Cave and the Mountain* (Stanford, Calif.: Stanford University Press, 1966), p. 310.

17. See Forster's pieces in *The Listener*, 2 December 1954, 977–8; and 5 December 1940, 801–2.

18. Stone, p. 301.

19. Malcolm Cowley, ed., *Writers at Work: The Paris Review Interviews* (New York: The Viking Press, 1958), pp. 26–7.

20. F. R. Leavis, *The Common Pursuit* (London: Chatto and Windus, 1952), p. 274. What Leavis sees as a failing at this point may more profitably be viewed as a complex effect. See my discussion in *The Achievement of E. M. Forster*, pp. 190–2.

21. P. N. Furbank, 'The Personality of E. M. Forster', *Encounter*, XXXV, No. 5 (November 1970), 67.

22. E. M. Forster, *Abinger Harvest* (London: Edward Arnold, 1936), pp. 59–61.

23. Review of Lawrence Binyon, *Poems of Blake*, *Spectator*, 2 April 1932, p. 274.

24. See 'The Human Abstract', William Blake, *Songs of Innocence and Experience*, facsimile with an introduction and commentary by Geoffrey Keynes (New York: The Orion Press, 1967), plate 47; and my discussion in *Interpreting Blake*, ed. M. Phillips (Cambridge: Cambridge University Press, 1978), pp. 215–16.

25. E. M. Forster, *The Hill of Devi* (London: Edward Arnold, 1953), p. 155.

26. Robbe-Grillet, p. 156.

27. See Keats' annotation to *Paradise Lost* in Harry Buxton Forman, ed., *The Poetical Works and Other Writings of John Keats* (London: Reeves and Turner, 1883), III, 24.

28. E. M. Forster, 'The Art and Architecture of India', *The Listener*, 10 September 1953, p. 420.
29. Rabindranath Tagore, *Gitanjali* (London: Macmillan, 1913), pp. 36–7. There is, of course, a strong yearning and waiting effect in Tagore's poem also (see, for example, pp. 32–4).
30. E. M. Forster, *Howards End*, ed. Oliver Stallybrass, Abinger edn. (London: Edward Arnold, 1973), p. 79.
31. Robbe-Grillet, pp. 54–5.
32. Robbe-Grillet, pp. 42, 47.
33. Robbe-Grillet, pp. 54–5.
34. See Clement Carlyon, *Early Years and Late Reflections* (London: Whittaker and Company, 1856), I, 193; and cf. Earl Leslie Griggs, ed., *Collected Letters of Samuel Taylor Coleridge* (Oxford: The Clarendon Press, 1956), II, 866. Coleridge says: 'In the Hebrew Poets each Thing has a Life of its own, and yet they are all one Life'.
35. Wordsworth, *The Prelude* (1850), vi, ll. 592–640; Geoffrey Keynes, ed., *Complete Writings of William Blake*, pp. 424–7; and see my *Wordsworth and the Human Heart* (London: Macmillan, 1978), especially pp. 240, 252–3; and *Wordsworth in Time* (London: Faber and Faber, 1979), pp. 158–61.
36. E. J. Morley, ed., *Henry Crabb Robinson on Books and Their Writers* (London: J. M. Dent and Sons Limited, 1938), I, 326.

Part III

The Novels

9 The Advance Beyond Daintiness: Voice and Myth in *Howards End*

Elizabeth Barrett

Behind the rather cozy domesticity of *Howards End* lies a full-scale attempt on Forster's part to create an English myth. His preoccupation with this idea is evident when the narrative voice muses:

> Why has not England a great mythology? Our folklore has never advanced beyond daintiness, and greater melodies about our countryside have all issued through the pipes of Greece. Deep and true as the native imagination can be, it seems to have failed there. It has stopped with the witches and fairies. It cannot vivify one fraction of a summer field or give names to half a dozen stars. England still waits for the supreme moment of her literature — for the great poet who shall voice her, or, better still, for the thousand little poets whose voices shall pass into our common talk.[1]

Forster, very likely, would classify himself among the 'thousand little poets'. Nevertheless, despite his characteristic concern with the significance of littleness, and its domestic manifestations, his attempts at myth-making are constructed around some centre as enormous in its archetypal implications as the fall from heaven to hell.

In *Howards End*, there are two distinct strands which together form the mythical fabric of the work. The first of these is concerned with the physical landscape, itself, and is usually conveyed by means of a narrative voice both overt and straightforward, in the 'poetic tone' noted by a number of critics.[2] The characteristics of this landscape remain more or less fixed, but not static. As a backdrop to the narrowly focused-upon drama of Schlegels, Basts and Wilcoxes, these physical features act as a constant, often ironic, reminder of what has been lost and what can be gained. Sealed inside this Eden is an intense psychological topography, through which the characters must travel, where both heaven and hell are experienced with an acute perception of detail.

In his development of this psychic landscape, Forster, unlike his Victorian predecessors, most notably Arnold, rejects a purely classical vision of tragedy. By adjusting his perspective to 'England', he manages to overcome the almost crippling limitations of a post-Victorian age and to use the materials at hand as the foundations of a local myth with implications that are universal. Such universality gains its momentum from the little worlds of tea-parties and concerts, discussion-groups and family breakfasts; indeed, these events are never without significance. Each word, each action reverberates, each person connects with his neighbour, usually unwittingly, until what seem to be tiny gestures 'performed in isolation' become revealed in their heroic proportions.

It is necessary, then, that the narrative voice appear as one that is both overtly, and sometimes intrusively, omniscient and omnipresent. A story as integrally concerned, as this one is, with the mythical dimensions of human behaviour must be approached by means of a narrator who is able to convince one that he apprehends the whole. If one cannot believe in this narrator's omniscience, one is bound to see only the parts, to fail, in fact, to make the connections. And because the characters' visions are so frequently faulty, although at times they see things clearly, the reader who is not scrupulously careful may find himself, as it were, travelling in the wrong direction.

The primary function of the narrative voice is to act as a most Hermes-like 'guide of souls'[3] through the complexities of Forster's psychological landscape. It directs the characters, most importantly Margaret, in the ways from innocence to experience. Consequently, Thomson's comments to the contrary,[4] Forster's 'good' characters must be morally responsible if their journey is to have any meaning. It is because of their capacity for vision, that it becomes imperative that this ability to see into the heart of things be exercised correctly.

Some characters, however, are more worthy of being tested than others. A case in point is provided by the narrator's comments on the behaviour of Henry Wilcox. When told that Wilcox was 'anxious to be terrible, but had not got it in him' (xxix, 243), one finds it amusing because it diminishes his stature by deflating his sexual ego. One proceeds, then, to the assumption that if he is not so terrible he might be rather nice — this is precisely what Margaret's view has been — and Henry is temporarily let off the adulterous hook. However, when seen from the perspective of Forster's own mythology, such a comment becomes a harsh, albeit humorous, indictment. Wilcox's lack of the 'terrible' excludes him absolutely from any real knowledge or value. Consequently, since Henry and his family are incapable of sustaining any real exertion of a moral or spiritual nature, the onus of responsibility must fall on those such as Margaret. The greater shortcoming, then, from Forster's point of view, lies not in Henry's insignificance but in Margaret's failure to perceive it. Authorial values become most clear when the point of view of narrator and character are juxtaposed. Sometimes their voices merge; more often they do not.

In *Howards End*, it is the narrative voice which most consistently conveys the author's viewpoints and in order to do so it draws upon four distinct characteristics. First, it speaks overtly for itself. This is the voice most obviously concerned with the description of the physical landscape associated with this myth: a good example presents itself in the opening paragraphs of Chapter 11. Mrs Wilcox has died and been buried and, because there is no one else to do it, the narrative voice delivers the elegy. As it speaks, it becomes apparent that there is joy in Ruth's death, the 'exaltation' of the earth gathering its own.

The woodcutter knows this instinctively. Watching over the funeral, perched up in a tree, somehow an inseparable part of that tree, he both dignifies Mrs Wilcox's death, in a way impossible for her family to comprehend, and insists through his presence alone on the joy of continuity: 'With a grunt, he descended, his thoughts dwelling no longer on death, but on love, for he was mating' (xi, 87). What *furor* that statement seems to have caused.[5] However, Forster does not view this woodcutter with disdain; on the contrary, the presence of this eminently natural man acts as something of a Greek chorus praising Ruth Wilcox and offering a commentary on the significance of her life.

In this particularly English atmosphere of romance, with its aura of an exhilarating and eternal battle between life and death, there is an ironic undercutting of the ways in which Wilcoxes express sorrow. Life and death are not the connected forces in Henry's mind; he only knows the world of marriages and funerals. The narrative voice, on the other hand, forges connections everywhere: between, for example, Margaret and the woodcutter. *He* takes *her* chrysanthemums to celebrate his 'night of joy'. She, then, by association must become admitted to the charmed circle of mythical figures and the ticket of admission has been her instinct.

Instinct is given but knowledge is earned. And since the search for experience is such an arduous one, both character and reader must have a reliable, although not always straightforward, guide. The technique used by Forster, in his development of the relation between voice and character, is a most effective one: he 'throws' a voice — not necessarily his own — into his character's mouth, much in the manner of a ventriloquist speaking through his 'dummy'. This brings us to this narrative voice's second characteristic: the character — most often Margaret — *appears* to speak for the author but in fact does not.[6] A look at one of her well-known speeches will illustrate what I mean:

> . . . You and I and the Wilcoxes stand upon money as upon islands. It is so firm beneath our feet that we forget its very existence. It is only when we see someone near us tottering that we realize all that an independent income means. Last night, when we were all talking up here round the fire, I began to think that the very soul of the world is economic, and that the lowest abyss is not the absence of love, but the absence of coin.
>
> (vii, 58).

From Forster's point of view, there is no question that the separation of man from money is a peculiarly English version of the ancient estrangement between man and God. However, it is not his voice, although it sounds rather like it, which defines the abyss as the 'absence of coin'. For to define hell as the absence of coin is to say that heaven is found in the presence of money. Unlike Margaret, what he mourns most must be the 'absence of love'.

At this point, Margaret cannot understand that by defining the abyss as she does, by acting as a spokeswoman for some English reality, she is, in fact, only emphasizing the degree to which she is learning to see the world through Wilcox eyes. Her assertion, then, is intimately bound up in a pattern of cause and effect with her rather arbitrary insistence, only moments before, that the 'Wilcox nerve' in Helen is dead. For all of her genuinely admirable qualities, Margaret has the kind of blindspot so characteristic of the 'English' hero: she is a little too ready to dismiss the 'doors of heaven'. An ironic contrast must be inferred between her statement regarding the absence of coin and her management — excellent manager she — of a situation in which Paul Wilcox, for one, finally and absolutely 'counts no more'.

The third characteristic of the narrative voice presents an instructive discrepancy between character and author that is even more subtle than the one just discussed: Margaret appears *not* to be speaking for Forster but if one carefully pays attention it is possible to hear his distinctly ironic tones. Furthermore, the intensity with which one must listen to hear his voice reinforces the importance of the moral choices confronting the heroine. Intense, however, need not mean solemn and the moment in question provides a very good example of the joke-playing aspect of the guide's personality.

Oniton Grange is the scene of a kind of dress rehearsal of Margaret's and Henry's marriage. And with their growing intimacy, if one can apply such a word to a Wilcox, comes a certain amount of moral smugness. Although Margaret appears rather ashamed of her evasive strategies for getting her husband-to-be to do what he ought, she is, in fact, quite proud of her ability to manage him. Patting herself on the back, so to speak, she concludes — fatal error: 'In dealing with a Wilcox, how tempting it was to lapse from comradeship, and to give him the kind of woman that he desired!' (xxvi, 226).

What Margaret considers to be the height of domestic diplomacy, becomes, when seen through the perspective provided by the narrative voice, something closer to outright dishonesty. And to underscore the degree to which she is moving, very rapidly indeed, towards the Wilcox world and away from Helen, Forster indulges in some ironic manipulation. One can hear Margaret's self-satisfied 'kind of woman that he desired' as a comment belonging to the narrative voice, so that what follows next is painfully appropriate.

Musing on the discrepancy between 'things as they are and as they ought to be', Margaret 'descends a mound' (xxvi, 228) and has a nasty little bump into reality: Jacky Bast. This, Forster seems to be saying, is what I mean by temptation and this is *really* the kind of woman Henry Wilcox desires. Here is authorial string-pulling at its most effective. It would seem that we readers are the witnesses to some unpleasant behaviour all round and this joke-playing narrator is as guilty as anyone else. However, the point is made: the complete estrangement between Margaret and Forster is intended to parallel the degree of separation between the pair who most matter — the sisters.

Characteristically, Forster makes the descent a tiny one and the fall itself is into the most hellish of conditions: confusion, banality and, most of all, squalor. As Margaret goes down from that mound a kind of incremental irony must accrue to her temptation, taking as it does the pathetic form of Jacky, 'a piece of cake in one hand, an empty champagne glass in the other, doing no harm to anybody' (xxvi, 228). Indeed, the harm which follows, and it is considerable, becomes part of *Margaret's* abdication of moral responsibility — most significantly in her writing of an acutely Wilcoxian letter to Helen, a letter which is both dishonest and, ultimately, deadly.

Look for a moment at its results. Helen is impelled to sleep with Leonard, an event which, as part of a complex chain of consequence, leads to his death. Of course, he is not actually murdered, which would be a burden of guilt too great for the sisters to sustain; were that the case, the work would be fatally weighted down. Rather, he only appears to be violently slain because the narrative voice tells us that Leonard's remorse 'cuts away', that he is 'driven straight through', that it is a 'knife that probes' (xli, 313). Such comments do more than act as a symbolic preparation for the blow from Charles. One becomes very nearly convinced that Charles actually runs him through the heart. All this focuses attention on Leonard: as his stature as tragic hero grows, Charles's dwindles away into the insignificance it deserves. Thus: Margaret writes a letter; Leonard dies. But he also gains a dignity, a dimension of greatness in death which is utterly denied him in life. And, from a structural point of view, he fathers the new life that will so appropriately come to be emblematic of the revivified relationship between the sisters.

It must be emphasized that the continuous authorial correction of Margaret's perceptions of herself occurs precisely because of her virtues, because of her huge capacity for seeing the unseen. The considerable importance that a number of humanist critics[7] have attached to her increasing attempts to connect the 'prose and the passion', to integrate Wilcoxes and Schlegels, is based for the most part upon a reading of Margaret's character by the same light with which she sees herself. However, as Forster points out again and again, that light may be faulty. Connection, in so far as Margaret is concerned during the time of her visit to Oniton Grange, is purely a matter of bridging the gulf between Henry as he is and Henry as he ought to be. It does not take into account the subtle, and most significant, relationships that have been implied by the authorial voice: those between Margaret and Jacky for example, or the similarity of Ruth Wilcox's position and that of Leonard Bast.

As one moves through the narrative, sharing the omniscient and omnipresent vantage point presented by this Forsterian voice, the real meaning of the relation between prose and passion becomes clearer. Indeed, the fusion of the two lies at the heart of Forster's myth-making. The testing of Margaret, or of any other character, is undertaken in order to facilitate connection. And, although Margaret's flaw, her weakness, lies in her undisputable prosiness, such prosiness is only 'bad' in so far as it inhibits her ability to connect with passion.

One can hardly call the delightful opening to Chapter 5 passionate, nor, with the possible exception of Helen who would do well with a little more prose, are the people who are attending this concert. But the passion is there. It is there, as Forster makes abundantly clear, in the music itself. It is somewhere else, too, and this is where the novelist's role comes in. For the basic premise upon which *Howards End* is constructed is this: 'How interesting that row of people was!' (v, 30). Here is the essential contradiction in Forster's mythology. The myth of England is, to him, a passionate one because he cares for it so deeply; it is animated by his interest. However, since this particular col-lection of people *are* English, for the most part they will be uncomfortable with grand gestures, violent landscapes, the overwhelming manifestations of emotion. Consequently, when Margaret has her moment of passionate apprehension, it will be no less intense for being small, intimate, quiet, and surrounded by an atmosphere of all-encompassing domesticity.

The most significant culmination of the connective pattern occurs in the coming together of the sisters and, in their reunion, at Howards End, they unite many of those mythical elements Forster associates with England. The shared past, for example, to which the two women return, is a past deeply rooted in the life of common objects. As they move back, through remembrance, to their childhoods, there is a parallel motion towards the well-springs of vision. 'The importance of youthful experience is one of Forster's main themes' says Thomson, and 'the insights and revelations of youth will be associated with specific experiences, specific persons and places. But for a certain number of years . . . they may flow into and illuminate some new locality or situation'.[8] This is precisely what happens and the luminosity of place, so characteristic of the house, spills over and infuses its contents as well.

This brings us to the fourth characteristic of the narrative voice: Margaret really does speak for Forster and her voice and point of view merge completely with the narrator's. His presence is not at all intrusive; for the most part he leaves the sisters on their own and his voice is interjected only to confirm what has already been dramatized: the splendour of shared vision and its accompanying transfiguration of the inanimate. As he joins his words to theirs, his words express their thoughts:

> And the triviality faded from their faces, though it left something behind — the knowledge that they never could be parted because their love was rooted in common things. Explanations and appeals had failed; they had tried for a common meeting ground, and had only made each other unhappy. And all the time their salvation was lying around them — the past sanctifying the present; the present, with wild heart-throb, declaring that there would, after all, be a future, with laughter and the voices of children. Helen, still smiling, came up to her sister. She said, 'It is always Meg'. They looked into each others' eyes. The inner life had paid.   (xxxvii, 296).

Stylistically, this final sentence is characteristic of Forster, in its understatement, its matter of factness, and its evocation of powerful affection. Indeed, it is a particularly effective example of how the contradictions inherent in an English mythology can be resolved; this, in effect, is what he believes. Prose and passion *are* connected, more than connected, as each takes on the other's attributes. The metaphor of England's commerce which has served as a structural principle of the work becomes transfigured by love. Those opposing forces — the inner life and the cash nexus — actually absorb each other's power.

Now that a common meeting ground has been earned, what Frye calls the 'broken current of memory'[9] is re-established. With this reconnection of the sources of power it becomes obvious that this meeting ground is not half way between anything; rather it is a wholly inclusive universe with extraordinary life-giving quali-ties. Even something as apparently ordinary as a dining-room chair, for example, can become transformed into something so alive as to seem to be almost breathing as when Helen says 'Their dear little backs are quite warm' (xxxvii, 294).

In Forster's mythology, then, such a common domestic object becomes a kind of sacred vessel and in doing so acts as an embodiment of the spiritual and psychological states of the person to whom it is attached. This atmosphere of domestic coziness, suggesting as it does a sense of enclosure and womb-like security, contrasts sharply with its satanic opposite — the dark, stuffy, imprisoning London, where men like Leonard live not on the earth but under it. And if this myth creates a universe that is both wholly inclusive and wholly English, it also intimates a human conditon that has the possibility of being perpetually embryonic.

Although the final picture is most definitely one of 'opening out', one must still question the significance of the material from which it has been constructed. In other words: can the embryonic coziness, the intrinsic littleness of English myth — and remember it is the little poets who are to voice it — provide the same aesthetic and emotional satisfaction as its classical and religious counterparts?

The development of *Howards End* rests on a most paradoxical foundation. On the one hand one is presented with extremely sophisticated, and successful, rhetorical techniques such as the handling of a multifaceted narrative voice. On the other hand, however, Forster's mythical structure reveals what one might call something approaching timidity, or perhaps reticence is the better word, particularly in comparison with the emotional confidence displayed by *The Longest Journey* and *A Passage to India*. In *The Longest Journey*, for instance, the fusion of classical myth with the characteristically detailed sense of English domesticity raises that work to the level of magic. That an incompetent hero can become a tragic one — as is the case with Rickie Elliot — somehow reinforces one's need to believe in the largeness of life.

Since the importance of personal relationships is emphasized throughout *Howards End*, there is one final aspect of Forster's attempt at making an English myth that should be considered: the nature of these human connections. It is obvious that the novels are not particularly approving of marriage; it is even more apparent that many of the short stories, the Italian novels, *The Longest Journey*, *Maurice* and *A Passage to India* imply that some, if not all, of the major relationships are likely to be between members of the same sex. However, in *Howards End* there are none of the strong sexual overtones of the earlier works: the closest one comes to the erotic is in the brief encounter of Helen and Paul in the garden.

This turning away from sexual tension — even in its most subtle manifestations — might have something to do with that timidity just noted. Or, more possibly, it is not so much a timidity, a fear, as a faltering of spirit, a kind of emotional exhaustion. Forster's England had done much, as he knew, to facilitate the friendly growth of affection; what it evaded was knowledge of physical love, especially between those of the same sex. The closeness of the two siblings, then, might be seen as a mechanism of displacement. In any case, the sisters' relationship is the significant one in *Howards End*. If nothing else it provides the pair pattern that is archetypally romantic. All else is subsumed by their movements of separation and reunion.

What is not being suggested in this emphasis on the sisters' connection is the point that Stone makes: that together these women are innately destructive and act out their roles as destroyers of men. His argument sees the ending in the hayfields as a travesty of harmony: 'The book ends with the two girls and their misbegotten heir in complete and undisputed possession of Howards End, in its real as well as its spiritual estate — and with all the human creatures they connected with either maimed, imprisoned, or dead. Once again things had gone on until there were no more men'.[10] This sounds rather like those earlier complaints that, in *The Longest Journey*, Forster killed off almost half of his fictional population.

Perhaps some of the reasons for this uneasy and most negative reading can be found in Stone's introductory comment. Suggesting that Forster may be 'hiding out' behind the guise of femininity, he goes on to argue that this 'oblique and feminine way of meeting opposition would suggest that Forster may be facing the great world more out of duty than inclination. Such possibilities make one question whether Forster will be able to give the problem of connection, especially connection between men and women, a fair trial . . . Forster's fictional transvestism does not increase our confidence that he will be an impartial mediator'.[11] Now, there may be something in this idea of Forster 'facing the great world more out of duty than inclination'. It would explain, in part, why there seems to be this desire to create a myth so embryonic in its coziness and sense of self-protection. However, there is still a serious problem with Stone's statement, for he starts like so many others from the premise that the only significant connection is that which occurs between women and men.

By taking most of what Margaret Schlegel says at face value and by making the unexamined assumption that her comments are almost always given authorial approval, many critics have placed emphasis on her attempts to connect with Henry Wilcox. I am not for one moment suggesting that her love for him is not a real and valuable one. What I would argue is that her reconciliation with Helen correctly aligns her loyalties, in so far as Forster is concerned, and in doing so provides the enlarging faculties of compassion which can take in a broken old man. But to say, as does Stone, that she and Helen are responsible for the Wilcox collapse is to ignore the directions provided by the narrative voice.

The virtuosity with which Forster uses this voice endows it with a presence, a personality if you will, both unique and endearing. And if the England behind Forster's myth-making is not always the stuff of great heroes, any limitations encountered might lie not so much in the mythic structure apprehended by his own imagination as in the materials provided by the English themselves. However, although Forster seems to imply that it is hard, and gets harder, to be passionate in a country, even in a landscape, so distrustful of the grand gesture, a very considerable compensation comes about through the unfailing resources of affection and humour. It is so typical of him that, after both character and reader have been conducted through an often hazardous, and sometimes agonizingly painful journey through experience, the playful aspect of his Hermes-like guide should triumph.

There is one final display of the ventriloquist's art. Unhappiness is over, order is restored, and surely it is not only Helen one hears saying: 'We've seen to the very end, and it'll be such a crop of hay as never!' (xliv, 340). Such a crop of hay, indeed.

NOTES

1. E. M. Forster, *Howards End*, ed. Oliver Stallybrass, Abinger edn. (London: Edward Arnold, 1973), p. 264.

2. Several critics have noted that the narrative voice has two distinct tones: the poetic and the humorously ironic in the manner of Jane Austen. Among them are Malcolm Bradbury, 'E. M. Forster's *Howards End*', *The Critical Quarterly*, IV (1962), 229–41; Francis Gillen, '*Howards End* and the Neglected Narrator', *Novel*, 3 (1970), 139–52; J. L. VanDe Vyvere, 'The Mediatorial Voice of the Narrator in E. M. Forster's *Howards End*', *Journal of Narrative Technique*, 6 (1976), 204–16.

3. See Judith S. Herz, 'The Narrator as Hermes: A Study of the Early Short Fiction', *E. M. Forster: A Human Exploration*, ed. G. K. Das and John Beer (London: Macmillan, 1979), pp. 17–28.

4. George H. Thomson, *The Fiction of E. M. Forster* (Detroit: Wayne State University Press, 1967). Thomson states — correctly I think — 'why [Forster] did not portray his bad people as morally responsible beings. To have done so would have given them too great a stature and spoiled the satire'. However, when he discusses the moral dimensions of the 'good' characters, it could be suggested that he makes an error. He says '. . . they resemble the bad people in this one respect only, that they are not morally responsible because their moments of vision are given. Though they are worthy of the revelation that comes to them, they cannot be said quite to have earned it' (p. 50).

5. For an example of an attack on Forster's 'élitist' attitude, see Kinley Roby, 'Irony and the Narrative Voice in *Howards End*', *Journal of Narrative Technique*, 2 (1972), p. 119.

6. Many critics assume, along with Stone, that 'Margaret can be said to speak for Forster'. She can do so, of course, but frequently does not. See Bradbury; Frederick C. Crews, *The Perils of Humanism* (Princeton, N.J.: Princeton University Press, 1962); Wilfred Stone, *The Cave and the Mountain* (Stanford, California: Stanford University Press, 1966); and VanDe Vyvere.

7. Bradbury; Crews; Frederick P. W. McDowell, '"The Mild Intellectual Light": Idea and Theme in *Howards End*', *PMLA*, LXXIV (1959), 453–63 and 'E. M. Forster: Romancer or Realist?', *English Literature in Transition*, XI: 2 (1968), 103–22; VanDe Vyvere.

8. Thomson, p. 53.

9. Northrop Frye, *The Secular Scripture: A Study of the Structure of Romance* (Cambridge, Mass.: Harvard University Press, 1976).

10. Stone, p. 263.

11. Stone, p. 237.

10 The Role of the Essayist-Commentator in *Howards End*

Paul R. Rivenberg

Were Henry James to have a celestial tea party, inviting Henry Fielding, Laurence Sterne, Jane Austen, Emily Brontë, George Eliot, William Makepeace Thackeray, Joseph Conrad and E. M. Forster, no doubt, as James himself might say, contradiction would grow 'young again over tea cups and cigars'.[1] One can imagine the restless spoons if the conversation turned to the role of the narrator in the novel. James, of course, would advocate viewing the actions of the story through a central intelligence, whose perspective would rule out the possibility of even an occasional authorial intrusion. Jane Austen and George Eliot would talk sense, Austen sympathizing with Eliot's need to establish, through authorial comment, norms against which her characters could be measured, and confessing that she too occasionally resorts to this tactic, though not nearly as often nor as extensively as Eliot. Miss Brontë might wait half the afternoon for Conrad to arrive, to ask whether her multiple and unreliable narrators in *Wuthering Heights* inspired techniques in his own fiction. Conrad, however, would not show up, preferring to hear about such parties second hand. Sterne would wait for Thackeray to reconsider his words against *Tristram Shandy*, and to realize how much the intrusive narrator of *Vanity Fair* has in common with Tristram.[2] Thackeray, however, would be busy defending himself, along with Fielding, against E. M. Forster, who, in *Aspects of the Novel*, criticizes their 'bar-parlour chattiness', noting that the intimacy this method allows 'is gained . . . at the expense of illusion and nobility'.[3]

That Forster should fault Thackeray and Fielding for the

intrusive nature of their narrators may seem a case of 'physician heal thyself' to those who have read *Howards End*, wherein the narrator, more persistently than in any of Forster's novels, stops the action to comment himself, in paragraph essays, in mid-paragraph, and in even in mid-sentence. Forster objects, however, not to authorial comment in general, as James does, but specifically to Fielding's and Thackeray's habit of exposing their own opinions of their characters. In *Aspects of the Novel* he explains, 'To take your reader into your confidence about the universe is a different thing. It is not dangerous for a novelist to draw back from his characters, as Hardy and Conrad do, and to generalize about the conditions under which he thinks life is carried on. It is confidences about the individual people that do harm, and beckon the reader away from the people to an examination of the novelist's mind' (*Aspects*, 57). That this reader has been beckoned away from the people to examine Forster's mind, or rather the mind of the essayist-commentator of *Howards End*, is perhaps an indication that Forster's narrator has more in common with those of Fielding and Thackeray than Forster would care to believe. We are prompted to ask if the narrator of *Howards End*, although calling attention to himself, avoids destroying the 'illusion and nobility' of the novel. Are his essays and commentaries integral to the work? Do they serve a purpose, or are they merely the undisciplined ramblings of an author who, having written essays since 1900, cannot help but riddle his novel with authorial comment?

That Forster felt comfortable with the essay as a form through which to express himself is evident even before the turn of the century. At the age of fifteen this form came naturally to him as a means of presenting Rooksnest, the house in which he had lived since the age of five. Although he originally wrote the essay in 1894, he added to it in 1901 — leaving off in mid-sentence — and again in 1947, at which point the essay becomes a selection of letters pertaining to the house. The additions lend this semi-autobiographical work an accidental air of Shandyan confusion.

Oliver Stallybrass suggested that Howards End is 'a conscious replica of Rooksnest',[4] observing that before the Forsters moved in, the house had been known as Howards. Certainly there are striking parallels between the Rooksnest of this early essay and the Howards End of the novel, the most significant being the wych-elm. The description of the tree in the essay, which mentions the fangs embedded in the trunk four feet from the ground and which ponders the bark's power to cure toothache, is rendered dramatically in the novel, in a conversation between Margaret and Mrs Wilcox (viii, 69).

Howards End further echoes this essay on a stylistic level. At fifteen years of age Forster is already using a conversational style, frankly admitting to his readers his uncertainty as to where to begin. In the second paragraph he writes, 'I suppose I had better begin with a description of the house', and in the third, 'I don't know what to speak about first but will perhaps tell about the house'.[5] The reader senses the same uncertainty in the opening sentence of *Howards End*: 'One may as well begin with Helen's letters to her sister' (i, 1). As in the 'Rooksnest' essay, the beginning, Helen's letter, is ultimately a description of the house.

Although he stopped writing novels in 1924 with *A Passage to India*, Forster wrote essays throughout his life, collecting many of them in two volumes, *Abinger Harvest* (1936) and *Two Cheers for Democracy* (1951). Comparing *Howards End* with these two collections one can see that Forster's concerns in the interjected essays of the novel are the same as those of some of his fully developed essays. Such topics as places, literature, music and personal relations are particularly likely to provoke Forster's editorial impulse.

In *Two Cheers for Democracy* Forster devotes ten essays to depicting places. His essay 'London is a Muddle' (1937) echoes commentary in Chapter 13 of *Howards End*. The premise of 'London is a Muddle' is that 'London is full of injustice, joylessness, and smugness, but there is good temper and rebelliousness in her too', that all in all the famous city is 'the muddle which need not be upleasant'.[6] It shows London to be a constantly changing city, and deals particularly with the architectural muddle, the tearing down and building up which has made London the sometimes charming, sometimes contemptible incongruity that is. Evidently this older Forster is milder than the Forster who in *Howards End* begins to comment by saying that 'To speak against London is no longer fashionable' (xiii, 106), and then proceeds to speak against her. The novel's commentator views London only as a bad muddle. If he admits that 'London fascinates' it is only because 'One visualizes it as a tract of quivering grey, intelligent without purpose, and excitable without love; as a spirit which has altered before it can be chronicled; as a heart that certainly beats, but with no pulsation of humanity' (xiii, 106). Forster sympathizes with all humanity caught in the flux of the ever-changing city, and in a pastoral mood waits for the public to forsake the cosmopolis for the country.

Forster artistically integrates this essay into the body of his novel by relating it, in the succeeding paragraph, to Margaret and her personal experience in the city. Margaret's troubled thoughts of how her home, Wickham Place, will eventually be destroyed and replaced by Babylonian flats, solidify the poetic-philosophic statement of the preceding paragraph: 'In the streets of the city she noted for the first time the architecture of hurry, and heard the language of hurry on the mouths of its inhabitants . . . . The particular millionaire who owned the freehold of Wickham Place, and desired to erect Babylonian flats upon it — what right had he to stir so large a portion of the quivering jelly' (xiii, 107). Margaret's personal worries, then, are a reflection of Forster's more general concern for humanity.

Art provides a relatively easy escape from London's 'quivering grey'. Music is one art form which strikes an editorial chord in Forster. In *A Room With A View*, the narrator tells the story fairly unobtrusively until he reaches the chapter entitled 'Music, Violets and the Letter S', at which point he cannot resist beating the kettledrums of commentary. As might be expected, many of his collected essays deal with this subject. The essay entitled 'Not Listening to Music' (1939) reflects Forster's commentary in Chapter 5 of *Howards End*. Forster begins his essay describing the temptation he suffers every time he enters a concert hall — to become inattentive. Like Helen he finds the concert situation a source for endless distractions. Just as Helen looks around her and ponders the horror of marrying a man like the cupids which decorate the ceiling, Forster, in 'Not Listening to Music', claims to be distracted by 'the tilt of the soprano's chin or chins . . . the backs of the chairs; the bumps on the ceiling; the extreme physical ugliness of the audience' (*TCD*, 122).

In the essay Forster also describes himself going through the same process of visualizing music which Helen goes through in the novel. He separates music into two groups — 'music that reminds me of something', and 'music itself' — confessing that he, in the early days of his musical appreciation, preferred the former. He says, 'When music reminded me of something which was not music, I supposed it was getting me somewhere.''How like Monet!" I thought when listening to Debussy, and "How like Debussy!" when looking at Monet. I translated sounds into colours, saw the piccolo as apple-green, and the trumpets as scarlet' (*TCD*, 124). Although he does not record Helen's vision of Goblins in Beethoven's Fifth, he does note that 'the slow start of Beethoven's Seventh Symphony invokes a gray-green tapestry of hunting scenes' (*TCD*, 123). Admitting his attraction to 'music which reminds me of something', Forster clearly favours 'music itself' (*TCD*, 122).

Chapter 5 in *Howards End* can be seen in part as a dramatized essay, its subject being the same as that in 'Not Listening to Music'. In the novel Forster establishes the two sides of the musical question in Helen and Margaret. Although the sisters do not debate the issue directly, Forster sets up the tension of debate (as he did in 'Not Listening to Music') by succeeding Helen's vision of Goblins in Beethoven's Fifth with Margaret's monologue to Leonard Bast about the mistake of seeing pictures in music. If Forster is the judge, however, neither sister wins. His description of Helen's interpretation of music implies that it is limited. He says, 'The notes meant this and that to her, and they could have no other meaning, and life could have no other meaning' (v, 32). Margaret too is limited by her inability to see value in any other artistic viewpoint. Like Forster, Margaret uses Debussy and Monet to make her point, saying, 'If Monet's really Debussy and Debussy's really Monet, neither gentleman is worth his salt — that's my opinion' (v, 36). One senses that Forster, in *Howards End*, is balanced somewhere between the two views, though leaning as always towards Margaret's, just as in 'Not Listening to Music' he admits the superiority of 'music itself', without denying the value of 'music that reminds me of something'.

If Margaret's views are not exactly those of Forster in this scene, they are at most other points in the novel. By merging Margaret's thoughts with those of the essayist-commentator, Forster makes her an extension of himself. She is well-suited for this responsibility, for she is, in effect, an essayist-commentator herself. She speaks in essays. Her monologue on the proper way to listen to music is just one example of the way 'Miss Schlegel puts everything splendidly' (ix, 73). Margaret even admits the essay-like quality of her talk when, after telling her aunt how the middle class stands 'upon money as upon islands', she says, 'While I have talked theories you have done the flowers' (vii, 58, 59).

That Margaret should speak essays seems somehow humorously appropriate in relation to the way she categorizes her aunt and her father, two people responsible for her upbringing. Margaret sees her aunt and Frieda as Journalism. Like newspapers they chatter about the possibility of something happening until they make it inevitable. Her father, on the other hand, 'with all his defects and wrong-headedness, had been Literature . . .' (vii, 60). If we were to categorize Margaret we would label her Essay, a form common to both Journalism and Literature. Margaret, however, is clearly her father's daughter, her essays being, like Forster's, more poetic than editorial.

While not formally categorizing herself as Essay, Margaret does compare herself, in her love-making, to prose. She tells her sister, '. . . there is the widest gulf between my love-making and yours. Yours was romance; mine will be prose. I'm not running it down — a very good kind of prose, but well considered, well thought out' (xix, 171). Her private prose relationship with Mr Wilcox could be compared to Forster's prose relationship with all Englishmen in his essay 'Notes on the English Character' (1920). Blaming the public school system for sending its pupils out into the world with undeveloped hearts, he says 'it is not that the Englishman can't feel — it is that he is afraid to feel',[7] Mr Wilcox is one such product of the public school system. Like Forster, Margaret understands all Mr Wilcox's faults, but does not blame him. She explains to Helen, 'He's afraid of emotion. He cares too much about success, too little about the past. His sympathy lacks poetry, and so isn't sympathy really' (xix, 171). His character is incomplete. Forster, in his essay, observes this characteristic in all his countrymen. The Englishman is necessarily incomplete because the true emotions inside him are distanced from his reserved, unsympathetic surface. In *Howards End* Forster implied, through Margaret, that to become complete one must connect 'the prose in us with the passion' (xx, 183). Margaret, creating this balance within herself, is able to connect outward with humanity. Mr Wilcox, who has walled his passion within himself, must remain incomplete.[8]

Margaret is so often motivated by Forsterian ideals that she can be viewed as a dramatized incarnation of the novel's essayist-commentator. When she speaks or thinks she exhibits not only the characteristics of an essayist in general, but the specific characteristic of Forster. She seems to agree with the commentary the essayist offers in the novel, her own thoughts often merging with or expanding on this.

This merging with Forster, however, does not make Margaret the constant standard by which the other characters are to be measured. To believe this would be to ignore her complexity and growth. Ironically, the same qualities that make her an ideal Forsterian commentator work against this growth. Margaret's wit, her love for literature and enthusiasm for current ideas, attract her to diversions and discussion groups which are at best intellectual pastimes. Just as Forster criticizes Bast for mistaking literature for life, for crediting his all-night walk to 'reading something of Richard Jeffries' (xiv, 118), he would criticize Margaret if she were to dwell on contemporary issues and hypothetical questions without moving beyond them to the problems of her own life. Forster applauds her when she begins 'to "miss" new movements, and to spend her time rereading or thinking', noting, 'she had outgrown stimulants and was passing from words to things . . . some closing of the gates is inevitable after thirty, if the mind is to become a creative power' (xxxi, 259). These words curiously echo a passage from 'A Note on the Way' (1934), in which Forster says, 'The arts are not drugs. They are not guaranteed to act when taken. Something as mysterious as the creative impulse has to be released before they can prop our minds' (*AH*, 88).[9] Margaret is beginning to allow this impulse to take hold, and is moving away from her role as clever, idealistic commentator, to become a woman who can both comment and creatively work her ideals into the realities with which she must cope.

Her growth reflects the movement in the final paragraph of 'Not Listening to Music', in which Forster observes that his own uncertain attempts at playing the piano help him to remain attentive to music during a concert. In a sense, Margaret is moving, like Forster, from the audience to the piano, from the public seat of a spectator to a private practice room. One senses that the narrator of *Howards End* would also like to move from the role of spectator to the role of participant.

To become such a participant, Forster would have had to develop a first-person stance either as himself or as a persona. Some critics, in an attempt to free the novel from authorial intrusion, suggest that Forster has in fact created a fictional persona in the novel.[10] This theory is misleading. The novel's commentary is so often comparable to the collected essays that the novel's narrator must be Forster himself. James might sigh and insist that such constant reminders of the creator behind the fiction will destroy for the reader the illusion of the novel. Francis Gillen, in his article '*Howards End* and the Neglected Narrator',[11] voices this argument, referring to those times when the narrator addresses the reader so directly or unexpectedly that the reader becomes distracted from the fiction.[12] Forster, however, is not out to destroy the illusion, just to pierce it. Had he wanted to destroy it completely, Forster, instead of making general comments about London or the dreariness of music halls, could have mentioned his own specific experiences — his conversations, his schooling, his friends — as he sometimes does in the collected essays. This would have allowed him a degree of participation and growth in the novel which his chosen point-of-view denies him. It would also have made him too much a first-person narrator to coincide with his omniscience. The conflict between the author's omniscience and his first-person point of view would have destroyed the reader's faith in the reality of the lives presented in the novel. *Howards End* would have read more like an essay heavily dependent for examples on a cast of contrived characters and hypothetical situations. Consequently, the reader's interest in and involvement with the story would have suffered. Forster's intrusions instead provide just enough tension to jar the reader into questioning the distinction between literature and life, an important distinction to make if the reader is to see literature not as a stimulating end in itself, but as a potential spark to his own creativity.

The number of essays in *Howards End* may convince some readers that the novel is essentially an essay in disguise, when it is simply the impulse behind the novel and the essays which is the same — an impulse to connect. Forster an essayist-commentator is a connector. He cannot use a middleman to reach his audience. He cannot, like Henry James, filter everything through a central intelligence who will endow it with the objectivity of drama. His contact with the reader must be direct, as it is in his essays. In *Howards End*, just as Margaret tries to break down the wall Mr Wilcox has built to protect his emotions, Forster tries to break down the wall between the narrator and the reader. He tries to connect directly with his audience through both interjected essays and brief, disruptive comments.

These interjections allow Forster to participate in the life of the story as much as is possible without sacrificing his omniscience to a first-person point of view. Only through an identification with Margaret can he leave the spectator world of the essayist-commentator, and enter the active life of the novel. This explains why Margaret is so much a Forsterian commentator herself. Through Margaret, even in the dramatic sections of the novel in which the essayist-commentator is silent, Forster has a voice, and can connect with the reader. In effect, then, Margaret's attempt to connect with Mr Wilcox and Leonard Bast suggests Forster's own attempt to connect with his audience. Just as Margaret hopes, by connecting with others, to realize eventually the comradeship of mankind, Forster perhaps hopes that his readers, by connecting with him, will release that 'creative impulse' he describes in 'A Note of the Way', and consequently will be pushed by their own feelings to connect outward. Indeed, Forster had made the distinction between life and literature clear enough in *Howards End* that, if his readers are inspired to connect after reading the novel, they should not say, as Leonard Bast might, 'Curious it should all come from reading something of E. M. Forster'.

NOTES

1. Henry James, *What Maisie Knew*, in *The Novels and Tales of Henry James*, New York Edition, XI (New York: Charles Scribner's Sons, 1908), pp. 6–7.

2. William Makepeace Thackeray, 'Sterne and Goldsmith', in *The Works of William Makepeace Thackeray*, ed. George D. Sproul, XXVI (New York: The University Press, Cambridge, 1904), p. 232. Thackeray's observation that Sterne 'never lets his reader alone' can as easily describe the intrusive nature of his own narrator in *Vanity Fair*.

3. E. M. Forster, *Aspects of the Novel*, ed. Oliver Stallybrass, Abinger edn. (London: Edward Arnold, 1974), p. 57.

4. See the introduction to E. M. Forster, *Howards End*, ed. Oliver Stallybrass, Abinger edn. (London: Edward Arnold, 1973), p. vii.

5. See the appendix to *Howards End*, p. 341.

6. E. M. Forster, 'London is a Muddle', *Two Cheers for Democracy*, ed. Oliver Stallybrass, Abinger edn. (London: Edward Arnold, 1972), pp. 350, 352.

7. E. M. Forster, *Abinger Harvest* (London: Edward Arnold, 1961), p. 13.

8. For other Forsterian comments on connection and personal relations in *HE*, see the 'tragedy of preparedness' essay (p. 104) and the 'Only connect' commentary (p. 183).

9. In *Howards End* Forster most strongly defines this approach to the arts in relation to Leonard Bast. For Leonard literature is a drug. He sits on the edge of gentility and waits for Ruskin to take effect. Although he experiences no 'creative impulse' when he reads 'The Stones of Venice' he is satisfied that this is a step in the direction of self-improvement.

10. Kinley E. Roby, 'Irony and the Narrative Voice in *Howards End*', *The Journal of Narrative Technique*, II (May 1972), 116–24. Roby suggests that the narrator is a condescending, prejudiced woman.

11. Francis Gillen, '*Howards End* and the Neglected Narrator', *Novel*, III (Winter 1970), 139–52.

12. The character of these interjections is perhaps best defined by listing a few examples:

    To Margaret — I hope it will not set the reader against her — the station of King's Cross had always suggested Infinity (ii, 9).

    If you think this is ridiculous, remember that it is not Margaret who is telling you about it; and let me hasten to add that they were in plenty of time for the train . . . (ii, 9).

    [Mrs Munt in the car with Charles Wilcox]: Mounting by her side, he put on gloves and spectacles, and off they drove, the bearded porter — life is a mysterious business — looking after them with admiration (iii, 15).

    [Margaret and Helen laughing upon contemplating the image of Queen Victoria in a 'clinging Liberty tea gown']: Bursts of disloyal laughter — you must remember that they are half German — greeted these suggestions . . . (v, 41).

11 Moments in the Greenwood: *Maurice* in Context

Ira Bruce Nadel

Contrary to E. M. Forster's private statements, the literary and personal influences that shaped his idea of homosexuality in *Maurice* were not unique. They reflected, in fact, a broader social and intellectual milieu that alternately inhibited and stimulated the behaviour and creativity of many writers at the beginning of the twentieth century. The nature of that climate and its impact on Forster is the subject of this paper which focuses, more precisely, on two aspects of the homosexual experience presented in the novel: blackmail and working-class lovers. It is useful to begin, however, with Forster's own assessment of England at the end of its Edwardian idyll and ask what he meant when he wrote that *Maurice* was part of 'an England where it was still possible to get lost. It belongs to the last moment of the greenwood'.[1]

Forster's retrospective statement is clearly enigmatic. Essentially, when Forster wrote the novel the greenwood that is the ideal of the book was extinct — with one possible exception: the classless, sexually uninhibited world of Edward Carpenter characterized by a healthy, out-of-doors homosexual life lived in robust physical affection and tenderness. Combined with the ideal of Hellenic friendship G. Lowes Dickinson summarized and the habits of personality Samuel Butler outlined in *Life and Habit*, read by Forster at the time he wrote *Maurice*, Carpenter actually and symbolically represented the possibility of life in the greenwood.

But when he began the novel in September 1913, Forster did not live in a country of unrestricted sexual mores. Homosexuality was a punishable crime that brought private shame and public dishonour; suicide was often the only remedy. The evasion that characterized the recognition of homosexuality at this period can be seen in the refusal of the British Museum to list Edward Carpenter's *The Intermediate Sex* in its General Catalogue until pressured to do so in 1913, although it had owned a copy for four years. Only three months before Forster began his novel, a homosexual scandal rocked the Austro-Hungarian Empire and threatened the military security of Eastern Europe. Personally, Forster's own homosexuality remained repressed and unfulfilled, seriously hindering his writing. Yet, in contrast to the English tradition of intolerance, suppression and punishment, Forster and his hero maintain a belief in a sexual Arcadia. What explains this paradox? The answer lies in the social and cultural matrix of Forster's age which he fondly recalled in 1960 as 'the greenwood'.

Before examining the sexual character of Forster's time and analysing his concept of homosexuality, it is necessary to understand the subject of *Maurice* in terms of a significant change in late Victorian and Edwardian literature: a radical alteration in the presentation of male relationships in the novel. In Victorian fiction the relationship that dominated male associations was that of fathers and sons as seen in such texts as *The Ordeal of Richard Feverel* or *The Way of All Flesh*. Towards the end of the century, however, this relationship began to assume a new shape. Instead of the conflict between paternal authority and youthful rebellion, the mother intervened and substituted her sometimes suffocating, sometimes threatening love. Mrs Yeobright in *The Return of the Native* is an early example; Mrs Morel in *Sons and Lovers* a later. Unable to attain an adequate spiritual or physical love, however, the son turns unhappily from the mother to a surrogate lover who, eventually, becomes rejected. Mme de Vionnet from *The Ambassadors* or Miriam in *Sons and Lovers* might be representative examples. In an effort to reinstate friendship and authority, the son searches for an acceptable parental figure among his peers or associates. Sometimes these figures — Strether or Leopold Bloom — stay safely within their sexual bounds as conservative father-figures but sometimes they do not, or cannot, and fulfil the needs of young men in covert and overt sexual ways. An historical illustration of this situation was the form of address of George Merrill to Edward Carpenter: 'My Dearest Dad', which was an echo of Peter Doyle's to Walt Whitman. Lord Henry Wotton's corruption of Dorian Gray illustrates an early literary example of this paternal affection; Aschenbach's attempted corruption of Tadzio in 'Death in Venice' a later.

Gradually, and surreptitiously, the homosexual novel in England emerged. Two early works were *The Sons of the Cities of the Plain* published in 1881 and *Teleny* which appeard in 1893, supposedly written, in part, by Oscar Wilde. By the beginning of this century, the poetry of Housman, the novels of Gide and the work of Proust began to represent homosexuality in more accomplished literary texts. A world of loving male relationships, idealizing the intimacy, affection and comradeship sought, but never achieved, by sons with their fathers began to characterize English fiction. In this new pattern of male friendship, *Maurice* has a central position. One critic, in fact, has stated that if the novel had been published when it was completed in July 1914, 'its positive treatment of homosexual love would have been at least as revolutionary as D. H. Lawrence's writings of the same period'.[2] It is true that the month Forster finished *Maurice* the British Society for the Study of Sex Psychology was established and that the massive study *Homosexuality of Men and Women* by the German sexologist Magnus Hirschfeld appeared. But these events had a limited impact upon the prevailing attitudes, in England, towards homosexuality, attitudes which prevented the appearance of a work such as *Maurice*.

What were some of the causes of the highly charged and dangerous climate for homosexuals at the end of the nineteenth century? One reason was the association of homosexuality and misconduct. The Cleveland Street Scandal of 1889–90 involving a homosexual brothel staffed by telegraph boys and visited by prominent aristocrats including, according to some, the son of the Prince of Wales, subjected the government to intense public criticism for its involvement and then attempted cover-up. The three trials of Oscar Wilde in 1895 further intensified the pressures placed upon homosexuals, although the law making illegal private as well as public acts of 'gross indecency' between members of the same sex had been passed ten years earlier. The death penalty for buggery, by the way, was not abolished in England until 1861; Scotland, however, kept it in force until 1889. The conviction of Wilde electrified England's homosexuals who rushed to the continent, as Frank Harris has reported:

Every train to Dover was crowded, every steamer to Calais thronged with members of the aristocratic and leisured classes, who seemed to prefer Paris, or even Nice out of season, to a city like London, where the police might act with such unexpected vigour . . . . Never was Paris so crowded with members of the English governing classes . . . . It was even said that a celebrated English actor took a return ticket to Paris for three or four days just to be in fashion.

Edward Carpenter less dramatically summarized the change within England:

Wilde was arrested in 1895 and from that moment a sheer panic prevailed over *all* questions of sex, especially . . . questions of the Intermediate Sex . . . .[3]

Four years before the Wilde trial, John Addington Symonds put forth the views regarding homosexuals shared to a very considerable extent by a misinformed public: 'It is a common belief that a male who experiences love for his own sex must be despicable, degraded, depraved, vicious and incapable of human or generous sentiments'. The public view had not changed much fifteen years later in 1906 when Lytton Strachey complained to Maynard Keynes that

It's madness for us to dream of making dowagers understand that feelings are good, when we say in the same breath that the best ones are sodomitical. If we were crafty and careful, I dare say we'd pull it off. But why should we take the trouble?

Only a hundred years later, Strachey predicted, there would be a change, although he could quip, long before that time, that if a man tried to rape his sister he would do the noble thing: 'he would attempt to interpose himself between them'.[4]

Until the 'Terminal Note' of 1960 no English novelist could write freely, openly or legitimately about homosexuality. The note is itself a testament to, and a rejection of, the legal, social and moral inhibitions that limited English writers from writing about homosexuality. Forster's remarks are a sign of a new phase and freedom. By way of contrast, Somerset Maugham's comment made late in his career summarized the repression that debilitated so many English writers of this period: 'I tried to persuade myself that I was three-quarters normal and that only a quarter of me was queer — whereas really it was the other way round'. Forster, of course, expressed a similar view when he wrote in 1964 that 'I should have been a more famous writer if I had written or rather published more, but sex has prevented the latter'.[5]

There was, however, an island of sexual freedom amid the restrictive landscape of Edwardian England: Cambridge and afterwards, Bloomsbury. At the turn of the century, the Cambridge Apostles were quite possibly the leading exponents of homosexual love as Keynes, himself, stated: 'The apostles repudiated entirely customary morals, conventions and traditional wisdom. We were, that is to say, in the strict sense of the term immoralists'. Keynes' use of the word directly echoes the meaning Gide imparted to it in his 1902 novel. In his autobiography, Bertrand Russell acknowledged the predominance of homosexuality during Strachey's leadership of the Apostles. Bloomsbury, in some ways a maturer Cambridge, extended the behaviour of the Apostles, as Quentin Bell realized when he rather exactly dated the shaping presence of homosexuality in the group: 'In 1908', he wrote, 'Bloomsbury had become licentious in its speech, by 1910 it was becoming licentious in its conduct, or rather license was no longer the privilege of its homosexual component'. Strachey, again, neatly expressed the new frankness when in 1908 he entered a room where Virginia Stephen and Vanessa Bell were sitting. Pointing a long, sinister finger at a stain on Vanessa's white dress, he uttered a devastating, one-word accusation: 'Semen?' Virginia Stephen recorded her reaction: 'Can one really say it? I thought & we burst out laughing. With that one word all barriers of reticence and reserve went down'.[6]

E. M. Forster was elected to the Apostles in February 1901, while Strachey was Secretary. G. E. Moore was then the intellectual leader of the 'club' promoting such ideas as 'the pleasure of human intercourse' and the 'enjoyment of beautiful objects'. P. N. Furbank reports that at that time homosexuality was 'talked about in a spirit of free and rational enquiry'; in this context, Forster realized that he was homosexual in temperament. However, his liberation was only mental, not physical. An accurate description of the freedom to be, yet failure to act, as a homosexual is found in J. R. Ackerley's summary of his experiences at Cambridge several years after Forster. Indeed, Ackerley's experience strongly parallel those of Maurice and Clive in the novel. Ackerley explains that

> In varying degrees and at various times I was attracted to a number of other undergraduates; I had sexual contact with none of them. So far as I know, all but one were normal boys . . . . But although I felt that, had I tried to kiss these normal, friendly boys who came so often to my rooms, my advances would not have been rebuffed, I could not take that step.[7]

The hesitancy and anxiety Ackerley describes and Forster recounts is no doubt characteristic of the majority of those young men who found themselves attracted to their peers but incapable of acting out those feelings.

In December 1910 Forster began his involvement with Bloomsbury, delivering in that month his popular paper, 'The Feminine Note in Literature', to the Friday Club. His association with Bloomsbury, sometimes at the centre and sometimes at the edge, continued for many years, although his own sexual development occurred independently of Bloomsbury's activities. Three points about the nature of homosexuality emerge from this brief review of the social and moral climate that surrounded it between 1895 and 1915: (1) society at large maintained and even enlarged its grounds for righteously condemning homosexuality as a vile, immoral act; (2) the designation of homosexuality as a criminal offence required from its adherents concealment, disguise and secrecy; (3) consequently it existed in relatively isolated institutions — public schools, universities, the military — where it was considered common practice. Forster was himself victimized by these contradictions which alternately demanded repression and respectability or expression and fulfilment. The struggle he experienced found its way into *Maurice* in the doubling that emerges in the text, most noticeably in the two voices of Maurice and his two complementary, not contradictory, lovers.

In *Maurice* the tension between social demands and private desires is epitomized by the narrator's remark that 'Cambridge had left him a hero, Penge a traitor' (xl, 191) and his subsequent concern with class as an aspect of homosexuality. In the over-dramatized dialogue between the two selves of Maurice, the middle-class Maurice debates with the rebellious Maurice, the former declaring 'I can't even now believe that it was with him' (xlii, 199) referring to his non-sexual affair with Clive. Almost immediately, however, Maurice reverses himself, complaining that he was a fool not to have possessed Clive 'in the hour of their passion' (xlii, 199). At that very moment, the King and Queen pass Maurice, enforcing his obedience to society through the dutiful removal of his hat. And at that moment, in·contrast, the Greenwood reappears: 'He was not afraid or ashamed any more. After all, the forests and the night were on his side, not theirs; they, not he, were inside a ring fence' (xlii, 199). Later, in the same chapter, he repeats this choice and his support of freedom when he compares the image of a shelter to a 'lair in the darkness' (xlii, 202). Maurice wants not the shelter with its limitations but the unrestricted existence that is found in a world of natural feeling and expression. But England limits Maurice repeatedly, as Lasker-Jones, the psychiatrist, summarizes when he answers Maurice's question, will England ever alter its laws concerning the prosecution of homosexuality: 'I doubt it,' he replies, 'England has always been disinclined to accept human nature' (xlii, 196).

England manifested this disinclination by creating a situation in which guilt and blackmail could flourish. Both elements are related to the complicated issue of class and both figure prominently in *Maurice* and enhance the truthfulness of its portrayal of homosexual life. The blackmail of homosexuals is a difficult subject to document although recorded cases go back to the 1760s; by the 1890s a play about the blackmailing of a young homosexual of a good family by two criminals was produced at the Prince of Wales Theatre, although it survived only for a single matinee performance. Wilde himself was repeatedly blackmailed in 1893 and is reported to have told one blackmailer who demanded £10 for an original letter sent to Lord Alfred Douglas 'Ten pounds? . . . You have no appreciation of literature. If you had asked me for fifty pounds, I might have given it to you'.[8] The Dublin Castle Scandal of 1907 involving the theft of the Irish crown jewels by two homosexuals who befriended the homosexual King of Arms was notorious because in this case the government was blackmailed by criminals who threatened, if they were arrested and tried, to reveal the names of highly placed homosexuals in government. Rumours at the time suggested that the investigation was halted by Edward VII, himself, who was afraid that his own brother-in-law might be implicated.

In the spring of 1913 a sensational international case of espionage and intrigue concentrated European attention on homosexual blackmail. The focus of the affair was Colonel Alfred Redl, a member of the Austrian Military Intelligence and of the General Staff Corps. Compromised by various homosexual alliances and in debt, Redl was blackmailed into providing vital military secrets to the Russians; discovered as a spy by his superiors, he was permitted to resolve the scandal by suicide before the charges became widely known. On 25 May 1913, Redl shot himself at the Hotel Klomser in Vienna, after a visit from members of the General Staff. The incident rocked the military, diplomatic and governmental branches of the Austro-Hungarian Empire.[9] John Osborne's 1965 play *A Patriot For Me* dramatized the Redl affair and the issue of blackmail. The arrest, trial and execution of Roger Casement for treason in 1916 echoed many of the issues of the Redl incident, although Casement's diaries contained incriminating details of his homosexual relations. After the trials of Oscar Wilde, Carpenter wrote with prescience that they 'opened wider than ever before the door to a real, most serious social and evil crime — that of blackmailing'. The leading investigator of homosexuality at the time, Magnus Hirschfeld, reported that out of 10,000 homosexuals he studied, nearly one-third had been blackmailed.[10] Blackmail was clearly a widespread and painful fact of homosexual life.

That Forster was unaware of this difficult aspect of homosexuality is disproven by the importance of blackmail in *Maurice*. The hero's fear of blackmail is a conditioned, middle-class reflex which begins, ironically, at his suburban home when he receives a telegram from Alec after their night together. Reading its terse invitation — 'Come back, waiting tonight at boathouse, Penge, Alec', Maurice thinks it contains 'every promise of blackmail' and that he dare not answer it (xl, 191). He fears not only the exposure of his homosexuality but of his involvement with one who is of the lower classes. In *Maurice*, having a relationship with a social equal, although it is unsatisfactory, is more acceptable than one with a gamekeeper. A second letter arriving at breakfast and read under 'his mother's eyes' further convinces Maurice that he may be victimized by Alec. The very objects in the room, as well as the people, seem to confirm his untenable position:

> His mother and aunt, the coffee he was drinking, the college
> cups on the sideboard, all said in their different ways, 'If you go
> you are ruined, if you reply your letter will be used to put
> pressure upon you. You are in a nasty position but you have
> this advantage: he hasn't a scrap of your handwriting, and he's
> leaving England in ten days' time. Lie low, and hope for the
> best'. (xl, 192)

Ominously, the narrator adds 'Butchers' sons and the rest of
them may pretend to be innocent and affectionate, but they read
the Police Court News, they know . . . .' Significantly Maurice's
fear and regret of his night with Alec are caused by the threat of
blackmail and public humiliation, not by personal dislike or
rejection of Alec.

In his meeting with Dr Lasker-Jones in the following chapter,
Maurice voices nervously his anxiety over blackmail and possible
court action as he blurts out 'He's an uneducated man; [but] he's
got me in his power. In court would he have a case?' (xli, 197).
Dr Lasker-Jones, the voice of conservative middle-class morality
upholding class differences and façades, replies that the letter
in Maurice's pocket cannot be 'construed as containing a
menace' and burns the letter as the hypnosis session continues.

A third letter, however, renews the danger of blackmail and
ends with the threatening statement, '*I know something*' (xlii, 201).
Maurice responds, arranging to meet Alec at the British Museum
which he describes in patronizing language as 'a large building.
Anyone will tell you which', adding wistfully to himself, 'Poor
B.M., solemn and chaste!' (xlii, 202). Chapter 43 is concerned
entirely with the threat of blackmail, beginning with Alec's
blustery threat that his brother is waiting outside so that Maurice
will pay up. But the unexpected and ironic presence of Mr Ducie,
who first introduced Maurice to the function of sex organs, is
the agent that shatters the threat of blackmail. Maurice's
announcement to Mr Ducie that his name is Scudder marks the
acceptance of a new identity and indirectly becomes a declaration
of his love for Alec. Credited by Alec with 'pluck' for his action
of challenging the possible blackmail, the repressed Maurice
bursts out with a description of how his middle-class position
would have protected him from any charges brought by a

gamekeeper. 'The police always back my sort against yours' (xliii, 209) he declares to Alec, although he admits that if he were brought to trial, he would have committed suicide like so many homosexuals trapped by public investigation. And at that moment, in the midst of his emotional outburst against Alec, Maurice confesses his love for him, shaming Alec into revealing that he attempted blackmail out of the hurt at not being loved by Maurice. Their fear of one another disappears as they recognize the emotional and sexual equality that was confirmed by their night together in a London hotel. Symbolically, this act certifies the acceptance of Alec in the world of Maurice, the world of the city; it marks the progress of their love from the pastoral world of Penge and its boathouse to the civilized urban landscape of London. Mediating between the two as the embodiment of historical time and culture is the British Museum.

A postscript to this theme of blackmail in *Maurice* lies in the reaction of Clive upon hearing from Maurice that he has fallen in love with Alec. At first fearing the threat posed to his election campaign by his association with Maurice, Clive, nonetheless, decides to 'rescue his old friend'. Feeling very much like a hero, Clive considers how to silence Alec and 'whether he would prove extortionate' (xlv, 230). In order to pursue this further Clive lamely invites Maurice to dine with him the following week at his London club. Maurice rejects the invitation and the novel's last vestige of blackmail. But this event, and not the idyllic renewal of love with Alec, may be Maurice's most idealistic act. Can he (and Forster) genuinely believe that blackmail would no longer plague him? The experiences of homosexuals during this period contradict such hopes.

The novel directly links blackmail with class through its insistence upon a working-class lover for a total, physical homosexual relationship. This was as true for Forster personally as it was artistically. 'I will not be treated as your servant' (xlii, 201) Alec writes to Maurice in his third letter and makes his acceptance as an equal a virtual prerequisite for their love. But Maurice is unable to do this completely; the merging of classes is more an ideal than a fact and an issue solved only by living 'outside class' (xlv, 223). In *Maurice* Forster suggests that there cannot be a complete homosexual relationship between equals, only unequals. Interestingly, this is a characteristic of Greek homosexuality. K. J. Dover writes that when the 'eromenos' (young lover) grew up and 'graduated from pupil to friend . . . the continuance of an erotic relationship was disapproved as was such a relationship between coevals'.[11] The need for class and social differences, in classical homosexuality, as the basis of a relationship is clearly and accurately transposed in Forster's account of early twentieth-century homosexuality. The classless relationship remained an ideal disproven by history and the actual experiences of Forster and his friends. Three examples among those who maintained working-class lovers were Edward Carpenter (George Merrill), J. A. Symonds (a Davos sleigh driver and a gondolier, Giorgio) and Sebastian Sprott (a variety of Nottingham slum characters).

The actions and statements of many homosexuals supported this fascination and involvement with lovers from the lower class. Forster, for example, in 1935 wrote 'I want to love a strong man of the lower classes and be loved by him and even hurt by him. That is my ticket'. In 1960 he said of Alec's character: 'I got to know him better partly through personal experiences'.[12] Ackerley in 1968 explained his fascination with working-class boys because he found them 'more unreserved and understanding' although he postulated that his 'guilt in sex [might have] obliged [him] to work it off on my social inferiors'. In fact, in 1925 Ackerley had written a play entitled *Judcote*, the story of a

> young, upper-middle-class, intellectual homosexual lonely, frustrated and sick of his family . . . [who] becomes emotionally involved with a handsome young workman . . . . Jude falls in love with him and, after various other happenings . . . runs away with him into a working-class life and they live happily together as mates ever after.[13]

Parallels to *Maurice* are, I think, obvious. Ackerley, however, was wantonly promiscuous with his lower-class lovers and often hurt by love. The involvement and need for lovers from the lower class has been crystallized by Christopher Isherwood writing of England in 1929:

> Christopher was suffering from an inhibition then not unusual among upper-class homosexuals; he couldn't relax sexually with a member of his own class or nation. He needed a working-class foreigner.[14]

Isherwood found him, of course, in Germany.

The stimulus for the pattern of class differences among English homosexuals during the early years of the present century may have been as much psychological as it was social. A working-class lover posed no threat to the middle- or upper middle-class male. He could be dominated financially, socially and intellectually. The working-class lover, however, had a naturalness, spontaneity and physical beauty that made him attractive to the middle-class lover in ways that members of his own class were not. Wilde supposedly said that he preferred working-class boys because 'their passion was all body and no soul'. However, several supporters of homosexuality found such unions the means for reconciling class differences, as J. A. Symonds explained to Edward Carpenter:

> The blending of Social Strata in masculine love seems to me one of its most pronounced, and socially hopeful features. Where it appears, it abolishes class distinctions, and open by a single operation the cataract-blinded life to their futilities.

Part IV of Carpenter's long Whitmanesque poem *Towards Democracy* contains an explicit description of the new millenium brought about by full and equal love between men of differing classes:

> The love of men for each other — so tender, heroic, constant
> . . . . Always so true, so well assured of itself,
> overlea[ps] barriers of age, of rank, of distance.

'Eros is a great leveller' Carpenter concluded.[15] The resolution of *Maurice* suggests this same theme but involves more fully such psychological complexities as mastery and humiliation, attraction and rejection.

In *Life and Habit*, which Forster read while writing *Maurice*, Samuel Butler explained that

> our own progress — or variation — is due not to small, fortuitous inventions or modifications . . . but to strokes of cunning — to a sense of need, and to study of the past and present . . . .[16]

A 'sense of need' and a 'study of the past and present': these are the causes of Maurice's self-awareness and acceptance of his homosexuality which is fulfilled totally only by Alec. But society had more difficulty in absorbing such feelings. The cultural attitudes and social reactions to homosexuality during Forster's life were reactionary at best and prohibitive at worst. Homosexuality threatened the continuation of the family and the Victorian ideal of the male; as it became associated with corruption, scandal and blackmail, it was soon perceived as a threat to the state. Tolerated as an aberration explicitly identified as buggery until the late nineteenth century, homosexuality, in its more social and indefinite form, became a state of mind and, to many, more seditious.[17] In this restrictive climate a 'greenwood' became essential. It existed, however, only imaginatively or mythically in that most interesting of forms, *Maurice*.[18]

NOTES

1. E. M. Forster, 'Terminal Note', *Maurice* (London: Edward Arnold, 1971), p. 240. All further references are to this edition.
2. Ian Young, 'The Flower Beneath the Foot: A Short History of the Gay Novel', *The Male Homosexual in Literature: A Bibliography*, ed. Ian Young (Metuchen, New Jersey: Scarecrow Press, 1975), p. 151.
3. Frank Harris in H. Montgomery Hyde, *The Other Love* (London: Heinemann, 1970), pp. 152–3; Edward Carpenter, *My Days and Dreams, Being Autobiographical Notes* (London: Allen & Unwin, 1916), p. 196.
4. J. A. Symonds, *A Problem in Modern Ethics* in Edward Carpenter, *The Intermediate Sex*, 2nd ed. (London: Swan Sonnenschein, 1909), p. 137; Strachey to Keynes in Roger Austen, *Playing the Game, The Homosexual Novel in America* (Indianapolis: Bobbs Merrill, 1977), p. 51.
5. Maugham in A. L. Rowse, *Homosexuals in History* (London: Weidenfeld and Nicolson, 1977), p. 241; E. M. Forster, 'Introduction', *The Life to Come*, ed. Oliver Stallybrass, Abinger edn. (London: Edward Arnold, 1972), p. xiv.
6. Keynes in Goronwy Rees, 'A Case for Treatment, The World of Lytton Strachey', *Encounter*, 30:3 (March 1968), 76. For Russell's comment see *The Autobiography of Bertrand Russell, 1872–1914* (Boston: Little Brown, 1967), p. 99; Quentin Bell, *Virginia Woolf* (New York: Harcourt Brace Jovanovich, 1972), I, p. 124.
7. P. N. Furbank, *E. M. Forster: A Life* (New York: Harcourt Brace Jovanovich, 1978), I, pp. 78–9; J. R. Ackerley, *My Father and Myself* (1968; New York: Harcourt Brace Jovanovich, 1975), pp. 118–19. All further references are to these editions.
8. See Arno Karlen, *Sexuality and Homosexuality, A New View* (New York: Norton, 1971), pp. 143–4; on *The Blackmailers* see Hyde, *The Other Love*, p. 164; Wilde in Philippe Jullian, *Oscar Wilde*, tr. Violet Wyndham (New York: Viking Press, 1969), pp. 282–3.

9. An excellent account of the affair is found in Robert B. Asprey, *The Panther's Feast* (London: Jonathan Cape, 1959). A similar scandal occurred in Germany in 1907, the Harden–Eulenberg affair which implicated the Kaiser in a homosexual clique.

10. Edward Carpenter, The Intermediate Sex, in Jeffrey Weeks, *Coming Out, Homosexual Politics in Britain* (London: Quartet Books, 1977), p. 21; Hirschfeld in Karlen, *Sexuality and Homosexuality*, p. 248.

11. K. J. Dover, *Greek Homosexuality* (London: Duckworth, 1978), p. 203.

12. Forster in Stallybrass, 'Introduction', *The Life to Come*, p. xiv; Forster, 'Terminal Note', *Maurice*, p. 219.

13. J. Ackerley, pp. 178–9.

14. Isherwood, *Christopher and His Kind*, 1929–1939 (New York: Avon, 1977), p. 3.

15. Wilde in Weeks, *Coming Out*, p. 40; Symonds in Weeks, *Coming Out*, p. 41; Carpenter, *Towards Democracy, Complete Edition* (London: Allen & Unwin, 1915), pp. 396–401; Carpenter, *The Intermediate Sex*, p. 114.

16. Samuel Butler, *Life and Habit* (1878; New York: AMS Press, 1968), p. 203.

17. Two interesting essays on the history of homosexuality in England are Randolph Trumbach, 'London's Sodomites: Homosexual Behaviour and Western Culture in the 18th Century', *Journal of Social History*, 11:1 (Fall 1977), 1–33; and Arthur Gilbert, 'Buggery and the British Navy, 1700–1861', *Journal of Social History*, 10:1 (Fall 1976), 72–98.

18. 'The wonder of the novel' wrote Isherwood, 'was that it had been written when it had been written; the wonder was Forster himself. . . putting these unthinkable thoughts into words'. *Christopher and His Kind*, p. 126.

12 *Maurice* as Fantasy

Kathleen Grant

In the course of his 'summing up' of E. M. Forster's *Maurice*, C. Rising maintains that the novel is a 'too-autobiographical justification for personal resentment so intensely felt that it robs its characters of charity and its symbolic devices of depth', and hence 'simply falls short of art'.[1] For him, '*Maurice* at best is personal therapy, at least a fumbling insight into a tortured soul. But is this enough? When one turns to our original question, "Has Forster done a good job?" the answer must be a resounding No followed by a quieter Yes'.[2]

Scholars frequently temporize in this inconclusive way as they strive for some sort of balanced judgement on *Maurice*, a novel that few seem to like, though most wish to be seen treating it with perhaps slightly ostentatious fair-mindedness. Jeffrey Meyers, however, produced a notably forthright 'resounding No', dismissing *Maurice* as a mere 'didactic *roman à clef*'[3] in which the homosexual theme that he saw as 'oblique, ambiguous and interesting' in *The Longest Journey* has surfaced to become 'flat, banal and dull'.[4] The most sympathetic attempt at a 'quieter Yes' is Evelyne Hanquart's, yet despite her readiness to be pleased, she characterizes the novel at last as 'une oeuvre "fabuleuse", idéaliste, qui manque de maturité'.[5] Yet the reader, she feels, 'conscient de l'importance et de la valeur de *Maurice* dans la vie de son auteur, ne peut le lire . . . sans une certaine émotion'.[6]

'Une certaine émotion' would be a mild term for some of the reactions the novel provoked in the less trammelled world of the review. Amongst the shriller voices was that of Cynthia Ozick, who denounced *Maurice* as a '*disingenuous*, an *infantile* book that pretends to be about social justice but is really about wishing',[7] with a flawed hero, Forster himself in grotesque costume, a character 'neither flat nor round, who is the ghost of undepicted, inexplicit coitus, of the missing pornography'.[8]

While Ozick was lamenting that *Maurice* was not a homosexual version of *Lady Chatterley's Lover*, Marvin Mudrick was complaining that it was. In a review notably lacking in *mesure*, Mudrick breezily advised the reader that 'if you've begun to suspect that a dozen years before *Lady Chatterley's Lover* Forster had already hit on the theme of sex as the solvent of English class distinctions, you'll be delighted by the information that Alec is a gamekeeper. Lady or lord, soft or sinewy, it's all in the same bag'.[9] Like Ozick, he considered *Maurice* bad, but while she denounced it as false, he proclaimed it Forster's 'only truthful book', contrasting it in particular with *Howards End*, which, he averred, is 'all lies'.[10]

Even the most temperate reviewers, such as Arnold Kettle[11] and Noel Annan,[12] judged the work as ultimately unconvincing, and focused their dissatisfaction on the character of Maurice, as a figure nobody could believe in.

This charge of lack of credibility was extended to Forster himself in at least one memorial notice. In 'The Strangeness of E. M. Forster', Simon Raven, who was up at Cambridge from 1948 to 1952, tells a number of gossipy anecdotes designed to support his contention that Forster's behaviour was sometimes at variance with his declared principles. One describes Forster refusing to attend a dinner because some undergraduates felt the subscription was too high. The second lies closer to our subject:

> One belief he most certainly and sincerely held was that everyone must be allowed freedom in his sexual affairs; and some friends who took him to the theatre were therefore very surprised when he started grumbling because, as he said, the play was about 'immorality flats' . . . . Which was all very well, as the friends told me later on: 'but after all, most of Morgan's life has been spent in 'immorality flats'.

Raven then cites an incident concerning the devotion J. R. Ackerley displayed in his love affair with his dog, which on one occasion caused him to cancel an arrangement he had made with Forster. Raven saw Ackerley's behaviour as both sensitive and loyal: 'I expected Morgan Forster to applaud it, since loyalty and sensitivity were two virtues which he never tired of extolling. But not so. "How can Joe be such a futile ass?" he said; "that *bloody* Queenie."'

He ends on this note:

> So which was the real Forster? The man who forewent a dinner which he might have enjoyed because others had complained that it was beyond their pockets: or the man who cursed Joe Ackerley for being faithful to his dog? And what about the man who was peevish over 'immorality flats'? Or who never gave a straight answer where a crooked one would do? Only connect, he used to say: I leave it to you.[13]

The irritation with Forster's elusiveness that comes through so crudely here seems to me to lie in more subtle forms behind much of the impatience or disappointment that readers have felt over *Maurice*. In his introduction to the novel, Furbank predicts that most readers will find it both 'masterly and touching',[14] Many may well have done so, but if so, have kept their admiration very quiet.

A number of factors seem to have worked against *Maurice*. It has often been judged in comparison with *Lady Chatterley's Lover*; its version of homosexuality seems to many quaintly dated; and its particular blend of realism and fantasy has proved confusing.

To complain that Forster's techniques are not those of D. H. Lawrence seems unreasonable. For Forster, *pace* Marvin Mudrick, sexuality simply is not 'all in the same bag'.

Similarly, to dismiss Forster's presentation of homosexuality in *Maurice* as dated is a crude oversimplification. Forster himself remarks of the book that 'it certainly dates — not only because of its endless anachronisms . . . but for a more vital reason: it belongs to an England where it was still possible to get lost. It belongs to the last moment of the greenwood' ('Terminal Note', p. 239). Of the book's presentation of homosexuality, however, he admits no such thing, but simply comments ruefully that his expectation that honesty would lead to understanding had in the event proved mistaken.

Of Forster's own homosexuality, one gathers that in middle life he had a good deal of experience with working-class lovers, one at least being a long-term commitment. The changes he made in the text of *Maurice* towards turning Alec into an individual rather than a symbol suggest that what had been wish in 1913 had been confirmed to some extent over the years by experience. The first volume of Furbank's *Life* gives a very good notion of Forster's sexual development and experience up to the point at which he produced the first version of *Maurice*.

As a child who was the centre of life for a female household, he was the 'Important One', markedly demonstrative and given to 'violent passions of love and fury'.[15] His love affair with his mother made his childhood radiant, and the whole impression of Forster in early years is of a highly emotional creature, eager for experience. A comment of his grandmother's is especially striking: 'One thing I don't believe anybody makes allowances enough for . . . is his intense enjoyment of this world and all it contains, and his proportionate misery when anything is withheld from him'.[16]

Unfortunately, much was likely to be, if not actually withheld, at least confusingly covered-up in the world of Forster's boyhood. From a home full of devoted female love and the happy companionship of gardener's boys, he emerged the most unlikely material from which 'to make a regular, manly English boy',[17] but this was the task begun by his tutor, continued by his prep school and persevered in by school itself. All these experiences were unfortunate. Forster first worshipped his tutor, only to find himself rejected in favour of cousin Percy. From prep school he writes: 'The worst of school is that you have nothing and nobody to love, if only I had somebody'.[18] Inevitably, he pinned his affections on a procession of other boys. For the naïve and sensitive Forster, the accumulation of such 'passions', the talk of other boys, an encounter with an exhibitionist, when all the while he had no possible confidant save a mother from whom sex 'was a dreadful subject and to be thought of as little as possible',[19] was to make for confusion, the sorry state he calls 'muddle' in *Maurice*. Further unsettling experiences in the hard-edged environment of real school completed the process of turning a vivid child into a demure and wary observer.

The King's of Oscar Browning and Lowes Dickinson came as a revelation, and by his second year, Forster was well on his way to enjoying his world and all it contained once more. His friendship with H. O. Meredith, whom some see as the model for Clive, dates from this point, and after Forster went down, this friendship became the focus of his emotional life. According to Furbank:

For Forster, H. O. Meredith meant more than all his other
friends. He regarded him as an emancipator, . . . he took him
as his model for the Deliverer, coming to rescue the hero or
heroine from muddle and self-deception. Now, sometime
during the winter it seems, this became closer than before —
indeed, in some sense or other, they became lovers. It seems to
have been an affair very much on the lines of that of Maurice
and Clive . . . that is to say, it was not a physical relationship, or
at least went no further than kisses and embraces. This was by
mutual agreement, according to Forster.[20]

Furbank suggests that Meredith took the lead, and that, to him,
the affair was an 'experiment', following affairs he had already
had with girls. For Forster, however, this experience 'was
immense and epoch-making; it was, he felt, as if all the "greatness" of the world had opened up to him. He counted this as the
second grand discovery of his youth — his emancipation from
Christianity being the first — and for the moment it seemed to
him as though all the rest of his existence would not be too long
to work out the consequences'.[21]

The record Furbank gives of the years between this grand
discovery of 1902 and the 1913 visit to Edward Carpenter that
Forster describes in his 'Terminal Note' to *Maurice* is hard to read
without Hanquart's 'certaine émotion'. The longing for physical
fulfilment, the attempts to convince himself that not finding it is
'better' ('I still want in all moods the greatest happiness but
perhaps it is well it should be denied me'),[22] the turmoil at seeing
Meredith marry and then become also his lover three years later,
his own abortive wooing of Syed Masood, the writing of erotic
stories to excite himself at the same time as he was persistently
attempting to control his 'gross' desires so as not to annoy others[23]
— all this makes it plain why he should have approached the
cottage of Carpenter and Merrill as a shrine.

Perhaps even more revealing than his delighted response to the
world of the Urnings, however, is the poem Forster had written
after visiting Henry James in 1908, when, coming away from
Lamb House he had seen a young workman leaning up against
a wall in the dusk, smoking a cigarette:

> I saw you or I thought of you
> I know not which, but in the dark

Piercing the known and the untrue
　　It gleamed — a cigarette's faint spark.
It gleamed — and when I left the room
　　Where culture unto culture knelt
Something just darker than the gloom
　　Waited — it might be you I felt.
It was not you; you pace no night
　　No youthful flesh weighs down your youth.
You are eternal, infinite,
　　You are the unknown, and the truth.
Yet each must seek reality:
　　For those within the room, high talk,
Subtle experience — for me
　　The spark, the darkness, on the walk.[24]

Echoes of this poem abound in *Maurice*, most obviously in
Chapter 27, in which the sterile talk within the drawing room at
Penge is set against Maurice's urge to be out of doors and his
encounters with Alec in the darkened garden. Forster's depiction
of 'the known and the untrue' life of Penge carries so heavy a
freight of satire that the novel can seem primarily a social tract,
a reading that is rather encouraged by Forster's early defence of
it to Forrest Reid:

> The man in my book is, roughly speaking, good, but Society
> nearly destroys him, he nearly slinks through his life furtive
> and afraid, and burdened with a sense of sin. You say, 'If he
> had not met another man like him, what then?' What indeed?
> But blame Society not Maurice, and be thankful even in a novel
> when a man is left to lead the best life he is capable of leading!
> . . . .
>
> My defence at any Last Judgement would be 'I was trying to
> connect and use all the fragments I was born with' — well you
> had it exhaustingly in *Howards End*, and Maurice, though his
> fragments are more scanty and bizarre than Margaret's is
> working at the same job . . .
>
> 　　　　　　　　　　　　　(*Maurice*, Introduction, p. vii)

Being asked to connect Maurice with Margaret Schlegel of the
'high talk' and 'subtle experience' draws the reader up short.
Maurice with Aziz, maybe. Maurice with Rickie, yes. Maurice

with Stephen Wonham, yes. Maurice with Lucy, yes, and Maurice with Helen, by all means. But Maurice with *Margaret?* This seems one of Raven's 'crooked' answers.

Yet there is a deep connection between *Howards End* and *Maurice* that we see reflected in Forster's remark that 'Only a little of my passion and irrationality was used up in *Howards End*'.[25] *Maurice* is very obviously the outlet for more of the Forster that D. H. Lawrence recognized as a deeply passionate and frustrated man.[26] Only for this one of all his novels does he describe a sudden rush of creative energy: 'The general plan, the three characters, the happy ending for two of them, all rushed into my pen' (*Maurice*, 'Terminal Note', p. 235). We are reminded of his accounts of the composition of 'The Story of a Panic' and 'The Road from Colonus', both works with a clear thematic link with *Maurice*. The whole of 'The Road from Colonus', 'a story of the chance of salvation lost' Forster said, ' "hung ready for him in a hollow tree" '.[27] Similarly, with 'The Story of a Panic', in a valley near Ravello, 'the first chapter of the story rushed into my mind as if it had waited for me there'.[28] This tale of 'the chance of salvation taken',[29] however, was not immediately satisfying, and in its original, inspired form, 'seemed unfinished'.[30] It would appear that the idea of actually taking the way of deliverance was not one that Forster could easily command, and this impression is strengthened when we read of his reaction to Charles Sayle's delightedly 'scandalized' response to the story:

'Oh dear', Sayle exclaimed to Maynard Keynes, 'oh dear, oh dear, is this young King's?'; and he explained to Keynes what the story was really about. Having . . . how should he put it . . . having had an unnatural act performed upon him by a waiter at the hotel, Eustace commits bestiality with a goat, then when he has told the waiter how nice it all has been, they try it on with each other again. 'While alive to the power of the writing, to its colour, its beauty, its Hellenic grace', fluted Sayle, 'I am still amazed . . . horrified . . . and *longing* to meet the author'. Keynes went about Cambridge spreading the story, . . . and . . . Forster was furious. He had had no thought of sex for his characters — sex simply hadn't been in his mind at all. So he said to himself; but years later he came to realize that, 'in a stupid and unprofitable way', Sayle had been right and that this had been the reason for his indignation. The story had excited him as he wrote it, and the passages that excited him most were the ones where 'something was up'. It was the same with the scene in *Where Angels Fear to Tread*, in which Gino tortures Philip by twisting his broken arm. It had stirred him to write it, though at the time he neither knew nor wondered why. But then, he asked himself, why should he have done? It had been his right as a young author to write about beauty and lust without knowing which was which or giving either a name.[31]

At this point, we might be forgiven if we begin to feel something of Raven's impatience with apparent inconsistency or Ozick's with disingenuousness. Yet the duality that is the basis of their charges is the essence of Forster, and fantasy often has given him his most supple means for expressing it. Like 'The Road from Colonus' and 'The Story of a Panic', *Maurice* is fantasy, and in each case Forster asks us to meet the demands that in his view fantasy lays upon us, the necessity 'to pay something extra':

> The other novelists say 'Here is something that might occur in your lives', the fantasist 'Here is something that could not occur. I must ask you first to accept my book as a whole, and secondly to accept certain things in my book'. Many readers can grant the first request, but refuse the second. 'One knows a book isn't real', they say; 'still, one does expect it to be natural, and this angel or midget or ghost or silly delay about the child's birth — no, it is too much.' They either retract their original concession and stop reading, or if they do go on it is with complete coldness, and they watch the gambols of the author without realising how much they may mean to him.[32]

The two stories we have seen as closely connected with *Maurice* in their kind of inspiration belong to the type of Forsterian fantasy that Stone has labelled 'light and unportentous'.[33] They are, in addition, rather vague in time and remote in setting. *Maurice*, in contrast, is for many heavy, portentous, and so firmly realistic in its presentation of both Cambridge and suburbia that its fantasy is very much of the kind Forster called the 'side-show':

> The general tone of novels is so literal that when the fantastic is introduced it produces a special effect; some readers are

thrilled, others choked off; it demands an additional adjust-
ment because of the oddness of its method or subject-matter
— like a side-show in an exhibition where you pay sixpence
as well as the original entrance fee.   (*Aspects*, vi, 75).

Just what we might call the particular side-show that is the
fantasy of *Maurice* is an interesting question. Perhaps, taking a
hint from Forster's description of *Tristram Shandy* (*Aspects*, vi, 77),
it might be termed 'Muddle: the Hidden God'; or, thinking of
Lawrence's poem of salvation refused, *Snake*, 'Alec: One of the
Lords of Life', or 'A Bundle of Voices', a name we could derive
also from *Maurice* (xxxv, 163), along with another possibility,
'The Shadow in the Glass' (ii, 13). I have elected to be more
mundane, however, and label the side-show simply 'The Great
Trial', on the basis of the last sentence of the Terminal Note:
'Clive on the bench will continue to sentence Alec in the dock.
Maurice may get off'.

In a novel of homosexuality, presenting the existence Clive
calls pejoratively, 'the land through the looking glass', we might
expect to find that it is Alec who sits on the bench, Clive who is
sentenced, while Maurice may get off, but if that were the case, we
should indeed have the immature romance that embarrasses
Hanquart, or the infantile wish-fulfilment that enrages Ozick.

I would suggest that the final effect of the novel is not that of a
'happy ending'. In *Maurice*, which might well have been called
Clive, we have Forster's most clearly defined story of the double,
one of those 'divings into and dividings of personality' (*Aspects*,
vi, 78) Forster distinguishes as one of the devices of the writer of
fantasy. Maurice's 'fragments' are indeed 'scanty and bizarre,'
and will make us only half a hero. For the sum, we need Clive, and
Maurice/Clive Forster presents himself in two *personae*, as he does
in *The Longest Journey* and in *Howards End*.

Regarded in this light, the question of 'believing' in Maurice
as a character becomes incidental. As the passionate self, who
finds expression only in childhood and in dreams and trances, he
exists in the novel as a version of Clive, his double, and wages a
battle for control with his rational counterpart in which he is
sometimes devil to it, and sometimes bedevilled by it.

After the Comedy of Errors that follows their apparently idyllic
day in the country, described in Chapter 13, we find Maurice and
Clive recalling the course of their relationship. 'Clive, you're a

devil' (xvi, 81), exclaims Maurice, as Clive instructs him in the worldly art of dealing with rules, regulations and Deans by lying. Clive, a little later in the scene, tells Maurice that the more he thinks it over, the more certain he is that it is Maurice that is the devil: 'I should have gone through life half awake if you'd had the decency to leave me alone' (xvi, 82).

Throughout their relationship, the inarticulate Maurice stands for the natural, the instinctive man, who advances through the irrational, gaining by yielding to impulse, and blindly seeking always to fly the nets to 'reality', the momentary glow of light in the darkness. Afraid of this darkness that he yet must seek, he is incapable of self-analysis, but is capable of losing himself in physical experience, whether it be the beauty he sees in Clive or the physical ugliness that he happily and naturally deals with during Clive's night of illness.

In contrast, Clive is the wilful, endlessly self-conscious seeker of equilibrium, a searcher for comfort rather than joy. Far more attractive to the reader than Maurice in the early part of the novel, he is nonetheless one who lives on lies self-administered, accepting a compromise deliberately worked for by the will. Unable to trust the body, in Lawrencian terms, he is caught in the net of what appears to be 'subtle experience' but is in fact a vulgar complacency more repellent than any Forster ever attributed to the world of Sawston.

Their apparently perfect day, the escape into the country in Chapter 13, is surely an ironic Forsterian pastoral. No reader of his other works, with their perpetually expressed distaste for the machine, will think that Maurice is anything but dead right when he says they are going to Hell on the powerful motorcycle with its noise, dust and stench. Similarly, when we meet the familiar Forsterian male bathing scene, Clive goes in only by accident, swims out as quickly as possible, to walk along calmly carrying Maurice's clothes while his lover joyously 'bathes properly', but alone.

Chapter 18 can be dismissed as a sentimental stylistic disaster, but it can also surely be read as an ironic indictment of Clive's rationalization of his fear of the physical. Its depiction of the lovers' 'extremely sensible' behaviour, and of the 'education' Clive gives Maurice prepares us for Clive's defection in Chapter 22, when seated in the theatre of Dionysus, all his self-conscious Apollonian control dissolves into a sense of vanity, which he cannot recognize as a willed denial of life:

> The stage was empty, as it had been for many centuries, the auditorium empty; the sun had set though the Acropolis behind still radiated heat. He saw barren plains running down to the sea, Salamis, Aegina, mountains, all blended in a violet evening. Here dwelt his gods — Pallas Athene in the first place: he might if he chose imagine her shrine untouched, and her statue catching the last of the glow. She understood all men, though motherless and a virgin. He had been coming to thank her for years because she had lifted him out of the mire.
>
> But he saw only dying light and a dead land. He uttered no prayer, believed in no deity, and knew that the past was devoid of meaning like the present, and a refuge for cowards.
>
> (xxii, 106)

Ultimately, Clive embraces Anne, and has never honestly contemplated any other course than this 'normality' which he pretends to his other self, Maurice, is a physical change come upon him against his will. We know he has always accepted this 'known' and 'untrue' role from the exchange he and Maurice have in Chapter 17, where he can speak calmly of himself as fathering children. Once abandoned by Clive, his conventional mirror image, Maurice can find the friend he has always sought but seen only in dreams only in his other double, the image of his shadow in the glass, a dark figure that had terrified him in boyhood even as it tempted him to summon it up: 'The trouble was the looking-glass. He did not mind seeing his face in it, nor casting a shadow on the ceiling, but he did mind seeing his shadow on the ceiling reflected in the glass. He would arrange the candle so as to avoid the combination, and then dare himself to put it back and be gripped with fear' (ii, 13).

This dark other self Maurice finds in Alec. On the realistic level, Alec is 'believable' enough, a man, like the others in the novel, who is a product of his class. As a figure of fantasy, he is, in Lawrence's phrase, 'one of the lords of life', whom Maurice must recognize and honour. His association with darkness, water, stolen fruit, his small snake-like head, flickering eyes — all connect him with the serpent and with the life of the earth. Working against Maurice's embracing him are all the forces of 'education', so that at one point Maurice feels himself a 'bundle of voices' (xxxv, 163), but none of them is Clive's, which has been potentially the most destructive. What Alec stands for, Clive cannot face, and so once Maurice has recognized and identified himself with his 'unknown' but 'true' double in Alec, the only possible ending to the novel, which centres on the relationship of Maurice/ Clive, is a Forsterian scene of separation. In Chapter 46, Clive 'feels' Maurice swaying snake-like before a 'wall of night' against which the evening primroses gleam, but for him Maurice is now 'essentially night', something he cannot comprehend.

As a story, in which we ask, 'and then?', *Maurice* works well enough, and is susceptible to the kinds of changes Forster made in it over the years, such as the addition of the passage making it clear how Maurice was to find Alec at the end. As psycho-fantasy, however, a side-show in which the irrational self rejects the intellect's fair semblance of sweetness and light to join the reality that glows momentarily in the darkness, the ending is not 'happy'. Rather it is a disturbing inner separation, a disintegration of the self that has nothing to do with the outer world. When the Clive part of E. M. Forster sits on the Bench, with Maurice/ Alec in the dock, Maurice, the impulse to reject authority and turn outlaw, may very well 'get off'. Alec, the force that underlies that impulse, certainly will not. 'Thought is free', and so, as Forster says, in that sense, 'Maurice and Alec still roam the greenwood' ('Terminal Note', p. 218). Yet the world that E. M. Forster chose to inhabit, or was unable to escape, may allow for outlaw moments, but these forays into the greenwood are, like the school outing that begins *Maurice*, only consciously contrived breaks from the norm, not moments of reality that are the stuff of life.

NOTES

1. C. Rising, 'E. M. Forster's *Maurice*: A Summing Up', *Texas Quarterly*, 17 (1974), p. 93.
2. Rising, p. 94.
3. Jeffrey Meyers, 'Forster's Secret Sharer', *Southern Review*, 5 (1972), p. 59.
4. Meyers, p. 61.
5. Evelyne Hanquart, 'Maurice et E. M. Forster', *Etudes Anglaises*, 28 (1975), p. 298.
6. Hanquart, p. 299.
7. Cynthia Ozick, 'Forster as Homosexual', *Commentary*, 52 (1971), p. 82.

8. Ozick, p. 83.
9. Marvin Mudrick, 'Fiction and Truth', *Hudson Review*, 25 (1972), p. 143.
10. Mudrick, p. 143.
11. Arnold Kettle, 'All for Love', *The New Republic*, 9 October 1971, pp. 26–28.
12. Noel Annan, 'Love Story', *The New York Review of Books*, 21 October 1971, pp. 12–15.
13. Simon Raven, 'The Strangeness of E. M. Forster', *Spectator*, 225 (1971), p. 237.
14. See Furbank's introduction to E. M. Forster, *Maurice* (London: Edward Arnold, 1971), p. ix.
15. P. N. Furbank, *E. M. Forster: A Life* (New York: Harcourt, Brace, Jovanovich, 1977), I, p. 14.
16. Furbank, I, p. 15.
17. Furbank, I, p. 31.
18. Furbank, I, p. 34.
19. Furbank, I, p. 37.
20. Furbank, I, pp. 97–8.
21. Furbank, I, p. 98.
22. Furbank, I, p. 121.
23. Furbank, I, p. 183.
24. Furbank, I, p. 165.
25. Furbank, I, p. 16.
26. Harry Moore, ed., *Letters of D. H. Lawrence to Bertrand Russell* (New York: Gotham Book Mart, 1948), pp. 29–31.
27. Furbank, I, p. 103.
28. Furbank, I, p. 92.
29. Furbank, I, p. 103.
30. Furbank, I, p. 92.
31. Furbank, I, pp. 113–14.
32. E. M. Forster, *Aspects of the Novel*, ed. Oliver Stallybrass, Abinger edn. (London: Edward Arnold, 1974), p. 75.
33. Wilfred Stone, *The Cave and the Mountain: A Study of E. M. Forster* (Stanford, Calif.: Stanford University Press, 1966), p. 135.

13 The Evolution of E. M. Forster's *Maurice*

Philip Gardner

I

Forty-seven years, to the month, after he had begun *Maurice*, E. M. Forster described it in his 'Terminal Note' of 1960 as still almost retaining 'its original form'.[1] Since there are, however, three versions of the novel, dated 1914, 1932 and 1959 respectively, I propose here to examine in detail the extent to which Forster's statement is accurate. A study over the past two years of its three typescripts, in the possession of King's College, Cambridge, has convinced me that an Abinger Edition of *Maurice*, with variants, would be of considerable value to students of Forster, and I offer what follows as a prolegomenon to such a work. Whether *Maurice* would in fact be included in the Abinger Edition seemed to its then editor, Oliver Stallybrass, early in 1978, sadly unlikely; one can only hope, a year later, that a favourable decision will eventually be made.

Variants apart, the need to have *Maurice* in the Abinger Edition may be indicated by a brief consideration of the text we have, published in 1971 with commendable piety but traces of editorial haste. This text, as P. N. Furbank points out in his preliminary Note, is essentially based on 'the typescript of 1960', which belongs in fact to 1959, and was made — presumably with the 1932 typescript as copy-text — as a result of Furbank's own help and enouragement.[2] But collation of the novel as published in 1971 with all three earlier typescripts reveals a number of incorrect or arbitrary readings. Some are the result of emendations, listed by Furbank in his textual note. Four of them, on pages 28, 34, 155 and 169, have no manuscript support; the last also lacks any point that might make up for this. On page 31

Furbank's adopted reading, 'watching for Durham',[3] replaces Forster's entirely feasible 'watching Durham': Featherstone-haugh's room, outside which Maurice waits for Clive to emerge, has a lighted window in which he may well be visible. On page 94, Clive is made to talk of 'us leisured classes coasting around in motor-cars'; here 'coasting' replaces the 1959 and 1932 'boosting' to which no contextually convincing sense can be attached. But the original 1914 word (for which 'boosting' seems to me a typist's error or perhaps 'correction') is 'hoosting', which, though quaint and dialectal, seems an apt pejorative description of cars from one who, on the evidence of *Howards End*, disliked them. It means 'coughing', particularly a kind of diseased cough emitted by cattle.[4]

Other errors in the 1971 text (though some of them just could be misprints) seem the result of want of zeal rather than excess of it. One may not be inclined to quarrel with the modernization of Forster's preferred spellings 'octette' (p. 80) and 'Tchai-kowsky' (p. 148); but the 'heaven' in which Clive does not believe (p. 114) is uncapitalized in all three typescripts, and 'science', one interview with which — in the form of Dr Barry — sufficed Maurice (p. 149), has no definite article. In the sentence 'So there would never be any question of this episode of his immaturity' (p. 151), 'would' should be 'could'; and the greeting which Simcox gives Maurice at the beginning of Chapter 39 — 'Cur-tains drawn, sir, nice sir, nice day for the match' — sounds more butler-like when one restores the weather — 'nice air' — to its proper place. At the beginning of Chapter 27, a slip of the 1959 typist's eye — 'The old gentleman evolved his leisure in evolving a new religion' — has been compounded by the substitution, not in Forster's hand, of 'employed' for 'evolved'; thus the missed 1914 and 1932 reading 'occupied' failed to get printed. More seriously, the 1914 description of life as an 'accident of conscious-ness' in Chapter 22 failed to find its way into the 1932 text; instead life became the possible, but in the context surely less likely, 'accident of consequences' we have now.

Perhaps the most important error in the book is a passage in Chapter 41 which must have caused many readers to do an uncomprehending double-take. On page 196 Maurice is talk-ing to Dr Lasker Jones about the happy days when 'Men of my sort could take to the greenwood'. He expands his notion oddly:

> It strikes me there may have been more about the Greeks —
> Theban Band — and the rest of it.

What Maurice actually said, in 1914 and 1932, was this:

> It strikes me there may have been more in that Robin Hood
> business than meets the eye. One knows about the Greeks —
> Theban Band — and the rest of it.

The omitted words form, in the 1932 typescript, a complete line which in transcription has been jumped, creating incoherence in 1971.

It would be incorrect to say that one could multiply examples, but even those I have mentioned reduce the authority of the current text of *Maurice*. But one change it makes from the previous versions does bear Forster's *imprimatur*. At a late stage he amended the second page of the 1959 typescript so that the hero's name, which from his birth some fifty years before had been 'Maurice Hill', should become the Maurice Hall we are now used to. The substitution (within the stockbroking firm of Hill and Hall) was easy to make, and one consequence is the amusing reference on page 24 to 'Chapman and Hall'. But the literary joke was inadvertent; the reason for the change was, as Forster expressed it elsewhere, 'to avoid identification'. In 1956 he noted having heard a talk by a distinguished geophysicist and Fellow of King's, Maurice Hill, FRS (1909–66), but not until a slight contretemps in April, 1964 does the awkward coincidence appear to have registered: 'The hero of my homosexual novel — written years before I ever heard of him — bears his name exactly!'

II

It was Forster's habit in writing his diary — by no means a day-to-day record — to use each December 31st as the receptacle for a summary of his year. His entry for 31 December 1913 begins: 'Maurice born on Sept. 13th'. It ends with the invocation: 'Edward Carpenter! Edward Carpenter! Edward Carpenter!' The latter, in effect, begat the former. Carpenter, an ex-clergy-man and Cambridge don, had 'dropped out' of society in 1874; when Forster visited him in 1913 he was 69, and had been leading his homosexual simple life on his farm between Sheffield and

Chesterfield for thirty years, a fact which needs to be considered if one is tempted to dismiss the happy ending Forster implies for Maurice and Alec. Forster's visit triggered off his novel, and particularly the touch on the small of his back by George Merrill, Carpenter's working-class 'comrade'. The 'touch' was built into the end of Part III some time in the nineteen-fifties, but the immediacy of its effect is already there in the 1914 text as Alec climbs the ladder: 'a little noise sounded, a noise so intimate that it might have arisen inside his own body'.

The writing-out of Forster's reaction produced what he termed at the end of 1913 '3 months of exaltation'. How far in the novel that feeling had taken him by then is not easy to establish precisely, but it seems likely that he had finished Parts I and II: the 1914 typescript of these is a very clean one and survives with only few and small changes in the printed text. But on 17 December 1913 he had already recorded a check: Goldsworthy Lowes Dickinson had read with 'disgust' one of his (presumably erotic) short stories and 'My smooth spurt is over'. Work resumed at the end of the year, but Forster was not yet sure how Maurice's life would turn out, asking himself 'will he ever be happy [?]'. Maurice's movement towards an eventual satis-factory relationship with Alec was almost disrupted by a visit Forster paid in March 1914 to his old King's friend Hugh Meredith, who was, if anyone was, the original of Clive. Like Clive he had 'become normal' and married, and one is tempted to ascribe some of the more sour notes in the novel's portrayal of Clive's latter-day character, especially in Chapters 37 and 46,[5] to the pain Forster felt at Meredith's attitude: he was 'reluctant to read' *Maurice*, then 'despised' it. Writing to his close friend Florence Barger a year later, Forster confided 'that Hugh can't again be in my life what he has been', and spoke of Meredith's 'utter indifference to *Maurice*'[6] which had so 'disconcerted' him that 'I nearly chucked it'.[7] Nevertheless he persevered, telling Florence Barger at the end of June 1914 that he had 'almost completed a long novel, but it is unpublishable until my death and England's'.[8]

Appropriately, the first person to read the completed, or virtually completed, novel was Edward Carpenter, in August. He was particularly pleased by the 'major chord' of the ending, which he thought 'the one bit of real romance'.[9] What Carpenter was referring to was not Chapter 46 but the Epilogue which followed it in the 1914 text. (More will be said of this later; other friends whose literary judgement Forster valued more highly were less happy with it and it was removed by 1932.) But in a letter to E. J. Dent in March 1915, Forster related Carpenter's comment on the ending — 'improbable but not impossible' — not to the Epilogue but to the presentation of Alec himself, which he said had been 'bad and unfinished' at that time. All one can say of this confusion is that a number of changes, manuscript amendments in the 1914 text, were made both to the rendering of Alec in Chapter 37 and to the latter part of the Epilogue, presumably between August 1914 and March 1915.

Goldsworthy Lowes Dickinson read *Maurice* at the end of 1914, its effect being to put him 'on a basis of comradeship at last'[10] with Forster. Forster's reply (13 December 1914) to his letter about the novel implies Dickinson's earlier acquaintance with it, and indeed at some point Forster had read parts of it to him.[11] Forster's reply also implies that Dickinson had criticized the Epilogue (in which the later life of Maurice and Alec was shown and not, as now, simply suggested), and appears to offer a half-hearted defence of it: 'The Scudder part certainly is better, but I agree. I might have been wiser to let that also[12] resolve into dust or mist, but the temptation's overwhelming to grant to one's creations a happiness actual life does not supply'.

The copy of *Maurice* which Dickinson read was circulated by him to two other Fellows of King's, John Sheppard and Maynard Keynes. Like all Forster's friends who saw the novel, they were asked to keep it 'as dead as a secret can be'. Their comments have not survived, but a letter of Forster's to E. J. Dent (the model for Philip Herriton in *Where Angels Fear to Tread*) gives us the responses of three other Cambridge friends who saw it early in 1915. Sydney Waterlow found it 'moving, and persuasive to all but bigots', yet better as a thesis than as a novel; whereas Roger Fry and Dent himself thought it 'beautiful and the best work I have done'.[13] After what in March 1915 he called the 'loneliness' of 'a year's work' (which suggests that he tinkered with the 1914 text at least until the autumn), Forster was pleased and comforted to find that his private vision could communicate artistically: 'I wrote it neither for my friends or [*sic*] the public — but because it was weighing on me; and my previous training made me write it as literature'. To his friend Florence Barger, who read and admired it in April 1915, he spoke of it in a letter from

Alexandria the following year as 'only one splash' of 'this enormous torrent in me that never stops' — a torrent of physical feeling which Forster was 'weary of controlling' in favour of 'all the unsubstantial fog of the spirit'.[14] The extent to which *Maurice* was the outlet for impulses and affections presented obliquely in his other novels is clear enough from this *cri-de-coeur*.

Very few of the favourable reactions to *Maurice* on the part of Forster's friends are of much help in a textual study of the novel, where among other things one is concerned with distinguishing between alterations made *currente calamo*; as a result of authorial second thoughts; and in response to specific criticisms. For one thing the reactions are too general; for another they are often preserved only as reflections in Forster's own letters. One notable exception is a letter of detailed comment sent by Lytton Strachey on 12 March 1915,[15] which is invaluable, when set beside the 1914 and the published texts, in showing Forster's variable willingness to make verbal alterations and in establishing a likely date (or *terminus ad quem*) for them. It also confirms the fact that certain changes in chapter numbering, visible in the 1914 text and implying a rather different initial shape for the latter part of the novel, had been made before Strachey saw it.

Most of Strachey's detailed objections were heeded by Forster, though it is interesting to note that not even his assigning the phrase 'ill-conditioned' (Ch. 31) to the vocabulary of Herbert Pembroke caused it to be altered. Forster's attitude to homosexuality, indeed to sex generally, was less emancipated than that of Strachey, who took much more lightly the kind of thoughts Maurice can be presumed to be having in the railway-carriage.[16] Nevertheless he removed the element of defensiveness which Strachey criticized in Chapter 43: the phrase in the British Museum scene distinguishing Maurice's love for Alec from his lust for Dickie Barry does not appear in the 1932 text, and had in fact been an afterthought in the text of 1914. Strachey's objection on the grounds of inconsistency to Clive's declaration in Chapter 9 — 'I love you as if you were a woman' — is registered by the 1932 text, where Maurice is only told 'I love you'. By then Forster had also removed the epithet 'Adamantine'; Strachey said of this 'it can't be right', when in 1914's Chapter 44 (containing most of the material of our present Chapter 45) it introduced the sentence 'He faced Mr. Borenius, who had lost all grasp of events' (p. 223).

Strachey found Maurice's love for Alec not entirely convincing partly because the 1914 text had made Maurice appear 'exaggeratedly upper-classish'. In so far as one can with any confidence attribute particular textural alterations to this more general objection, they seem to have taken two forms. One is small-scale excision. Maurice's first sight of Alec is of 'a gamekeeper dallying with two of the maids' in the grounds of Penge (p. 153); in 1914 'he fixed the trio with a haughty stare'; in 1932 'he stared at the trio, feeling cruel and respectable'. But as most of Chapter 34's first paragraph was originally a manuscript addition to the 1914 typescript, one cannot be sure of its relevance here. Better evidence of a possible response to Strachey occurs in Chapter 40, when Maurice is told that the man he has by now slept with is the son of a butcher: in 1914 his mental response was 'A butcher's son's about the limit', the snobbery of which was at least disguised by 1932's 'This is about the limit'. And Maurice's description of himself to Dr Lasker Jones (Ch. 42) as one who 'always kept servants in their places' is cancelled in the 1914 text itself. Larger-scale additions to Chapter 37 (mentioned above in connection with Forster's letter to E. J. Dent of March 1915) may also, in part, have been meant to create an air of greater ease and friendliness between Maurice and Alec. Their encounter on page 172 was part of an addition in Forster's hand to the 1914 text, as was Maurice's warm view of Alec at the top of page 176; and their encounter in the shrubbery (p. 177) had been added by 1932.

A final example of Strachey's criticism leads directly to a consideration of the nature of the 1914 text held by King's College, Cambridge. If Strachey was unable to persuade Forster to call Maurice's thoughts in the railway-carriage something other than a disapproving 'ill-conditioned', he was it would seem able to modify Forster's view of Maurice's resort to masturbation in Chapter 32. He complained that Forster called it a 'malpractice' for which Maurice paid the price of 'a creeping apathy towards all things'. This, for Strachey, was making altogether too much of it: 'as often as not the effects are simply nil'. The phrasing of the published novel, which is identical with the 1932 text here, suggests some compromise between Forster's view and Strachey's:

. . . in his despair he turned to the practices he had abandoned

> as a boy, and found they did bring him a degraded kind of peace, did still the physical urge into which all his sensations were contracting, and enable him to do his work.   (p. 149)

It would be natural to expect the 1914 text to display the earlier phrasing Strachey objected to. Instead, there is no trace of it; the relevant passage is exactly the same as that quoted above. The likely conclusion is that Strachey read a different copy of the 1914 text, which has not survived and which at least at this point embodied a soon discarded reading. The 1914 text we have, whose later chapters have been renumbered, itself suggests the existence of an earlier structure which has vanished; but since Strachey's copy agrees with ours in giving the number 44 to the 'crisis' chapter (the one at Southampton), that cannot have been it. Nevertheless, were the lost Strachey copy (which may have been the one read by Florence Barger later) ever to be found it might establish a clearer forward line of development for *Maurice*, as evidence both internal and external makes it most unlikely that the 1914 text now at King's was used as the copy-text for the 1932 typescript.

III

The copy of *Maurice* which E. J. Dent read in February 1915 was borrowed not from Forster himself but from a friend of his named Leonard Greenwood, to whom Dent was instructed by Forster to return it. In 1967, two years after Greenwood's death, the almost-blind Forster recorded the receipt, from Greenwood's executors, of 'the M.S. I lent 40 or so [years] ago'; it had been discovered in a disused safe. Found again among Forster's papers in 1970, this is the text of the 1914 *Maurice* we now have. The story of its lucky, and I feel devoted, preservation is not known; whatever it was, scholars of Forster are deeply in Greenwood's debt.[17]

His care for the text itself is manifest. Whereas the versions of 1932 and 1959 are uniform typescripts, each of 347 pages, the earlier one incorporating a fair quantity of Forster's ms. amendments, the version of 1914 is altogether richer and more multifarious, consisting of 227 larger pages which can be broken down into six distinct sorts. The greater part of the text is typescript carbons, purple in colour; the typeface from Chapter 7 onwards is bigger than that which precedes it. Throughout this large grouping there are many amendments in Greenwood's careful and elegant script, fewer in Forster's more rapid one. But, within it, some pages are entirely in Forster's hand, notably additions to the present Chapter 37; others, particularly the first four pages of the British Museum chapter, are in Greenwood's. Of especial interest is the fact that there are two complete and parallel versions of the present Chapter 46 (numbered 45 in 1914). One is a black typescript carbon, or possibly top copy, with alterations and cancellations in Forster's hand; the other is a blue carbon, amended in Greenwood's hand. Greenwood's amendments would seem to follow Forster's, but there are some which he does not include, which suggests to me that Forster made further revisions at some later point. The fact that the 1932 and subsequent texts incorporate *all* Forster's changes in Chapter 46 joins with the external evidence (Greenwood's having kept his copy until his death in 1965) in implying that the 1932 version of *Maurice* was made not from Greenwood's 1914 text but from Forster's, only Chapter 46 of which has survived. In support of this view one may cite, *inter alia*, an addition in Forster's 1914 Chapter 46 which is not found in Greenwood's copy but which is transmitted through the 1932 text: the phrase 'or even in England' near the top of page 228.[18] One may also note that the end of Greenwood's Chapter 9 contains, unshortened, the phrase 'I love you as if you were a woman', of which Lytton Strachey successfully complained in 1915.

Parts I and II of *Maurice* — his years at school and at Cambridge — are little different in Greenwood's copy from the printed text. For the benefit of students of the history of slang, it is worth underlining two instances of this fact — the use of the term 'a shit' in connection with Risley's cousin the Dean (p. 25), and the knowing, jokey reference by Maurice to his relationship with Clive as 'a queer business' (p. 82). One might think these locutions fairly recent, but both date from the 1914 typescript. Other 1914 words and phrases were changed, some of them perhaps very early on. In Chapter 17, Maurice originally 'coloured crimson' (p. 86) when Clive's mother mentioned the possibility of her son's marriage; Clive's revulsion from Maurice (Ch. 24) originally caused him not to faint but to vomit, and 'All his thoughts turned nauseous and bitter' (p. 109). These readings were cancelled in the 1914 text, as was a phrase in Chapter 20 which expanded on the restraint and fastidiousness of Clive's love for Maurice: 'they had only saluted a dozen times in the two years'. But for some unspecified time (until the 1932 typescript was made) the division between Parts I and II fell at a different point, the end not of Chapter 11 but of Chapter 12, which concluded with the triumphant, climactic phrase 'They had won' (p. 65).[19]

In Parts III and IV significant differences from the printed text increase, indeed to such an extent that only an edition of the novel could do justice to Forster's first thoughts; if, that is, the 1914 text in our possession contains all of them. Judging from alterations made to the 1914 chapter numbers in that text itself, Part IV at least does not, and to pursue the matter involves a potentially confusing comparison of numbering in the present and 1914 versions. A divergence in numbering first appears at the present Chapter 34: this, in 1914, was two chapters, 34 and 35, the division coming after the sentence 'As twilight fell, he entered a new circle of torment' (p. 156). Thus the 1914 numbers are one digit ahead of the printed text, and Part III ends with Chapter 38. One would therefore expect 1914's Part IV to begin with Chapter 39. Indeed it does, and its situation (though not its wording) is that of our present Chapter 38 — Alex and Maurice in bed at Penge. But the 1914 chapter number 39, and the heading 'Part IV', are pencilled alterations to an original typed number '40' (XL). It would seem reasonable to infer the existence of an *earlier* and now missing Chapter 39, with which Part IV presumably once began; but whether this chapter was substantially different or only a different frame for material we still have it is impossible to tell, though it is worth remarking, again, that 1914's Chapter 38 (our Chapter 37) contains large manuscript additions that may replace discarded passages. There is also — since these altered chapter numbers persist to the end of the 1914 text — the strong possibility of a vanished chapter later in Part IV, a Chapter 45 which would have occurred between the present Chapter 42 (containing Alec's long letter to Maurice) and the present Chapter 45, in which Maurice sees the *Normannia* off. Such palimpsest hints of an 'ur-*Maurice*' are tantalizing, and complicate further the richness of variation visible between 1914 and later texts.

There are too many of these 1914 variants to discuss. Some of them are involved in the delineation of the Penge milieu, and as a sidelight on one of its denizens, the strangely named rector Mr Borenius, one may note a possibly revealing slip of Forster's pen in a manuscript passage added to (our) Chapter 37: Forster wrote 'Mr. Bons' — the culture snob of 'The Celestial Omnibus' — immediately changing this to 'Mr. Borenius — how dry!' (p. 172). His 'sinister' quality is insisted on in a later manuscript passage replaced by 1932: 'he paid no attention to the sophisticated — they were lost souls — but went for the impressionable and young. And Maurice was unsophisticated enough himself to be afraid and to be sorry for the village lads'.

One of these, of course, is the young gamekeeper Alec Scudder — his age is indicated by the 1914 text as about 23 — and the most important of the 1914 variant passages concern Maurice's developing awareness of, and relationship with, him. In 1914 the passages in which Maurice 'struck against corduroys' (p. 174) and later talked with Alec in the shrubbery do not exist. Instead, Alec's physical attractiveness is rendered more explicit in the section describing his entry at Maurice's window at the end of Part III. More lyrical than the shorter, twice-revised final paragraph in the present text, this begins:

> He seemed to crackle and burn and leaping round saw the ladder's top quivering against the moonlit air. Who was climbing up to him, who? From whom did the maddening vibration ascend? From an athlete, beautiful and young, who desired him and whom he desired.

His emotions confused, Maurice invites Alec in, and initial physical reluctance is replaced by a conclusion of generalized rapture:

> All broke. They forgot society and the law and the fruitless knowledge that they were unlike most men. The world became mist, its censure a murmur of leaves. Locked in the glimmering night they established perfection, perfection of a sort, perfection for a time.

The 1914 version of Part IV is structurally, as well as verbally, different from the published text. The conversation between Alec and Maurice which begins it is both shorter and less substantial — more 'dreamy' — in keeping with the partial vision of Alec

as an idealized athlete.[20] Its expansion by 1932, and the filling
out of Alec's individuality by means of details from his everyday
life, may have prompted the (rather awkward) division into two
chapters (38 and 39) of what in 1914 was a single one (39). This
ended, as now, with Maurice 'green-white' of face, fleeing from
the cricket match to his room; but once there he is not 'violently
sick', rather he 'succumbed to a racking fit of laughter'. That this
mocking defiance of society is touched with hysteria and shame
is, I think, implied by a melodramatic sentence — ending in
Chapter 40, truncated by 1932: 'He had abused his host's
confidence and defiled his house in his absence, he had insulted
Mrs. Durham and Anne so foully that were they to know of it they
might go insane'. To generalize from a number of scattered 1914
variants, one may say that Maurice recoils more extremely than
he is made to do later from an idealization of Alec into an
outraged fear of the likelihood of blackmail. His response to
Alec's first letter (p. 192) points this up: 'Maurice — who had
sometimes yearned for some sentimental child of nature — felt
only alarm when the dream came true'. And far from thinking
judiciously that 'if he played his cards carefully he might still get
through' (1932), in 1914 'All Maurice's sex-passion had now
curdled into anger and disgust', tinged with a wish to believe true
the love he now views as a dangerous illusion.

The ingredients of an instinct to blackmail, on Alec's part, and
a responsive fear on Maurice's — both of which are ultimately
conquered — are present in the 1914 British Museum chapter
(numbered 43, as now) which, much and complicatedly re-
arranged, forms the basis of the present text. Curiously enough,
however, Alec's bluff about his brother Fred outside, and his
mention of a 'serious charge' to Mr Ducie, are first found in the
1932 version. Elements not found in the 1932 chapter include
Maurice's statement that 'There are supposed only to be two
sorts of people, but there may be heaps' (which recalls Margaret
Schlegel's 'eternal differences' in Chapter 44 of *Howards End*),
and a harsh authorial comment on the British Museum itself,
which, though 'supposed catholic' (p. 209), nevertheless 'allows
no book on their subject [i.e. homosexuality] to enter its readers'
hands'. But the salient structural difference between the 1914 and
later versions resides in the absence from it of Chapter 44, in
which Maurice and Alec spend the night together in a hotel,
fruitlessly 'talking plans'. Instead, 1914's Chapter 43 diverges

from the present one after the sentence 'By now they were in love with one another consciously', and concludes with a rather didactic but touching conversation as Maurice and Alec walk the wet streets. The possibility of their staying together is considered indirectly and by reluctant negatives: a life 'as mates', it transpires, is poetry, or only for 'heroes', which they are not. Their parting is more noble, less bitter, and thus perhaps less realistic, than that of our present Chapter 44, added by or about 1932. These are some of Maurice's thoughts as he drives away (a middle-class touch) in a 'car' whose prosaic materialization is not described:

> He might for a moment have felt arms round him, and kissed, while yet he was young, the lips of a young man. Yet the pleasure procured would have been reminiscent. They had grown, and he could not desire a better farewell [. . . .] What had Alec made out of the sermon? His manliness had grown inscrutable, and he had never looked back when he tramped coughing into the rain.

From this pre-Hemingway stoicism, the 1914 text goes straight to Southampton, where Maurice sees Alec's boat off. This act is against his better judgement, as in 1932 and now, but the wording of the opening is different: 'The unconquerable longing for happiness bore him down', to be succeeded by 'disillusion' and 'an attack of class nausea' as he confronts 'the sight and smell of the third-class passengers' and Alec's relatives, 'a meaner edition of the type he had loved'. Forster tinkered with details of the rest of this chapter up to the nineteen-fifties, but the present text broadly preserves the matter of 1914. Except, that is, for the ending: in both the 1914 and 1932 versions the chapter finished with an extended form of conversation with Mr Borenius (p. 224), in which Maurice, having exultantly realized 'that Alec was stopping', indicates his intention to return to 'Penge and then London'. His last words are the joyful exclamation 'Oh look at the sky . . . . It's as if it's on fire'. The 1914 Penge chapter, our final Chapter 46, was revised in numerous small details (notably the wording to Clive of Maurice's physical relations with Alec), but its material was not essentially changed. It is worth emphasizing this *à propos* the beautiful penultimate paragraph, in which Maurice vanishes from Clive's life, to leave ultimately nostalgic memories of 'the scent and sounds of the May term'. David Craig, reviewing *Maurice* in 1971,[21] aptly called this a 'dissolve', but was wrong in supposing the passage a late revision: it dates from 1914.

But one element in the 1914 text was unique, and had disappeared from *Maurice* by 1932. This was the epilogue (it had no chapter number): five pages of blue carbon typescript, with alterations in Greenwood's hand, and a lacuna of unknown size (but probably not large) near the end. Forster's memory of its date of composition, in his 'Terminal Note' of 1960, seems confused: he says that he 'was encouraged to write an epilogue' partly by others, which suggests it was an afterthought to the main text. But Carpenter read it in August 1914, and, in March the following year, Lytton Strachey. Nor was Forster quite accurate in saying that the Epilogue 'gave universal dissatisfaction', to judge from the surviving documentary evidence. Rather, some friends felt reservations about it: Goldsworthy Lowes Dickinson for one, and Strachey, to whom 'your Sherwood Forest ending' seemed 'slightly mythical'. It occurs in autumn, five years later, in 'a haggard country' of plantations, somewhere in Yorkshire, in which Maurice's sister Kitty, bicycling on a solitary holiday, encounters Maurice and Alec working together as woodcutters. Kitty is a curiously sympathetic young spinster of 27, and whatever the awkwardness of her being used as an intermediary to supply the reader with the suburban repercussions of Maurice's disappearance, there is a sexually ambiguous quality in her isolation which makes her a suitable person to realize, suddenly, what pressure has brought her brother and 'his friend' to abandon the accustomed world. From her reflections the conclusion of the Epilogue jumps to the practical effect of the encounter on Maurice and Alec, and in a passage dovetailed in Greenwood's hand on to the typescript,[22] to a final authorial statement of their precarious achievement:

Couched in a shed near their work — to sleep rough had proved safer — they shared in whispered review the events of the day before falling asleep. Kitty was included, and they decided to leave their present job and find work in a new district, in case she told the Police or returned. In the glow of manhood 'There we shall be safe' they thought. They were never to be that. But they were together for a moment, they had stayed disintegration and combined daily work with love; and who can hope for more?

IV

Writing to E. J. Dent in August 1915, Forster said that '*Maurice* appears to be my swan song', adding however the hope that 'perhaps something else will occur'. Shortly afterwards he sailed for Alexandria, where he spent the war working for the Red Cross, and what occurred there was not further fiction, but his love affair with a handsome Egyptian tram-conductor, Mohammed el Adl. This is likely to have had in due course its effect on the text of *Maurice*, since in letters to Florence Barger Forster talks of the relationship in terms of the novel. On 4 April 1918 he wrote of a meeting in el Adl's room which was a 'crisis', tinged, it would seem, with fear and class-mistrust on Forster's side:

> I thought he had meant to insult me, and left in a fury. He was puzzled and distressed, but very dignified. All through it is *I* who have endangered the thing — curiously like Maurice towards the end of the book. I have found it so hard to believe he was neither a traitor or [sic] cad.

A month later, he wrote glowingly of el Adl's superiority to 'the people one meets in offices and clubs . . . people of position dank with self-righteousness', and concluded:

> How gloriously right E.C. [Edward Carpenter] has been! and 'Maurice' wrong chiefly because of my timidity and doubt whether human emotion, unaided by social labels, could attain so much.

It seems as if Forster's experience with el Adl (who died of consumption in 1922 but was long and tenderly remembered[23]) provided a realization of Maurice's gradual movement from Clive, and his own class, to a viable relationship with one of lower class. Thus I should suggest that much of the expansion of Alec visible in the 1932 text, particularly the more realistic conversation of Chapter 38 and the addition of Chapter 44, results from this actual experience, and from the reinforcement it provided for Forster's dream of homosexual love.

We have, however, insufficient evidence by which to date precisely these and other small changes[24] to the 1914 text. Forster left his locked diary behind when he went to Alexandria, so there are no entries between October 1915 and April 1919, the year when he returned to England. P. N. Furbank has advanced 1919 as a year when revisions were made, but Forster's letters suggest 1920. He had offered to lend the 'unpublished thing' to Bob and Bessie Trevelyan in February 1920, having 're-read it lately, with less approval than I expected. Parts are good, and I like the style, but there are grave faults some of which I may alter some day'. In fact, he tidied up the manuscript 'in the hope of giving you a more favourable impression of it'[25] by early March, and received within days a 'very fine and encouraging letter' about it from Bessie Trevelyan. It is a pity this has not survived, since it was obviously also a detailed letter. One can only infer her particular comments, and any action Forster possibly took later as a result of them, from his reply of 18 March 1920:

. . . now I find myself thinking less of it. The end is certainly wrong — dead rather than wrong, but that's as bad or worse. I see what is wrong with it, I fancy, and what Scudder ought to be; there's too much theory about him. But I don't think I shall rewrite him. You are right too about the changes of method, though the fault here was that of technical incompetence. I couldn't think how to convey the necessary information.

If the phrase 'changes of method' refers partly to the Epilogue, which looks at events from a quite new viewpoint, that of Kitty, Bessie Trevelyan's objection may have led Forster to abandon it, especially if, as seems likely, it was the 'wrong' or 'dead' ending referred to. Certainly Forster's reason given in his 'Terminal Note — that the Epilogue, five years after the action's date, 1912, would have landed Maurice and Alec in the First World War — is not entirely convincing, since his completion of the 1914 text overlapped the start of the war. But its scrapping by 1932 may have had a more cogent internal point: the picture of Maurice and Alec in an idealized 'simple life' future may have seemed less necessary, and artistically unbalanced, once more material showing them together in the present had been added to earlier sections of Part IV. Still, though the Epilogue is absent from the 1932 typescript, Forster was not even then absolutely decided about it. Christopher Isherwood, who was shown the novel in April 1933, has written recently of discussions between him and Forster as to the merits of various endings, the Epilogue clearly being one of them.[26]

It is from the 1914 text, as substantially modified by the version 'typed in final form, 1932',[27] that the published text of *Maurice* derives. But a few changes of detail, and one large addition, were still to be made, and these are found, some in blue-black ink, a few in green, written in Forster's nineteen-fifties hand in the 1932 typescript, from which they were copied into the final version typed in 1959. Most of these are likely to date from 1952, on the last night of which Forster sat for a long time in King's College (not in his own rooms there) 'revising *Maurice*'s end' — not, it would appear, just the last chapter but the whole of Part IV, and perhaps also at this time the last paragraph of Part III. The 1932 text had abbreviated the 1914 union of Maurice and Alec into two sentences: 'Everything broke. Locked in the glimmering darkness he established perfection, perfection of a sort, perfection for a time'. Twenty years later Forster replaced this with the quieter, more circumstantial single sentence we have now.

The changes in Part IV are all small, but interesting; though they can only be sampled. One is rather strange: the phrase at the end of Chapter 38 — 'and took up the gun that had guarded them through the night' (p. 183). This is a green ink replacement for 1932's typed 'and went as they had come'; but it, in its turn, was crossed out by Forster in black ink. It still appears, however, in the 1959 typescript. The remaining changes are textually straight-forward, and are concentrated in the last three chapters. Chapter 44 adds the phrases 'all troubles over' (p. 213) and 'There's bin enough fighting' (p. 214); 'put forth violence' (p. 215) replaces the 1932 'desperately violently'; and on page 217 Alec's 'I don't want no unpleasantness to finish with' is added, perhaps to relocate the spirit of the excised phrase — 'and what he mustn't do was to say anything which might fester afterwards' — which in 1932 followed Maurice's 'He had lost'. In Chapter 45, Maurice's answer — 'It . . . was advertised' — to Mr Borenius's query about the boat's sailing time replaces 'Why could he not answer?' found in 1914 and 1932. In Chapter 46, Clive is shown reacting strongly (and perhaps stagily) to Maurice's news about his night with Alec at Penge: 'Maurice — oh, good God!'. In 1914 his reaction had been the oddly weak 'Is — is that all?', which Forster had cancelled but found no substitute for. On page 230 Maurice is asked to dine with Clive 'the following week' and 'Next Wednesday', instead of 'the following day' and 'Tomorrow then — ' (1914 and 1932). And since the rhythms of endings are a matter of concern to writers and readers, the very last phrase of *Maurice*, changed no fewer than three times, should be recorded. The original 1914 reading was 'meditating how best he could conceal the deplorable incident from Anne, his wife'. 'Deplorable' was then cancelled in the 1914 typescript. In 1932 the whole phrase became 'to correct his proofs and to devise some method of concealing the affair from his wife'. Finally 'his wife' was changed to 'Anne', giving the satisfying cadence with which the novel now closes.[28]

But the last word of the novel was not the last word Forster wrote. In 1958, as P. N. Furbank has recorded in his biography,[29] Forster's attention was drawn to the inconclusiveness of the Southampton chapter. Having exultantly realized that Alec has not caught the boat, how, Forster was asked, was Maurice 'actually going to find' him? By 1959, the chapter no longer stopped at the promise of a 'sky on fire', but was extended by some handwritten pages now to be found in the 1932 text along with the typed version made of them; they are represented by pages 224–5 of the printed text. This beautifully paced passage, lyrical yet sober, inserted conveniently and with no sense of strain into the already existing time-scheme, shows Maurice returning to Penge, where he finds Alec waiting for him in the boathouse. Maurice's belief, at Southampton, that 'England belonged to them' — itself a sort of answer to the question posed in Chapter 19 of *Howards End* — is given substance by the quiet confidence of their reunion, which adumbrates the future and, at last, makes Forster's Epilogue artistically superfluous. 'And now we shan't be parted no more, and that's finished' are the last words of the revised chapter. The final phrase is, also, Forster's appropriate farewell to a novel which had been in his mind, intermittently, for forty-five years,[30] and which contains some of his sparest, tautest writing, as well as some of his most impassioned.

NOTES

1. E. M. Forster, *Maurice* (London: Edward Arnold, 1971), p. 235.
2. See P. N. Furbank, *E. M. Forster: A Life* (New York: Harcourt Brace

Jovanovich, 1977), II, p. 306. Furbank records that the typescript was handed over to Forster at the end of May 1959.

3. This is the Penguin (1972) 'reading adopted'; that listed (but not actually printed) in the Arnold (1971) edition is 'waiting for Durham'.

4. Joseph Wright, *English Dialect Dictionary* (London: H. Frowde, 1902). Its provenance is given as Shropshire (which Forster had visited in 1907); also Somerset and Devon.

5. An especially nasty touch (only found in the 1914 text of Ch. 46) is Forster's description of Clive's attitude to the 'luminous petals' in Maurice's hand (p. 229): 'though they were worthless Clive felt a regret for property destroyed'.

6. Forster, letter to Florence Barger, 10 August 1915.

7. Forster to Florence Barger, 27 April 1915.

8. Forster to Florence Barger, 29 June 1914.

9. Edward Carpenter to Forster, 23 August [1914]. Printed in *E. M. Forster: The Critical Heritage*, ed. Philip Gardner (London: Routledge and Kegan Paul, 1973), p. 428.

10. Forster's diary, 31 December 1914.

11. Forster to E. J. Dent, 8 February 1915: 'I wanted a word with you, but hadn't the opportunity. That *was* my own novel that I was reading to Dickinson, but it is unfortunately unprintable and indeed unmentionable'.

12. The precise force of 'also' is unclear. I can only suggest that Forster is thinking of the relationship between Maurice and Clive, which resolves into dust and mist.

13. Forster to E. J. Dent, 6 March 1915.

14. Forster to Florence Barger, 6 October 1916. This letter, unusually revealing and written in pencil, appears not to have been sent.

15. This is printed in full in *E. M. Forster: The Critical Heritage*, pp. 429–31.

16. See my remarks in *The Critical Heritage* in connection with *Ermyntrude and Esmeralda*, p. 429.

17. Not much is known about Greenwood's friendship with Forster. A New Zealander, born in 1880, Greenwood came as a Classical Scholar to King's in 1889, and he and Forster were both Apostles. From 1909 to the end of his life, Greenwood was a Fellow of Emmanuel. He spent the Christmas of 1913 with Forster and his mother at Weybridge, and was perhaps the first to know about *Maurice*, sharing Forster's view at the end of the year that its hero had 'become an independent existence'. (Forster's diary, 31 December 1913.) The nature and duration of the friendship is suggested by a cryptic entry in Forster's diary at the end of 1914, in which he took stock of various relationships: 'L.H.G.G. I am to blame. I ought not to have. It worries me that entirely through my own fault my feelings have altered . . .' A further visit in 1923 is merely noted by Forster, and the lack of material makes futile any speculation on the possible extra-bibliographical connection between Greenwood and *Maurice*.

18. An opposite instance is found in the present Ch. 45 (p. 219). The description of Scudder — 'Alec's main charm was the fresh colouring that surged against the cliff of his hair' — is crossed out in Greenwood's 1914 text, but appears in the 1932 typescript. Presumably this was an excision about which Forster later changed his mind.

19. When the division was moved, this strong phrase was presumably no longer needed. However, it is interesting to see it surfacing again at the

end of Forster's 'Little Imber' (1961), the incomplete tailpiece to which
concludes 'Males had won'. (See footnote 30 below.)

20. His physique is graphically indicated in 1914's Ch. 39. The present
     sentence beginning, 'He was in white flannels' (p. 187) then concluded:
     'and strode obvious under them; the lame lady had to turn her head
     away in case she admired him'. The 1914 version, including its Epilogue,
     particularly stresses Alec's physical attractiveness to *women*, and one
     recalls Gerald in *The Longest Journey*. It is perhaps relevant here to note
     that all the men Forster loved (Meredith, Masood, Mohammed el Adl,
     Bob Buckingham) got married.

21. David Craig, *The Times Higher Education Supplement*, 15 October 1971.
     Craig's mistake results, I think, from a misunderstanding of P. N.
     Furbank's introduction to the 1971 *Maurice*.

22. The alterations to the Epilogue are difficult to date. In a letter to Dent, 6
     March 1915, Forster wrote: 'About the epilogue, I quite agree, and it shall
     be altered'; but dissatisfaction with 'the end' (Epilogue or Part IV?) is
     also expressed in a letter to Bessie Trevelyan, 18 March 1920.

23. Among Forster's papers at King's are two Alexandria tram-tickets. He
     also kept a pencil belonging to el Adl, with which he recorded in his diary
     the completion of *A Passage to India*.

24. As examples of small changes made by 1932, one may instance the final
     phrases of Maurice and Dr Lasker Jones (pp. 169–70); this conversation,
     in 1914, ended: 'The doctor told him to read *Punch* for a few minutes in the
     waiting room before he started'. Alterations were also made to the
     phrasing of Alec's second letter (p. 201): for instance, instead of 'It was
     before you came' 1914 has, 'I know how Mr. Durham treated you. That
     was not fair, now you are not fair', and the next sentence originally read:
     'It is natural to want a girl when no gentleman signs to you, you cannot
     go against human nature'.

25. Forster's letter to R. C. Trevelyan, 7 March 1920.

26. See Christopher Isherwood, *Christopher and His Kind* (New York: Farrar,
     Straus, Giroux, 1976), pp. 125–7.

27. Possibly some changes were made the year before: a letter from Forster to
     T. E. Lawrence in 1931 has the sentences: 'How good Mauriac is. I am
     just reading Genetrix', but for 'Mauriac' Forster first wrote 'Maurice'.

28. One should add, perhaps, a more revealing personal change. The phrase
     'old age' in reference to Clive (p. 230) was also supplied by Forster in the
     1950s. Previously the word used was 'senility', but by now Forster was
     over seventy and may have felt it to be unduly harsh.

29. Furbank, II, p. 304.

30. It was not, however, Forster's farewell to fiction. His last work was a short
     story, 'Little Imber', written in November 1961. Set in a Huxley-esque
     future, it triumphs if only in fantasy over the sterility of homosexuals
     deplored in Ch. 17 of *Maurice* (and perhaps suggested obliquely in Ch. 23
     of *The Longest Journey* by Rickie's dream of his mother saying 'let them die
     out'). The story offers the possibility of a *fruitful* homosexual union. 'Little
     Imber' — a sort of Alec-figure — is named after the now derelict and
     inaccessible village of Imber, located in a military firing-range on Salisbury
     Plain — the last occurrence of Wiltshire, a country which haunts Forster's
     fiction.

14 Annotating the Imagination

Elizabeth Heine

The editing of an author's drafts of a novel or a story is itself a form of annotation, less obviously so than explanatory notes on literary allusions or geographical and historical references but just as important for tracing the paths followed by the author's imagination in creating the fiction. The occasional direct annotations necessary to mark a doubtful manuscript reading are only the surface indications of a continual process of decision, for readings of semi-legible words are often interpretations dependent on the reader's sense of the author's imagination — imagination rather than style because the style of the finished work usually results from the author's revision and polishing of an initial way of seeing. The thing described or the idea indicated in the drafts may be fully present in the imagination before it is fully expressed and styled in the way most fitting to the author's intentions for the work as a whole. Or an idea may be less well-imagined, and the process of polishing may bring a subtly different idea into expression. In either case there is no guarantee that the word one might expect to see in a finished work is the word that appears in the draft, though one's expectations may lead one to see it. The editor is thus most neutral when most accurate, and least neutral when manuscripts are difficult to decipher and to organize in terms of the finished work. Since I contributed to Oliver Stallybrass's edition of *The Manuscripts of A Passage to India* (Abinger Edition, vol. 6a)[1] as a minor annotator of doubtful readings, I would like to indicate some of the measures taken to ensure as much accuracy as possible in that volume, before going on to consider some of the problems of annotation which turned up as I confronted the task of completing the edition of *Arctic Summer and Other Fiction* (Abinger

Edition, vol. 9).

Anyone wishing to study the manuscripts of *A Passage to India* now has the inestimable advantage of two thorough representations of their substance, each made with a different end in view. Robert L. Harrison's 1964 dissertation[2] is essentially a transcription of the manuscripts, visually oriented to the look of the manuscript pages and set within the frame of the text of the first British edition. Oliver Stallybrass, as in his edition of *The Manuscripts of Howards End* (Abinger Edition, vol. 4a), presents the evolution of the text of the Abinger edition of *A Passage to India* (vol. 6)[3] with as much attention as possible to the order of the mental processes reflected in the changes from the manuscripts. The existence of Harrison's work meant that the accuracy of Stallybrass's could be checked against that rarest of sources, a reading provided by someone not involved in the same project, and the difference in purpose meant that Stallybrass could not simply depend on Harrison's transcription, but was instead forced to consider its accuracy at all points. As someone who was called on to re-examine points of difference against the manuscripts, I would say that the few words still undeciphered are likely to remain so, although there is always the possibility that another pair of eyes may see more clearly.

Directed always to look at troublesome passages, I sometimes forgot that most of the manuscript can be read without too much difficulty. Even three hundred queries are few in a manuscript of five hundred leaves, and many of the questions I considered arose simply because all doubtful marks in the photocopy of the manuscript at King's College, Cambridge, had to be checked against the original at the Humanities Research Center in Austin, Texas. Oliver Stallybrass did much of the checking in person; I made a useful double-checker. In some ways the physical distance between the editor and the original, necessitating the use of the photocopy, was an aid rather than a disadvantage in the pursuit of accuracy. Editor and assistant checked Harrison and the photocopy in England; the editor checked the results against the originals; near Austin and already familiar with Forster's handwriting, I could check problems against the manuscripts once again. In so far as both different readers and different readings, distinct for reasons of distance in space and time, are a prerequisite for accuracy, the Abinger edition of the manuscripts benefited from both Harrison's work and the need for the photocopy.

Answering queries, I often did no more than ascertain whether an unusual punctuation mark apparent in the photocopy was or was not an aberrant fleck of some sort, or offer an opinion about an order of succession which might depend on inks indistinguishable in photocopy. The reconstructions of orders of composition marked 'tentative' in the Abinger volume reflect the editor's best judgement of the author's track through heavily deleted passages; however tentative, the reconstructions are indispensable guides for anyone confronting the manuscripts in person. At the very least practically all the words will have been deciphered. Queries would be sent to me in a neutral form and I usually worked without reference to Harrison. Thus I often found that I was simply justifying either a Stallybrass or a Harrison reading, usually by a descriptive annotation; my note might read, 'The word is *tried*, with the cross on the *t* acting like a hat over the *e*, and no dot for the *i*' (*tried* replaces *were careful* on leaf A212 and appears on p. 319 of the Abinger *Manuscripts*). Sometimes, as in reading *unalarming* for Harrison's *unbecoming* (leaf A226; *Manuscripts*, p. 336), I might see easily what had been detected as a possible misreading but not clarified in photocopy. Or I might do no better than to accede to the dreadful asterisks which indicate unresolved illegibility. One nearly asterisked word particularly pleases me because I wrote out the struggle to decipher it, and the act of writing not only recorded the process but triggered the solution. The question was something like, 'What is that word followed by *in love*?' In my notes the answer reads: 'Beats me. Looks like a mixture of *bountiful* and *beautiful* and *bumpkin* corrupted by a *harrumph* — *housefly*? *butterfly*? (I'd better give up.) — [New and triumphant line:] How about *triumph in love*, with the cross for the *t* over by the *p*?' Sometimes a cheerful mood is as much an aid in manuscript decipherment as a kinesthetic trigger, for it seems to me that the joky *harrumph*, did the trick. From the last line of A77, a placement which helps to account for its ill-formation, *triumph* now appears on p. 93 of the Abinger *Manuscripts*, replacing Harrison's *b***** but still accompanied by an editorial question mark, a direct annotation indicating less certainty, or more prudence, than I felt in the pleasure of discovery.

All three of the examples above occur in draft passages fairly far removed from the final text. *Tried* appears in the single paragraph, showing a group of men in the Club who 'tried to keep cool' in their reactions to Aziz's arrest, which was revised to focus on the Collector alone before broadening to the general response (Abinger *Passsage*, xx, 174). The same phrase appears in an earlier version of this much rewritten passage, where the men are responding to the Collector's restraint of his rage. In the final version only the Collector restrains himself; the others 'behave naturally' and demand revenge. The change from *were careful* to *tried* is in part stylistic but also accords with Forster's gradual shift away from showing such an attempt on the part of the men. In the end he emphasizes their lack of restraint. *Unalarming* occurs in the earlier of two extant versions of the description of the 'small tazia', an emblem of a famous tomb, commemorating murder and religious warfare. Finally 'a frivolous and flimsy erection, more like a crinoline than the tomb of the grandson of the Prophet' (*Passage*, xxi, 182), it is at first 'childish and unalarming'. Probably the later mention of a crinoline, important primarily for its shape, triggered Harrison's reading. *Triumph* appears in the draft of the paragraph about the 'thrilling game' Aziz plays in trying to persuade Professor Godbole to speak of the Marabar Caves (*Passage*, vii. 68). Considering the nature of the crucial events in the caves, this last of the three most deserves annotation. There is inescapable irony in the suggestion that for Aziz obtaining an answer from Godbole would be 'the intellectual equivalent of a triumph [?] in love'.

In each of the examples above the suitability of the deciphered word in its context supports the reading. Another problem of decipherment can serve to illustrate both Forster's skill in finding *le mot juste* and the differences between the Stallybrass and Harrison representations of the manuscripts. When Ronnie Heaslop meets Aziz at Fielding's tea party (*Passage*, vii, 69) he restrains his desire to 'retort' to Aziz's provocations and silently identifies his 'type' as the 'spoilt westernized'. The corresponding entry in the manuscript volume shows that the whole clause — 'and this was the spoilt westernized' — was an added element, and that in it *spoilt* replaced *semi*, not immediately, continuing on the same line *currente calamo* [with running pen], but later, for *spoilt* is marked as an insertion. Harrison's transcript shows that *spoilt* in fact appears only in the text of the novel, not in the manuscript, but *semi* is not deciphered, probably because its placement in the manuscript is odd. What Harrison's transcription indicates is an indecipherable four-letter word above the deleted 'as he said afterwards' which initially followed 'retort'. In the manuscript, however, there is also an obsure hook which connects the four-letter puzzle to *Westernized* below, in the added clause inserted above the line in such a way that *semi* had to be inserted higher on the page; the context makes the prefix clear. But neither representation shows the progressive insertions exactly, for in Stallybrass's edition the deciphered *semi* is shown merely as a deletion within the major insertion. Harrison provides more of the look of the page and a clear distinction between the manuscript stage and changes made later; Stallybrass gives the more accurate reading, emphasizing substance and order rather than appearance and stage. In general, as their different purposes would suggest, Stallybrass is the better guide to the process of the novel's evolution, but Harrison remains useful because in his presentation changes can be traced to a given manuscript leaf and placed more easily in the manuscript context.

As for those ultimate annotations of the manuscript editor, emendations in the text of the finished work, Oliver Stallybrass is scrupulously clear about his reasons for his choices. In the sentence beginning, 'Others praised Him with attributes' (*Passage*, xxxvi, 304), logic alone justifies the change to *with* from the clearly wrong *without* of all previous editions, but the manuscript also reads *with*. The same combination of logic and manuscript support explains the return to the manuscript *earth* from the *vault* of previous editions in the last sentence of the third paragraph of the novel, the first clause of which now reads, 'The distance between the earth and them is as nothing to the distance behind them'. For almost all of the more than forty emendations based on manuscript readings, there is the same sense of 'Yes, of course, that's certainly right'. In a very few cases, where a return to the manuscript reading chiefly affects style rather than logic, some debate may continue. Forster was certainly not a perfectionist in his proofreading, but it is always possible that a typist's misreading may have suited him. It makes little difference whether squirrels *squeal* or *squeak* (*Passage*, x, 105), or whether one *hears* or *learns* a proverb (*Passage*, xvi, 151), but I suspect that interesting stylistic arguments about the placement of 'in the bazaars' in the seventh sentence of the novel (at the beginning, or at the end?) are now inevitable.

Two particular questions of emendation, one resulting in a change and one not, illustrate how the final decision depends both on the logic of facts and on the editor's sense of Forster's style and imagination. In both cases the logic of facts determined the final choice, but the debates touched matters so fundamental to the structure of the novel that the editor arranged the annotations to encourage continued discussion. The unimplemented change appears as a suggested alternative in the textual notes to the novel. It would have been a substitution of *slyly* for *shyly* in the statement that Godbole 'looked shyly down the sleeve of his own coat' as he proposed that the 'evil action' said to have been performed in the Marabar Hills was performed by all, including himself, his students, Fielding, Aziz, and even Adela Quested (*Passage*, xix, 169). The essential fact supporting the suggested change is that Forster's l's and h's are often indistinguishable. The editor's annotations show his conviction of the need for discussion of the possibility as well as his reason for not making the change. In *Passsage*, he notes only that *slyly* 'is a tempting alternative reading of the MS . . . . The doubtful letter is, however, marginally more like a Forsterian h than a Forsterian l'. In *Manuscripts*, he shows *slyly* as his preferred reading, with a reference to the comment in the first volume, thus compelling discussion. And the question is certainly worth discussing, if only because it forces one to define as clearly as possible one's opinion of Godbole's character. Increased sensitivity to the word, moreover, led me to notice that after the trial Adela, talking with Fielding about the same question of the 'act' performed in the caves, is described as 'looking at him shyly' when she asks him about his disbelief in heaven (*Passage*, xxvi, 228). The words are not in the manuscript draft of the conversation, and I suspect Forster added them as an intentional echo of the earlier *shyly*, reinforcing the balance between the two discussions. But then I prefer *shyly* in any case. For me, Godbole is indeed 'sly and charming' at the beginning of his interview with Fielding, when he exasperates him with his complementary proposal of naming a school after him, making him a hero-king. Moments later, forced to speak of sexual matters in terms of his fundamental beliefs (or vice versa), Godbole seems to me quite reasonably *shy*, rather than again *sly*; he seems to me here like Adela, who also finds no words to describe her visionary experience.

The second question of emendation, resulting in the change which was made, affects the colours which appear in the clouds when the 'friendly sun of the monsoons' shines on the palanquin of the 'Ark of the Lord' (*Passsage*, xxxvi, 296). In all previous editions 'pink and green skeins of cloud' appear; they are now 'pink and gray' because my query about the possibility of an echo of the colours in the granite 'skin' of the Marabar Caves (*Passage*, xii, 118), supported by a fragment of manuscript describing pink clouds 'flecked by small and swiftly moving clouds of grey', convinced Oliver Stallybrass that the change was justified. Credited with the suggestion in the note, I would like to indicate some of the other, unstated arguments also considered. There was the high probability that a typist could produce *green* for *grey* when reading ahead to *skeins* (the spelling *gray* is a consistency not for Forster but for the Abinger Edition), and the equally high probability that Forster would not catch such an error in the typescript. The later paling of the water of the tank 'to a film of mauve-gray' (*Passage*, xxxvi, 297) is another assurance that Forster imagined a scene in which pink and gray colours marked both sky and water. The only remaining question would be whether he might have consciously permitted *green* to remain in the text, perhaps because he felt the echo of 'pink and gray' might be growing too obvious, perhaps because the curtains behind which the image of the god finally retires are unquestionably 'magenta and green' (*Passsage*, xxxvi, 305), a complication of the colour scheme. In this case the probability of typist's error, the certainty about the visual elements of the scene, and the conviction of the importance of the echo moved the editor to make the change. The debate also led me, doubtfully but dutifully following the echoes, to suggest a possible association with Fielding's remark about the 'pinko-gray' colour of supposedly 'white' skin (*Passage*, vii, 56). This connection seemed improbable both to me and the editor at the time, but the more I am aware of Forster's propensity to re-examine the metaphors of ordinary language with both literal exactness, like Mrs Honeychurch in *A Room with a View*, and imaginative subtlety, like Rickie Elliot in *The Longest Journey*, the more it seems to me possible that there may be an association of the colours of human skin with those marking the elemental barriers which separate water and sky and stone.

Very close attention to the manuscripts of *A Passage to India* leads one to see structural connections to the whole of the novel in the smallest details of the manuscripts, even as the question of accuracy is a continual reminder of the limits in the perception of any one reader. One of the great pleasures of working with Oliver Stallybrass was his scrupulous fairness, whether in debating the pros and cons of an interpretation or in verifying the existence of a comma. Certainly I learned from him that the chagrin I felt when I saw my own misreadings was an inevitable part of the task, far outweighed by the pleasure of getting facts right. I also learned how important it was to respect Forster's use of facts, how the best check of a difficult reading might lie outside the manuscripts, in the details of a *Baedeker* or the colours of a sunset. All these lessons I found to be essential as I worked to complete *Arctic Summer and Other Fiction*, for I soon discovered that the techniques of assuring accuracy in transcription were just as necessary in preparing the general notes. In particular, I discovered that a literal-minded approach to Forster's metaphors and allusions, though often effective in identifying the factual nature of a reference, would not always take me far enough. One example from each of Forster's unfinished novels, *Nottingham Lace* and *Arctic Summer*, will serve.

In *Nottingham Lace* there is an allusion to a picture called 'The Soul's Awakening', which I judged from the lack of description to be a real picture, in 1900 very well-known. But if real, it was certainly no longer well-known. Moreover, there is no easy way to track a forgotten painting by title alone. The librarians of King's College, helpful as always, came up with Holman Hunt's 'The Awakening Conscience', but this picture of a woman springing from her paramour's lap hardly seemed likely to be the 'amiable and domestic' scene hanging in the bedroom of the hero's conservative aunt. Then another reference turned up, in a letter Forster wrote to his mother early in 1907. He was visiting his friend H. O. Meredith in Manchester, and Meredith, in high spirits, responded to the idea of a 'picture' tea by proposing to go as 'a fish sitting up in bed yawning — the Soul's Awakening!' Literal as ever, I wondered whether Hunt's conscience-stricken woman, somewhat agape, could be considered fish-like — or should I search for some kind of death-bed scene? Only after Miss C. A. Parker of the Royal Academy identified the painter as James Sant and referred me to a reproduction in Mary Clive's book of reminiscences, *The Day of Reckoning* (Macmillan, 1964) did the shackles fall from my mind. This sweetly pretty girl, clasping a prayer book and gazing heavenward, had no more to do with a fish than the sole of a shoe. Meredith's pun was outrageously simple, but inaudible to me precisely because I was so intent on discovering what the picture looked like, not sounded like.

A different combination of literal-mindedness and ignorance of 'general' knowledge almost caused me to miss a much more complex pun in *Arctic Summer*. In that novel Martin Whitby refers to the *Saturday Westminster* as 'that sea-green incorruptible'. Taking Forster's literal use of facts for granted, I set out to discover whether this journal existed, was incorruptible, and was green. And indeed, the *Westminster Gazette* was a highly respected organ of Liberal opinion, its pages still faintly tinged with green. As I browsed through the greenish pages of the newspaper I became rather fond of it, for its Saturday issue was literary, with contests several times won by Rupert Brooke; moreover, it presented an advertisement for a Brunsviga office machine which at last convinced me that by 1912 everyone, like Aziz (*Passage*, vii, 60), really was talking about Post-Impressionism: 'There is nothing Impressionist or Post-Impressionist or Picassoist about the Brunsviga. It is Pre-Raphaelite in its clearness, completeness, and attention to detail' (9 February, 1912). Pleased with my discoveries I reported them to the same essential King's College librarians, to learn that only in testing my new knowledge could I advance beyond the literal. In my ignorance I had had no idea that the English response to 'sea-green incorruptible' is 'Robespierre'! There in the *Oxford Dictionary of Quotations* is the reference to Carlyle's *French Revolution*. There in G. L. Dickinson's edition of Carlyle's history is the description of Robespierre, the 'Incorruptible', sea-green with fear. In fact, as far as I could determine, the original elements of fear and nausea have gone from the 'sea-green' which is now taken to suggest a clear, cool incorruptibility. But there was my literal reference, transformed by others' knowledge into a colourful pun, a multi-levelled allusion, an infinitely more interesting annotation of Forster's imagination.

The limits of the knowledge with which any reader reads thus become hazards for the editor, perils to accuracy when unknown, amusing only in retrospect. However, much as I found myself wishing to know more about such things as Forster's recurrent use of folksongs, or his awareness of the customs of interior decoration — would rooms with a view ever have Nottingham lace curtains? — what I would most like to see as an aid in the annotation of Forster's imagination is a concordance flexible enough to show the images which recur in varied forms not only in each work but also draft to draft and work to work. The 'fists and fingers' of the Marabar Hills are so familiar that I was startled to find mountains described in terms of an upthrust hand in one of Forster's earliest extant stories, now called *Ralph and Tony*. And in the manuscripts of *A Passage to India* there is a recurrence of an early association of Alpine mountains and Gothic cathedrals, also linked to the Marabar Hills. In *Arctic Summer and Other Fiction* I could note only the few such echoes which I recognized, but there must be many more. Signifiers of patterns long-persistent in Forster's imagination, they too need annotation.

NOTES

1. E. M. Forster, *The Manuscripts of A Passage to India*, ed. Oliver Stallybrass, Abinger edn. (London: Edward Arnold, 1978).
2. Robert L. Harrison, 'The Manuscripts of *A Passage to India*', unpublished dissertation, University of Texas, 1964, *Dissertation Abstracts*, XXV (1965), 474.
3. E. M. Forster, *A Passage to India*, ed. Oliver Stallybrass, Abinger edn. (London: Edward Arnold, 1978).

15 *A Passage to India*: The Dominant Voice

Barbara Rosecrance

A Passage to India moves toward catastrophe and symbolic revelation with the visit of two English ladies and their Indian host to the famous Marabar Caves. As Mrs Moore, Adela Quested, Aziz, and their entourage of servants enter the first cave, Forster describes their passage:

> The small black hole gaped where their varied forms and colours had momentarily functioned. They were sucked in like water down a drain. Bland and bald rose the precipices; bland and glutinous the sky that connected the precipices; solid and white, a Brahmany kite flapped between the rocks with a clumsiness that seemed intentional. Before man, with his itch for the seemly, had been born, the planet must have looked thus. The kite flapped away . . . . Before birds, perhaps . . . . And then the hole belched, and humanity returned.[1]

Perhaps the most startling aspect of this description is the remoteness of its perspective. For the cave entrance to appear as 'a small black hole' the speaker must be quite far away. Moving toward the cave, the party had 'climbed up over some unattractive stones . . .' (xiv, 138). The small black hole is similarly uninviting; those who enter it are commensurately reduced to its scale. The diction projects a sense of ominous foreboding. The combined effect of perspective and diction is to emphasize the insignificance of the human actors. The rhythmic inversions and repetitions enlarge the importance of setting. Every word contributes to the implication of man's pettiness, to his helpless lack of dignity before the most elemental forces of the universe. From the narrator's distant perspective, the human beings are merely forms and colours; even as these their agency in the scene is highly transitory — they have only 'momentarily functioned'. Their entrance into the black hole places them in the grip of powers beyond their control as beyond their ken; Forster's verb and simile — they are 'sucked in like water down a drain' — reduce their dignity still further. When the people return, they are expelled from the caves, again as if by an overwhelming force: 'the hole belched'; in the context of this personification, man is merely an unpleasant excretion.

With *A Passage to India* the reader moves into a world which, however implied in the earlier novels, shares far less with them than they did with each other. Though fraught with apprehensions about the encroachments of the modern world, though occasionally hysterical in tone and hollow in its affirmations, Forster's voice maintained a hopeful posture in that pre-war era which saw the composition of five of his six novels. But the dregs of Edwardian optimism vanished in the abyss of the Great War. When Forster came to his last novel, he turned his narrative techniques to the expression of a vision more distinctly modernist than anything seen in his earlier work. The brush with apocalypse suggested by the goblins of *Howards End* has become a pervading statement of man's potential doom. The novel's central symbol of caves which generate evil not because of their own attributes but because of the human inadequacy which they echo is explicitly the metaphysical abyss that confronts contemporary man.

But to describe *A Passage to India* as modernist in subject and symbolistic in method is to give a very partial impression. For Forster, continuing the practice of omniscient narration derived from an earlier tradition, is no less present here than in his early works; in fact, his narrative voice is more pervasive. Yet this voice differs in important ways from the narrative language of the earlier novels. In *Passage*, Forster has created a narrative voice that is controlling, from the opening phrase of the first chapter, 'Except for the Marabar caves', to the concluding statement, 'No, not there'.

Forster's unique achievement in *Passage* lies in the union of a narrative voice that speaks in new accents with the cumulating reiterations of phrase and image that E. K. Brown and others, following Forster's own terminology in *Aspects of the Novel*, have called 'rhythm'. The combination of Forster's voice with his rhythmic use of image and symbol, the way in which he controls the variations that reveal his major themes in their complexity, gives *Passage* its extraordinary sense of structural coherence. The narrator's interventions are both integral and primary to the expression of theme and to the context that engenders the novel's complex symbolism. That the narrative voice and the developing symbols project a vision in which chaos and disorder dominate the faint glimpses of an ordered universe in no way reduces the quality of verbal and artistic order in the novel itself.

To study authorial presence in *Passsage* is both to define the quality of Forster's narrative voice and to view the effect of its relationship to the rhythmic repetition of words, phrases and images that suffuse the novel with symbolic implication. Such consideration should correct the view, both implied and directly stated by some critics, that because Forster develops an intricate symbolism in *Passage*, he does not comment significantly in his own voice. E. K. Brown, for example, distinguished between 'the interweaving of themes' through rhythm that he considered Forster's prevailing mode and 'a much blunter instrument, comment' that is 'the usual Victorian means'. Brown's demonstration of Forster's command of rhythm was meant to imply Forster's fortunate abandonment of the 'blunter instrument'.[2] Wilfred Stone asserts directly that '*A Passage to India*, unlike earlier books, is almost totally lacking in editorial or didactic comment'.[3] While Brown's view that narrative commentary is crude does injustice to the complexity and subtlety of Forster's narrative interventions, his belief that Forster does not significantly employ these does not reflect the reality of Forster's practice in *Passage*. I would take even more direct issue with Professor Stone's statement. As answer to such critics, the opening chapter of *A Passage to India*, one of three in all the novels devoted entirely to the narrator's language, provides dramatic refutation of the idea that Forster is neither editorial nor didactic.

The first chapter is an extraordinary achievement. Simple and concentrated, it encapsulates the major thematic polarities that inform the novel, includes the central concepts whose symbolic importance Forster will develop, projects the novel's salient and startling view of man, and through diction, tone and perspective creates the narrative voice that evokes and controls all the important terms of meaning.

Forster's first sentence reads, 'Except for the Marabar Caves

— and they are twenty miles off — the city of Chandrapore presents nothing extraordinary'. Frank Kermode has noted the inversion of principal and subordinate clauses that makes caves the intial object of the reader's attention and associates them, as every future reference will, with the adjective 'extraordinary' — 'The excepted is what must be included if there is to be meaning'.[4] But more than this, the narrator's first sentence effectively suggests the novel's major polarity. For action and comment will assert that human life is a condition of exclusion: living in invidious separation from his fellows, man is isolated from meaning and from God. The 'passage to India', a complex and sombre transformation of the title to Whitman's poem,[5] is a voyage of the soul, a search for meaning, the attempt to discover a unity that includes man, the natural world and all matter in a transcendent vision of divine love.

Kermode's analysis indicates the rhetorical function of so apparently casual an arrangement of clauses and suggests the profundity of implication that underlies the deceptively simple concreteness of Forster's description of Chandrapore. But his characterization of Forster's words as 'easy, colloquial, as if with a touch of the guide-book',[6] does not represent the substance or suggest the bleak and detached tone of the opening chapter. For Forster conveys, within the framework of exclusion and inclusion, the terrifying vision of man's insignificance that demonstrates itself as the novel's most basic assumption.

Far from presenting a travelogue, the opening chapter suggests a view of man whose emphases are outlined in the first paragraph.

Except for the Marabar Caves — and they are twenty miles off — the city of Chandrapore presents nothing extraordinary. Edged rather than washed by the river Ganges, it trails for a couple of miles along the bank, scarcely distinguishable from the rubbish it deposits so freely. There are no bathing-steps on the river front, and bazaars shut out the wide and shifting panorama of the stream. The streets are mean, the temples ineffective, and though a few fine houses exist they are hidden away in gardens or down alleys whose filth deters all but the invited guest. Chandrapore was never large or beautiful, but two hundred years ago it lay on the road between Upper India, then imperial, and the sea, and the fine houses date from that period. The zest for decoration stopped in the eighteenth

century, nor was it ever democratic. In the bazaars there is no
painting and scarcely any carving. The very wood seems made
of mud, the inhabitants of mud moving. So abased, so monotonous is everything that meets the eye, that when the Ganges
comes down it might be expected to wash the excrescence back
into the soil. Houses do fall, people are drowned and left
rotting, but the general outline of the town persists, swelling
here, shrinking there, like some low but indestructible form of
life.   (i, 2)

Forster's careful discriminations in this paragraph are micro-
cosms of his developing thematic preoccupations. It will later
be seen that the fundamental characteristic of the Marabar Caves
is that 'Nothing, nothing attaches to them' (xii, 117). The
conjunction in the first sentence between 'nothing' and 'extraordinary' presents a highly condensed suggestion of the caves'
significance. That it is an active suggestion is not evident on first
reading; as Kermode says, the words 'lie there, lacking all
rhetorical emphasis, waiting for the relations which will give
them significance . . . but they are prepared for these relations'.[7]
    The first sentence implies more than the importance of in-
cluding the excepted. In distinction to the caves, the city is
'nothing extraordinary'. In contrast to the caves, which have no
attributes and are in any case not described here, the city has
many, none of which is extraordinary. The attributes of the city
share two major characteristics. They are abased, and they reveal
an indistinction of city from rubbish, man from city, and man
from rubbish. The reduction of distinctions anticipates the
climactic message of the caves, in which everything is characterized by a negative sameness, in which the smallness of the
universe becomes embodied in an echo that says 'ou-boum' to
whatever is said.
    In the second sentence Forster separates nature's work from
man's and suggests that between man and garbage there is little
difference. Nature forebears to cleanse man — the Ganges edges
rather than washes the city. The ensuing sentences of this
paragraph develop the degraded associations of man and his
works and intensify the implication that man is too loathsome
or insignificant even for nature's purifying attention.
    With an implied contrast between the 'panorama of the stream'
and the bazaars that shut it out, the third sentence hints at the

haphazard quality of man-made distinctions and categories —
the Ganges 'happens' not to be holy at this place. Forster
introduces another major theme by suggesting the elusively
changing quality of reality, the difficulty of clear-cut identification. Not only is the view 'wide and shifting', the initial observation that there are no bathing-steps on the river becomes the
assertion that 'indeed there is no river front'. Later in the novel
Forster claims that 'nothing in India is identifiable, the mere
asking of a question causes it to disappear or to merge in
something else' (viii, 78). The constant alteration of matter,
illustrated frequently in the novel, is connected with those
changes that move constantly from one apparent absolute to the
next, seeking an answer to the fundamental question of which
all other questions and appeals are but a version: 'Beyond the
sky must not there be something that overarches all the skies,
more impartial even than they? Beyond which again . . . [sic]'
(v, 34).

The fourth sentence details the city's degradation. The 'mean'
streets, the 'ineffective' temples, the 'filth' of the alleys specify
and support the earlier identification with 'rubbish'. This sentence also begins the important metaphor of invitation. The
alleys of Chandrapore ironically exclude most of the humanity
they presumably exist to accommodate; only the 'invited guest'
may penetrate the filth. The fatuity of man's invitations and
exclusions is suggested here, and Forster will develop a view of
the futility of man's attempts to exert control over his destiny
through assertions of will in a series of variations on the idea of
invitations. The brief reference here places the concept of invitation in the context of the repugnant character of man's offerings.

If a guide-book quality can be said to characterize any part of
the opening chapter, it appears in the next three sentences, but
even here Forster's meaning transcends the apparent simplicity
of description. Sentence five explains the largely excluded: the
paucity of beauty or decoration in the city is historically conditioned. The next sentence enlarges an implication of the
'invited guest' who figures in sentence four. The activity of
decoration was temporary, its beneficiaries were few. Most of
the population was excluded — the little art that existed was not
'democratic' in its application. The next sentence illustrates this
contention: as the seat of common humanity, the bazaars are
characterized by the absence of art. The uncarved wood is

scarcely distinguishable from mud, the lack of differentiation extends from man's works to man himself, 'mud moving'. The ninth sentence passes specific and general judgement: 'abased' derives from the primitve lowness of mud, 'monotonous' from the monochromatic similarity of wood and man; the statement is also a comment on all that has gone before — the adjectives culminate in 'everything', the remainder of the sentence defines all of Chandrapore as an 'excrescence'. The speaker's observation that the river 'might be expected' to wash the city back into the soil is an enlargement of the initial hint provided by the 'edged rather than washed' of the second sentence. Rather than presenting a harmony, man and nature are in tension: so repelled is nature by man's abasement and filth that her forbearance to purge herself of the 'excrescence' surprises. The last sentence of the paragraph suggests small movements of flux within a primordial continuity. The context is death and decay — 'houses do fall, people are drowned and left rotting'. Apathy not agency characterizes man; at the very bottom of the scale of life, his sole activity is to 'persist'. The final image of the city with its rotting dead is that of an amoeba, 'swelling here, shrinking there'. Its lowness is matched only by its capacity to survive: beyond this, Forster does not accord man a single positive characteristic.

From this extraordinary bleak picture of human incapacity, Forster moves in the second paragraph to develop the comparison between nature and man. Viewed from the rise of the civil station above the city, 'Chandrapore appears to be a totally different place'. The languid river that shrinks from contact with man has become a 'noble river' and washes 'a tropical pleasuance'. Water imagery is associated in all the Forster novels with fecundity and a regenerative power. The narrator has already suggested that for the river to exercise its cleaning function would be to rid itself of man altogether. But for the vegetation, water performs its accustomed services. Besides the river, 'ancient tanks nourish' the tropical trees. Nature asserts itself: the trees hide the bazaars as the bazaars hid the view of the river. Forster contrasts the energy of the natural world with the limitations of man. 'Endowed with more strength than man and his works', the trees are motivated also by their desire to escape from the inglorious confines of man's world: they 'rise', they 'burst out of stifling purlieus and unconsidered temples', they 'soar above the lower deposit' to find light and air, to greet each other, and 'to build a city for the birds'. From this perspective, the city is 'a city of gardens', 'a forest sparsely scattered with huts', finally, 'a tropical pleasuance'. This view is possible only because the works of nature hide the works of man. Only as a city for the birds can Chandrapore be seen as beautiful. Forster suggests again the illusory quality of reality by the conjunction of the verb 'appears' with Chandrapore, and he reminds us that nature's glorification does not present the 'real' city, by noting the 'disillusionment' of the newcomer, once driven down from the rise.

With a brief description of the civil station whose roads 'intersect at right angles' (i, 3), a triumph of sensible planning that will not take man very far into the realms of spirit, Forster reiterates the suggestion of separations and exclusions: the civil station 'shares nothing with the city except the overarching sky' (i, 3). Again the idea of exclusion and the concept of 'nothing' mean more than the apparently straightforward statement seems to say. In sharing nothing except the sky, the civil station shares all, for the chapter's final paragraph asserts the dominion of the sky: 'the sky settles everything'. Anglo-Indians and natives have nothing in common: the exclusions are man-made.

The final two paragraphs move from consideration of the nature that is more beautiful and more powerful than man but yet shares a sense of scale with him to the larger aspects of nature that dominate both: earth, sun and sky. Earth is vast but like man helpless, dependent on sun and sky. To the image of the 'prostrate earth' is contrasted the phallic energy of the 'fists and fingers' of the Marabar Hills. In Forster's final sentence, the inversion with which he began the chapter culminates in the reintroduction of the caves, emphasized further by their reiterated association with the adjective 'extraordinary'.

Diction, tone and perspective create a controlling narrative voice. Detached and impartial, the speaker seems to regard all he sees as unsurprising. But what his diction develops as 'nothing extraordinary' is a view of man as degraded. Verbs describing the city are low in energy, as in 'it trails along the bank', or as in the frequent forms of 'to be' that coupled with adjectives or verbal participles reveal the city as 'mean', 'ineffective', 'abashed', 'monotonous', 'rotting'. The nouns similarly reiterate the negative character of Chandrapore, a rare strong verb is attached to 'filth' — 'filth deters', and Forster offers in summary the intensely repellent noun, 'excrescence'.

The deliberately impassive tone combines with a perspective that moves from near to far. The inclusion of the cosmic intensifies the insignificance of man, and in the increasing remoteness of the narrator's point of view, the human scale is reduced further. The speaker bounds Chandrapore by size and shape; the city not its inhabitants is the object of initial consideration, and they are not mentioned until after rubbish, filthy alleys and inartistic bazaars have been noted. Barely differentiated from these, even at the point of the narrator's focus upon it, humanity is low and small.

The perspective withdraws to include civil station and city in the cosmos, then farther still, to contemplate the distance between sky and stars and thence between stars and infinity. Seen from here, man is almost incongruously tiny. As the perspective recedes, it can be seen that change is the only constant. In the second paragraph, 'the prospect alters'. The third paragraph discusses the 'changes' of the sky and moves to consider the distance behind the stars, by implication beyond change, 'beyond colour, last freed itself from blue'. Each change in perspective engenders a different view of reality, and each such change identifies the alteration of matter not only with the idea of appearance and reality — viewed through trees the city's illusory beauty hides the grim truth of Chandrapore — but with an ever enlarging series that moves from one apparent absolute to the next. In the systematic movement from city to infinity, structure and perspective become aspects of the narrative voice in rendering Forster's preoccupation with the nature of reality and the existence of God.

A Passage to India moves between polarities of exclusion and inclusion, separation and unity, discord and harmony, negation and affirmation, the emptiness of the caves and the fullness of a universe animated by divine presence, the reductive vision and the inclusive vision. The novel's burden is the demonstration of discord, the search for unity its motive power. Bridging the oppositions is a continuous appeal, an invocation of divine presence that seeks to transcend the prevailing chaos and isolation of human existence. Although the opening chapter provides illustration of ways in which Forster's narrative voice defines these informing concepts and categories, their full meanings arise only as they appear and reappear in changing contexts. The first chapter demonstrates the novel's crucial unity of voice with theme and setting and reveals the dominating agency of Forster's narrative voice in rendering a vision that was, for him, both new and final to his practice of fiction.

NOTES

1. E. M. Forster, *A Passage to India*, ed. Oliver Stallybrass, Abinger edn. (London: Edward Arnold, 1978), Ch. xiv, p. 138.

2. E. K. Brown, *Rhythm in the Novel* (Toronto: University of Toronto Press, 1967), pp. 63, 86.

3. Wilfred Stone, *The Cave and the Mountain* (Stanford, California: Stanford University Press, 1966), p. 340.

4. Frank Kermode, 'Mr. E. M. Forster as a Symbolist', in *Forster*, ed. Malcolm Bradbury (Englewood Cliffs, New Jersey: Prentice-Hall, 1966), p. 92.

5. Walt Whitman, 'Passage to India', *Leaves of Grass*, ed. Harold W. Blodgett and Scully Bradley (New York: New York University Press, 1965), p. 418.

6. Kermode, p. 92.

7. Kermode, p. 92.

16 E. M. Forster and Hindu Mythology

G. K. Das

> Why has not England a great mythology?
> Our folklore never advanced beyond
> daintiness, and the greater melodies about
> our countryside have all issued from the
> pipes of Greece. Deep and true as the
> native imagination can be, it seems to have
> failed here. It has stopped with the witches
> and the fairies.
>
> (*Howards End*, Ch. xxxiii, p. 264)

One of Forster's main discontents with English culture and way of life was their lack of a strong mythological tradition. His own creative imagination was enriched initially by recourse to Greek mythology, and the Hellenistic world predominated and was idealized in his early work. In *The Longest Journey* and *Howards End* he attempts apparently to transplant the mythical life of ancient Greece among the downs and farms of England, but the effect that is achieved in these two novels — and the same can be said about *Maurice* also — is an element of consumate fantasy rather than a fuller, 'mythic' rendition of life as there is in *A Passsage to India*. Indeed one sees in the background to his approach to Hindu myths a feeling of disenchantment with the world of Pan as expressed in *Howards End*: 'Of Pan and the elemental forces, the public has heard a little too much . . .';[2] as he turns to explore Hindu myths in *A Passage to India*, he is at once struck by their intriguing novelty, their complex symbolism and the unique phenomenon of their living continuity.

The mythical core of *A Passage to India* is wholly Hindu

Buddhism, being centrally concerned with the pursuit of enlightenment, has no room for myth; similarly, Islam, with its avowed claim to historicity, is also anti-myth. It is the Hindu world that is ahistorical and richly myth-oriented, and is presented as such in the novel. Personally Forster was attracted by the Hindu's mythical imagination, which he describes as 'a constant sense of the unseen',[3] and he looked at it as a higher power than any set religious faith — whether Buddhist, Moslem or Christian. One of the main achievements of his Indian novel is the creation of that living sense of the unseen by the use of various Hindu myths. Critics like Frank Kermode, John Beer, Frederick Crews and Wilfred Stone have variously explored the symbolic, visionary and mythical aspects of the book; the purpose of this essay, therefore, is not to establish a new dimension, but to throw light on some relatively less explored points concerning Forster's interpretation of Hindu myths and his use of these myths for achieving particular kinds of effects.

References to Hindu myths in Forster's early writings serve purposes both of fantasy and critical investigation concerning various rival religious faiths. The fantasy presented in the story 'Mr Andrews', for example, has the god Vishnu seated in Heaven beside Buddha, Allah, Jehovah and many other gods, who are described as cruel, coarse, peevish, deceitful and vulgar; with Mr Andrews we no doubt realize that Vishnu, the supreme preserver of Hindu mythology, is as powerless as the other gods, unable to fulfil the aspiration of humanity. In a similarly agnostic vein are several allusions to Hindu deities in Forster's Indian Diary and letters from India of 1912–13. In these private papers, Vishnu, Siva, Krishna, Rama, Ganpati, Durga, the Monkey-god, bullock gods, and trees and stones daubed with paint, all figure primarily as unwieldy objects of curiosity; also an overall sense of bewilderment is expressed in an entry in the Diary of 18 March 1913 which describes Hindu religion in general as 'capricious'.[4] But alongside such a picture, one also sees in the young Forster, especially after his first Indian visit, a marked inclination to study Hindu mythology more seriously and a growing sense of discovery. This phase of his development is demonstrated in some discerning pieces that he published on the subject prior to *A Passage to India*.

Among these writings the three pieces that I want to look at in particular are: 'The Gods of India' (May 1914), 'The Age of

Misery' (June 1914) and 'The Churning of the Ocean' (May 1920). Forster's thoughts in these writings are to be examined in relation to three main lines of interpretation of Hindu myths which were current at that time. First, there was the work of Christian missionary scholars, who were keen to demonstrate that Hindu myths and rituals were all vulgar, age-old superstitions and barbarisms. Secondly, there were the pioneering anthropological investigations of Frazer which brought to light various meaningful connections between Hindu myths and rituals and those of other ancient religions. Thirdly, there were also distinguished contributions made by scholars of comparative thought and art like E. J. Rapson, E. B. Havell and Alfred Lyall who studied Hindu mythology as a valuable means to explore India's complex spiritual heritage. Viewed in this perspective, Forster's own approach to the subject shows a distinctiveness that cannot be missed.

It is somewhat ironical that a full-scale introduction to Hindu myths was available to Forster, who was generally sceptical of missionaries, through the work of a Wesleyan missionary, the Rev. E. Osborn Martin. Martin's book *The Gods of India* (1914) was full of interesting details meant for the general reader; it was also wider in its survey than the few previously published specialized studies in the field like W. J. Wilkins' *Hindu Mythology, Vedic and Puranic* (1882) and A. A. Macdonell's *Vedic Mythology* (1897). It was read and analysed by Forster with keen interest. In Martin's classification the first category of Hindu gods includes the 'Vedic' gods, i.e. those gods who were worshipped by the early Aryans and continue to be worshipped by the Hindus even today. They are: the Earth, the Sky, the Fire-god, the Sun-god, the Rain-god, etc. While Martin's chief interest in studying them was to establish parallelisms between these gods of the Hindus and the gods of the ancient Greeks and Romans and thus to deny any distinction to Hindu myths, it will be seen that Forster's depictions of several of these myths in *A Passage to India* show their distinctively living force, which Greek or Roman myths do not possess.

The second category of Hindu deities according to Martin includes the 'Puranic' gods and goddesses, such as Brahma, Vishnu, Siva and his consort Parvati, the ten incarnations of Vishnu which inlude Krishna, etc. These deities are more numerous than the Vedic ones, and the myths relating to them are more complex and have yielded to varying interpretations in post-Vedic literature — the Epics and the Puranas. It is in respect of these myths that Martin's denunciation of the Hindu tradition is particularly scathing; to him the myths are all entirely absurd, immoral and evil. Forster does not share such a view and comments that it was typical of missionaries, who could scarcely be objective:

> Deity after deity is summoned before the tribunal of Wesleyan-ism, and dismissed with no uncertain voice. Krishna stole butter as a baby, and worse later. Jagganath is a goggle-eyed log. Brahma 'has an unenviable moral record', and his head was once cut off by the thumbnail of Siva's left hand . . . . Some goddesses are Satanic, like Kali, others corrupt, like Radha. And as are the deities, so are some of their followers: lustful, cruel.[5]

In Forster's view, Puranic myths are valuable for two striking reasons. First, he sees that these myths represent the divine and the earthly not in exclusive compartments but in a continuous process of fusion embodying the Hindu idea of creation. 'The divine is so confounded with the earthly that anyone or anything is part of God'[6] is a belief which is central to the myths concerning Krishna, and which appeals to Forster. Unlike Martin, who condemns Krishna worship as immoral and deplorable, he is struck by the Hindu notion that the licentious lover of Radha and numerous milkmaids is also the supreme Lord of the universe. The second notable feature of Puranic myths, and of all Hindu myths in general, according to Forster, is that they present all deities both as gods in their physical manifestations and as emblems of the inconceivable and the eternal: they are a goal to be realized and also the means to apprehend a further goal — 'They are steps towards the eternal'.[7]

Martin's last category of Hindu myths includes those con-cerning what he calls the 'inferior gods and godlings'. These, according to him, are sacred rivers, animals and birds, the Monkey-god, trees and stones, saints, the spirits of the dead, etc. These deities are widely worshipped in the villages, and the myths connected with them are expressions of local belief, which Martin dismisses as petty, crude and primitive: 'Inferior lamps are sometimes lighted, and fire sacrifices and petty offerings

presented. Very frequently near the shrine, on a rough mud
platform, little clay images of elephants and horses are found in
rows. These are said to form the equipage or vehicle of the
god . . . .'[8] Forster's own reaction to these local myths is quite
different from Martin's: it is a mixture of bewilderment, as is
reflected in several places in *The Hill of Devi*, and a positive sense
of attraction as can be seen, for instance, from his account of a
meeting between him and a Hindu fakir at Benares in 1913.
There is a reference to this meeting in the first volume of P. N.
Furbank's biography,[9] but a fuller picture will be available if one
reads the relevant entry in Forster's Indian Diary along with the
piece 'The Gods of India'. The fakir, who was also in touch with
Sir William Rothenstein and had been visited by Lowes Dickinson and R. C. Trevelyan, told Forster that to the Hindu any deity
— whether Siva, or a sacred river, or the sky — was not the goal
but the means to realize God indirectly. With the help of an
illustration of a human frame drawn by him the fakir explained,
as Forster puts it: 'God was in the brain, the heart was a folded
flower. Yoga unfolded the flower, and then the soul could set out
on its quest of God. Two roads lay open to it. It could either
proceed directly . . . or indirectly through one of the Hindu
deities . . . .' When Forster asked which road was the best, the
fakir replied that the direct road was quicker but 'those who take
it see nothing, hear nothing, feel nothing of the world. Whereas
those who proceed through some deity can profit by — ' he said,
pointing to the river, the temples, the sky, and added, 'That is
why I worship Siva'.[10] The mythic trust of the fakir — shared also
by Forster's Hindu friends in Dewas and Chhatarpur (and by
masses of Hindu believers today) — that all deities, high or low,
mediate between the individual and the unseen, making the
latter's immediacy felt, proved for Forster a compelling force; he
used it to counteract the tendency among Christian interpreters
to demolish Hindu myths.

With secular interpretations of Hindu myths, on the other
hand, Forster felt more congenial. Although there is not much
evidence of any strong influence of Frazer on him, there are in
Forster's thinking several distinct echoes which prompt a comparison. For example, his description of Hindu worship of sex
— 'symbolically in Saivism and actually in some Sakti rites'[11] —
and his frequent allusions to Indian representations of Siva and
Parvati in terms of what he calls 'fertility symbols'[12] are Frazerian.

In *A Passsage to India* we notice even clearer connections both in the structure and the themes: Frazer seems the stimulus behind the tripartite division of the novel corresponding to the cycle of the Indian seasons, as well as the presentation of the water ceremonies, the dying king, and the ritualistic sacrifice of gods and 'scapegoats'[13] in the final section. But the main difference between Frazer and Forster in their treatment of Hindu myths is that they bring varying kinds of interests to play upon the subject. While Frazer is looking for *fact* and *notion* behind myth and is interested in conveying to his readers 'some *notion* [my emphasis], however dim, of the scenery, the atmosphere, the gorgeous colouring of the East',[14] Forster is interested in capturing with the help of myth glimpses of the unseen — what he calls 'a life beyond facts'.[15]

Forster sees that compared to anthropological and historical world-views of western scholars, the Hindu mythological vision is profounder, and he is stimulated by its grasp of the eternal. As he observes:

> There are four ages, teaches the Hindu, of which the historical is the most miserable and the last. These four make up one Great Period of about five million years, while one thousand Great Periods make up one single day in the life of Brahma. Facts are a sign of decay in the world's fabric. They are like dust crumbling out of the palace walls which Brahma, after the thousand Periods that are his night, will rebuild . . . we are the palace and the palace is we, and when the soul glances hither and thither among the fallen masonry it is really looking for the soul.[16]

The spiritual aspect of Hindu myths stimulated Forster's thought, and his views in this respect were influenced by the works of two noted Indologists, named earlier in this essay, E. J. Rapson (author of *Ancient India*, 1914) and E. B. Havell (author of *The Ideals of Indian Art*, 1911, 2nd edn 1920). Both Rapson and Havell emphasized that the distinctiveness of Hindu mythological vision as compared to Hellenistic vision lay in the fact that the former celebrated the joys of the spirit, to which the latter remained indifferent. Havell drew attention to the mythical third eye of Siva or Durga, for example, which in a simple way denoted spiritual consciousness to the Hindu peasant as well as the intellectual Brahmin, whereas a western classical scholar 'would expect a Greek nymph, or a Roman Sybil, with an explanatory label'.[17] Rapson similarly drew a contrast between the Greek concern with an enchanting form or object and the Hindu concern with the contemplative enchantment of soul, and argued that the Hindu vision remained supremely triumphant before and after the advent of Hellenism in India. Such a picture seemed to Forster an eye-opener; to seek what was lacking in Hellenistic culture he now felt stimulated to look to the Hindu world, in what seemed the right perspective. 'Professor Rapson puts all in a truer perspective', he says.

> He shows that whatever Alexander [in his military tour of India] might have done, he did nothing, and it is to later immigrants that we are to attribute such Hellenism as was established along the Indus Valley. Even that died. Greece, who has immortalised the falling dust of facts, so that it hangs in enchantment for ever, can bring no life to a land that is waiting for the dust to clear away, so that the soul may contemplate the soul.[18]

Forster sees an intriguing representation of Hindu spiritual vision in a myth like the 'churning of the ocean'. Following Havell's interpretation he sees that the myth, in its depiction of gods and demons striving together to produce the nectar of immortality by churning the cosmic ocean of milk, illustrates how individual beings and objects constantly participate in the eternal, and how barriers between high and low, good and evil, male and female, human and non-human, etc. are broken in this universal process. Forster is struck by the immense sense of freedom, power and possibilities that the myth inspires:

> gods and mountains, snakes and milk, pass into and out of one another, until we lose all sense of individuality. Once inside the churn, anyone becomes everyone or anything. Vishnu is bound to no form or sex. Siva, wroth with the gods, tries simultaneously to save them. And in other legends Siva can be Vishnu, and both can be Brahma, and Brahma either of them; for not only is matter a veil that hides reality, but the meshes of the veil are themselves interchangeable . . . .[19]

Forster learnt from Havell that such a mythic vision of the boundless spirit, and its various representations in literature and art, could be appreciated by the westerner by abandoning 'our individualistic formulae and the academic rules that we have derived from the practice of Rome and Greece'.[20]

To Forster, as to Havell, the Hindu mythological tradition is richer than the Greek or Roman tradition, but his approach to the subject is different from Havell's in a significant way. While Havell looks at the myths as an embodiment of the glory of Vedic India, which he sees as a golden age of the Hindus in terms of spiritual attainments, Forster is sceptical about such an interpretation. Describing himself as 'incurably tepid on the subject of a Golden Age', he doubts, as he says, whether 'in Vedic times, when rishis were frequent and devas sat at human feasts, all the achievements of future ages existed in the form of thought'.[21] Unlike Havell, he is led by his interest in Hindu myths not to idealize a past phase of civilization, but to look for continuities between the past and the present orders.

Forster's main discoveries concerning Hindu myths, as outlined above, are embodied in *A Passage to India*. The opening chapter of the novel introduces us to the Hindu vision of the unseen. It depicts the river Ganges, the overarching sky, and the sun over the city of Chandrapore as living spirits having superhuman powers. In contrast to the city itself, which 'presents nothing extraordinary' — its streets are 'mean', temples 'ineffective,' and its little civil station 'provokes no emotion' — the Ganges, the mythical mother of Hindu tradition,[22] is portrayed with 'its shifting panorama' as a 'noble river'. Though near Chandrapore it happens 'not to be holy' — for purposes of ritualistic bathing — as it is elsewhere, according to Hindu belief, its presence is that of a supremely benign deity; by washing 'the excrescence back into the soil', it has nourished the earth, the woods and the vegetation. Similarly, the sky and the sun, two divine spirits of the earliest Hindu triad,[23] are described as living presences in their full resplendence and power: '. . . when the sky chooses, glory can rain into the Chandrapore bazaars, or a benediction pass from horizon to horizon. The sky can do this because it is so strong and so enormous. Strength comes from the sun, infused in it daily . . .' (pp. 3–4).

We see that the mythical undercurrent steadily assumes a stronger force in the novel and that in subtle ways it influences the mind of the westerner, who is alien to Hindu vision. In Chapter 3, Mrs Moore, Adela and Ronny watch the Ganges in its radiance, awe and mystery, and are struck by its uniqueness: 'It belonged neither to water nor moonlight, but stood like a luminous sheaf upon the fields of darkness . . . the dead bodies floated down that way from Benares, or would if the crocodiles let them . . . "What a terrible river! [exclaims Mrs Moore] What a wonderful river!"' (p. 26). Such a vision of the life and power of the Ganges comes to Mrs Moore attended with a sense of oneness with the heavenly, which was unknown to her in England: 'In England the moon had seemed dead and alien; here she was caught in the shawl of night together with earth and all the other stars. A sudden sense of unity, of kinship with the heavenly bodies, passed into the old woman . . .' (p. 24).

Conflict between western science and Hindu myth is the keynote in the beginning of the second part of the novel, and myth eventually emerges as more potent. It is argued in the opening paragraph of Chapter 12 that geology, a western invasion of Hindu belief, has robbed the Ganges of its mythical heritage: 'The Ganges, though flowing from the foot of Vishnu and through Siva's hair, is not an ancient stream. Geology, looking further than religion, knows of a time when neither the river nor the Himalayas that nourish it existed, and an ocean flowed over the holy places of Hindustan' (p. 116).[24] We are then given a scientific and historical account of the formation of the Indo-Gangetic plain and told that Dravidia, the Southern peninsula, is older than Himalayan India, the 'immemorial' abode of the Hindu deities. But as we proceed further, the resources of science, history and archeology are shown to be limited and they give way to accumulated mythical wisdom: '. . . if mankind grew curious and excavated, nothing, nothing would be added to the sum of good and evil' (p. 118).

The towering myth in this part of the novel is the Hindu vision of the absolute, the infinite and the unaccountable which precedes and comprehends all creation. It is represented through an extraordinary complex of mythical forms: the primordial sun, the 'sun-born rocks' of the Marabar, and the dark and empty caves inhabited by echoes and skirted by stones and water.[25] We are told that there is nothing in the world like these rocks — they are without proportion, indescribable in human speech and 'older than all spirit' — and that on their summit is a boulder with a cave — 'a bubble-shaped cave that has neither ceiling nor floor, and mirrors its own darkness in every direction infinitely' (p. 118). This clearly is the non-Christian, non-scientific, myth-inspired Hindu vision of the primal void and the egg and the womb of creation; a creation hymn in the *Rig-Veda* describes thus the state before creation:

> There was then (in the beginning) neither nonentity nor entity; there was no atmosphere, nor sky above. What enveloped (all)? Where, in the receptacle of what (was it contained)? Was it water, the profound abyss? Death was not there, nor immortality; there was no distinction of day or night. That One breathed calmly, self-supported; there was nothing different from, or above, it. In the beginning darkness existed, enveloped in darkness . . . .[26]

The journey to the Marabar gives the western visitors what Martin Heidegger would call 'dread' that reveals 'nothing'. In terms of Hindu thought, it is a perception of 'not-being'; if the river Ganges had stimulated Mrs Moore to a vision of universal 'being', the equally myth-laden Marabar leads her to a vision of universal 'not-being', which to her Christian mind appears nihilistic: 'Everything exists, nothing has value' (p. 140). Mrs Moore's collapse after Marabar is indeed the novel's comment on the failure of Christianity to deal with the unknown, the unseen and the unnamable. For the Hindu Godbole, on the other hand, the 'nihilistic' role of Marabar is as significant as everything else in the life of the spirit: 'everything is anything and nothing something . . . absence implies presence, absence is non-existence . . .' (p. 169).

The positive value attached to 'not-being' is a central point in Hindu mythology of all times. As the Vedic myths conceived of the formless in terms of various spiritual and impersonal forms, so did the Puranic myths of later times embody it in various forms of physical and personal incarnations. These mythical representations, whether impersonal or personal, by virtue of their combination of paradoxical significances — being and not-being, known and unknown, and seen and unseen — cannot meet the western demand for a norm, be it the Christian norm of good or the Greek norm of beauty. By western notions, Hindu myths are, as the Krishna festival in the last part of *A Passage of India* apparently is, a 'frustration of reason and form' (p. 275), a 'great blur' (p. 306); but the novel no doubt discards Christianity and science[27] firmly and aspires to rest its faith in the myths.

The mythical theme in the final section of the novel is mainly concerned with the birth of Krishna. Myth here is enacted in the form of rituals, which are a vital part of the Hindu way of life. There are mimetic performances in Raja's palace at Mau of some Vedic myths, such as the one depicting Vishnu as he strides in three steps over the triple universe of the earth, the sky and the firmament, but the ceremony of Krishna's birth is the culminating and all-embracing event. At the hour of the birth, Mau is like an 'extended' temple[28] illumined and vibrant with the spirit of Krishna, lover of the whole universe. The very houses seem dancing; Godbole and the whole community of Hindu villagers participate in the spiritual elation, feeling that the god before and after his birth is always present with them. For them myth is more than reality; the little silver image of Krishna is not a mere idol, as the westerner thinks, but the god actually present in their rapturous congregation:

> The assembly was in a tender, happy state unknown to an English crowd, it seethed like a beneficent potion. When the villagers broke cordon for a glimpse of the silver image, a most beautiful and radiant expression came into their faces, a beauty in which there was nothing personal, for it caused them all to resemble one another during the moment of its indwelling, and only when it was withdrawn did they revert to individual clods.
>
> (p. 275)

The Krishna myth means for Forster many things at once. He sees it as an embodiment of the Hindu vision of complete being. Illogical and imperfect by traditional western notions, Krishna is incredibly mundane and spiritual, human and superhuman, a lascivious lover and saintly renouncer — all in the same being; in conceiving such a god Hindu imagination has excelled the Greek or the Christian conception of spirituality. Forster writes in admiration of the many 'imaginative legends' and 'profound thoughts' which, along with many pleasant trivialities of life, have been woven into the Hindu myth: 'Warrior, counsellor, randy villager, divine principle, flautist, great king: these are some of Krishna's aspects, and to them must be added the destroyer of dragons, the Hercules-Seigfried hero who makes the earth habitable for men. It is no wonder that in India so varied a deity exercises a wide appeal'[29] The poetic presentation of the myth, accordingly, is an apt finale to the novel.

In writing the novel Forster was pursuing a mythical quest, as he says, of 'the universe as embodied in the Indian earth and the Indian sky . . . the horror lurking in the Marabar Caves and the release symbolised by the birth of Krishna'.[30] He found Hindu worship of Krishna spiritually far more meaningful than the technological or political idolatry of the West. It is the spirituality of Godbole and the Hindu community of Mau during the Krishna ceremony that he wishes to affirm against the false gods of empire, race or power.

NOTES

1. The pagination is that of the Abinger edition of *Howards End* (London: Edward Arnold, 1973), ed. Oliver Stallybrass.
2. *Howards End*, Ch. 13, p. 106.
3. See 'The Gods of India', *The New Weekly*, 30 May 1914, 338.
4. The MS of Forster's Indian Diary is in the Forster archive at King's College, Cambridge. I am grateful to the Provost and Scholars of King's for permission to consult it.
5. See 'The Gods of India'.
6. 'The Gods of India'.
7. 'The Gods of India'.
8. The Rev. E. Osborn Martin, *The Gods of India* (Delhi: Indological Book House, 1972), p. 203.
9. See P. N. Furbank, *E. M. Forster: A Life* (London: Secker and Warburg, 1977), I, pp. 245–6.
10. 'The Gods of India'.
11. 'The Gods of India'.
12. Forster uses the term in his essay on 'Erotic Indian Sculpture', *The Listener*, 12 March 1959, 469–71.
13. cf. 'Thus was He thrown year after year, and were others thrown . . . scapegoats, husks, emblems of passage . . .' — *A Passage to India*, Abinger edition, ed. Oliver Stallybrass, (London: Edward Arnold, 1978), Ch. 36, p. 304. All subsequent references to the novel are to this edition; page numbers of references are indicated within parentheses.
14. See *The Golden Bough IV: Adonis, Attis, Osiris*, Vol. 1 (London: Macmillan, 1963), p. vi.
15. See Forster's essay (a review of E. J. Rapson's *Ancient India*) 'The Age of Misery', *The New Weekly*, 27 June 1914, 52.
16. 'The Age of Misery'.
17. E. B. Havell, *The Ideals of Indian Art* (London: John Murray, 1920),

p. xviii.

18. 'The Age of Misery'.
19. 'The Churning of the Ocean', *The Athaeneum*, 21 May 1920, 667–8.
20. 'The Churning of the Ocean'.
21. 'The Churning of the Ocean'.
22. In Hindu mythology, Ganga, the personified Ganges, is the daughter of the Himalayas and is worshipped by the Hindus as the great mother.
23. The Three supreme deities of The *Vedas* are Surya, Agni and Vayu.
24. We recall the Hindu myth of creation, 'The churning of the ocean', referred to earlier in the essay; the opening of Chapter 12 of *A Passage to India* seems to reconcile western scientific theories to Hindu belief as it describes the birth of new creations and the destruction of old ones as a continuing process resulting from the sea's action: 'As Himalayan India rose, this [Dravidian] India, the primal, has been depressed, and is slowly re-entering the curve of the earth. It may be that in aeons to come an ocean will flow here too, and cover the sun-born rocks with slime. Meanwhile the plain of the Ganges encroaches on them with something of the sea's action. They are sinking beneath the newer lands.'
25. cf. 'They skirted the puddle of water, and then climbed up over some unattractive stones, the sun crashing on their backs' (Ch. 14, p. 138).
26. Cited in Martin, *The Gods of India*, pp. 85–6.
27. Repudiation of science is intended in several statements in the novel, e.g. 'Life [to Aziz] is not a scientific manual (Ch. 31, p. 268); and '. . . the human spirit [during the Krishna ceremony] had tried . . . to ravish the unknown, flinging down science and history in the struggle' (Ch. 33, p. 278).
28. cf. Rose-leaves fall from the houses, sacred spices and coconut are brought forth . . . It was the half-way moment; the God had extended His temple . . .' (Ch. 36, p. 300).
29. See 'The Blue Boy', *The Listener*, 14 March 1957, 444.
30. Forster, 'Three Countries', typescript of a paper in the possession of King's College Library, Cambridge (cited in Robin J. Lewis, *E. M. Forster's Passages to India*, Delhi, Oxford University Press, 1979, p. 146).

17 Muddle Et Cetera: Syntax in *A Passsage to India**

Molly B. Tinsley

If we had to decide which of the legacies of Ancient Greece has meant more to Europe and mankind, we might well nominate the complex sentence. Along with Greek philosophy, there grew up a language able to express its fine distinctions and carefully ordered thought.[1]

It is with some notion of the connection between culture and sentence structure that E. M. Forster begins his treatment of Leonard Bast in *Howards End*. Leonard, bent on escaping the abyss where no one counts, reads *Stones of Venice* assiduously, memorizing cadences and trying to adapt Ruskin's complex structures to his own mediocre experience. But Leonard is just sensitive enough to realize the inappropriateness of his efforts. The glorious rhythms of Venice are not for him. He must stick to simple sentences like 'My flat is dark as well as stuffy'.[2] Oddly enough, Leonard Bast anticipates Forster's own struggle later to develop sentences that would aptly reflect the experience of India. He too had to leave behind the harmonies of the Mediterranean, the 'spirit in a reasonable form', as inappropriate to a muddled civilization where 'everything was placed wrong'.[3] If, as Turner suggests, orderly hypotaxis is a correlative for European civilization, it is not surprising to find the Forster of *A Passage to India* exploring ways to discard or at least disrupt it.

In fact, the sentence that establishes itself in *A Passage to India*, if

---

*This chapter was first published in *The Journal of Narrative Technique*, Vol. 9 (1979), No. 3.

not as the norm at least as a conspicuous motif, is a loosely
co-ordinated sequence that sputters along, refusing the potential
emphasis of parallelism, and falling into subordinate structures
not so much to clarify distinctions as to introduce tangential
detail. Aziz's quest for the picnic elephant, for example, unwinds
its syntax, finally illustrating the contingency of grand events
on minutiae. Semi-official, this beast

> was best approached through Nureddin, but he never answered
> letters, but his mother had great influence with him and he was
> a friend of Hamidullah Begum's, who had been excessively
> kind and had promised to call on her provided the broken
> shutter of the purdah carriage came back soon enough from
> Calcutta.   (xiv, 130)

Sentences like this, muddled and lumpy as an Indian landscape,
seem to have relinquished two conventions of Western form —
climax and closure. In so doing, they enforce stylistically the
issues at the heart of Forster's theme.

The details of Adela's assault comprise another loose amalgam
of co-ordinate and subordinate structures:

> She had struck the polished wall — for no reason — and before
> the comment had died away, he followed her, and the climax
> was the falling of her field-glasses.   (xxii, 185)

This sentence contains in its own ironic comment on climax: the
potential for syntactic emphasis is thrown away on the second of
the three co-ordinated elements, the left-brancher, while the
assertion of climax in the third is undercut by its identification
with 'falling', the cadence of 'field-glasses', and, of course, by its
evasion of the sexual implication. There is a similar play on
western form in the recounting of the legend of the water tank:

> It concerned a Hindu Rajah who had slain his own sister's son,
> and the dagger with which he performed the deed remained
> clamped to his hand until in the course of years he came to the
> Marabar Hills, where he was thirsty and wanted to drink but
> saw a thirsty cow and ordered the water to be offered to her
> first, which, when done, 'dagger fell from his hand, and to
> commemorate miracle he built Tank'.   (xix, 170)

Godbole's conversations, we are then told, often 'culminated' in a cow. Certainly the disintegrating syntax of this single sentence mocks all notions of the culmination.

Anticlimax, of course, acquires thematic resonance in *Passage*. The Indian sunrise, the picnic, the trial, the Hindu festival — all are its manifestations. It is the condition of the time-bound, fact-bound world which denies men the 'poetry' they 'yearn for', denies joy grace, sorrow augustness, and infinity form (xxiv, 201). It is what one is left with when 'God' has passed, and he is always passing. Thus, the dwindling festivities of the 'Temple' section:

> Some of the torches went out, fireworks didn't catch, there began to be less singing, and the tray returned to Professor Godbole, who picked up a fragment of the mud adhering and smeared it on his forehead without much ceremony.
>
> (xxxvi, 305)

Here the fluctuating imprecision of the clauses joins with Godbole's gesture of humility to mark the dissolution of vision.

Forster's sentences in *Passage* fight closure as consistently as they undermine climax. Numerous final ellipses as well as three 'etc.'s violate the rhetoric of well-made sentences, and more than a dozen times in the course of the novel, Forster adds extra elements to his sentences by means of a simple, unsubtle 'also'. In many instances these afterthoughts represent the pressure of the lower 'inarticulate world' which in India 'is closer at hand and readier to resume control as soon as men are tired' (x, 105). Thus Adela lies passive in shock:

> She had been touched by the sun, also hundreds of cactus spines had to be picked out of her flesh.   (xxii, 184)

During the May festival, the inarticulate world is invited to encroach and be loved — 'birds, caves, railways, and the stars' (xxxiii, 278).

> A cobra of papier-mache now appeared on the carpet, also a wooden cradle swinging from a frame.   (xxxiii, 278)

[The Rajah] could witness the Three Steps by which the

Saviour ascended the universe to the discomfiture of Indra,
also the death of the dragon, the mountain that turned into an
umbrella, and the saddhu who (with comic results) invoked the
God before dining.   (xxxvi, 294)

Snakes twist their way through the narrative of *Passage* as images
of those lower pressures so dangerous to civilization. It seems
appropriate, then, that the cobra should take a final, casual bow
at the parting of Aziz and Fielding, by means of an 'also':

Presently the ground opened into full sunlight and they saw a
grassy slope bright with butterflies, also a cobra, which crawled
across doing nothing in particular.   (xxxvii, 307)

Along with the anticlimactic sentences, then, these additions
seem to pay tribute to the ragged edges, the formlessness of the
Indian experience. No sentence, in other words, is so sacred that
it cannot be reopened and altered by the emergence of a new fact.
In this Forster affirms stylistically that Hindu sense of heaven
which so horrified the western missionaries. 'Oranges, cactuses,
crystals and mud? And the bacteria inside Mr. Sorley' — it was
'going too far' to include all these in their Lord's mansions. In
an ironic comment that forecasts the exploded rhetoric of *Passage*,
the missionaries insist, 'We must exclude someone from our
gathering or we shall be left with nothing' (iv, 32).

Perhaps the most recurring departure in *Passage* from the
refined logic of hypotaxis is the comma-spliced sentence. In
certain cases, spliced co-ordination seems to evoke the rapid
overlay of thought or action that approximates the jumble of
simultaneity. The verdict is delivered, for instance,

then the flimsy framework of the court broke up, the shouts of
derision and rage culminated, people screamed and cursed,
kissed one another, wept passionately.   (xxiv, 219)

Interestingly enough, these run-on sentences are expressive not
only of chaos but also of ecstasy. Thus Godbole achieves his
limited communion with the Other:

Chance brought her [Mrs Moore] into his mind while it was in
this heated state, he did not select her, she happened to occur

among the throng of soliciting images, a tiny splinter, and he
impelled her by his spiritual force to that place where completeness can be found . . . . His senses grew thinner, he
remembered a wasp seen he forgot where, perhaps on a stone.
He loved the wasp equally, he impelled it likewise, he was
imitating God. And the stone where the wasp clung — could
he . . . no, he could not, he had been wrong to attempt the stone,
logic and conscious effort had seduced, he came back to the
strip of red carpet and discovered that he was dancing upon
it . . . . He danced on.   (xxxiii, 277)

As this blur of sentences suggests, vision in India has little to do
with either climax or closure, completeness being simply the
product of the same subjective, emotional shift that converts
muddle to mystery. In fact the festival as a whole, as a process of
collective ecstasy, is without an 'emotional centre' and finishes
in 'unsatisfactory and undramatic tangles' (xxxvi, 305–6).

It may be illuminating to compare the syntax of Godbole's
dance to some sentences that render such a thematically
resonant event in *Howards End*. When Margaret and Helen
Schlegel take their shelter for one night in Howards End, they are
able to renew their intimacy and enjoy the rewards of allegiance
to the 'inner life' (xxxvii, 296).

The present flowed by them like a stream. The tree rustled. It
made music before they were born, and would continue after
their deaths, but its song was of the moment. The moment had
passed. The tree rustled again. Their senses were sharpened,
and they seemed to apprehend life. Life passed. The tree
rustled again.   (xl, 312)

This succession of simple clauses would seem to have declined the
intellectual sophistication of hypotaxis, to be approaching
stylistically the multiplying co-ordination of Godbole's dance.
Yet the difference in effect is radical. Despite the emphasis on
'connecting' in *Howards End*, the economy and discipline of these
sentences seem to insist on a sharp line between chaos and vision.
Punctuation is tight; there are no detours into dependent structures. Set against the more abundant, chaotic process of the
Hindu festival, the sentence 'Life passed' suggests how rigid and
exclusive that line may become in *Howards End*. Finally, the image

which embodies this transcendent experience, an image which Margaret, awakening at midnight, witnesses from an upstairs window, is one of clarity and stasis:

> The house had enshadowed the tree at first, but as the moon rose higher the two disentangled, and were clear for a few moments at midnight.   (xl, 312)

Margaret sees; Godbole dances. Margaret achieves a heightened power of discrimination; Godbole participates in the power of indiscriminate loving. Margaret's effort is to sort things out, into orderly sentences. Godbole's is to include everything in an endless sentence.

The comma splice does more, however, than approximate immediate experience at its emotional extremes, thus suggesting the immanence of mystery in muddle. Compared to syntactical alternatives that integrate sets of elements through subordination, spliced clauses can appear as separate, impenetrable worlds. As Ronnie discovers when he tries to settle the Mohurram dispute by rerouting a procession or shortening a tower, 'the Mohammedans offered the former, the Hindus insisted on the latter' (viii, 87). In the linking of concrete details, the splice seems to sharpen their discreteness:

> The trees were full of glossy foliage and slim green fruit, the tanks slumbered;   (xxv, 222)

> A sentry slept in the Guest House porch, lamps burned in the cruciform of the deserted rooms.   (xxxvi, 297)

> Thorns scratched the keel, they ran into an islet and startled some cranes.   (xxxvi, 302)

Each splice seems to reinforce the separateness of things and people that India decrees in her hundred voices. At the same time, the splice points towards a unity beyond, or maybe among, all the hard, disparate parts. When Ronnie leaves Fielding's party in a huff,

> there was a moment of absolute silence. No ripple disturbed the water, no leaf stirred.   (vii, 72)

The positive absence of motion, for horizontal water and vertical trees, seems suddenly to join them into one coalescence. In a more tactile way, as Aziz's friends tumble out of his bungalow into the heat,

> the space between them and their carriages, instead of being empty, was clogged with a medium that pressed against their flesh, the carriage cushions scalded their trousers, their eyes pricked, domes of hot water accumulated under their headgear and poured down their cheeks.   (x, 105)

In these spliced clauses we find the disconnected symptoms of one implicit fact — the April sun is overpowering the earth. In Forster's commitment to splices, then, there is detectable an issue central to his novel's theme. Juxtaposition begins to suggest identity, and just as the syntax of chaos may become the syntax of ecstasy, multiplicity and unity may coexist. Perhaps the most charming image of this paradox explores its social dimension. On the return from the picnic,

> Mrs. Moore slept, swaying against the rods of the howdah, Mohammed Latif embraced her with efficiency and respect.
> (xvi, 160)

Here people rather than things are afforded Forster's contiguous treatment. They are definitely each alone, yet tenuously together.

One last recurrence in *Passage* dramatizes stylistically this paradoxical affirmation of both the separateness and unity of things. Another version of strained co-ordination — and sympathetic to the dangling addition — the unwieldly catalogue erupts in the narrative to assert the irrepressibility of life against the tidiness of sentences. Two characteristics of the catalogue in *Passage* invite thematic insight into the extraordinary world of that novel. Of the seven catalogues, first of all, that function as the direct objects of verbs (and persons), all but one enumerate things with illusory status. As Aziz returns from his picnic, he surveys the landscape from atop the rented elephant, 'a Mogul emperor who had done his duty'.

> He watched the Marabar Hills recede, and saw again, as provinces of his kingdom, the grim untidy plain, the frantic and

feeble movements of the buckets, the white shrines, the shallow
graves, the suave sky, the snake that looked like a tree.

(xvi, 150)

But at the very moment of this complacent vision, Adela is making
the deposition that will shatter Aziz's 'kingdom'. In fact, the
description within the catalogue betrays its own unmanage-
ability: untidy, frantic, shallow, and with that protean snake.
Also in catalogue form are the tongue-tying places Mrs Moore
'would never visit' (xxiii, 199) and the various performances the
Rajah *would have* witnessed if he had not died the night before
the final ceremony. One object catalogue stands out for its
deceptive air of things competently reconstructed — McBride's
account of the happenings at the Caves:

> He spoke of Miss Derek's arrival, of the scramble down the
> gully, of the return of the two ladies to Chandrapore, and of
> the document Miss Quested signed on her arrival, in which
> mention was made of the field-glasses.   (xxiv, 212)

Actually, the methodical calmness of this catalogue, the careful
parallelism, the passively appended field-glasses make all the
more ironic the discrepancy between ' circumstantial evidence'
and inscrutable reality. The issue is again illusion. And the point,
perhaps, of all these direct object catalogues — the error of
suppressing the agency and power of 'things', of the Other, of
objective experience, which is fate.

But, most frequently, the catalogue in *Passage* functions as an
appositive, giving nouns the freedom to multiply, and one thing
to lead to another. As the picnic starts out,

> much has still to enter the purdah carriage — a box bound with
> brass, a melon wearing a fez, a towel containing guavas, a step-
> ladder and a gun.   (xiii, 121)

There is the sense here, in the relative weakness of the word
'much' balanced against its concrete particulars, of a general
category falling into its components, threatening the very processes of generalization, categorization. There is the same
implication in the confusion that follows the trial, when Adela is
carried out into the streets of Chandrapore:

The faint, indescribable smell of the bazaars invaded her, sweeter than a London slum, yet more disquieting: a tuft of scented cotton wool, wedged in an old man's ear, fragments of pan between his black teeth, odorous powders, oils — the Scented East of tradition, but blended with human sweat as if a great king had been entangled in ignominy and could not free himself, or as if the heat of the sun had boiled and fried all the glories of the earth into a single mess.   (xxv, 220)

The category 'smell' at the beginning of this passage is only briefly adequate to classify the following appositives: tufts of wool, pan, powders, oils. Then a second attempt to generalize, 'the Scented East of tradition', must be adjusted by a further concrete, 'human sweat', and by two similes, the second of which finally resolves the particulars of the catalogue into perhaps the only generalization possible of Forster's India, a sensuous 'mess'.

Yet while many catalogues dramatize the stubborn diversity of things, of experience, they may also conjure up images of unity, by seeming to enumerate the terms of an infinite equation in which everything is equal to every other thing, and ultimately equal to God. In the appositive catalogue, each developing is linked to the primary noun, and by analogy to each other noun:

The signs of the contented Indian evening multiplied: frogs on all sides, cow-dung burning eternally; a flock of belated horn-bills overhead, looking like winged skeletons as they flapped across the gloaming.   (xxxvi, 297)

Sings=frogs=cow=dung=hornbills. This sense of a mystical equation emerges finally from what can be read as two sets of posterior appositives to the noun 'God Himself':

Thus was He thrown year after year, and were others thrown — little images of Ganpati, baskets of ten-day corn, tiny tazias after Mohurram — scapegoats, husks, emblems of passage.
     (xxxvi, 304)

Cosmic homogeneity is solidly realized, though inverted, in the message Mrs Moore hears in the cave: 'Pathos, piety, courage — they exist, but are identical, and so is filth. Everything exists, nothing has value' (xiv, 140). A second anterior appositive reiterates this theme: 'Hope, politeness, the blowing of a nose, the squeak of a boot, all produce "boum"' (xiv, 139). In the 'Temple' section, 'Boum' becomes 'Radhadkrishna' or 'God si love', and the negative proposition of the caves is modified to affirm that everything exists, everything may have divine value. It is with a last anterior appositive catalogue, though, that Forster reminds us that the moment with God, when the universal equation receives its completing central term, is brief. And just as 'it becomes history and falls under the rule of time', so must the friendship of Aziz and Fielding succumb to the India of separate and disparate pieces, united only in denial:

> The temples, the tank, the jail, the palace, the birds, the carrion, the Guest house, that came into view as they issued from the gap and saw Mau beneath: they didn't want it, they said in their hundred voices, 'No, not yet', and the sky said, 'No, not there'.   (xxxvii, 312)

It is this India, of autonomous things, insoluble muddle, that strained and perhaps finally defeated the complex sentences of E. M. Forster the novelist.

NOTES

1. G. W. Turner, *Stylistics* (Harmondsworth, Middlesex: Penguin Books, 1973), p. 71.
2. E. M. Forster, *Howards End*, ed. Oliver Stallybrass, Abinger edn. (London: Edward Arnold, 1973), p. 47.
3. E. M. Forster, *A Passage to India*, ed. Oliver Stallybrass, Abinger edn. (London: Edward Arnold, 1978), p. 270.

18 Forster's Inner Passage to India

Vasant A. Shahane

E. M. Forster's *A Passage to India* is his most significant artistic achievement. As a vision of the Whitmanesque 'Passage' to the 'soul of India', it becomes, indeed, a 'Passage' of the Forsterian soul to primal thought in the Indian setting, a kind of spiritual circumnavigation of the world, from west to east, through Alexandria to the Hill of Devi. In doing so it owes something to Whitman's articulation of *his* soul's voyage:

> O soul, repressless, I with thee and thou with me,
> Thy circumnavigation of the world begin,
> Of man, the voyage of his mind's return,
> To reason's early paradise,
> Back, back to wisdom's birth, to innocent intuitions,
> Again with fair creation.[1]
>
> ('Passsage to India' ll. 169–74)

In 'the voyage of his mind's return to reason's early paradise', Cyril Fielding undertakes another sort of Forsterian journey as he returns to the Mediterranean norm.

> [He] re-embarked at Alexandria — bright blue sky, constant wind, clean low coast-line, as against the intricacies of Bombay. Crete welcomed him next with the long snowy ridge of its mountains, and then came Venice. As he landed on the piazzetta a cup of beauty was lifted to his lips, and he drank with a sense of disloyalty. The buildings of Venice, like the mountains of Crete and the fields of Egypt, stood in the right place, whereas in poor India everything was placed wrong. He had forgotten the beauty of form among idol temples and

lumpy hills; indeed, without form, how can there be beauty? Forms stammered here and there in a mosque, became rigid through nervousness even, but oh, these Italian churches! San Giorgio standing on the island which could scarcely have risen from the waves without it, the Salute holding the entrance of a canal which, but for it, would not be the Grand Canal! In the old undergraduate days he had wrapped himself up in the many-coloured blanket of St. Mark's, but something more precious than mosaics and marbles was offered to him now: the harmony between the works of man and the earth that upholds them, the civilization that has escaped muddle, the spirit in a reasonable form, with flesh and blood subsisting. Writing picture-postcards to his Indian friends, he felt that all of them would miss the joys he experienced now, the joys of form, and that this constituted a serious barrier. They would see the sumptuousness of Venice, not its shape, and though Venice was not Europe it was part of the Mediterranean harmony. The Mediterranean is the human norm.[2]

Forster chose his own passage through an exit from the Mediterranean to the Indian Ocean. Thus his view and vision of 'Alexandria Visited' are, in some ways, linked to his vision of India.

Edwin Thumboo has perceptively pointed out the connecting links between the ideas of Plotinian Christianity and those of the Bhakti cult in Hinduism.[3] Forster explains in *Alexandria: A History and a Guide* that Plotinus believed that:

> God has three grades . . . The one is — Unity, the One . . . it has no qualities, no creative force, it is good only as the goal of our aspirations. But though it cannot create, it overflows (somewhat like a fountain), and from its overflows or emanation is generated the second grade of the Trinity — the 'Intellectual Principle' . . . . It is the Universal mind that contains — not all things, but all thoughts of things, and by thinking it creates. It thinks of the third grade — the All Soul — which accordingly comes into being. With the All Soul we near the realm of the comprehensible. It is the cause of the Universe that we know.[4]

These ideas of Plotinus's are reflected in the Hindu view of the universe. Plotinus underscores the emotional, the imaginative aspect of the divine, which is also embodied in Professor Narayan

Godbole's ecstatic vision of God. Indeed, his attempt to become one with God and to include everything in the universe into his own ambit is very close to the Plotinian view outlined by Forster: 'We are all parts of God, even the stones, though we cannot realize it; and man's goal is to become actually, as he is potentially, divine . . . .'[5] In fact, Godbole's difficulty with the stone in his attempt at inclusion seems almost a continuation of the Plotinian theme in *Alexandria: A History and a Guide.* At one stage Forster speaks of the vision of oneself and the vision of God being 'really the same' because each individual is God. This is absolutely true, not only of Godbole himself but also of the *gopis* (milk-maidens). Thus, Alexandria paves the way for Forster's 'Passage to India'.

Both Fielding's tea party and Professor Narayan Godbole's song illustrate Forster's fictional mode of circumnavigation: the criss-cross of characters and events in the narrative and symbolic structure which characterizes *A Passage to India.* Fielding's 'tea' is actuated by a desire to foster a pleasant get-together. It aims at friendship, though in effect, it frustrates it, whereas Professor Godbole's song,[6] which is expected to be a mere casual entertainment, effectually functions as an instrument of harmony.

The meaning of Godbole's song is woven into the symbolic structure of the novel. Its theme is the desired spiritual union between Lord Krishna and His *gopis.* These milk-maidens love their Lord and also look upon Him as a human figure. They are eager to be in a state of close and intimate communion with Him. As the song emphasizes, a woman's total self-surrender to her companion-in-love is analogous to a religious devotee's complete self-surrender to God. The *gopi* worships Krishna, 'Love, come to me only', but he refuses to come. This refusal sets the negative tone characteristic of the Marabar Caves. Mrs Moore innocently asks Godbole, 'But He comes in some other song, I hope?' 'Oh, no, He refuses to come', repeats Godbole (vii, 72).

The song itself is a poetical utterance expressing an idea fundamental to the *bhakti* cult: the devotee's total self-surrender to God. This cult uses poetry and song to demonstrate the combination of the divine and erotic elements in human passion. Indian folklore and devotional poetry, especially that of Meera Bai, amply illustrate this synthesis of the sexual and the religious. The song may also imply a belief in an Immanent God, a concept of Pantheism, suggesting that God is, in effect, within the human heart. Therefore, when the milk-maidens ask God to come to each one of them, they overlook the fundamental truth that God is, indeed, within them. God's refusal to come, therefore, is an assumption of these *gopis*, which is dramatically used by Forster in the fabric of his fiction. Forster calls the song a significant part of the 'stream of events' having a peculiar and subtle effect upon Mrs Moore and Miss Quested. The effect is described in words which conceal more than they reveal: 'Ever since Professor Godbole had sung his queer little song, they had lived more or less inside cocoons, and the difference between them was that the elder lady accepted her own apathy, while the younger resented hers' (xiv, 125). It is clear that Godbole's song has had a far-reaching effect on Mrs Moore and Adela Quested in their search for the real India.

It is interesting to explore the genesis of the enigmatic Professor Narayan Godbole. Undoubtedly, many qualities of both Sir Tukoji, the Maharajah of Dewas, and the Maharajah of Chhatarpur are compounded in Godbole's personality. When Forster had 'a Krishna conversation' with the 'fantastic and poetical Maharajah of Chhatarpur' the latter told him: '. . . I can meditate on love, for love is the only power that can keep thought out. I try to meditate on Krishna. I do not know that he is a God, but I love Love and Beauty and Wisdom, and I find them in his history. I worship and adore him as a man'.[7]

In a letter to Mrs Alyward, dated 6 March 1913, Forster describes the spiritual attitudes of Sir Tukoji III, the Maharajah of Dewas, especially, his 'belief in a being who, though omnipresent, is personal, and whom he calls Krishna'.[8] Godbole also embodies the Maharajah's devotion to the *bhakti* cult and his attitudes to food and fasts. He is, of course, a Chitpavan Brahmin, but his connection with the great tradition of the rebellious Tilak or of the moderate Gokhale, as suggested by G. K. Das,[9] needs further scrutiny. The Brahmin-Kshatriya or Brahmin-Maratha differences are as old as Hinduism itself, but, in my view, these have only a limited relevance to Godbole's mind and personality. Godbole as an educator or education minister is as disappointing as Sir Tukoji III was as the ruler of Dewas State Senior. Their greatness and magnificence lie in their inner life.[10]

Whereas Forster's inner passage to India is primarily projected through the personality of Godbole, it is also envisioned and expressed in the person of Mrs Moore. An understanding of the complexities of her experience in the Marabar Caves is crucial to the comprehension of Forster's fictional and spiritual journey. It is equally important to trace, analyse and interpret the connections between Mrs Moore's experience in the Caves and Professor Godbole's mystic, visionary moments during the Temple ceremonies. In this context, Forster's comment, that 'Temple' represents the same thing as the scene in the Cave 'turned inside out'[11] is very revealing. Godbole's ecstatic dance recreates through memory and a wish for spiritual fulfilment that is marked by a total merging of his self with the Absolute, the image of Mrs Moore.

The basic question about Mrs Moore's experience, its quality and range, has been raised by Forster himself: was it a vision or nightmare?

> She felt increasingly (vision or nightmare?) that, though people are important, the relations between them are not, and that in particular too much fuss has been made over marriage; centuries of carnal embracement, yet man is no nearer to understanding man. And today she felt this with such force that it seemed itself a relationship, itself a person, who was trying to take hold of her hand. (xiv, 127)

Her apparent loss of interest in personal relationships is the outcome of her experience in the Caves. She is turning her back on the world of matter and phenomena, the world of the senses and rational distinctions. She is preparing herself for the final act of dying by moving towards a state of almost complete isolation and detachment.

The atmosphere at the Marabar expedition is unusually depressing and is infected by intangible elements of strange omen. A spiritual silence seems to have invaded the human senses, and neither sounds nor thoughts can develop. 'Everything seemed cut off at its root, and therefore infected with illusion' (xiv, 132). This almost cosmic despair prepares the ground for her profoundly disturbing experience. The echo gets hold of her mind and begins to undermine her hold on life: 'Coming at a moment when she chanced to be fatigued, it had managed to murmur: "Pathos, piety, courage — they exist, but are identical, and so are filth. Everything exists, nothing has value"' (xiv, 140).

Mrs Moore thus seems to have been overwhelmed by an apparently valueless world. The Marabar has even robbed infinity of its vastness and expanse. In this peculiar mental state, Christianity appears before her as a feeble religious force and it too is confronted by the echo, the 'boum':

> Then she was terrified over an area larger than usual; the universe, never comprehensible to her intellect, offered no repose to her soul, the mood of the last two months took definite form at last, and she realized that she didn't want to write to her children, didn't want to communicate with anyone, not even with God. She sat motionless with horror, and when old Mohammed Latif came up to her, thought he would notice a difference. For a time she thought, 'I am going to be ill', to comfort herself, then she surrendered to the vision.
>
> (xiv, 141)

The effect of the Caves on Mrs Moore is in part negative and in part positive.[12] Her loss of interest in personal relationships, her indifference and the collapse of her will form the negative elements of her experience. On the other hand, these same attributes have been termed 'religious' and can be centred in the 'twilight of the double vision' in which elderly persons of a reflective, religious nature are sometimes involved:

> If this world is not to our taste, well, at all events there is Heaven, Hell, Annihilation — one or other of those large things, that huge scenic background of stars, fires, blue or black air. All heroic endeavour, and all that is known as art, assumes that there is such a background, just as all practical endeavour, when the world is to our taste, assumes that the world is all. But in the twilight of the double vision, a spiritual muddledom is set up for which no high-sounding words can be found; we can neither act nor refrain from action, we can neither ignore nor respect Infinity.   (xxiii, 198)

Mrs Moore's vision, or anti-vision, suggests the twilight state which approximates the ambivalence between light and darkness, knowledge and ignorance, hope and despair, joy and sorrow. Her vision, then, is in tune with the progression of her being from the state of the living to the state of the dead. Critics have stressed this emphasis on death since, for a true Christian, life is a preparation for death and her vision appears at a time when she is initiated into the act of dying. Death in Forster's novels, says F. R. Leavis, endows events and characters with a religious sanctity.[13] In this context Forster's account of Mrs Moore's death is significant: 'Dead she was . . . and her body was lowered into yet another India — The Indian Ocean' (xxviii, 244).

Mrs Moore's experience has also been interpreted as being 'religious' in the context of the Hindu view of supreme spiritual isolation known as *Kaivalya*. From this Indian perspective, she approaches the Absolute, which is beyond both time and space and which can be reached only by those who turn their face away from the world of the body, the physical universe of attachment, the life of pleasure. She gains a vision of the vast immensity of the Absolute through her experience in the Caves which themselves embody the concept of roundness and wholeness. The echo, then, is a positive and valuable 'sound', a kind of 'oum', the sacred syllable of the Hindus. It is in this light that Mrs Moore's experience has been interpreted by McConkey as a religious quest for the unity of man and cosmos.[14] It is my view that Forster has subtly shown that the experience of Mrs Moore and the mystical trance of Godbole are two facets of a single religious experience.

Love, in its universal context, and *bhakti*, in its Hindu and Vaishnava context, play a major part in the narrative and symbolic modes of reconciliation among the principal characters. The third section of the novel, 'Temple', is highly significant in its dramatization of the impact and limitations of universal love and recent critics of Forster's fiction have accorded it a very important place in the novel's overall structure. Forster's own view of the 'Temple' is recorded in an interview:

Interviewer: What was the exact funtion of the long description of the Hindu festival in *A Passage to India*?
Forster: It was architecturally necessary. I needed a lump, or a Hindu temple if you like — a mountain standing up. It is well placed: and it gathers up some strings. But there ought to be more after it . . .[15]

Professor Narayan Godbole, the voice of the *bhakti* cult, becomes the chief instrument of Forster's strategy of reconciliation in 'Temple'. Godbole's appearance suggests harmony, peace and love as if he were inwardly inspired to bridge the gulf between the East and the West, between the Indians and the Anglo-Indians, between the Caves and the Temple. Hundreds of miles west of the Marabar Hills, in Mau, he stands in the presence of his personal God. Two years have elapsed since the incidents in the Marabar Caves had darkened the atmosphere and the minds of men. Godbole celebrates the birth of Lord Krishna which occurs at midnight, although paradoxically, Lord Krishna transcends the processes of birth and death — 'He is, was not, is not, was' (xxxiii, 274). Merriment is obtained at the expense of good taste since 'all spirit as well as all matter must participate in salvation' (xxxiii, 279). The Lord and Godbole stand at opposite ends of the carpet and the mystic, clashing the cymbals, sings and dances before his God. He sings of Tukaram:

> Tukaram, Tukaram,
> Thou art my father and mother and everybody.
> Tukaram, Tukaram,
> Thou art my father and mother and everybody.
> Tukaram, Tukaram,
> Thou art my father and mother and everybody.
> Tukaram, Tukaram,
> Thou art my father and mother and everybody.
> Tukaram . . .   (xxxiii, 274)

It is significant that in this song, Godbole offers his obeisance not to God but Tukaram, the greatest mystic saint of Maharashtra, the seventeenth-century Marathi poet whose *abhangas* have been enshrined in the hearts of millions of common folk. He is the pre-eminent exponent of the *bhakti* cult and its emphasis on man's union with God through love. This *bhakti* cult is one of the most significant strands of Hindu belief as it is practised by the people. The concept of love as the true pathway to God is part of the preachings of both Hinduism and Christianity, and provides a setting to the spiritual affinity established between Professor Godbole and Mrs Moore.

Godbole's invocation, 'Radhakrishna, Radhakrishna' is again a prayer to a personal God, an *avatar* of Vishnu. He represents the voice of Vaishnavism, a principal concept of Hinduism, and one which is central to the third section of the novel. He does not openly voice the beliefs of Advaita Vedanta as a few critics, especially McConkey, have affirmed: the emptinesss in the Marabar has been explained as an aspect of the Absolute, and the echo is stated to be the sound of Mrs Moore's inadequate awareness of it. While *Om* or *Oum* is believed to signify the non-dualist *Vedanta*, *Ou-Boum* has been interpreted as the voice of the dualistic point of view. Both of these sounds either help or hinder the process of the characters' attempts at merging with the Absolute. In my view, Professor Godbole does not represent the voice of the monistic *Advaita Vedanta*; on the contrary, he is in the opposite position of affirming the non-monistic view of reality: an intuitively held belief in a personal God. His is the true voice of the Hindu belief in the unity of God: *Man-Tattvam-asi* — 'That Thou art' — and the idea that the whole world is Brahma: *Sarvam-Khalu-Idam-Brahman.*

However, the western mind may have some difficulty in apprehending Godbole's mysticism. Writing about metaphysical nihilism, William Ralph Inge has this to say: 'It is a common criticism brought against mysticism of the Indian type, that it ends in metaphysical nihilism. The mystic who tries to apprehend the infinite grasps only zero. As applied to the actual teaching of Indian thinkers, this criticism is based largely on Western misunderstanding of Eastern thought'.[16]

Forster, in presenting the nihilistic elements of Mrs Moore's experience — whose indifference to the body and renunciation of things earthly suggests Plotinian Christianity — seems to underscore western misconceptions of Indian thought. In doing so, he points out that the seeds of Professor Godbole's attempts to merge with God, the source of divinity, can be seen in Plotinus's attempt to merge with the Absolute. Plotinus, himself, says:

The one who has experienced understands what I mean: how the soul takes on another life as it approaches God. Having come into His presence, it rests in Him, it merges in Him. It knows Him as the Dispenser of the only true life. Everything earthly is stripped away; bonds that fetter us are loosened so that we may adhere to Him, no part remaining in us, but with it we may cleave to God. Then shall we be worthy to behold Him and ourselves in a single light; but it will be a self lifted into splendour, radiant with spiritual light, nay, itself become a light, pure, buoyant, incandescent, identical with Godhead.[17]

A similar concept of the Infinite´ is effectively described and praised in *Shrimad Bhagavatam*:

Thou art the cause, thou art the effect;
Thou art the work, thou art the doer;
Thou art the instrument, thou art the action;
Thou art all in all,
There is nothing beyond or about thee.
From thee all religions spring forth,
Thou art the source of all Scriptures,
Thou art the fountain of all knowledge;
Yet none of these can reveal thy infinite nature,
For verily thou art supreme;
Infinite, absolute, impersonal, beyond all name and form art thou.

It is this Infinite in Indian philosophic thought that Forster seeks to discover through a process of circumnavigation of the spirit — through Mosque, Caves, Temple and principally through Mrs Moore and Professor Godbole. This is the pattern of Forster's inner passage to India: a never-ending journey constantly moving towards the expansion, not completion, of the horizons of consciousness.

NOTES

1. Walt Whitman, 'Passage to India', *Leaves of Grass*, ed. Harold W. Blodgett and Sculley Bradley (New York: New York University Press, 1965), p. 418.
2. E. M. Forster, *A Passage to India*, ed. Oliver Stallybrass, Abinger edn. (London: Edward Arnold, 1978), p. 270.
3. 'E. M. Forster's Passage to India: Dewas, Alexandria and the Road to Mau', presented at the Forster Seminar, Hyderabad, January 1979. It is necessary to note two other essays, Mohammad Shaheen, 'Forster's Alexandria: the Transitional Journey' and John Drew, 'A Passage via Alexandria?' in *E. M. Forster: A Human Exploration*, ed. G. K. Das and John Beer (London: Macmillan, 1979), pp. 79–101. These essays deal with the same theme as my paper does; however the substance as well as the points of view differ greatly.
4. E. M. Forster, *Alexandria: A History and a Guide* (Garden City, N.Y.: Doubleday, Anchor Books, 1961), p. 70.

5. *Alexandria*, p. 71.

6. For an account of Forster's meeting with Mr Godbole, see P. N. Furbank, *E. M. Forster: A Life* (New York: Harcourt, Brace, Jovanovich, 1977), p. 249. 'Mr. Godbole sang to him. "There are scales appropriate for all hours of the day", he noted. "That for the evening was the scale of C Major, but with F# instead of F"'.

7. E. M. Forster, *The Hill of Devi* (London: Edward Arnold, 1953), p. 30.

8. *Ibid.*, p. 30.

9. G. K. Das, *E. M. Forster's India* (London: Macmillan, 1977), Chapter 6.

10. Both the Dewas dynasty and Professor Godbole sing of Tukaram, the eminent Maharashtrian saint poet. Forster writes in *Hill of Devi* 'Tukaram, Tukaram thou art my father and my mother and all things, "we would sing, time after time, until we seemed to be worshipping a poet"' (p. 117) and in *A Passage to India* Godbole and his choir of six colleagues sing: 'Tukaram, Tukaram, Thou art my father and mother and everybody'. (xxxiii, p. 275). I believe that this couplet is the English version of a Marathi Prayer and is probably derived from Poet Kacheshwar's *aaratees* of Tukaram. The original Marathi version is:

> *Tukarām, Tukarām, toochi māza baap, toochi māzi maya*
> *Tukarām, Tukarām, toochi sarwaswa māze . . .*

When I read this 'probable Marathi original' to Forster in his room at King's, he smiled over it.

11. Alan Wilde, *Art and Order: A Study of E. M. Forster* (New York: New York University Press, 1964), p. 151.

12. Although from the western point of view, Mrs Moore experiences 'Nothingness', this 'Nothingness' is itself viewed from a very different angle in the Hindu view of the cosmos. For instance, statements such as 'Everything exists, nothing has value' may from the Hindu point of view be interpreted as 'Neti, Neti' (not-this, not-this). The Hindus believe that the Absolute is beyond good and evil, beyond all distinctions, beyond logical categories. And, therefore, it has to be expressed in purely negative terms (Neti, Neti). In this light, the negative elements of Mrs Moore's experience could be endowed with a deeply religious significance.

13. F. R. Leavis, *The Common Pursuit*, (London: Chatto and Windus, 1952), p. 264.

14. James McConkey, *The Novels of E. M. Forster* (Ithaca, N.Y.: Cornell University Press, 1957).

15. P. N. Furbank and F. J. Haskell, 'E. M. Forster', *Writers at Work*, ed. Malcolm Cowley (New York: The Viking Press, 1958).

16. William Ralph Inge, *The Philosophy of Plotinus*, 2 vols. (London: Longmans, Green and Co., 1929), p. 117. See also Clive W. Johnson, 'Plotinus and Vedanta', *Vedanta and the West*, 179 (May–June 1966), an illuminating study of the resemblances between the concepts of Plotinus and Hindu religious thinkers such as Shankara and religious texts such as the *Upanishads*.

17. Johnson, p. 15.

19 E. M. Forster and India

Ahmed Ali

So much as been written about *A Passsage to India* that one cannot see the artist, or the civilized Englishman, or even Forster himself, separate from his own novel, with an identity and personality of his own. Any life outside of that one book becomes obscured so that across Forster's life span of ninety-one years only one word seems ingrained — INDIA — covering up the thirty-three years before his first visit to that sad country, and the twenty-five after his last in 1945.

Thus, often in my vacant moods I begin to wonder: was there ever a real E. M. Forster, or was it all a legend, figment of imagination, the echo of his own creation, boum ou-boum. Yet even the doubts and affirmations, questions and answers, themselves get lost in that hall of enigma, the Marabar Caves, where the mystery of each individual mind in its overpowering darkness, the horror of isolation of man from man in the absence of understanding, sympathy and affection becomes indistinguishable from the gift of kindness and more kindness which lights up the spark of love.

The symbolic meanings of the novel have been lost in preoccupations with the right and wrong, the why and wherefore of the particular view of Anglo-India Forster chose to present. Consequently, the India Forster saw and presented takes on the phantom-like appearance of his own cow in *The Longest Journey*; was it there or was it not there? For the India that he visited, knew, and came to love, was not the India of popular imagination, not the India of the Anglo-Indians, or of the freedom-fighters, or of the India — divided in the minds of Hindus or Muslims — of a later moment of history. It was, essentially, the India of the poet's desire for a friend, of the seeking hand stretched out for affection and acceptance.

When we think of India, it is either a picture of rajahs or

elephants that rises before our eyes; or one of Gandhi squatting half-naked with a spinning wheel, making salt to defy the might of the British Empire; or of an India torn in two, Hindus and Muslims killing one another and splitting the country apart like the shell of a peanut. This was not the India Forster visited. The India he presented took its life and form from his vision. It was the India that on a smaller scale, in a different way, I tried to describe in my own novel, *Twilight in Delhi*,[1] a likeness that Forster noticed in the preface of the Everyman's edition of *A Passage to India*.

So much have his readers and friends read into him of their own selves or ideas of him, that in this confusion we forget that E. M. Forster was first and foremost an artist and humanist. His art was enlightened by his humanism, and his humanism by his art. He came out to India not with any professional or political motive and not in order to promote good will among nations as did his friend and tutor Goldsworthy Lowes Dickinson who, with R. C. Trevelyan, accompanied him on the visit. He came to meet his friend Syed Ross Masood, whom he had met in 1906, and who had returned to his own country a few months before. His mission was thus one of affection and friendship. He had no occasion to form any preconceived notions, or, in fact, any idea about India other than that it was the home of the friend.

Being a thoughtful man, however, he had read a variety of books before embarking on the journey in October 1912: Lyall's book about the British in India, for instance, and the life of Sir Syed Ahmad Khan, grandfather of Ross Masood and founder of the Anglo-Oriental College of Aligarh. The enthusiasm behind his preparation lay in the excitement of his anticipated experience, and he kept his mind open to what he was going to find and see.

Intense as his emotional engagement with India may have been, however, it was not, at the time, to lead to a novel. In fact, in January 1913 he wrote to Forrest Reid:

> I am dried up. Not in my emotions, but in their expression. I cannot write at all. You say I helped you once — have a shot at helping me for I need it . . . . It often makes me very unhappy. I see beauty going by and have nothing to catch it in. The only book I have in mind is too like *Howards End* to interest me . . . . I want something beyond the field of action and behaviour: the

waters of the river that rises from the middle of the earth to
join the Ganges and the Jamuna where they join. India is full
of such wonders, but she can't give them to me . . . .[2]

The letter is imbued with the eternal sadness of the artist caught
between the desire for creation and the inability of the spirit to
respond, the emotion to detach itself in order to search for that
'something' beyond action and behaviour, the mystery and
miracle of life, which only the very great have looked for and
captured for the joy of mankind.

His companions on the visit, Dickinson and Trevelyan, were
horrified by the squalor and muddle, the meaningless of the life
they saw in India, and were repelled. Forster, in the greatness
of his imagination, accepted the muddle and the squalor, and
whatever else India offered, with sympathy and love and all
humility of heart. With his passion for human contacts, lack of
haughtiness, openness to new experience, politeness and gene-
rosity, all rooted in his own culture and humanism, he transcended national, racial and psychological barriers that stood in
the way of so many of those new to India. He thus easily made
friends and was appreciated by all Indians and taken to their
bosoms. He was rewarded: wonderful vistas of thought and
imagination opened up before his mind and provided a sense of
peace surpassing understanding. In turn, he left a gift of love in
the form of two great books — *A Passage to India* and *The Hill of
Devi*, dedicated to two other friends who were India and much
more to him — books that serve as a monument to friendship and
a bridge across all barriers in life as in death.

All that I wish to emphasize here is that Forster was not a
political person in the sense the word is understood today; nor
was he a missionary or social worker bent on reforming India's
caste system. If anything, Forster was areligious. He had his
beliefs, but he put his faith in human relations. He was also
sensitive to the idea of transcendence, the purpose beyond the
world of action and behaviour, and he had a feeling for contemplation and the appreciation of something bigger that lies
behind human life, the wonder and mystery of existence which
becomes religious in the finest meaning of emotional experience.
He was drawn to Nature and its varied moods and beauties, to
ruins and mosques which communicated, in their silence, the
message of something deeply mystical and eternal. Towards the

end of his life he came to believe in the possibility of other life in the universe. As he said in one of his very last letters to me: '. . . I don't admit that my view of human nature has been invalidated, though economical and political affairs are being led by science at an increasing rate towards disaster. I have been interested lately — (and in an astronomical setting) in the possibility — indeed the probability — of other and non-human forms of life elsewhere in the universe . . . .'

How much this religious feeling is derived from the evangelical past of the Thorntons and Forsters or is a result of his intense experience with India is a subject for speculation. However, the feeling was there, intense, emotional, felt and evidenced in a spiritual kind of absorption whenever he was in the old ruins, the monuments and mosques of Islam. Furthermore, there is an appreciation of the spirit behind the rituals that celebrate the birth of Krishna; behind the mystical devotionalism of his friend the Maharajah of Dewas, transferred in the novel to the yearnings of Professor Godbole for the friend who never came; or behind the desire of the Rajah of Chhatarpur for the appearance of the love god, the sought-for friend. He had a genuine respect for what was truly religious in other people's behaviour — the act of prayer in the loggia by a group of more orthodox Muslims after the very unorthodox wedding at Simla; the search for God by Chhatarpur; the acts of devotion by Dewas Senior. I have seen him with tears on his face after such experiences. He had less sympathy for Christianity which he found negative and too 'self-important'. Personal relations meant much more to him, for they were part of universal love, what he saw behind the festival Gokul Ashtami in the novel: 'They loved all men, the whole universe, and scraps of their past, tiny splinters of detail, emerged for a moment into the universal warmth . . . .'[3]

When this wholeness is shattered, when man becomes isolated from man, as was the case with Anglo-India, with Mrs Moore's separation from Adela Quested, from her son, even from Aziz, he is swallowed up by the diabolical darkness of the Caves, by his own flaying mind, to be driven to acts of suspicion, devilish outrage and antagonism. Like splinters of fear lighting up a hellish conflagration of hate, the Marabar Caves symbolize the terror of loneliness, isolation, and the darkness of the mind, echoing in exact measure and imitation each person's own thoughts and fears apart from other human beings and from one another, snapping in a macabre act the strings of the heart so that it becomes for ever immune to the call of love, the boum ou-boum of the all-forgiving past, the equalizing power of eternity. All that can now be heard are the terrifying echoes of time exploding, wrenched-away atoms splitting in the vacuum of the human mind. Not until the release at the end, symbolized by the birth of Krishna, is harmony restored at last and life redeemed.

Thus one could say that Forster's search for union with the divine was in many ways like the search of his friend the Maharajah of Dewas. The Rajah of Chhatarpur expressed it exactly. Looking at the blazing colours of the sunset, he said: 'I want a friend like that'.[4] Such an affirmation is behind Forster's statement, quoted in the introduction to *A Passage to India*, that the novel is about 'the search of the human race for a more lasting home, about the universe as embodied in the Indian earth and the Indian sky'.[5]

NOTES

1. Ahmed Ali, *Twilight in Delhi* (London: The Hogarth Press, 1940).
2. P. N. Furbank, *E. M. Forster: A Life* (New York: Harcourt Brace Jovano-vich, 1977), I, p. 249.
3. E. M. Forster, *A Passage to India*, ed. Oliver Stallybrass, Abinger edn. (London: Edward Arnold, 1978), Ch. 33, p. 276.
4. Furbank, I, p. 235.
5. In the introduction to *A Passage*, p. xxv, Stallybrass quotes from this still unpublished essay, 'Three Countries'. The manuscript-cum-typescript of the 1950s is at King's College, Cambridge.

Part IV

Writers' Panel

Writers' Panel:
An Introduction

Robert K. Martin

Although he lived much of his life at Cambridge, E. M. Forster never held a regular academic post, and although he wrote often on the subject of fiction, he wrote as a critic or fellow-novelist rather than as a scholar. When he wrote about English fiction he imagined 'all the novelists . . . at work together in a circular room' while 'we' (that is, he and his readers, who are also of course their readers) 'look over their shoulders'.[1]

Forster's image suggests a continuity of time in which it is not merely the past that informs the present, but also the present that informs the past. Pursuing Forster's metaphor may lead us back to its possible source, Pater's 'imaginary portrait' of 'Denys l'Auxerrois', where Denys, the spirit of Dionysus 'reincarnated' as a mediaeval monk, is observed as he 'in cowl now with tonsured head, leaned over the painter, and led his work, by a kind of visible sympathy, often unspoken, rather than by any formal comment.'[2] That the monk who is painting is illustrating an edition of Ovid completes the circle; the figure who leans over him brings together the spirit of the past as well as that of the present, the flesh as well as the soul.

With such 'visible sympathy' all artists everywhere share the same circular room, provided only that they let themselves be guided by imagination, 'our only guide into the world created by words',[3] as Forster put it. As we organized the centenary conference, it seemed important to allow writers an opportunity to talk about the ways in which E. M. Forster had been an important presence in their lives, an unseen figure occasionally guiding their pens. Each of the writers who participated could acknowledge a particular way in which Forster had entered into his or her life as an artist.

James McConkey is both a critic who has written one of the

earliest studies of Forster's fiction and a writer of short stories and novels that bear the mark of Forster's spirit. Like Forster he makes out of the reworkings of his own life the material for a moving and tender exploration of a man's search for some understanding of his own experience and for the identification of human relationships as the most difficult and most valuable of human goals.

Bharati Mukherjee's work also stands in a clear relationship with Forster's. As an Indian writer, she inherited a landscape that had been charted for English literature by Forster. It is a sign of that uneasy relationship that she began her literary career by parodying Forster, thereby making that familiar gesture of homage and emancipation. She has had to create her India, and in order to do so, has observed it from without. Her acute observations of herself and of her Canadian husband display a Forsterian sense of muddle, incomprehension and good will.

Eudora Welty, the most distinguished author of the American South, inhabits a world far from Forster's experience. But, like Forster, she has been sensitive to place and has known how to draw upon her intricate knowledge of the ways of her country to create memorable characters as full of the mythology of Mississippi as Forster's were of that of England. Like Forster she celebrates, with love, even when indulging in the wildest of fantasies or drawing for us characters at once probable and improbable. And in her critical essays on Forster's writing, she expressed the affinity she felt for the 'comic glint', the ironic conclusion, and above all, the 'moral iron'.[4]

Her fellow Mississippian, Elizabeth Spencer, is perhaps best known for her stories and her novel (*The Light in the Piazza*) set in Italy. Like Forster's Italian novels and stories, Miss Spencer's works wittily explore the confrontations between cultures. Her wealthy Americans seem but cousins to Forster's travelling Englishmen and women, and their sudden coming to awareness is as likely to produce high comedy as any of Forster's 'eternal moments'.

Although comedy is certainly a characteristic mode for Forster, it is by no means his only one. Marie-Claire Blais, Quebec's most highly regarded novelist and the winner of the French Prix Goncourt, responds to Forster above all as the author of *Maurice*. Blais, several of whose novels have explored the nature of homosexual love under the condition of social oppression, has been interested in the ways in which Forster led the way for future writers to explore homosexual life. For her *Maurice* is important as a novel which began to chart new territory, by simultaneously revealing the possibility of love and the reality of fear.

All the participants have shared with Forster the belief that 'If human nature does alter it will be because individuals manage to look at themselves in a new way'. Forster saw that 'Every institution and vested interest is against such a search', but he also saw that 'a very few people, but a few novelists are among them'[5] would continue their contemplation and so contribute to the development of humanity. It was to that end that he looked over their shoulders, and to that same end that we may hope that the circular room continues to expand and to make room for the record of those who are now brought together in the proximity of a shared craft.

NOTES

1. E. M. Forster, *Aspects of the Novel* (London: Edward Arnold, 1974), pp. 8–9.
2. Walter Pater, 'Denys l'Auxerrois', *Imaginary Portraits* (London: Macmillan, 1914), p. 71.
3. E. M. Forster, *Anonymity: An Enquiry* (London: Hogarth Press, 1925), p. 23.
4. Eudora Welty, Review of *The Life to Come*, in *The Eye of the Story: Selected Essays and Reviews* (New York: Random House, 1978), pp. 232, 233.
5. E. M. Forster, *Aspects of the Novel* (London: Edward Arnold, 1974) p. 118.

Writers' Panel

Participants: Elizabeth Spencer, Bharati Mukherjee,
Marie-Claire Blais, James McConkey,
Eudora Welty

I — The Panel

Elizabeth Spencer:

The encounter of writer to writer is a very important thing to talk about. I have never taken a class on Forster but I've known him as a writer one admires although I have not been particularly conscious of the influence. We have a meeting ground in that instead of taking a passage to India, which seemed a little far to think about, I took a passage to Italy and saw my loves among Forster's novels flow from that coincidence. *Where Angels Fear To Tread* is probably my favourite of Forster's work. I've jotted down a few notes on how my acquaintance with Forster began and I had to search my memory to locate it. Finally it came up just whole and like a scene out of something one might have read because I remembered the whole circumstance, once I started thinking about it. Once long ago in the forties when I was working on my first novel in a beat-up old rooming-house in Nashville, Tennessee, a friend dropped in for coffee on a warm spring morning. He asked me if I had ever read a novelist called E. M. Forster. I said I'd heard the name but, no, had never read him. He forthwith produced a book — being quite carried away he'd brought it along — and said 'I'm so excited by his work'. 'Why', I said. I must have been in a grumbling mood since I was writing myself. 'Well it's hard to define', he said; then he tried. He said 'You go reading along in what seems to be an existence made of daily life, trivial, witty, well observed, but not much else and then suddenly, suddenly' — he lacked for words. 'Suddenly what?' I asked. 'Well, just let me read you this', he said, and he read something. It's a passage I have now forgotten. I sometimes after all these years think I can remember it and all my reading has not brought that particular passage to light. I shall keep on reading Forster 'til one day I will find it. But I remember the feeling, and I know that it excited me too. We read some more and we talked a long time. I since have read nearly all of Forster I think, some of his books many times over and so have encountered this feeling my friend referred to in many passages over and over. It is as though one were proceeding on a horizontal plane and then suddenly found that plane vertically cut through by the upward/downward reach of a remarkable perception. This perception is generally marvellously unpredictable, it is the totally honest response of the mind of Forster to the tangle called life. It is original, penetrating, devoid of dogma. Its revelations so modestly rendered stun us without attempting to stun. 'All literature', he disengagingly remarks, 'tends towards a condition of anonymity . . . .'[1]

No writer likes to admit to being influenced. But on rereading a passage like the one I shall read, a very brief one, from *Where Angels Fear To Tread*, and a passage from my own work (obviously I proceed at my peril), it is obvious that this modestly woven manner of expression achieves its own rhythms and that though I have never consciously absorbed them I've been caught like many another in their net.

Italy, Philip had always maintained, is only her true self in the height of the summer, when the tourists have left her, and her soul awakes under the beams of a vertical sun. He now had every opportunity of seeing her at her best, for it was nearly the middle of August before he went out to meet Harriet in the Tirol . . . .

They travelled for thirteen hours downhill, whilst the streams broadened and the mountains shrank, and the vegetation changed, and the people ceased being ugly and drinking beer, and began instead to drink wine and be beautiful. And the train which had picked them at sunrise out of a waste of glaciers and hotels was waltzing at sunset round the walls of Verona . . . .

And on the second day the heat struck them, like a hand laid over the mouth, just as they were walking to see the tomb of Juliet. From that moment everything went wrong. They fled from Verona. Harriet's sketch-book was stolen, and the bottle of ammonia in her trunk burst over her prayer book, so that purple patches appeared on all her clothes. Then, as she was going through Mantua at four in the morning, Philip made her look out of the window because it was Virgil's birthplace, and a smut flew in her eye, and Harriet with a smut in her eye was notorious. At Bologna they stopped twenty-four hours to rest. It was a *festa*, and children blew bladder whistles night and day. 'What a religion!' said Harriet. The hotel smelt, two puppies were asleep on her bed, and her bedroom window looked into a belfry, which saluted her slumbering form every quarter of an hour. Philip left his walking-stick, his socks, and the Baedeker at Bologna; she only left her sponge-bag. Next day they crossed the Appennines with a train-sick child and a hot lady, who told them that never, never before had she sweated so profusely. 'Foreigners are a filthy nation', said Harriet. 'I don't care if there are tunnels; open the windows.' He obeyed, and she got another smut in her eye. Nor did Florence improve matters. Eating, walking, even a cross word would bathe them both in boiling water. Philip, who was slighter of build and less conscientious, suffered less. But Harriet had never been to Florence, and between the hours of eight and eleven she crawled like a wounded creature through the streets, and swooned before various masterpieces of art.[2]

The following is from my own best known work on Italy, *The Light in the Piazza*.

To the traveller coming down from Florence to Rome in the summer-time, the larger, more ancient city is bound to be a disappointment. It is bunglesome, nothing is orderly or planned, there is a tangle of electric wires and tram lines, a ceaseless clamour of traffic. The distances are long, the sun is hot. And if, in addition, the heart has been left behind as positively as a piece of baggage the tourist is apt to suffer more than tourists generally do. [And I thought Forster hadn't influenced me.] Mrs. Johnson saw this clearly in her daughter's face . . . . [The story that I was telling in this book was about a woman travelling with her daughter, the daughter falls in love with an Italian in Florence, is swept away to Rome.]

At night, after dinner, Mrs. Johnson assembled her guide books and mapped out strenuous tours. Cool cloisters opened before them, and the gleaming halls of the Vatican galleries. They were photographed in the spray of fountains and trailed by pairs of male prostitutes in the park. At Tivoli, Clara had a sunstroke in the ruin of a Roman villa. A goatherd came and helped her to the shade, fanned her with his hat and brought her some water. Mrs. Johnson was afraid for her to drink it. At dusk they walked out the hotel door and saw the whole of the city in the sunset from the top of the Spanish Steps. Couples stood linked and murmuring together, leaning against the parapets.[3]

One gets caught very easily in the net of this style which seems to be so plain.

Bharati Mukherjee:
Elizabeth just mentioned that writers don't like to admit to influences. Probably for American, Canadian, Quebec writers it is an insulting question or a tiresome question. But for someone like me, who's a Third World expatriate writer, it becomes a very difficult and heart-breaking question. Whom do I have as a model to follow, literary model or political model? Who can articulate best for me the post-colonial consciousness? Sometimes when people discover that I like to write they ask me who has influenced me, expecting me to answer R. K. Narayan, Raja Rao, or Mulk Raj Anand, and they're quite visibly angry, or disappointed anyway, when I say Forster and V. S. Naipaul. Forster is a strange sort of choice for me. I grew up in the 1950s in the India that Forster had written about in the 1920s. I didn't of course read Forster when I was growing up. The school I attended was run by Irish nuns who did not approve of Forster. Perhaps the nuns had stayed too long in India and had accurately discovered a subversive element in Forster's life and literature. The object of the school was to turn out English-speaking native women who could flutter graciously like Forsterian extras at garden parties to be hosted by the post-Colonial descendants of Ronnie Hislop. It wasn't until I was twenty and a graduate student in a muddled middle western America that I discovered Forster and *A Passage to India*. Until then, as a well brought up post-colonial I had assumed that India and Indians were not

worthy of serious literature, that the India I knew had no legitimacy in fiction. The wonder in reading Forster was that forty years before, he had written about a society I thought I could still recognize. Though he.couldn't provide me with a literary model, only another post-colonial writer could do that (and here I'm thinking of V. S. Naipaul as my ancestor), he had validated for me a fictional world. The chaos that I had been trained to perceive by the Anglos as a deformity, as a weakness of the Indian character, was really the life-renewing muddle and mystery of Forster. For India-born writers like myself the fictional concerns remain, and here I'm almost embarrassed to admit, faintly Forsterian. I cannot ignore Forster when I set my characters or my fiction in India. I have somehow to take into account that Forster wrote about that country. But, we heard this morning how Forster had to deal with the fag end of a decent age. I unfortunately was born at the beginning of a less decent age and so I'm writing without viewing the world as a whole as Forster did, and so when I write with the omniscience of a Forsterian point of view I'm writing as a satire of Forster. I can only parody the omniscient wisdom of a Forsterian narrator. I'd like to read the very first page of fiction I ever wrote, which is quite deliberately an imitation and a parody of Forster, only in my fictional world palaces have shrunk to rented hotels and Hindu Rajahs have become *nouveaux riches* multi-millionaires, aggressive multi-millionaires, and the Mau tank has become a swimming pool full of dried leaves and lizards and snakes:

> The Catelli-Continental Hotel on Chowringhee Avenue, Cal-cutta, is the navel of the universe. Gray and imposing, with many bay windows and fake turrets, the hotel occupies half a block, then spills untidily into an intersection. There are no spacious grounds or circular driveways, only a small square courtyard and a dry fountain. The entrance is small, almost shabby, marked by a sun-bleached awning and two potted hibiscus shrubs. The walls and woodwork are patterned with mould and rust around vertical drains. The sidewalks along the hotel front are painted with obscenities and political slogans that have been partially erased.
>
> A first-floor balcony where Europeans drank tea in earlier decades cuts off the sunlight from the sidewalk. In the daytime this is a gloomy place; only a colony of beggars take advantage

of the shade to roll out their torn mats or rearrange their portable ovens and cardboard boxes. The area directly in front of the Catelli's doorway is littered with vendors' trays, British mystery novels and old magazines laid out on burlap sacks, and fly-blackened banana slices sold by shrivelled women. At night neon tubes from tiny storefronts flicker over sleeping bodies outside the hotel, then die before breaking of the violent Calcutta dawn.

The Catelli is guarded by a turbaned young man, who sits on a stool all day and stares at three paintings by local expressionists on permanent display by the hibiscus shrubs. He's unusual for a doorman of any hotel: he is given to sullen quietness rather than simple arrogance, as though he detects horror in the lives of the anonymous businessmen who pass through his doors each day. A doorman is an angel, he seems to say. He is not without love, however, this guardian of the Catelli-Continental Hotel. He loves the few guests who come every day but do not stay. He sees flurries of exquisite young women in pale cottons and silks and elegant old men carrying puppies and canes, and he worships them. While small riots break out in the city, while buses burn, and workers surround the warehouses, these few come to the Catelli for their daily ritual of expresso or tea. And the doorman gathers them in with an emotional salute.

There is, of course, no escape from Calcutta. Even an angel concedes that when pressed. Family after family moves from the provinces to its brutish centre, and the centre quivers a little, absorbs the bodies, digests them, and waits.[4]

This then is my playful working on Forster and it runs throughout that novel. In writing what became an accidental autobiography, *Days and Nights in Calcutta*, the having to cope with Forster became less direct. But the concerns remained unabashedly Forsterian — where is the real India and what is the real India — even for someone like me.

I would like to read just a small section which gives an idea of the schizophrenic cultural life that educated Indians of my generation and background suffer:

As a very small child, before I learned to read, I used to listen to my grandmother (my father's mother), reciting ancient stories

from the Puranas. But after I started missionary school in
earnest, the old gods and goddesses and heroes yielded to new
ones, Macbeth and Othello, Lord Peter Wimsey and Hercule
Poirot. I learned, though never with any ease, to come and
go talking of Michelangelo, to applaud wildly after each scene
in school productions of *Quality Street*, and to sing discreetly
as a member of the chorus in *The Gondoliers*. School exposed me
to too much lucidity. Within its missionary compound, multi-
headed serpents who were also cosmic oceans and anthro-
pomorphic Gods did not stand a chance of survival. My
imagination, therefore, created two distinct systems of carto-
graphy. There were seas like the Dead Sea which New
Testament characters used as a prop to their adventures and
which the nuns expected us to locate on blank maps of Asia
Minor. And then there were the other seas and oceans, carved
in stone on walls of temples, bodies of water that did not look
like water at all which could never be located on maps supplied
by the school.

The mind is no more than an instrument of change. My
absorptive mind had become treacherous, even sly. It had
learned to dissemble and to please. Exquisitely self-conscious
by its long training in the West, it has isolated itself from real
snakes and real gods. But the snakes and gods remain, waiting
to be disturbed during incautious sabbaticals.[5]

Marie-Claire Blais:

I think my two colleagues expressed very well their views in a
very touching way, a very impressionist way, their views as
writers, and as persons, to Forster. I have just a few ideas that I
want to share with you. I was struck by what you just said,
Bharati, and I was also struck by what Elizabeth said because
it is extremely true, this idea of the literary lightning that you get
from Forster. But I also agree with you that there is something
that we, that our time of living betrayed. His was a very peaceful
time of life although it's true that you could satirize it. In many
ways his work is pure and literary like Proust's but when you read
it in our time and age and generation you are struck by a certain
insensitivity both to suffering and to the search for the truth in
oneself. I think for me a very impressive book that he wrote was
Maurice. It is a self-searching book about self-knowledge. He was
very sensitive to the pain of people but he was living in a society

which was very insensitive and he had to make some compromises. When I read his works again I'm extremely sensitive
to this compromising way not only of writing but probably of his
own being and for me that's why *Maurice* is a very important book.
Also in *Howards End* he accuses society of indifference and in other
books he described the rebellions of many women, many characters who refuse to be the medieval women as he called them. And
I think he respects woman, the idea of the real woman, but I still
feel that there is something very male chauvinist about his way
of thinking about us, probably because of his time. I think that
he also, like James, was extremely conscious of the social
oppression, and oppression of the individual, and he was troubled
by that. There is a kind of complaint of the self — that agonizing
self that nobody understands — that's very clear for me through
all the books and specially in *Maurice*. Also, the relationship is
fascinating of men in front of women. They are always separate,
always in groups. The men go swimming and they are all together
and speak about this pure life of the body. It seems to be
concerning men only all the time. It's not only because of his
sexual preference there; it seems an absolutely social distinction
between women and men which is something I didn't notice in
my first reading. And something that struck me very much also
is the secret aspiration to freedom, self-freedom, and also this
great need of being secure with his time and in peace with his
time. And he was extremely worried as we are, maybe more than
we are even, because he was more romantic, very worried about
the future not knowing that his future would be very, very
terrible. And also, there is in his nature something that struck
me very much, it is a fear in his works for women or men to be
themselves completely whether bad or good but this is a fear of
unity of the self. That's what strikes me most, for the moment.

James McConkey:
Forster has been such an influence in my life that I really don't
know where to begin. I understand that many people who visited
Forster were readers of his novels who felt a closeness to him — a
friendship — simply from reading the novels; they were responding to the accents of his voice as it is heard in his written work. I
first felt Forster to be a friend in this way when I was a young
man, and because of my affection for him I wanted to write a
book about his fiction. After I did write such a book, I thought

it time for me to sit down and write a book of my own, a novel that reflected my own values. I have that book at home in a desk drawer. It's a novel about a young man who's really quite nice, but who looks with detached irony on life; he's incapable of making commitments. He becomes entangled in a shoddy scheme and ultimately someone whom he loves dearly dies in a violent little episode as a consequence of his lack of commitment. Although he learns something from that death, he's still uncommitted as the novel ends. Forster wrote that novel before me — in *Where Angels Fear to Tread* — but so fully had I been under Forster's influence that I didn't even recognize my indebtedness.

There are many aspects of Forster that have influenced me, I think. I know in everything I've written there's some element of Forster. Actually my two favourite fiction writers of the past — of the immediate past — are Forster and Chekhov. I don't want to get into a discussion of what they have in common except to say that both of them judge human beings in reference to a spiritual totality that lies beyond human consciousness and can only be intuited now and then. A novel that I recently published, *The Tree House Confessions*, has its source in such an intuited moment of my own life. But how do we know to what degree moments which we can loosely call mystical are the consequence of books we have read as well as events in our own lives? Augustine's great moment at Ostia and those other moments in which he felt that he was able to sense the divine light were prepared for by his reading of neo-Platonic documents; in his visions he was seeing in part that which he had learned from his very reading. The seed of my novel came from my own psyche and experiences, and yet I'm sure it was a consequence too of my reading of Forster and Chekhov — and Augustine.

I'd like to speak briefly of my one meeting with Forster. He wrote me a letter after my critical study had been published and said he had liked the book. He had some nice things to say about it, and he also pointed out some errors. I called Eleanor Lavish 'Lydia'; that's a typical enough scholarly error, isn't it? He said, in a postscript, '*Eleanor* Lavish, not Lydia, but she is too delighted to be included to mind'. In that same postscript he added he hoped we would meet some day. When I saw him at King's College he was alone for the summer. He'd had a heart attack. He'd bought a cake and made tea, using a faucet of his old-fashioned Victorian bathtub to fill the tea-kettle up. He wanted to be hospitable and kind, though I must have been a difficult guest. For when I climbed the steps and saw the faded letters of his name on the door, what immediately came to my mind was that reference in *The Longest Journey* to the 'grey ghost' of another name beyond Rickie Elliot's name on his Cambridge door. When Forster opened that door and I saw an elderly man who obviously had been quite ill, I burst into tears, which made it rather difficult for me to speak. I protested over and over again during that meeting that I had come not for any benefit that might accrue to me as a scholar or critic. I didn't care about that, I said. I had come just to tell him how much he had influenced my life — I said that so much I must have been a pest. He really wanted to talk, and, in a sense, I refused to listen. We had a long discussion during which I said some things that displeased him. Since I'd been living in Paris, he asked me if I preferred Paris to London. I knew what I was supposed to say, but I said 'yes'. He said he disliked Paris so much that on his trips to the South of France every year he took a big arc around it.

Toward the end of the discussion, he said something that embarrassed me so much that for years — before I came to understand it — I felt ashamed for him and myself. He said he'd made one major mistake as a young man. I said, 'What was it?' and he said, 'I trusted people too much', words that shocked me. The mistake I made was to think that his remark invalidated the purpose of my visit to see him, that it meant I could not develop a genuine personal relationship with him. I wouldn't meet the remark directly. Instead, to indicate that I understood its spiritual implications, I said, '*A Passage to India* reminds me of the later quartets of Beethoven'. He replied very frostily that he didn't like the later quartets of Beethoven, he liked the earlier ones.

Then he told me he was not writing any more but destroying manuscripts, and in my attempt to be impartial and not to intrude I said nothing about saving them. Toward the end of the discussion we were really far apart. I said I had to leave. He said he'd go down the steps with me. I said he didn't need to do that. (He was alone in King's College and the steps were worn and the cobblestones in the courtyard were quite difficult to get over, especially for a person who was elderly and unsteady on his feet.) Very acidly, he said, 'I owe it to you for your book'. We walked very slowly down the steps and across the courtyard and out the gate. As he stood next to the Victorian style pillar-box just beyond the gate, I said, 'I like that mail box very much.' I *did* like it, and felt a connection existed between it and Forster. He said, 'I like that pillar-box very much too', and then he smiled at me in such a warm way it seemed we might conceivably have embraced. I waved and he went back in. For years I never told anyone what he had said to me, about trusting people too much, but I think all of us here could expound on those words for an hour and understand it in reference to what we know of Forster from his novels.

Eudora Welty:
In a way mine is a sort of the obverse of Jim McConkey's because it is about a letter I got from E. M. Forster when I was a beginning writer. That is a meeting at a different point in life from when you met which was a real meeting. I had published a number of short stories but I wasn't known anywhere, and I received this letter one day where I live in Jackson, Mississippi. It was written in New York City, and dated 28 April, 1947. I copied it off to bring:

> Dear Miss Welty: Finding myself in your country I feel I should like to give myself the pleasure of writing you a line and telling you how much I enjoy your work 'The Wide Net'. All the wild and lovely things it brings up have often been with me and delighted me. I am afraid that I am unlikely to have the good fortune of meeting you while I am over here since my itinerary keeps me to the North and to the West. Still there are meetings which are not precisely personal and I've had the advantage of one of these through you, and I would like to thank you for it. With kind regards and all good wishes. Yours sincerely, E. M. Forster.

Well, it was several moments before I was able to read the signature, partly it was his handwriting and partly it was my disbelief. The letter was kindness, undreamed-of kindness. It was also something that belongs to another realm, another kingdom in the sense of animal, vegetable or mineral kingdoms. It was response. It was what I knew Mr Forster meant me to receive from him. It had been received and had given pleasure. The letter carries some marks of tears and when I copied it off to bring to this conference my tears came back. This is the only time I've ever shared this letter, mailed to me thirty-two years ago, because it seems appropriate that I should read it in this company, who well know the value it had for the young writer I was, and has for that writer today, and who can see it with me in its lasting and undimmed light. I thought that would fit in with what I was asked to do, to talk of what Forster had meant to me in my work.

I have tried to think of the other things he meant to me. He must surely have strengthened my recognition of place as a prime source of enlightenment in fiction. He gave me help, help not abstract, but directly useful toward identifying in place my own most trustworthy teacher. And he crystallized for me an instinctive belief that mystery in human relationships exists *per se*, that some relationships and that occasional human actions, perhaps of great import, may occur outside satisfactory explanations and still need to be taken into account. And I believe I've apprehended through Forster's novels something I would have otherwise missed about form. Out of itself a work may abide by, adhere to, a felt composition, a structure building itself or building upon itself. What mounts up is not so much the progress of events as the intensity of awareness of the events, the advance made by way of human revelation; that is the plot, an advance toward light. Indeed, in *Aspects of the Novel*, Forster suggested that the idea the novelist must cling to is not completion, not rounding off, but opening out. 'When the symphony is over we feel that the notes and tunes composing it have been liberated, they have found in the rhythm of the whole their individual freedom. Cannot the novel be like that?'[6] Yes, I think it can. That is the real essence of what Forster has meant to me. I think he is so present to, so pervasive in, my understanding of experience that I can only be general about it, I can only say these fundamental things.

II — Questions

(Only members of the panel are identified in the following discussion.)

Question 1:

Bharati Mukherjee: May I ask Jim a question. I'm stunned by that revelation of Forster's confession that he had trusted too much. I don't know why you kept it to yourself all this time, and why you've revealed it to us now, but, you know that's like Mrs

Moore. He has become Mrs Moore, my God!

James McConkey: There are passages in the biography[7] which suggest that his very large belief in human relationships was followed by moments in which he wondered if people were really that important, which is very much in keeping with what you're saying too. For a while I thought he said that to me because he thought he needed to give me a warning as a very naïve young American. But it was more than that I think. If you think of Forster in some sense as Rickie Elliot, as much as a fictional character is ever one and the same with the author behind it, you can see that Rickie Elliot's tragedy is in part a consequence of trusting people too much. What he does with his half-brother Stephen, for example, is to make him something he is not out of his desire to have something solid and eternal there in front of him. And it is true in human relationships that if you trust people too much, you expect them to be eternal and constant and when they refuse to be that way you become bitter and dismiss them. And it took me a long time to realize that, in part, in talking about himself, he undoubtedly was talking about that aspect.

Eudora Welty: But he felt he could trust you, so he said this, he might not have said it to anybody. What I mean is, the reason he brought this up, this thing of trust, was that at least you would understand what he meant. Also maybe that's just the way he felt, sometimes. His favourite word was eternity. And he was measuring everything by eternity and you can't do that every day.

Question 2:

(From the audience): I wonder what he meant by trust and what you mean when you're using it, for there are so many levels of trust. In the early novel, *Where Angels Fear to Tread*, trusting seems to be something like stupidity. The poor girl is practically punished for not being sophisticated enough for what she tries to do. Does Forster mean that when he speaks of his early tendency to trust? And there are the Anglo-Indians who come to India trusting absolutely in their suburban values. Are they indulging in another kind of trust?

James McConkey: Of course I don't suppose he meant all those things at that moment, because he meant it as a personal statement. Human relationships were of crucial importance to him, although he knew one couldn't make human relationships absolute, even if in his own early life, he may have tried to do just that. Of course, he was an elderly man, and he certainly changed a lot of his attitudes in the years after I saw him. For example he said he would not allow *Maurice* to be published under any circumstances, and I did ask 'Why?' about that and he said simply because it was so dated, and it was written for a social purpose, to try to alter or change attitudes that needed to be changed, but of course he couldn't publish it; and that problem had now been resolved as best it could be, and the book had lost its reason and was old-fashioned and he decided he would not permit it to be published. A few years later of course he did.

Question 3:
(From the audience): Miss Welty, I know that a sense of place is very important in your fiction. I was interested in what you said about a sense of place as a source of Forster's fiction. Could you be a little more specific about what you've seen in Forster's work?
Eudora Welty: Well, I guess the example that would occur to us first is *A Passage to India*, especially in the episode in the Marabar Caves. This is a place that has existed before the beginning of people, before anything. It is the great empty thing, the place that was there in itself without any way to describe it; it was without anything by which human beings could identify. This is the absence of what place meant for Forster. Everywhere that Forster had laid a novel, place meant something specific, in *Howards End*, and of course in the Italian novels and in many of the fantasies such as 'The Road from Colonus'. Really the forming influence of the story can come out of place, and I had felt this way myself, you know. From where I was, I responded to what he said about those things because I felt the same way, that something can come out of a place, some kind of life, an enduring life, something that receives the experience and holds it. It is really something about which words don't exist so much. Even in *Marianne Thornton*, the book he wrote about his great-aunt, you see how place meant so much to all of them. And that was the house he grew up in, so as an infant, as a little tiny boy, there must have been born in him the seed of all that. And this anchoring of belief in a place is also connected with a sense of changelessness. He spoke of how convinced his great-aunt was in her beliefs. She

didn't question the rightness of things and the belief in God and the belief that you could live a life that would not hurt others but would help other people. She would never have felt distrust you would think or gone through any of the things that Mrs Moore went through. There are different things but they are somehow connected, you know, the anchoring of beliefs with something that does not change.

Question 4:
(From the audience): I would like to ask Marie-Claire Blais a question. You mentioned something about men and women in Forster which I think is very true, that they are always in separate groups, and you said you didn't think this had to do with his sexual preferences but with his culture. Could you say more on this? How would you see *Maurice* in connection with this? What do you think of the portrayal of women in *Maurice*?
Marie-Claire Blais: Do you remember any women in *Maurice*? There are not many.
Questioner: Yes, the women are the people they marry! They are afraid that the women will take the men away from them.
Marie-Claire Blais: Oh yes that's true, that's not flattering at all. But it seems to me that it's more social, it's more of his time than his own personal view. I think he really loves women but understands what problems there are for them. He describes Lucy as a person who doesn't like this kind of view men have of women. He has a sense of injustice about the way women suffer particularly when they are alone. He describes women who are alone much better it seems to me than when they are in the pursuit of a man or a fortune which is when they are in what you could call a social grip. But in *Maurice*, it's true you are right, but that's because they are the enemy then. It's mostly personal probably, and it's a very personal book, so maybe his view of women is not entirely there. I don't see in him a bitterness or misunderstanding of women's nature. I think he is very close to women's nature, as Proust was. For me he's more of a Proustian man than a Gidean man, he's not like Gide who really felt cut off from women altogether. I think he's more ambiguous than that, he has a very ambiguous nature.

Question 5:
(From the audience): My question is about manuscripts. What keeps a manuscript in your drawer, and what makes a manuscript that you destroy rather than keep? It's really a question for all of you.

Eudora Welty: What makes you keep them and what makes you tear them up? I think as long as they're alive or have a spark of life you respect that in them. You'd better watch that and be sure it's dead before you throw it away. But also you may not know; I think time is such an element in writing that you want to give it its full due, that is, give it a certain amount of distance in time and space and look back at it 'til you can really tell. I've destroyed a number of manuscripts for different reasons and I haven't destroyed some that I think I'll go right home and destroy. I have a good friend who is a novelist and short story writer and he told me once that he had written thirteen versions of a story and stuck them all in a drawer and he waited for I don't know how long and went back and it was number seven that was the right one. So, you see, you don't know. You can write too long on one, and just because you've written it later may not mean it's better. I keep telling myself that.

James McConkey: Maybe it's because I don't write enough, but of what I do write, all I want left is the purity of what seems to me my best version, and I destroy all my traces, no manuscript copies, no versions. They all get burned up the moment the version that's closest to what I feel inside myself has been done. I don't want anybody to see all those impurities.

Elizabeth Spencer: I keep everything that isn't completely finished because, even though every spark of vitality dies out of it, even though it's terrible, even though I wouldn't read it on a bet, there's still something in my frame of mind at that time that may in some way tell me what led me to this and might just by veering off lead me into something else that might be profitable. The other thing is that as Eudora said there may be a spark, a seed or something that's growing in the dark that might come up out of that, but once something is finished and I'm satisfied I go and burn up every trace of it that led up to that. It's funny you all mentioned it, I thought I was the only person that did that. We had a house in Lachine, Quebec, for a while, just outside Montreal, and in the middle of the hot summer I had finished a novel that was going to come out. I put all these manuscripts in

an empty fireplace on a very hot day and built a fire and set fire
to all this. Shortly later there was a ringing at the doorbell. Once
a year the city sends round chimney-sweeps, who never thought
on this hot day . . . they rang the doorbell and one said, 'Qu'est-ce
que vous faites aujourd'hui, il fait très chaud et vous avez . . .',
they thought I was mad. I told him I was an 'écrivain' and he said
'Oh' and he understood that all writers are crazy. Once it's done
and it's the best I can do and it is going to be published, I don't
want to know how it got there.

Bharati Mukherjee: I guess I must be bizarre then in hanging on to
all the drafts. My versions are so different, even the names of
characters are different in each of these versions that it's only
my Hindu imagination that says they are all really drafts of the
same novel. And I think that if I were a short story writer perhaps
I would have this under better control, I would have a more
rational way of dealing with it. I think one learns with experience
and I'm still very inexperienced at this game. For me the hardest
thing is to find the right voice, the right point of view, and, until
I've found the right point of view to tell a story from, I know that
it's not right, until I can hear that voice inside my head dictating
the fiction, it's not right. The cosmetic part is easy, but it's getting
the larger story captured, you have to know what really was the
story that you wanted to tell, which may not be the story you
started out with.

Question 6:
(From the audience): May I ask whether any of you find that
Aspects of the Novel illuminates your own acts as novelists?

Eudora Welty: Before I came up here, I reread *Aspects of the Novel*,
which I just think is marvellous. I put some notes down of what I
thought were the best things but that's not an answer to the
question. I just kept writing down the wonderful things he had
said: '[A fictional character] belongs to a world where the secret
life is visible'.[8] That's a volume right there. Or he gives a definition
as to when a character in a book is real: 'it is real when the novelist
knows everything about it. He may not choose to tell us all he
knows . . . but he will give us a feeling that though the character
has not been explained it is explicable, and we get from this a
reality of a kind we can never get in daily life'.[9] That's just like a
sky rocket you set off. You know everything comes out from

sentences like that and to me the whole book is like that.

Questioner: Is this influence or is it an articulation of that which you've already felt?

Eudora Welty: No I don't connect it with myself. I just connect it with the wisdom of a writer about a novel. Of course it couldn't help but teach anybody many things, but it's so penetrating to me because it goes straight to the very heart of fiction.

James McConkey: What you mentioned before about expansion, that comes right out of *Aspects of the Novel*. I think that's affected many writers, the notion that not completion but expansion is what is important.

Bharati Mukherjee: And a sense of story and rounded and flat characters. Henry James and Forster remain for me marvels of a writer working from the inside out. I had read *Aspects of the Novel* initially as a literary theory and although it was very intriguing it didn't mean anything to me as a writer. Then once I was writing fiction and went back to Forster's *Aspects* suddenly it was like skyrockets going off. It was a totally different experience, an articulation of what I felt.

James McConkey: In an assessment of Forster after his death some critic said, 'We really have to dismiss generally Forster's criticism, for we really can't accept the notion, it's not a serious notion, that all writers can be seen sitting around a table, from Dante to the present time'. But that notion is very serious. It's crucial to *Aspects of the Novel*, it's crucial to Forster's novels, it's crucial to my interest in Forster's novels and it's crucial to my favourite of all the essays that he wrote, 'Anonymity', and it's very crucial to me. If you understand that essay you understand something that's very important about Forster and *Aspects of the Novel*.

Question 7:

(From the audience): May I ask the members of the panel if they have had ecstatic or mystical experiences?

Eudora Welty: If you'd ask the question in other terms, I think I could answer it. The whole act of fiction is to imagine yourself in a leap out of your mind and body into characters or another person. You make that leap which transcends sex and race and age and time and place in writing about any character. You wouldn't call it mystical, but it is an act of the imagination which is your guide when you're writing. It is a tool of your work and an aspect of your sympathy and your wish to identify something out of yourself in the world, to connect. But I don't call that mystical. I don't really know what mystical is.

Question 8:
(From the audience): Can you suggest why it seems to be harder each year to convince undergraduates to like Forster? They find it hard to believe, for example, that people really spoke like that.
Bharati Mukherjee: Is your question: is it a dated novel? I certainly don't think so. Because I think fiction is about other fiction, that it has nothing to do with an accurate representation of real life. no literature is finally dated to me.
James McConkey: In high school I didn't like Forster and I remember the first time I read *A Passage to India*, as a very young person, I became irritated. It seemed elusive. There was a story to tell that he was not telling properly. It seemed that for some reason he was avoiding his subject. It was only the second time I read it — after I'd come back from military service and was a little more experienced — that it seemed as if I understood it. I guess maybe I was not old enough to understand it when I was seventeen. Is that possible?
Eudora Welty: I didn't read him too much 'til later but I still remember the first time I read *A Passage to India*. I was thrown into a deep depression by it. I didn't understand that was what the problem was, and I had to. It was a couple of years later when I read it again that I began to understand; it began to flicker.
James McConkey: In that respect I heard something in the panel this morning that I should have said something about, for it meant a great deal to me. It was a reference to the manuscripts, to a comment Forster made about Henry Fielding. I've always associated the Fielding in *A Passage to India* with Henry Fielding. Forster's own reservation about Henry Fielding was that he wouldn't go into the 'unknown country'. Some critics feel that Forster's Fielding is to be equated with Forster himself but the Fielding of *A Passage to India* is, in a sense, consciously being limited on the author's part because he, too, cannot go into unknown country. If we could only feel that Fielding represented the values of the novel, how much easier it would be for a high school student to understand it.

Question 9:
(From the audience): How does the panel respond to Forster's notion of inspiration that he described in the preface to the short stories, that he went for a walk and the story came to him?

Elizabeth Spencer: I don't recall the passage — I must have read it at some time or other — but I think stories do just seem to drop out of the air sometimes. It will just come into your head almost as a whole and it seems like a gift then, or sometime the central core, more often the central core of the thing will occur to you. But, as Bharati put it, sometimes you start out writing it wrong and you have to go back.

Eudora Welty: Didn't he say that it was only once when this happened to him, you know, when he wrote that first story and thought it marvellous? He said, 'it is the only time I ever sat down on a story like an ant hill'.[10] He wrote it and he thought the story was a success and it sold and he thought his fortune was made, so he just had to take another walk and it never happened again. He said he learned that that was not really the way such things happened and I would go by what he said.

NOTES

1. E. M. Forster, 'Anonymity: An Enquiry', *Two Cheers for Democracy*, ed. Oliver Stallybrass, Abinger edn. (London: Edward Arnold, 1972), p. 81.

2, E. M. Forster, *Where Angels Fear to Tread*, ed. Oliver Stallybrass, Abinger edn. (London: Edward Arnold, 1975), pp. 75–6.

3. Elizabeth Spencer, *The Light in the Piazza* (New York: McGraw-Hill, 1960), pp. 57–8.

4. Bharati Mukherjee, *The Tiger's Daughter* (Boston: Houghton Mifflin, 1972), pp. 3–4.

5. Clark Blaise and Bharati Mukherjee, *Days and Nights in Calcutta* (Garden City, N.Y.: Doubleday, 1977). pp. 171–2.

6. E. M. Forster, *Aspects of the Novel*, ed. Oliver Stallybrass, Abinger edn. (London: Edward Arnold, 1974), p. 116.

7. P. N. Furbank, *E. M. Forster: A Life* (New York: Harcourt Brace Jovanovich, 1977).

8. Forster, *Aspects of the Novel*, p. 44.

9. *Aspects*, p. 44.

10. See Forster's introduction to his *Collected Short Stories of E. M. Forster* (1947; rpt. London: Sidgwick and Jackson, 1975), pp. v–vi. His exact words are: 'Of these two processes, the first — that of sitting down on the theme as if it were an anthill — has been rare'.

Part V

A Review of Recent Forster Studies

'Fresh Woods, and Pastures New': Forster Criticism and Scholarship since 1975

Frederick P. W. McDowell

The publication of P. N. Furbank's authorized *E. M. Forster: A Life* (London: Secker and Warburg, Vol I, 1977. Vol. II, 1978; 2 vols. in one, New York: Harcourt, Brace, Jovanovich, 1978) and the large number of other books and essays written on Forster since 1975 indicate that interest in him continues unabated. The authors of these studies are convinced of Forster's importance to his posterity, though the adulatory tone and the tendency, once noteworthy among his Indian disciples, to regard him as a saint have virtually disappeared. The impact, for better or for worse, of Furbank's biography and of the posthumously published homosexual works has been to make us see Forster plain, and indeed, in a different light. His eminence as a novelist remains unassailed, it seems to me, whereas the new revelations about him and his newly published fiction have sometimes seemed to strengthen, and then sometimes to diminish, our conception of him as public presence, humanist sage and dedicated artist. Forster will undoubtedly occupy a place somewhat less august in the annals of contemporary literature than he did in the years 1945 to 1970, but it is safe to say that he will never sink to the obscurity that overtook him, in the period 1930 to 1943, as an important novelist. A juster and more solidly based estimate of his work — such, it seems to me, ought to be the primary goal for contemporary Forster scholarship. Many of the recent writings on him represent, I think, steps toward the achievement of this end.

In any case, Furbank's *E. M. Forster: A Life* remains the single most important and comprehensive book on Forster in recent years. The biography is, in one sense, definitive and magnificent; we learn things otherwise impossible to have ascertained, and we have had the factual record set straight concerning the life and the career. Furbank quotes copiously from unpublished sources in the Forster Archive at King's College, Cambridge; and he has had contact with many of those who knew Forster well or who were his intimates. Such details as those concerning Forster's loss of West Hackhurst as domicile, a tale spreading over the 1930s and ending in 1946 and involving continual misunderstandings between Forster and his aristocratic relatives, form a comic saga, have their dramatic value, and could not have been reconstructed without Forster's records.

Furbank's book is complete in all externals, but also gives us new windows through which to see Forster, the man. If his socializing among London lower-class men at times seems faintly disreputable, we can yet recognize that he was honest about his own nature and how its demands might be best satisfied. Most important, it seems to me, is that Furbank, with his own novelistic eye, has recreated for us as living people the individuals who formed or influenced Forster. Invaluable, therefore, are the portraits of his familiars such as Marianne Thornton, his mother, his aunt Rosie Whichelo, his aunt Laura Forster, E. J. Dent, Nathaniel Wedd, Oscar Browning, H. O. Meredith, Goldsworthy Lowes Dickinson, Syed Ross Masood, R. C. Trevelyan, Mohammed el Adl (Forster's beloved in Alexandria), Sir Malcolm Darling, Lytton Strachey, Forrest Reid, D. H. Lawrence, T. E. Lawrence, Virginia and Leonard Woolf, Siegfried Sassoon, Florence Barger, Sebastian Sprott, J. R. Ackerley, Christopher Isherwood, William Plomer, Harry Daley, May and Bob Buckingham, and Benjamin Britten, to name the most important. Furbank has filled his pages with living people; this feat underlines the most important of values for Forster, the sanctity of personal relationships. A mine of biographical data, imaginatively ordered, such is the contribution that Furbank has made to Forster studies.

In another sense, Furbank's biography raises as many questions as it settles. It reorients us as to Forster's career and achievement, and it both embellishes and magnifies the man; but in a sense, somewhat difficult to define, it also diminishes him.

The emphasis upon the personal life tends to stress that aspect out of all due proportion, while the ongoing intellectual life fades. Furbank not only fails to give us much sense of Forster's intellectual Gestalt, he also does not reveal very cogently the relationships existing between the life and the work. One must except from such a judgement Furbank's full documentation of Forster's public activities in the 1930s and the 1940s when he emerged as the surprisingly vigorous champion of liberal values at the time that they were being challenged by economic depression, Naziism, Communism, the tightly organized state, an aggressive capitalism, censorship and militarism. But if he scants Forster as an adventuring mind and as a creative artist, he has supplied the materials and many of the data from which Forster's inner biography can at some time be fashioned.

In fact, three tentative studies in this direction of achieving a synthesis between Forster's life and work have appeared. John Colmer in *E. M. Forster: The Personal Voice* (London and Boston: Routledge and Kegan Paul, 1975) presents an overview of Forster's work, throwing it into new perspective because he makes use of papers in the E. M. Forster Archive and of the homosexual fiction. Colmer's performance is notable, especially since he did not have Furbank's life to draw upon. *E. M. Forster: The Personal Voice* is a fresh and illuminating study which consolidates or modifies earlier judgements in the light of the new materials available to the critic. In a brief notice it is impossible to cover the many brilliant aspects of this study, but let me mention Colmer's viewing of *The Longest Journey* in the light of Greek tragedy and Ibsen's *Ghosts*, the analysis of the rescue motive in *Howards End*, and the establishment of a contrast in *A Passage to India* between a harmony achieved through reconstruction (in Adela and Fielding) as opposed to a fuller harmony achieved through completeness (in Mrs Moore, Godbole and Aziz). If Colmer fails to contribute an originative dimension to Forster studies, he has nevertheless written a substantial study to which the student of Forster must constantly refer. Philip Gardner in his pamphlet, *E. M. Forster* in Writers and Their Work Series (London: Longman Group, 1978) presents in short compass much shrewd and illuminating commentary as he surveys Forster's work and career. From this short study a general reader can learn more about Forster than from any other source, and the advanced student can also read the essay with profit. I can only cite one of its many provocative insights, the 'Caves' in *A Passage to India* as representing 'the enigmatic and frightening side of spiritual experience, the sense of chaos and nothingness whose effects spill over and make the conclusion of the novel equivocal'. Gardner's undertaking is a model of its kind, at the same time that it does not entirely supplant the earlier critique in this series by Rex Warner (1950; revised by John Morris, 1960). Glen Cavaliero in his book, *A Reading of E. M. Forster* (London: Macmillan; Totowa, N.J.: Rowman and Little-field, 1979) writes an overview of the literary *œuvre*, an intelligent but by no means indispensable book in view of the many studies similar to it already regarded as standard. It does not carry Forster studies further than Colmer does, but it is well written and approaches the whole of Forster's writings with a fresh sensibility. Cavaliero is especially discerning in his treatments of style and aesthetic effects in the fiction. His enterprise is somewhat relaxed and lacking in rigor, but some insights make the book worth consulting; for example, Stephen Wonham of *The Longest Journey* viewed as 'almost a fool of God . . . . a romantic conception subjected defensively to deromanticising treatment' or the significance of Forster's homosexuality for his artistry: 'The transformation of a private and personal estrangement into an engaged concern with the very society which implicitly re-jected him is one of Forster's triumphs as humanist and artist'. At this point I should also mention Francis King's *E. M. Forster and His World* (London: Thames and Hudson; New York: Charles Scribner's Sons, 1978). It is more challenging than the usual run of books in the series of which it is part. Whereas King does not quite fuse Forster's life with his vision as artist, he goes over much of the same material covered by Furbank, but in more concise, concentrated form. He is excellent on Forster's life, both the inner and outer, and has some new insights into Forster the man as a result of his having known him. And the pictures are super.

1977 saw the publication of my compendious *E. M. Forster: An Annotated Bibliography of Writings about Him* (DeKalb: Northern Illinois University Press). The bibliography is reasonably complete through 1974. I have also abstracted the most important reviews of the posthumously published works and included the items then available to me in 1975. In 1979 *E. M. Forster: The Human Exploration, Centenary Essays* (London: Macmillan; New York: New York University Press) appeared, under the editorship of G. K. Das and John Beer. The contributions of the volume are all interesting and many are profound. In general, they reach a higher level of competence and insight than those appearing in the volume of ten years back, *Aspects of E. M. Forster* edited by Oliver Stallybrass (London: Edward Arnold; New York: Harcourt, Brace and World). At selected points in this present overview I shall cite the most important of the essays; and perhaps I can now mention my own 'Forster Scholarship and Criticism for the Desert Islander' (pp. 269–82), in which I discuss those secondary works that seem to me of absolute importance for the Forster student to have studied.

The other recent important book-length studies relate to Forster's greatest achievement, *A Passage to India*. In 1975 V. A. Shahane edited *Focus on E. M. Forster's 'A Passage to India'* (Madras and New Delhi: Orient Longman), a compilation of essays on *Passage* by Indian critics, half of them published for the first time in this book. It reveals as did the 1964 *E. M. Forster: A Tribute*, edited by K. Natwar-Singh (New York: Harcourt, Brace and World) the respect in which Forster's Indian critics hold him as well as the stimulus he has provided for them. Easily the best essay is Chaman L. Sahni's 'The Marabar Caves in Light of Indian Thought', which may come to be a definitive analyis of its subject. In Sahni's view the 'Caves' of Part II embody the superhuman Brahman without attributes while the 'Temple' ceremonies of Part II embody the personal Brahman. Jane Lagouidis Pinchin's *Alexandria Still: Forster, Durrell, and Cavafy* (Princeton: Princeton University Press, 1977) is a well written and thoroughly informed book concerning three major men of letters. Pinchin documents how fully the relaxed atmosphere of Alexandria and the influence of Cavafy contributed to the more expansive and inclusive scope and the less provincial quality found in *A Passage to India*, in comparison with the other novels. Forster's personal development in Alexandria and the consummation of his homosexual passion there may also have led, she says, to the breadth and to the firmer grasp of experience characteristic of *Passsage*. G. K. Das's *E. M. Forster's India* (London: Macmillan, 1977; Totowa, N.J.: Rowman and Littlefield, 1978) is an impressive marshalling of facts about Indian history and society in the nineteenth and twentieth centuries and about Forster's view on India. The nineteenth-century attitudes of the British toward India, especially the Platonic concept of a

ruling élite who act as wise guardians for supposedly less
developed colonial populations, led directly to the twentieth-
century problems which Forster appreciated from his contact
with Indians during his stays in the subcontinent. Whereas Das
etches in masterfully the contemporary Indian agitations reflected in the novel, he does not discuss as fully as he might its
religious dimensions. Robin Jared Lewis in *E. M. Forster's Passages to India* (New York and Guildford: Columbia University
Press, 1979) presents a detailed version of Forster's travels in
India, personally verifying many aspects of his visits there and so
enlarging our knowledge of the circumstances concerning his
exposure to India and to things Indian. He quotes judiciously and
extensively from Forster's diaries, other unpublished sources,
and interviews with people who knew Forster. Lewis' book
provides, in short, a valuable amplification and supplement to
the chapters on Forster's sojourns in India to be found in
Furbank.

The other book-length studies on Forster are either less important or somewhat specialized. V. A. Shahane's second book
on Forster was published in 1975, *E. M. Forster: A study in Double
Vision* (New Delhi: Arnold-Heinemann). Shahane focuses upon
the dualities present in Forster's fiction: the rational as opposed
to the irrational, vision as opposed to anti-vision, the material as
opposed to the immaterial. The author is appreciative, though he
offers little that is new and profound. John Sayre Martin's *E. M.
Forster: The Endless Journey* appeared in 1976 in the British
Authors: Introductory Critical Studies series, sponsored by the
Cambridge University Press. It is a reliable, readable, enthusiastic and comprehensive introduction to Forster, but less that
is challenging gets said in the book than could be said. Even for
an introductory book, it is focused at too elementary a level, in
contrast to Philip Gardner's pamphlet described above; and too
little reference is made to the vast body of criticism already
existing on Forster. Norman Page's *E. M. Forster's Posthumous
Fiction* came out in 1977 in the English Literary Studies series of
monographs put out by the University of Victoria. Page gives us
informed and careful discussions of *Maurice* and of the stories in
The Life to Come, though he refers hardly at all to the bulky
criticism already existing on these works by 1975. The result is
that we have once again one critic's private view of some of
Forster's fiction without any attempt having been made to

indicate the consensus view already formed on the works that are being discussed.

Any reviewer of Forster scholarship within the last few years must pay tribute to the monumental, continuing, *The Abinger Edition of E. M. Forster*. The Edition had been under the expert, meticulous and enthusiastic editorship of Oliver Stallybrass whose untimely death has robbed us all of our foremost Forsterian. His death has even cast the future of the Edition in doubt, though it is to be hoped that a new editor or editors can be found to complete it along the lines that Stallybrass envisioned in 'The Abinger Edition of E. M. Forster' (*English Literature in Transition*, 16, 1973, 245–56). The last volume that he worked on, *Arctic Summer and Other Fiction*, was co-edited with Elizabeth Heine and has just been published as Volume 9 in the Abinger series. All Forsterians thus hope that this monument to a foremost modern writer will not be left only half erected.

The recent volumes in the Abinger Edition have, moreover, been all of them impressive, each containing a definitive text (compared with the manuscript where it exists and the various editions collated, with the purpose of unearthing substantive corrections), a glossary where appropriate, notes, and illuminating introductions, often making use of unpublished materials which provide in detail the circumstances of composition and the critical reception for the given work. In 1975 *Where Angels Fear to Tread* appeared as Volume 1, *A Room with a View* appeared in 1977 as Volume 3, and in 1979, to help with the celebration of Forster's centenary, *A Passage to India* appeared, along with *The Manuscripts of 'A Passage to India'*, as Volumes 6 and 6 A. The latter will obviate the necessity for most scholars to use Robert L. Harrison's hitherto definitive thesis on the manuscripts and to visit the Humanities Research Center at the University of Texas to consult the actual manuscript. Of subsidiary but great interest is Volume 3 A, *The Lucy Novels: Early Sketches for 'A Room with a View'*. The fragments reveal the true Forsterian touch and allow us to see how the novel was composed and what Forster dropped from the completed version. The unused fragments but reinforce one's consciousness of Forster's consummate Austen-like mastery of social comedy.

E. M. Forster's Commonplace Book was published in a beautiful but limited facsimile edition by the Scolar Press in 1978, under the editorship of P. N. Furbank (a trade edition is promised for

1982). The work is important in providing some materials for a fuller analysis of E. M. Forster's mind, career and artistry than would be otherwise possible; and the Forsterian aspect of the entries makes many of them truly beguiling, so that we will look forward also to the publication of Forster's letters and diaries whenever that may occur. Elizabeth Heine in an essay-review of the *Commonplace Book* in the *Contemporary Review* (234, May, 1979, 251–5) pinpoints the importance of the publication of this book for Forster scholars, and I can do no better at this point than to refer the reader to her full discussion. Here may be the place to mention that P. N. Furbank and Mary Lago are undertaking a two-volume *Selected Letters of E. M. Forster*, an enterprise authorized by the Trustees for the Forster estate.

Important general accounts of Forster have been written by James R. Baker, Roger Bowen, Eugene Webb, Evelyne Hanquart, Alan Wilde, John Russell and Wilfred Stone. Baker in 'Forster's Voyage of Discovery' (*Texas Quarterly*, 18:2, 1975, 99–118) maintains that Forster followed a circular route in his career, in effect ending where he had begun, in a backwater where personal relations are all-important. En route he travelled out into the disturbing world, as the malaise pervading *Howards End*, *A Passage to India*, *Abinger Harvest* and *Two Cheers for Democracy* attests; and it is this very disillusion with 'scientific humanism' that underscores the modernity of his outlook. Baker's thesis is interesting, though he fails to define it sharply enough and to trace its total ramifications in Forster's works. Bowen in 'A Version of Pastoral: E. M. Forster as Country Guardian' (*South Atlantic Quarterly*, 75, 1976, 36–54) provides a careful but scarcely compelling analysis of the pastoral element in the fiction and of Forster's increasing difficulties in domesticating it in art. Webb in 'Self and Cosmos: Religion as Stategy and Exploration in the Novels of E. M. Forster' (*Soundings*, 59, 1976, 186–203) sees in Forster's fiction the poles of the need for order and of the prevalence therein of disorder, with the result that Forster attempts to reconcile these disparate forces in an increasingly complex way. If this analysis is sound, it is not particularly arresting. Less ambitious but in some ways more intrinsically interesting is Evelyne Hanquart's 'E. M. Forster's Travelogue from the Hill of Devi to the Bayreuth Festival' (*E. M. Forster: A Human Exploration*, pp. 167–82). She gives us a full summary of Forster's travels, using unpublished materials to supplement the information previously available. She is especially interesting on Forster's experiences in Africa which he visited in 1929 with the Bargers.

The best of these general treatments are those of Alan Wilde, John Russell and Wilfred Stone. Wilde in 'Desire and Consciousness: The Anironic Forster' (*Novel*, 9, 1976, 114–29) presents his controversial interpretation of Forster's career in terms of his use of irony. Irony is muted in the early fiction, according to Wilde, because integration and then transcendence (especially in *Maurice*) are desired. Irony becomes pronounced in *A Passage to India* where transcendence is still desired but not so easily to be attained. The anironic Forster emerges, Wilde contends, with the homosexual short stories in which direct sensual experience, the unexamined life, is the value celebrated. In his book, *Modern British Fiction: Studies in Joyce, Lawrence, Forster, Lewis and Green* (Baltimore and London: Johns Hopkins University Press, 1978), John Russell analyses in Chapter 4, 'E. M. Forster *Howards End, A Passage to India*' (pp. 89–122) the elements of Forster's style. He finds, as distinguishing features of the prose, compound sentences of an aphoristic or exemplum sort, the use of antithetical constructions, and the presence of positive modal verbs ('do/did' construction) and of various sorts of negatives, in contrast with the work of the other writers that he discusses. Wilfred Stone in 'Forster on Profit and Loss' (*E. M. Forster: A Human Exploration*, pp. 69–78) focuses on the ultimately Christian metaphor basic to *The Longest Journey, Howards End*, and to much of his later thought, 'the division between earthly and spiritual coin'. For Forster the claims of both ranges of our experience are important, but Stone emphasizes how Forster, though conscientious on the subject of money, is even more insistent on his search for ideal value; and he also notes how Forster's exclusionary élitism sometimes confused his thinking on economics and social justice.

There are two recent articles that relate Forster to the Bloomsbury milieu. The first by Elizabeth Heine, 'E. M. Forster and the Bloomsbury Group', appeared in the E. M. Forster special issue of *Cahiers d'Etudes et de Recherches Victoriennes* [since 1978 called *Cahiers victoriens et édouardiens*] (Montpellier, Université Paul Valéry, 1977, Nos. 4–5, pp. 43–52). Heine finds that Forster's activities in and attitudes toward the group were ambivalent; that he reflected this ambivalence in *The Longest Journey, Howards*

End and *Maurice*; and that he gained from his contact with members of the group, even if he did not feel himself to be completely at one with them. In 'Forster and "Bloomsbury" Prose' (*E. M. Forster: A Human Exploration*, pp. 161–6), P. N. Furbank stressed the qualities of lightness, flexibility and evoca‑ tion of personality as traits that Forster shared with Bloomsbury writers; his somewhat obsessive concern with metaphor and a constantly shifting angle toward his materials were peculiarly his own. In the most extended recent account of Bloomsbury, *Bloomsbury: A House of Lions* (Philadelphia: Lippincott; London: Hogarth Press, 1979), Leon Edel drops Forster from detailed consideration, despite Leonard Woolf's listing him as one of the original group; his friendships with Strachey, the Woolfs and others; his being a disciple, though not a close student, of G. E. Moore (as *The Longest Journey* attests); his Cambridge connections at the turn of the century, especially with King's College and the Apostles group; his having written in *Howards End* the most consumate representation of Bloomsbury attitudes and values in literary art; and his having written many essays, especially the famous 'What I Believe', which embodies the Bloomsbury *Weltanschauung*.

Some of the most challenging of recent investigations have connected Forster with other writers. John H. Stape in 'Meredith and *Howards End*' (*Cahiers*, pp. 53–60) analyses Forster's in‑ debtedness to Meredith more completely than anyone has yet attempted, emphasizing the specific influence upon him of *The Egoist, Beauchamp's Career* and *Diana of the Crossways*. H. K. Trivedi in 'Forster and Virginia Woolf: The Critical Friends' (*E. M. Forster: A Human Exploration*, pp. 216–30) maintains that attrac‑ tion yet wariness toward each other marked the relationships between the two writers. For Woolf Forster was ultimately too much the devotee of an Arnold Bennett kind of realism, while for Forster Woolf seemed in her work to be overly concerned with its pattern and texture. They were in accord, however, in their emphasis upon liberal culture, upon the personal, upon vision and upon humanistic values. James McConkey in a contribution to *E. M. Forster: A Human Exploration*, 'Two Anonymous Writers, E. M. Forster and Anton Chekhov' (pp. 231–44) argues con‑ vincingly that the writers are most alike in their sensitivity to the elusive relationship existing between the specific and the universal, between the outward self and the inner self, especially as that latter seeks for identification with a force that unites, at least fitfully, the forms of existence. The resemblances and differences between Forster and yet another influential modern writer, T. S. Eliot, are the subject of G. K. Das's revealing 'E. M. Forster, T. S. Eliot and "The Hymn Before Action"' (*E. M. Forster: A Human Exploration*, pp. 208–15). Das notes the correspondences existing between 'The Waste Land' and *A Passage to India* and the responsiveness of both authors to Buddhistic and Hindu values, though Forster was more critical of disinterested action and of the alleged beneficent effects of suffering than was Eliot.

Perhaps the deepest affinity between Forster and any of his contemporaries was with D. H. Lawrence. Friction and misunderstandings, however, tempered their continued friendship and mutual regard and prevented them from becoming close to one another. Two critics in *E. M. Forster: A Human Exploration* analyse this relationship. C. E. Baron in 'Forster on Lawrence' (pp. 186–95) and John Beer in '"The Last Englishman": Lawrence's Appreciation of Forster' (pp. 245–69). Baron in his essay emphasizes what we all know, Forster's high regard for Lawrence as artist, particularly at the time of Lawrence's death. Baron also demonstrates Forster's sense of the unity of Lawrence's thought by directing attention to the similarity of meaning existing between the natural symbols of *The White Peacock* and those of *The Plumed Serpent*, an aspect of Lawrence's work that Forster had alluded to in passing in his obituary on Lawrence. Beer in his turn documents the similarities in the development of Forster and Lawrence as novelists by citing books that have parallel themes and characters. He also observes their affinities with paganism and a possible mutual indebtedness in this respect to the work of Kenneth Grahame. He cites their critical attitude toward Bloomsbury, he stresses their mutual sense of the mother as an abiding (if sometimes reluctantly acknowledged) spiritual influence, and he notes the inclusiveness of vision in the two men.

As Forster's most considerable achievement, *A Passage to India* continues to attract scholars and to stimulate them into writing about it. Several major discussions of it from 1975 have appeared in journals and books and include essays written by Elaine Showalter, Edwin Thumboo, John Colmer, Benita Parry, Michael Orange and Michael Ragussis. Elaine Showalter in '*A Passage to India* as "Marriage Fiction": Forster's Sexual Politics'

(*Women and Literature*, 5, 1977, 3–16) observes that Forster seems distrustful of marriage as an enforced condition in which women become victims, particularly when they are subject to other repressions such as purdah. She also notes that Aziz is arrogant toward women and reprehensible in his views toward Adela Quested. While Forster recognized Fielding's marriage as embodying a hope for continuance and reconciliation, his uncertain presentation of it, she says, also indicates his own scepticism toward it as a solution to the human dilemma. Edwin Thumboo in 'E. M. Forster's *A Passage to India*: From Caves to Court' (*Southern Review* [Adelaide], 10, 1977, 112–44) stresses the dynamic and changing aspects of the relationships charted in the novel. Adela Quested, for instance, grows in understanding, especially when she becomes aware of the natural force emanating from the courtroom punkah. Mrs Moore and Godbole, Thumboo says, transcend the other religions present in the novel by aligning themselves with Hindu values; and Ralph and Stella, Mrs Moore's children, make a leap into this faith at the end. Here we have a challenging if somewhat loosely organized essay, the original insights of which are sometimes difficult to separate from other existing commentary on this novel. John Colmer organizes a coherent discussion in 'Promise and Withdrawal in *A Passage to India*' (*E. M. Forster: A Human Exploration*, pp. 117–28). He stresses the contradictions in the British ruling class, in the tradition of romantic liberalism, and in the tradition of British imperialism as they are expressed in *Passage*; and he defines also, as a basic pattern in this novel, the ironic contrast developing when expectation and promise are undercut by disappointment and withdrawal. Another contrast, between the power of verbal expression and the limits of such expression, forms the subject of Michael Orange's 'Language and Silence in *A Passage to India*' (*E. M. Forster: A Human Exploration*, pp. 142–60). In a subtle critique Orange demonstrates how Forster's language, with some effort and much mastery, accommodates the contrasting sensations of flux and stasis, connects the mundane and the divine, and modulates into silence as the novelist attempts to give articulation to the mystical.

Among the most admirable of these comprehensive essays are those by Benita Parry and Michael Ragussis. Parry in '*A Passage to India*, Epitaph or Manifesto?' (*E. M. Forster: A Human Exploration*, pp. 129–41) is concerned with still another dichotomy present in the novel, the contrast between the coherence expressed in the design and the symbolic organization of the novel and the open-ended, refractory and contradictory nature of the novel's deeper structure. There exists, she says, a disjunction between the mythopeic mode of the novel which suggests the possibility of achieving unity and its grim and pessimistic realism which suggests division, not reconciliation. The multivalent significance of *Passsage* is also the aspect of the novel stressed by Michael Ragussis in 'E. M. Forster: The Vision of Evil in Fiction: The Narrative Structure of *A Passage to India*' (*The Subterfuge of Art: Language and the Romantic Tradition*, Baltimore and London: Johns Hopkins University Press, 1978, pp. 133–71). Ragussis argues that the complexities of meaning in the novel derive from the multiple perspectives from which Forster observes character, action and setting. Each of the major characters, the principles of science, the ideas of Hinduism, and the narrator who is involved in the action and develops through it provide these alternating, enriching, complicating perspectives. Ragussis pursues an original approach to this much analysed novel, though his arbitrary equation of the Caves with evil and his assumption that a narrator independent of the author controls the novel are at best debatable.

I should mention in passing a few other general discussions of Forster's great novel. D. C. R. A. Goonetilike in 'Difficulties of Connection in India: Kipling and Forster' (*Developing Countries in British Fiction*, London and Basingstoke: Macmillan, 1977, pp. 134–69) argues convincingly that Forster's novel presents a true picture of conditions and people in India, despite the opinions to the contrary expressed by Nirad Chaudhuri and some others. M. M. Mahood in 'The Birth of Krishna: Forster's *A Passage to India*' (*The Colonial Encounter: A Reading of Six Novels*, London: Collins; Totowa, N.J.: Rowman and Littlefield, 1977, pp. 65–91) recreates the historical circumstances against which the action and the characters in *Passage* must be seen. She reinforces similar findings by G. K. Das in his book and by Jeffrey Meyers in *Fiction and The Colonial Experience* (Ipswich: Boydell Press; Totowa, N.J.: Rowman and Littlefield, 1973). Mahood is especially illuminating when she defines the tensions in the novel and the limitations of each of the characters and then when she suggests that a sacramental, non-rational view of life may neutralize the forces of evil more fully than would a more self-conscious, intellectualized philosophy of experience. In 'Love and Friendship in *A Passage to India*' (*Cahiers*, pp. 121–30) Joseph Dobrinsky argues that for Forster friendship is the most valued state existing between two people, transcending in importance an intellectual relationship or sensual love.

A number of recent accounts of Forster focus on his Egyptian sojourn; almost inevitably the writers of these studies see the sojurn in relationship to Forster's Indian experiences and his Indian novel. In fact, one of the best of recent scholarly inquiries into Forster's mind is that of John Drew, 'A Passage via Alexandria' (*E. M. Forster: A Human Exploration*, pp. 89–101). Drew fully charts in this treatise Forster's indebtedness to Plotinus and his neo-Platonism. On the basis of this study we will now have to reckon with Plotinus as an influence upon Forster in his depiction of Godbole and as a supplement to the Hinduism assimilated in *Passage*. For Mohammad Shaheen in 'Forster's Alexandria: The Transitional Journey' (*E. M. Forster: A Human Exploration*, pp. 79–88) neo-Platonism was not the only aspect of Alexandria that was formative upon Forster; his stay in the city also gave him a sense of detachment as requisite for the intellectual life, and an insight into the importance of the shifting point of view which he was to use so brilliantly in *A Passage to India*. In 'A Note on the Government of Egypt' (*Cahiers*, pp. 113–20), Philippe Daumas suggests how the anti-imperialist attitudes later voiced in *Passage* and Forster's ambivalent view on Indian national independence had their partial inception in his Egyptian stay and their partial expression in his 'Notes on Egypt'.

I should also note in passing three essays concerned with various facets of the background for *A Passage to India*. Sujit Mukherjee in 'The Over-arching Sky: Forster and the Tradition of Anglo-Indian Fiction' (*Cahiers*, pp. 160–73) sees Forster's novel as crucial in the development of a tradition dealing with colonial themes in fiction. *Passage*, he says, consolidated certain materials and attitudes and led to other books (he mentions many of them), dealing with other Indian themes: imperial, racial, political, communal and universal. J. Birje-Patil in 'Forster and Dewas' (*E. M. Forster: A Human Exploration*, pp. 102–8) notes the similarities between Forster's accounts of his stay in Dewas and 'Temple' in *Passage*; and he makes the penetrating observation that Dewas becomes for Forster a kind of greenwood of escape from the pressures of modern life (Forster celebrates the greenwood in his Terminal Note to *Maurice*). V. A. Shahane in 'Life's Walking Shadows in *A Passage to India*' (*E. M. Forster: A Human Exploration*, pp. 109–16) makes a strong case for regarding Aziz as formed not only on Syed Ross Masood but upon another of Forster's close Indian friends, Saeed Yar Jung.

Critics have been less attentive to *Howards End* than *A Passage to India*. Peter Widdowson in his monograph, *E. M. Forster's 'Howards End': Fiction as History* (Sussex University Press, *Text and Context*, 1977) views the tensions, the ambiguities and the irresolutions to be found in this novel as indicative both of an affirmation of liberal humanist values and as a realization of their vulnerability. The critic is searching enough in his definition of the weakness of *Howards End* but less sure in ascertaining its strengths. In his essay Widdowson attacks Forster's mixture of the realistic and poetic modes (the attack first launched by Virginia Woolf in 1927) and the inefficaciousness of Forster's liberalism (a critique similar to that in C. B. Cox's *The Free Spirit*, London and New York, Oxford University Press, 1963). The typical student of Forster will feel, I think, that the dimensions of Widdowson's study are finally constricting rather than expansive. J. L. VanDe Vyvere in 'The Mediatorial Voice of the Narrator in E. M. Forster's *Howards End*' (*Journal of Narrative Technique*, 6, 1976, 204–16) follows the fashionable, if critically dubious, trend of separating the author from the narrator of his fictions, and this critic finds, accordingly, that it is the narrator in *Howards End* who achieves the balanced perspectives put forward in the novel as the foremost positive value. In the *Cahiers* Forster issue, Henri Quéré in 'Écriture et idéologie: le discours des formes dans *Howards End* de E. M. Forster' (pp. 61–84) sees *Howards End* as a work which illustrates the premises behind 'écriture', premises which stress a viable connection between the form and the ideology of the novel, moving it towards a synthesis of opposing impulses. Quéré's discourse is basically more concerned, it seems to me, with questions of theory than it is with the interpretation of *Howards End*, though I may not be adequate to assessing his work. Easily the best of the recent accounts of *Howards End* is that by R. N. Parkinson, 'The Inheritors; Or a Single Ticket for *Howards End*' (*E. M. Forster: A Human Exploration*, pp. 55–68). This commentator observes that Forster in this novel is concerned with completeness — 'the completeness of a carefully mediated symbolic pattern and the completeness of a comprehensive view of human nature'; and he stresses the skill with which Forster uses antithetical patterns to reinforce his values. The critic's unapologetic tone in writing about this novel is refreshing, and his defence of Henry Wilcox as a man whose moral obtuseness is balanced by a spiritual acuteness, charm, commonsense and clear-sightness is spirited and justifiable.

Critics and scholars have paid less attention to Forster's other novels within the last few years. Only one article has appeared on *Where Angels Fear to Tread*, Alina Szala's 'North and South: Civilisation in E. M. Forster's First Novel' (*Cahiers*, pp. 27–41). This critic sees Forster as the champion of civilization in *Angels* rather than as its opponent, though Forster prefers, she says, the enlightened civilization of Italy to the repressive culture of Sawston in England. Wider in its scope and the questions it raises is Judith Scherer Herz's 'The Double Nature of Forster's Fiction: *A Room with a View* and *The Longest Journey*' (*English Literature in Translation*, 21, 1978, 254–65). Herz perceptively asserts that much of Forster's strength as a novelist depends on the tension generated in his works of fiction by the collision of two story lines: the surface heterosexual romance and the interior homosexual romance. In '*The Longest Journey*: E. M. Forster's Refutation of Idealism' (*E. M. Forster: A Human Exploration*, pp. 32–54), S. P. Rosenbaum makes a definitive case for the influence of G. E. Moore in the formation of the world-view which Forster dramatized in *The Longest Journey*. Rosenbaum persuasively presents Stewart Ansell, in spite of some of his misperceptions and waverings, as Forster's spokesman and as a representative of Moorean realism in the novel; his function, as a result, is to educate the misguided Rickie Elliot as to the fallaciousness of his fixed perceptions which are idealistic in both the popular and the philosophical sense.

A number of recent accounts of Forster have been concerned with his homosexuality, with the posthumously published fiction, and with its implications for an interpretation of his career. I have been unable because of limitations of space to consider several short articles which interpret a single story, though possibly George Thomson's interesting detective work in 'Where Was the Road from Colonus' (*E. M. Forster: A Human Exploration*, pp. 28–31) should be mentioned in passing. Mention should also be made here of a model bibliographical study, listing important manuscript variants and textual errors for the stories in *The Life*

to *Come*, Oliver Stallybrass's and George H. Thomson's 'E. M.
Forster's *The Life to Come*: Description of the Manuscripts and
Typescripts at King's College, Cambridge' (*Papers of the Bibliographical Society of America*, 72, 1978, 477–503). Judith Scherer
Herz has turned her attention to the early stories as a group in
her 'The Narrator as Hermes: A Study of the Early Short Fiction'
(*E. M. Forster: A Human Exploration*, pp. 17–27). She finds that
these stories are serious rather than whimsical works, being
mythical in their ramifications; and she suggests that Hermes, as
a beautiful and mischievous young man and as a god who spans
the realms of life and death and love, is the informing presence
behind these tales rather than his son, Pan. Dennis Altman in
'The Homosexual Vision of E. M. Forster' (*Cahiers*, pp. 85–96)
regards homosexuality as a force which kept alive Forster's
resistance to middle-class conventions at the same time that these
conventions prevented him from expressing himself openly on sex
in his fiction and in his public utterances during his life time. He
was thus forced to be essentially false to himself and was unable
to transcend the limits imposed on him by British liberalism; as
a result his work and career will have to be examined in light of
what we now know about him. Whether Forster could have been
as open in his life time about his sexual predilections as Altman
would wish is perhaps a debatable issue. Evelyne Hanquart in
'"Dearest my Joe": une lecture des lettres de E. M. Forster à
J. R. Ackerley (1922–1966)' (*Cahiers*, pp. 97–112) provides an
extended glimpse into a fascinating correspondence. The letters
describing Forster's problems with 'The Other Boat' are especially illuminating. Elizabeth Wood Ellem has written most
provocatively about the early fiction, down to and including
Maurice in 'E. M. Forster's Greenwood' (*Journal of Modern Literature*, 5, 1976, 89–98). The greenwood is, in its simplest form in
the early stories, a refuge from the civilized and intellectual life;
then it is a place, in the rejected chapters of *The Longest Journey*,
where the secrets of nature can be joyously learned; and finally,
in *Maurice*, it is a place of exile from an uncomprehending world.
A. O. J. Cockshut in 'The Male Homosexual' (*Man and Woman:
A Study of Love and the Novel*, London: Collins, 1977, pp. 162–85)
is more favourable to *Maurice* than many writers on Forster have
been. He attributes the flaws in the earlier fiction to the com-
pulsion to render homosexual themes in terms of heterosexual
situations and characters. *Maurice*, in contrast, is an honest,

intelligent and fascinating book, and successful for the most part except when Forster's animus against the later Clive obtrudes.

The most thoughtful of the essays which integrate Forster's homosexuality and his homosexual works into his entire career are those by two eminent Forsterians, Alan Wilde and Wilfred Stone. In 'The Naturalisation of Eden' (*E. M. Forster: A Human Exploration*, pp. 196–207) Wilde asserts that in the fiction through *Maurice*, Pan serves chiefly as an emblem of friendship and desired connection, whereas 'panic' in this fiction represents the intrusion of a more violent aspect of Pan, Pan as physical love, upon this desired state of friendship and potential harmony. In *A Passage to India* Mrs Moore achieves, says Wilde, the most violent confrontation of all with Pan, though panic is neutralized in the novel by irony; and in the stories that follow, Pan is replaced by Priapus, 'platonic love by unobstructed and fulfilled desire'. The involutions of Wilde's presentation resist summarization; suffice it to say that the essay does something to connect the early stories with the late ones and to integrate Forster's career as artist. Stone in '"Overleaping Class": Forster's Problem in Connection', (*Modern Language Quarterly*, 39, 1978, 386–404) explores the difficulties experienced by the homosexual in achieving integration — connection as self-fulfilment and connection as social and political being. In the homosexual fiction a great gulf exists between desire and such fulfilment, Stone contends; and fulfilment most often entails the sacrifice of an individual from a lower class, except in 'The Other Boat' and 'Dr. Woolacott' (the best of these fictions) in which the hero suffers his saviour's fate. This is a thoughtful essay, and we can accept its conclusions to the degree that we regard the Scudder-Maurice sequences in *Maurice* as a failure to cross the barriers of class.

What of Forster's career and of his continuing significance as artist and man of letters? Some approximation to an answer is provided by John Beer in 'Introduction: The Elusive Forster' (*E. M. Forster: A Human Exploration*, pp. 1–10). Beer celebrates Forster for his elusiveness, his union of reason and sensibility especially in *A Passage to India*, his valuation of intellectual pleasure, his continued search for sources of vitality in nature and in mankind, and his withdrawal from extreme positions. The oscillations in his mind are constant between recognition of a truth and a withdrawal from it in order to subject it to further scrutiny. For me Forster matters a great deal as the man who was capable, in the dark days of 1940, of utterances like the following: 'Our chief job is to enjoy ourselves and not to lose heart, and to spread culture not because we love our fellow men, but because certain things seem to us unique and priceless, and as it were, push us out into the world on their service'. The sense of something uniquely human that is too precious to be lost — the conveying of this in his fiction and non-fiction is the secret, I think, of his continuing appeal to the intellectual and to the general reader alike. It is the steel of Forster's temperament, not the charm, that finally counts.